P9-BIV-744

Intimate Relations

Intimate Relations:
Family and Community in Planter Nova Scotia, 1759-1800

Edited by
Margaret Conrad

Acadiensis Press
Fredericton, New Brunswick

1995

© Acadiensis Press 1995

Canadian Cataloguing in Publication Data

Main entry under title:

Intimate relations

(Planter studies series; no. 3)

Proceedings of the Planter Studies Conference sponsored by the Planter Studies Committee and held at Acadia University in the fall of 1993.
Includes bibliographical references and index.
ISBN 0-919107-42-7

1. New Englanders — Nova Scotia — History — 18th century — Congresses.
2. Nova Scotia — History — To 1784 — Congresses.*
3. Nova Scotia — History —1784-1867 — Congresses.*
I. Conrad, Margaret.
II. Acadia University. Planter Studies Committee.
III. Planter Studies Conference (1993: Acadia University)
IV. Series.

FC2321.25.I67 1995   971.6'00413   C95-950085-5
F1038.I67 1995

AUGUSTANA UNIVERSITY COLLEGE
LIBRARY

 PRINTED IN CANADA

INTIMATE RELATIONS
FAMILY AND COMMUNITY IN PLANTER NOVA SCOTIA, 1759-1800
Edited by Margaret Conrad

ACKNOWLEDGEMENTS

Despite appearances to the contrary, conference proceedings do not edit themselves, nor does the editor do the job unaided. Brenda Naugler, who was essential to the successful organization of the 1993 conference, was also central to the editorial process. Paid in part by a grant made available from a SSHRC Small Universities Research Fund, Brenda brought order to the computer disks that arrived in various formats and conditions, kept files on my correspondence with contributors, and patiently entered the many editorial changes that were required. Pat MacNutt, one of the world's most efficient secretaries, helped to get the final manuscript off to the printer and did some last-minute proof reading.

In what has now become a time-honoured tradition, the members of the Planter Studies Committee gave me the freedom to handle the project as I saw fit and were generous with their time and expertise when I asked for it. Most contributors were prompt and professional in their response to my questions and I am grateful to them for making my task so easy.

As with previous publications in this series, I am grateful to the Occasional Conference Jury of SSHRCC, the juries of Acadia's Research and Graduate Studies Division, and the Esther Clark Wright Endowment for the funds necessary to produce this volume. Finally, and most importantly, I am indebted to Gail Campbell and the members of the Board of Acadiensis Press who agreed to publish our third volume of proceedings. Without their willingness to take on this project, it might never have seen the light of day. It should also be said here that Acadiensis Press has been instrumental in shaping the "new history" of the Atlantic Region, a major scholarly achievement for which we in the Planter Centre are most grateful.

Margaret Conrad

Introduction

In the fall of 1993 the Planter Studies Centre, Acadia University, hosted the third Planter Studies Conference in Wolfville, Nova Scotia. The focus of the three day conference, "Family and Community in Planter Nova Scotia, 1759-1800," was chosen to fit into the program developed by the Wolfville Centennial Committee to celebrate the anniversary of the town's incorporation. As this volume indicates, the topic stirred genealogists, public historians, and university scholars into a potent brew. Twenty of the thirty presentations heard by the nearly 150 people who attended the conference were submitted for publication.

The Esther Clark Wright Lecture, endowed by the woman who did so much to focus attention on the Planters, was delivered by Philip Greven, Jr., Professor of History, Rutgers University. When his study, *Four Generations: Population, Land and Family in Colonial Andover, Massachusetts,* appeared in 1970, it was immediately recognized as a benchmark in family and community studies. One of Professor Greven's great strengths as a historian is his ability to draw links between the past and present. In subsequent books, *The Protestant Temperament* (1977) and *Spare the Child* (1991), he continued to explore the inner and inter-personal aspects of human existence in earlier times and to show how historically-generated behavioural patterns continue to influence our contemporary world. Professor Greven readily admits that his work sometimes pushes "the boundaries of historical scholarship beyond the limits that scholars find comfortable," but no one can accuse him of failing to push back the frontiers of historical inquiry. True to form, in his conference presentation on recent trends in New England family and community history, Professor Greven left his listeners with much to think about. His fine paper inspired the title of this volume and magnificently frames its entire content.

The other four papers in the first section, entitled "Approaches to Family History," also provide new ways of exploring the past. In her ground-breaking survey of the treatment of widowhood in Canadian family history, Bettina Bradbury alerts researchers to the problems associated with failing to take into account the death of a spouse. She points out that, in the past, family breakup through death was an experience as common as divorce is today and therefore it warrants more attention than it has hitherto received. By focusing on the personal letters of Maritime Loyalists, Ann Condon opens a window on the history of eighteenth-century emotions and family values. Her observations about Loyalist families offer suggestive avenues for Planter scholars. Inspired by her work on literary sources, Althea Douglas underlines the importance of the "female connection" in genealogical research. She suggests that livestock breeding and genetic software programs may well serve genealogists better than the conventional computerized formats they currently use to trace their ancestors.

Concentrating on the nuts and bolts of genealogical research, Ronald Illsley surveys the variety of computerized sources available at the Old Kings Courthouse Museum for people tracing their Planter ancestors.

The conference was testimony to the remarkable growth of scholarly interest in the Planters. In her paper, Patricia Norred, a Fulbright scholar whose doctoral work focuses on the history of the Connecticut Planters, underlines the great changes taking place in family and community values in pre-revolutionary New England. Her conclusion, that the migrants to Nova Scotia may have been more "Yankee" than the people they left behind, challenges scholars to do further research on the forces that prompted the Planters to leave their New England homeland. Of course, migration in itself can be a transforming process, a point underscored by Barry Moody in his close examination of Granville Township, where New England values and institutions were altered by the environment, new political arrangements, and association with other settlers.

"Others" were certainly part of the Planter story. Joan Dawson's paper on Joseph Pernette explores the development of New Dublin Township, an area of Nova Scotia that is now associated more with the "foreign Protestants" of Lunenburg County than it is with the Connecticut Planters to whom it was originally granted. In his paper on settlement in Lunenburg County, Kenneth Paulsen demonstrates that culture does, indeed, make a difference in family relationships and inheritance patterns. Tanya Dawson's study of Oliver Lyman, a deputy surveyor in Horton Township, suggests that Planters were also adept at assimilating "others" who lived among them. Even within families there were differences in the way that culture was perceived and transmitted. Through a careful reading of the diaries of father and daughter in the Seccombe family, Gwendolyn Davies exposes the gendered responses to daily life in one Planter family.

One of the most striking features of Planter scholarship is the extent to which it has been embraced by the local Maritime community. Not long after the first Planter conference in 1987, the term "New England Planter," which we had consciously adopted to differentiate the New Englanders from other "pre-Loyalists" who settled in the old province of Nova Scotia, began to be widely used. Now, in the Wolfville area, there is a Planter Square (a subdivision), Planter exhibits (at the Kentville Courthouse Museum) and Planter picnics. A more astonishing example of scholarly transfer to the local community is the adoption of a Planter "look." In their article on Planter clothing, Clary and Sharon Croft describe the kind of wardrobe worn by "ordinary" adult New Englanders who came to Nova Scotia. They also produced a colourful drawing to illustrate their article, which was copied by costume designers. Even before this manuscript went to press, Planters could be seen, in July 1994, docking at Newport Landing, clad in costumes designed according to the images provided by the Crofts. A few months before this dramatic event, Hugh MacNeil, on behalf of the enterprising citizens of Newport, consulted the Planter Studies Centre for assistance in staging a re-enactment of the Planter landing. With the permission of the Crofts, the Centre made available a copy of their paper and drawing from which the breeches, aprons and other articles of apparel were fashioned. I doubt if there was ever a better example of how tradition is "invented," and those of us from the Planter Studies Centre who witnessed the event were suitably impressed by the degree to which our research interests influenced our surrounding community. Because it is likely to continue to shape how we "see" the Planters in the future, the Crofts' paper is a fitting piece with which to open the section on "Community and Culture," which includes five articles that explore exciting new areas of Planter scholarship.

In the 1970s, James Snowdon developed a scholarly interest in the Planters which was gradually focused on Planter furniture. His paper, at last, provides in writing the information that Jim has long shared with antique collectors who, it must be conceded, are often the first to recognize the importance of material culture. Another piece of material culture — late eighteenth-century ledgers from the Dewolf general store at Horton Landing — are analyzed with great dexterity by Elizabeth Mancke to yield our first insights into women's role in the Planter economy. Although legal records offer Planter scholars a rich treasure trove, they have remained largely untapped. For that reason the papers by Judith Norton, drawing on the Chipman Collection to explore domestic violence, and Julian Gwyn, using the Chancery Court records to trace the fortunes of four entrepreneurs in Planter Nova Scotia, are significant contributions to our understanding of the Planters.

In our material age, we sometimes forget that most Planters, even Julian Gwyn's would-be capitalists, held strong religious convictions that shaped the way they viewed their world. The final section of this volume includes four papers on religious themes in Planter Nova Scotia. In his paper on New England Baptist preacher Isaac Backus, Stanley J. Grenz adds an important chapter to the religious context of the New England Planters. Dr. Grenz's presentation was sponsored by the Acadia Centre for Baptist and Anabaptist Studies and scheduled to coincide with our conference. We are delighted that he agreed to permit us to publish his paper here. George Rawlyk, our 1990 Planter Scholar, focuses on the role of "believer's baptism" in the rise of the Baptist Church in the Maritimes. Gwen and Stuart Trask explore three sides — Planter, preacher and patriarch — of Jonathan Scott, Congregationalist minister in Yarmouth, Nova Scotia, while Beatrice Corbett discusses two members of the Moulton family who played prominent roles in the religious and educational history of the Maritimes and Ontario.

It is unfortunate that published proceedings are unable to include the "ancillary" activities that take place during a conference. Three, in particular, should be mentioned here. A Planter exhibit, sponsored by the Parks Canada, was opened with great fanfare at the Kentville Courthouse Museum on Friday, 1 October. A model of its kind, the Museum has done much to bring the story of the Planters to the wider community. During the banquet at the Old Orchard Inn on the following evening, John Duncanson, whose studies of the Hants County townships of Falmouth, Newport, Rawdon and Douglas add immeasurably to our knowledge of Planter history, was proclaimed a Planter Scholar. His citation, written by James Snowdon, concludes this volume. On Sunday morning, the Covenanters Church was the site of an "event" which featured a fine meditation by Dr. J.R.C. Perkin, former President of Acadia University, and a very special presentation by the Elastic Millennium Choir on the evolution of choir music over 500 years. The plain style of the meeting house, the colourful autumn environment, and the inspiration of speaker and choir proved a fitting end to our program.

Those of us working at the Planter Studies Centre no longer ask if there is any Planter history left to explore. In the closing session, Janet Guildford, who, at the time, was teaching at Mount Saint Vincent University, and David States, a historian with the Parks Canada, offered useful suggestions for future research. Meanwhile, we at the Planter Studies Centre try to arrange our many priorities to fit our meagre budget. Despite dwindling funding sources, *New England Planters in the Maritime Provinces of Canada, 1759-1800: A Bibliography of Primary Sources*, compiled by Judith Norton and published by the University of Toronto Press, appeared in the spring of 1993. In its computerized form it is available on Internet. Judith is now compiling a genealogical database on the Planters for the New England Historic Genealogical Society. Our newsletter, *Planter Notes*, appears regularly under the capable editorship of John Thomas. Although we have yet to develop the archival collections policy demanded of us by Provincial Archivist Carman Carroll at our 1990 conference, Acadia Archivist Pat Townsend continues to receive documents relating to the Planters. All but 150 of the original print run of 1500 of our first volume of proceedings, *They Planted Well*, have been sold and the second volume, *Making Adjustments*, continues to find a market. With *Intimate Relations,* I have finally managed to produce an index. Indexes have been developed for the previous two volumes and can be included in a future printing.

MARGARET CONRAD
May 1995

Family and Community in Early America

Philip Greven
Professor of History
Rutgers University, New Jersey
1993 Esther Clark Wright Lecture

Nearly a quarter of a century has now elapsed since the publication in 1970 of three studies of families and communities that helped transform the ways in which we perceived and understood the social history of colonial America. The studies of Plymouth colony, Dedham, and Andover, Massachusetts, by John Demos, Kenneth Lockridge and myself, together with Michael Zuckerman's analysis of New England towns, seemed to herald a new departure in the methodology of social history, combining both demographic and psychological perspectives on families and communities that promised to alter our understanding of life in the seventeenth and eighteenth centuries among the immigrants to New England and their offspring.[1]

The early 1970s proved to be a very exciting moment for early Americanists since there was an intense interest suddenly in issues that had been neglected by previous generations of historians, and a burst of enthusiasm for the analysis of people's lives and experiences — rooted in the detailed reconstruction of their families and communities — that augured well for the future of the field of early American history. Now, however, looking back at the previous two decades, the feeling of excitement and the sense of promise seem to have been somewhat excessive, given the research and writing that have been forthcoming in recent years. This conference provides an opportunity to reappraise some of the accomplishments of the past two decades and to anticipate possible directions for future research in the combined fields of family history and community studies.

When I first began research on families in Andover, Massachusetts, in the very early 1960s, I had no idea where my research would take me. I had begun a search for materials on New Light separatists and evangelicals during and after the Great Awakening — the first major religious revival in New England in the 1730s and 1740s — but I ended up studying a community that was Old Light and anti-revivalist, the antithesis of what I initially set out to explore. By choosing to focus upon Andover, however, I ended up writing a dissertation and subsequently a book — *Four Generations* — that have come to be regarded as

---

1   John Demos, *A Little Commonwealth: Family Life in Plymouth Colony* (New York, 1970); Kenneth A. Lockridge, *A New England Town: The First Hundred Years* (New York, 1970); Philip J. Greven, Jr., *Four Generations: Population, Land, and Family in Colonial Andover, Massachusetts* (Ithaca, N.Y., 1970); Michael Zuckerman, *Peaceable Kingdoms: New England Towns in the Eighteenth Century* (New York, 1970).

virtual classics in the field of family and community studies. How I wish I could have known the future fate of my project when I was actually doing my research! Perhaps my anxiety would have been somewhat reduced by the thought that what I was doing would prove to be of use and interest to many other people in the years to come.

The problem was that there were no models for me to draw upon to help make sense of the multiplying piles of minute details that accumulated during my inquiry into the lives of Andover's first four or five generations. I either had to invent my own guidelines or discover analogous work done elsewhere by other historians far removed from colonial Andover.[2] I am quite certain that this experience was true for the others who were studying towns and families in the 1960s, because we all worked in an intellectual vacuum, devoid of adequate guidance in terms of knowing how to make sense of the detailed information being gathered from town records, church records, probate records, deeds and vital records, which collectively produced vast quantities of isolated bits and pieces of information. We had data in abundance, but how could anyone make sense of them or discern patterns of common experiences embedded in such microscopic and seemingly trivial detail?

Obviously each historian found ways of coping with the chaos inherent in local records and the results — polished, carefully considered, and severely pruned — appeared in our books and articles during the 1970s and 1980s. But my own encounters with the settlers of Andover and their descendants for four generations probably were similar to those of anyone who ventures to study families and communities in the seventeenth and eighteenth centuries, whether they be located in New England, the Chesapeake, Nova Scotia, New Brunswick or any other locale. Doing local history involves certain common problems which I want to consider briefly before commenting upon some of the results of more than two decades of historical inquiry into these subjects.

The first and most obvious problem involves sources. For New England, town records, tax lists, church records, vital records, probate records and deeds offer a rich array of information, but information that is highly fragmented and partial. Names, dates, acts, decisions and sometimes wishes can be recovered in relative abundance, but so much of the time this material seems to be meaningless and opaque since it rarely reveals the thoughts, feelings and motivations of people. Most records are bare-boned, skeletal remains of human lives that once

2   However, several important community studies were published during the 1960s that helped shape our inquiries: Sumner Chilton Powell, *Puritan Village: The Formation of a New England Town* (Middletown, Ct., 1963); Darrett B. Rutman, *Winthrop's Boston: A Portrait of a Puritan Town* (Chapel Hill, 1965); Richard L. Bushman, *From Puritan to Yankee: Character and the Social Order in Connecticut, 1690-1765* (Cambridge, Mass., 1967).

were fleshed out and experienced in all the rich complexity of sensual being — felt with the body, thought with the mind, imagined with the fantasies of living human beings now turned to dust.

Learning to listen to the dead speak and observing their actions are what being a historian is really all about. Unfortunately, much of the evidence that survives for us to decode only lets us hear distant echoes of voices and see distant images of the lives people actually led three or four centuries ago. Mostly, we are able to see them only from the outside, their external lives made visible by the spare records generated by individuals and groups for us to decipher.

When I began to do my research in Andover, I realized that I had almost no material that could be considered personal, apart from the manuscript wills of many men and a few women, and even these were mostly impersonal standardized documents that told little about the actual individuals themselves. Still, as any reader of *Four Generations* will discover, it is amazing how much can be recovered in terms of people's actions and deeds — how they chose to distribute their property, to whom, under what circumstances, and how these choices altered under different circumstances. Inheritances can prove to be remarkably revealing, in terms of parents and children, and especially fathers and sons. But still their voices are muffled, and their individuality rarely emerges from these documents.

The same is true of the external characteristics of their families. Only by a careful and laborious process of reconstruction, using probate records, deeds and vital records, can anything substantive be recovered to illuminate the outward lives of people in these towns in early British America. Again, I had few clues at the outset about ways in which to find out about the families in Andover. But I had the good fortune to be given the manuscript for Peter Laslett's article on two English villages in the seventeenth century — Clayworth and Cogenhoe — which, for the first time, used census information to analyze the composition of households and to explore the nature of family structure while also examining the level of population mobility in these two communities.[3] Laslett's results concerning household size, family structure, population mobility and demography proved to be startling, given the assumptions current then, and I realized that I could do something similar, with very different sources, in my study of Andover.

Family structure — which sociologists and anthropologists had long considered essential — suddenly became an issue for historians to consider as well. I began to realize that my disparate array of bits and pieces of information about

---

3   Peter Laslett and John Harrison, "Clayworth and Cogenhoe," in H.E. Bell and R. L. Ollard, eds., *Historical Essays, 1600-1750, Presented to David Ogg* (London, 1963). Also see Peter Laslett, *The World We Have Lost* (New York, 1965) and *Family Life & Illicit Love in Earlier Generations: Essays in Historical Sociology* (Cambridge, England, 1977).

individuals and families in Andover could be collated in terms of what they revealed about family life in relation to households and kinship networks. By reading sociological studies of English rural and urban communities in the twentieth century as well as Laslett's study of seventeenth-century communities, I realized that I had found models that would help me make sense of the chaotic detail that I was gathering for Andover's inhabitants.[4] Similarly, I discovered that I could make use of all the information in the town's vital records — incomplete and frustrating though they often proved to be — together with the conscientious labours of genealogists of Andover's families, some published, much in manuscript, because I also became aware of the field of demography, the history of populations. Again, historians had done little or nothing with such information, having no sense that these records could be analyzed or reconstituted into usable information about people's lives. But models existed in the early 1960s, mostly in Europe with historical demographers such as Louis Henry, Pierre Goubert and Anthony Wrigley, who pioneered in using the technique which came to be known as "family reconstitution."[5] By modifying their techniques to fit the records in Andover, I began to reconstruct the life-histories of Andover's families, using birth, marriage and death records, and thus created what turned out to be one of the first studies of historical demography for an early American town. It remains, for all its flaws, one of the few done to date.[6]

In retrospect, the analysis of the life-histories of individuals in families as well as the collective biographies of townspeople as a group has proven to be one of the most rewarding methodologies that historians of the family can use. What I discovered — and what other historians also began to discover independently — was that the previous assumptions made by historians about life in New England in the seventeenth and eighteenth centuries were largely false.

---

4   Two such studies were especially revealing: W.M. Williams, *The Sociology of an English Village: Gosforth* (London, 1956) and *A West Country Village, Ashworthy: Family, Kinship and Land* (London, 1963).

5   See Louis Henry, *Anciennes familles Genevoises: Étude demographique: XVIe-XXe siècle* (Paris, 1956) and "The Population of France in the Eighteenth Century," in D.V. Glass and D.E.C. Eversley, eds., *Population in History: Essays in Historical Demography* (Chicago, 1965), 434-456; Pierre Goubert, *Beauvais and le Beauvaisis de 1600 à 1730: Contribution à l'histoire sociales de la France du XVIIe siècle* (Paris, 1960); E.A. Wrigley, "Mortality in Pre-industrial England: The Example of Colyton, Devon, over Three Centuries," *Daedalus* (Spring 1968), 546-580, and *Population and History* (London, 1969). For further examples, see the bibliography in Greven, *Four Generations.*

6   See, however: Maris A. Vinovskis, ed., *Studies in American Historical Demography* (New York, 1979); Robert V. Wells, *The Population of the British Colonies in America before 1776: A Survey of Census Data* (Princeton, 1975).

People lived far longer, married later, often had fewer children and smaller families, than most historians had thought. But my study of Andover also demonstrated that people's lives often changed, sometimes dramatically, over the course of time, generation after generation.[7]

In terms of the history of families and communities, the late 1960s and early 1970s proved to be a period of true methodological innovation and the results remain useful even when many of these studies have been scrutinized and criticized for flaws in their techniques or data. Family reconstitution, demography, and the analysis of family structure, kinship and mobility transformed the ways in which historians could explore and analyze the familial and communal worlds of early Americans. Even though most of the work done from such perspectives remains external — the outer aspects of people's life-experiences being more readily visible than the inner dimensions — the techniques that were used by historians during this period remain invaluable for any study of families or communities.

During the mid-1970s, many of us believed that our studies would be the beginning of an on-going collective historical effort to explore the demographic history of early America, with local history becoming a major enterprise among the professionals concerned with the history of the family. Our anticipations and projections, alas, have turned out, more often than not, to have been just fantasies. The reality of scholarship during the past two decades (with several important exceptions) has not sustained our hopes and anticipations of increasing amounts of evidence about some of the most intimate aspects of people's lives, from birth through marriage to death.

To be sure, some historians during the past decade or so have made substantive contributions to our understanding of the histories of populations both in New England and the Chesapeake. Daniel Scott Smith and M.S. Hindus, for example, were able to decipher hidden patterns of sexual behaviour by analyzing the cycles of conception embedded in the evidence of marriages and births, thus

---

7   Similar transformations affected the Chesapeake region as well, but in the opposite direction from those characteristic of so many early New England communities. In the Chesapeake, life in the early phases of settlement was short, risky and harsh, with early marriages and even smaller truncated families at the outset, while later generations lived longer, married later, and had larger families. Demographic evidence has proven to be immensely helpful in grasping the quality of life for those people living in different regions of British America.

    See especially: Darrett B. Rutman and Anita Rutman, *A Place in Time: Middlesex County, Virginia, 1650-1750* (New York, 1984); Allan Kulikoff, *Tobacco and Slaves: The Development of Southern Cultures in the Chesapeake, 1680-1800* (Chapel Hill, 1986); Lois Green Carr, Russell R. Menard and Lorena S. Walsh, *Robert Cole's World: Agriculture and Society in Early Maryland* (Chapel Hill, 1991).

probing aspects of experience that hitherto had been inaccessible to historians and other analysts.[8] Linda Auwers Bissell and Douglas Lamar Jones explored the issue of mobility in the context of three New England towns, Windsor, Connecticut, and Wenham and Beverly, Massachusetts.[9] Jones, in his book *Village and Seaport: Migration and Society in Eighteenth-Century Massachusetts,* used the techniques of family reconstitution and demographic analysis, together with attention to inheritance and family structure, to dissect the levels of spatial and economic mobility in two communities.[10]

Unfortunately, interest in historical demography in New England seems to have dissipated as most scholars turned their attention to other regions and other issues. As a result, historians in the 1990s will not have the accumulated body of evidence — based upon family reconstitutions and a series of local demographic studies — that many of us expected to see forthcoming when we first undertook our own individual studies of localities. The records are there still, certainly, but the focus now is elsewhere.[11] Regrettably, historical demography is no longer a compelling methodology among early Americanists.

Much the same can be said for the analysis of family structure and kinship, despite the publication of several studies which have explored certain aspects of these issues by focusing upon inheritance and patriarchy, which were central

8   Daniel Scott Smith and M.S. Hindus, "Premarital Pregnancy in America, 1640-1971: An Overview and Interpretation," *Journal of Interdisciplinary History,* V (1975), 537-70. Also see Daniel Scott Smith, "A Perspective on Demographic Methods and Effects in Social History," *William and Mary Quarterly,* XXXIX (1982), 442-68.

9   Linda Auwers Bissell, "From One Generation to Another: Mobility in Seventeenth-Century Windsor, Connecticut," *William and Mary Quarterly,* XXXI (1974), 79-110; Douglas Lamar Jones, *Village and Seaport: Migration and Society in Eighteenth-Century Massachusetts* (Hanover, N.H., 1981). See also Roger Thompson, *Mobility and Migration: East Anglian Founders of New England, 1629-1640* (Amherst, MA., 1994).

10 In the context of the Chesapeake, Lorena Walsh, Lois Carr, Russell Menard and others have done remarkable studies of the demographic histories of seventeenth-century Maryland and Virginia, despite the lack of vital records and adequate sources. Their ingenuity has transformed our consciousness of basic patterns of life in these regions in terms of marriage, death and family size, and provided us with a measure by which to judge the unusual conditions prevalent throughout so much of New England for the better part of a century. See, for example: Lois G. Carr and Lorena S. Walsh, "The Planter's Wife: The Experience of White Women in Seventeenth-Century Maryland," *William and Mary Quarterly,* 3rd Ser., XXXIV (1977), 542-71.

11 In many regions and contexts, however, records do not exist or exist only in highly fragmented forms: see, for example, Stephanie Grauman Wolf's *Urban*

themes in *Four Generations*. The excellent analysis of inheritance in Connecticut by Toby Ditz in *Property and Kinship* confirms many of the earlier arguments in my own book, but extends our understanding of family dynamics by exploring the experiences of the female members of families as well as the male members in terms of their property and inheritances.[12] Real property, in the form of land, was the prerogative of males during the eighteenth century in Connecticut, just as it was elsewhere in the colonies. In the Canadian context, Barry Moody's analysis of "Land, Kinship and Inheritance in Granville Township, 1760-1800" is a superb inquiry into these issues in Nova Scotia, many of whose early settlers were originally from Massachusetts and other parts of New England. These Nova Scotians brought with them experiences and traditions which dovetailed with the earlier studies of Andover and Plymouth colony. What emerges from Moody's persuasive account is the degree of transformation, of change rather than continuity with older patterns of patriarchal control by fathers over sons. Migration to Nova Scotia clearly altered many of the ways people lived their lives and shaped their family relationships. As Moody observed, "There is little evidence here of attempts to control or manipulate the children, to play the patriarch."[13] This is not overly surprising, actually, given the timing of their exodus from Massachusetts to Nova Scotia, for many mid-eighteenth-century fathers, even in towns like Andover, were no longer able to play the patriarchal roles available to their own fathers and grandfathers.[14]

Despite the contributions of such studies, the issues of family structure and kinship remain marginal, at best, in most recent studies of families and communities in New England and elsewhere. Christine Heyrman's sophisticated exploration of the communities of Gloucester and Marblehead from the late-

Village: Population, Community, and Family Structure in Germantown, Pennsylvania, 1683-1800 (Princeton, 1976).

12   Toby L. Ditz, *Property and Kinship: Inheritance in Early Connecticut, 1750-1820* (Princeton, 1986).

13   Barry Moody, "Land, Kinship and Inheritance in Granville Township, 1760-1800," in Margaret Conrad, ed., *Making Adjustments: Change and Continuity in Planter Nova Scotia, 1759-1800* (Fredericton, 1991), 175.

14   Most of the studies of families in the Chesapeake done in recent years have based their analyses on techniques that rely more upon literary sources than upon the reconstruction of life-experiences from deeds, probate records and other locally-based sources which underpinned most of the earlier studies of family structure and kinship. Daniel Blake Smith's *Inside the Great House: Planter Family Life in Eighteenth-Century Chesapeake Society* (Ithaca, N.Y., 1980), for instance, explores the issues of gender, parenting, child-rearing and kinship in considerable detail, but uses letters, diaries and other personal sources generated by the gentry during the eighteenth century.

seventeenth to the mid-eighteenth centuries in her book *Commerce and Culture* makes many references to kinship and family, but does not provide a systematic structural analysis of these subjects in their local contexts.[15] Families are not unimportant, but they also are not central to her study. The same can be said of Helena Wall's study *Fierce Communion: Family and Community in Early America*.[16] Her perspective on families is multi-regional and broad-based, not localized nor scrutinized in the depth and detail that characterizes most demographically-rooted analyses. Family structure and kinship do not engage her interest, even though she is sensitive to the interactions and relationships among neighbours and members of nucleated families.

With few notable exceptions, younger scholars have not chosen to make use of the methodologies of the 1960s and 1970s. They appear to have reverted to the more general literary techniques available to historians in earlier generations, even though their work is more sophisticated and informative than much of the work done in the 1940s and 1950s.

Families usually are studied in the contexts of communities, and the whole issue of the nature and functioning of communities in the colonial era has been a major concern for several decades now. Community studies became a focus for the inquiries of the late 1960s and early 1970s, and New England was the centre of focus for most scholars. The earlier work by Sumner Chilton Powell on Watertown and Sudbury alerted historians to the problem of tracking English immigrants into their new American towns and communities in order to discover what stayed the same and what changed in terms of their culture, society and polity. The subsequent studies of the English origins of many New England communities by David Grayson Allen emphasized the persistence of distinctive patterns of life in various English regions.[17] This perspective was enhanced by David Hackett Fischer's massive study of first and second generation folkways

---

The intensive analysis of the life-histories of all the residents of Middlesex County, Virginia, in the seventeenth century by Darrett and Anita Rutman in their superb book *A Place in Time* confirms the centrality of kinship networks for the English residents who lived and died in early Virginia. Their sources, however, are radically different from those used for previous studies of New England towns and families.

15   Christine Leigh Heyrman, *Commerce & Culture: The Maritime Communities of Colonial Massachusetts, 1690-1750* (New York, 1984).

16   Helena M. Wall, *Fierce Communion: Family and Community in Early America* (Cambridge, Mass., 1990).

17   David Grayson Allen, *In English Ways: The Movement of Societies and the Transferal of English Local Law and Custom to Massachusetts Bay in the Seventeenth Century* (Chapel Hill, 1981).

in *Albion's Seed*, which also argues that replication rather than transformation was the central fact of life for the early settlers of the British colonies in seventeenth- and eighteenth-century America.[18] Continuity, not change, is the basic emphasis of these studies of communities and societies.[19]

The issue of change and continuity actually was the subject of the earlier Planter Studies Conference in 1990. Certainly this has been the central theme of much of the research and writing concerning early Anglo-American communities in the seventeenth and eighteenth centuries, from the Chesapeake to Nova Scotia. In the early 1970s, Kenneth Lockridge's analysis of Dedham and my analysis of Andover both emphasized changes over the course of time, from the first to the fourth and fifth generations. Even the study of *Winthrop's Boston* by Darrett Rutman focused upon changes in the community from the initial effort to create a unified and cohesive social order to a fragmented and disorderly town two decades later. Lockridge described the creation of a "Christian Utopian Closed Corporate Community" in Dedham which subsequently dispersed and disintegrated into a far more individualistic and privatized township within the first hundred years.[20] Andover, too, began as a relatively cohesive community and then people dispersed about the town's lands as farms were carved out of wilderness and families chose to live upon their scattered acres distant from the original town center. Paul Boyer and Stephen Nissenbaum linked such processes of communal transformation to the phenomenon of witchcraft in their fascinating study of *Salem Possessed*.[21] While individual towns may have experienced such changes over the course of time, Bruce Daniels demonstrated in his analysis of *The Connecticut Town: Growth and Development, 1635-1790* that such processes were endemic throughout the colony.[22] In essence, his book detailed the "transition from communalism to in-

---

18 David Hackett Fischer, *Albion's Seed: Four British Folkways in America* (New York, 1989).

19 See, for example, Virginia De John Anderson, *New England's Generation: The Great Migration and the Formation of Society and Culture in the Seventeenth Century* (New York, 1991).

20 Lockridge, *A New England Town*, 16.

21 Paul Boyer and Stephen Nissenbaum, *Salem Possessed: The Social Origins of Witchcraft* (Cambridge, Mass., 1974).

22 Bruce C. Daniels, *The Connecticut Town: Growth and Development, 1635-1790* (Middletown, Ct., 1979).

dividualism" that Richard Bushman had noted earlier in *From Puritan to Yankee* and other historians of local communities had described as well.[23]

Among the crucial questions asked either implicitly or explicitly in many of the community studies have been these: Were these communities orderly and harmonious? If so, why? If not, why not? My study of Andover emphasized orderliness and harmony. I actually wrote that "the fundamental elements shaping the characteristics of family life in seventeenth-century Andover were profoundly important factors in transforming the utopian ideals of community and social order set forth by Governor John Winthrop into practical reality." I also argued that "the small agricultural towns like Andover probably proved to be excellent places in which to realize the goals of order, hierarchy, and the closely-knit community." Indeed, I went so far as to insist that "In no significant sense were the lives of the first and second generations in disorder, once their permanent roots had been firmly established in early Andover."[24] So I wrote, but was and is it true?

The answer must be somewhat ambiguous even now. It all depends upon who and what one looks at. What I neglected to note, even though I was fully aware of the facts, was that Andover was a community that had more people accused of witchcraft and confessing to being witches than any other town in Massachusetts in the early 1690s. For this one relatively brief moment in time, at least, the town was not orderly, not harmonious, and not peaceful. Several of Andover's inhabitants died as a result of the controversy over witchcraft, yet one would hardly know this from reading *Four Generations*. I must say, however,

---

23 Daniels, *The Connecticut Town,* 175. Also see Bushman, *From Puritan to Yankee.*

The themes embedded in so much of the literature on early New England communities also pervade the analysis of the entirely different context of the Chesapeake by Darrett and Anita Rutman, in their reconstruction of life and community in Middlesex Country, Virginia (*A Place in Time*). Their study proves conclusively that one need not create a town in order to form a community. Counties can serve just as effectively, because it is the human networks of kinship and friendship and neighbourliness that actually make communities function. But even they perceive a change over the course of time, as the population began to disperse, the social structure began to solidify, and slavery began to have a profound impact upon people's lives and culture. The internal workings of Middlesex County communities changed significantly over the course of time, just as was true in so many New England towns. Although they do not emphasize this point, it is clear that the harmony of the later period experienced by many whites depended upon the repression and enslavement of large numbers of blacks.

24 Greven, *Four Generations,* 170-171.

that readers could take note of the fact that William Barker, a second generation son, confessed that "he has been in the snare of the devil three years" — but that is all that a reader would discover from my book, except for one footnote which points out that Martha Carrier was "put to death as a witch."[25] Perhaps there were things happening in Andover that my analysis could not explain. Perhaps, indeed, the orderliness of the early generations that I emphasized was illusory. Perhaps I made a serious mistake of judgment by leaving out Andover's witches from my account, even though, in truth, this brief episode seemed to have almost no sustained impact upon the lives that unfolded in the documents that I explored. In terms of inheritances, family structures and demography, witchcraft seemed to be irrelevant, or nearly so. But in terms of the nature of the community itself, surely this was not the case. In 1970, however, there was nothing available in print to clue me into other ways of making sense of this community, and little to alter my perception of the continuities and orderliness of the lives of Andover's inhabitants. Witchcraft, as Perry Miller once noted, seemed a momentary aberration, not a revelatory event.[26]

More recent scholarship has transformed our understanding both of communities in early New England and the nature of witchcraft itself. It is the community, however, that I wish to focus upon here rather than the specific issue of witchcraft, fascinating as it may be. Boyer and Nissenbaum demonstrated that family disputes, neighbourly dissension, and subsequent factionalism were at the root of the witchcraft accusations in Salem Village. There was a long complex pre-history which enabled them to explain the outburst of such seemingly irrational behaviour, and their study helped make sense of what hitherto had seemed inexplicable.

More recently, John Demos has transformed our sense of early New England communities by his probing analysis of the social, communal and psychological roots of witchcraft in *Entertaining Satan*.[27] By not focusing on Salem Village, but exploring the phenomenon throughout New England, he reveals the persistence of conflicts among neighbours in various communities throughout the region. The central theme — which builds upon the analyses of witchcraft in England by Keith Thomas and Alan Macfarlane — is the conflict between concepts of community and concepts of individualism, between organicism and autonomy.[28] The ideals emphasized unity, order and harmony, but the realities of

25 Greven, *Four Generations*, 87, 107n.

26 Perry Miller, *The New England Mind From Colony to Province* (Cambridge, Mass., 1953), 191.

27 John Putnam Demos, *Entertaining Satan: Witchcraft and the Culture of Early New England* (New York, 1982).

28 Keith Thomas, *Religion and the Decline of Magic* (New York, 1971); Alan Macfarlane, *Witchcraft in Tudor and Stuart England* (New York, 1970).

daily life frequently belied such hopes and expectations. Demos demonstrates persuasively that witches served as communal lightning rods for the repressed and expressed anger, aggressiveness and hostility felt and experienced by vast numbers of people in the seventeenth-century colonies. Life was far more complex and difficult than most historians had realized. As a result, his analysis of several communities, together with the detailed exploration of individual and collective life-histories, makes absolutely clear the fact that towns like Andover were not Winthropian utopias after all, being riddled with disputes and disagreements throughout their histories.

More recently, Helena Wall's analysis of families and communities adds further confirmation of this assessment of early American community life. In one chapter she examines "The Tyranny of Neighbours" in terms of "Slander" and gossip. In several other chapters, she explores aspects of the family that reveal repeated instances of violence, abuse and domestic conflict, as well as parental neglect and harm to children. She, too, emphasizes the shift from a tightly knit communal world to a more loosely knit and individualistic world by the end of the eighteenth century. She concludes by observing that "By the late eighteenth century...many of the daily realities of family and community life, many of the assumptions and conditions on which that life had rested throughout the colonial period, had changed or weakened." Indeed, she argues that "Redefining the boundaries of the community and the purposes of the family constituted a revolution in private life in eighteenth-century America."[29] Whether or not this is true remains to be seen, but clearly she believes that a major transformation in both family and community life had occurred between settlement in the early seventeenth century and the revolution in the late eighteenth century.

Although so many historians of early American communities have emphasized a transition from order to disorder, from communalism to individualism, Christine Heyrman has managed to turn this assumption on its head in her analysis of Gloucester and Marblehead, Massachusetts. Her book's central theme can be described as the evolution of communities from disorder, bordering on chaos, into order bordering upon a realization by 1750 of the ideals that shaped John Winthrop's Puritans more than a century earlier. She notes that her study "departs from most other town studies by emphasizing continuity rather than change as the central characteristic of colonial New England's history." In effect, she does not read her stories in terms of "decline" but of solidification and cohesion, communities being formed into relatively harmonious entities. As she notes, "Instead of confirming the conventional view that the Puritan communal order collapsed under the pressure of economic expansion, the evolution of Gloucester and Marblehead illustrates the strength and

---

29   Wall, *Fierce Communion,* 137, 147.

resilience of traditional patterns of association and inherited beliefs and values."[30] Her subtle and sophisticated exploration of these two communities is one of the very finest local studies done recently. But it also confuses the issue still further for anyone who tries to tease out the long-term patterns of development and of meaning to be associated with communities in pre-revolutionary British America.

So far, most of the emphasis by scholars has been upon the outer or external histories of people's lives, with both families and communities being scrutinized in detail from a distance. We also need to consider some of the more intimate aspects of life. What have we learned about the psyches and thoughts of the people whom we study in such numbers and with such intensity? What do we know about the ways in which people's characters and beliefs were actually formed and shaped by the experiences of childhood, youth, and adulthood?

When John Demos published his first book in 1970 — *A Little Commonwealth* — he made use of demographic analysis for his exploration of Plymouth Plantation's inhabitants, but he also pioneered an entirely different direction in the study of families and communities by making use of the psychological theories and insights of Erik Erikson. Erikson's book *Childhood and Society* had a profound impact upon the way in which Demos framed his own historical analysis of the people in Plymouth colony, whose life-cycles unfold in the evocative prose of Demos's sensitive reconstruction.

Other historians also began to explore aspects of childhood and early life-experiences in the seventeenth- and eighteenth-century Anglo-American worlds. The massive exploration undertaken by Lawrence Stone in his book on *The Family, Sex and Marriage in England, 1500-1800* demonstrates that child-rearing and family life changed dramatically over the course of several centuries, oscillating between intensely repressive and extremely permissive periods of disciplining children, with repercussions for virtually all aspects of English life, society and culture.[31] Stone delineates brilliantly many of the most profound personal implications of these varying ways of rearing children and living in families and kinship groups. His analysis remains one of the most provocative and informative studies of the childhood roots of distinctive patterns of personality and cultural forms yet done by any historian.[32]

---

30 Heyrman, *Commerce and Culture,* 15, 18.

31 Lawrence Stone, *The Family, Sex and Marriage in England 1500-1800* (New York, 1977).

32 More limited in scope, but also important, is the work done by Linda Pollock on English and American childhood, using autobiographies and other literary sources to explore various aspects of childhood experience, discipline and rearing over the course of several centuries. She shares my view that there was far more continuity in many basic aspects of childhood experience than most historians would be prepared to believe. Her collection of sources on childhood and family

I would like to believe that the same can be said of my own subsequent book on *The Protestant Temperament*, which explored *Patterns of Child-Rearing, Religious Experience, and the Self in Early America* and was published the same year as Stone's massive book.[33] Unlike Stone's analysis, however, *The Protestant Temperament* ignores time and change over the long period from the early seventeenth century to the early nineteenth century, and argues that people's experiences — in terms of fundamental patterns of child-rearing and religious life — did not alter significantly over more than two centuries. Not surprisingly, this assumption disturbs most historians, who are trained to think in a linear mode, change usually being more important to them than continuity. My book also assumes that childhood is the formative matrix for adulthood, and that adulthood cannot be understood adequately without some awareness of the early life-experiences that shape the personalities of individuals and groups.[34] This assumption also bothers most historians, since they are trained to deal mostly with *adults* who write, speak and act, and whose records provide us with most of the evidence that we use to recover the past. My book also explores the emotional life of people of different temperaments — the self-repressing Evangelicals, the self-controlling Moderates, and the self-expressive Genteel. People's psyches are as important as other aspects of their lives and thought. Most historians are still uncomfortable with emotions — even those once felt by people long dead. They often resist trying to fathom the complexities of personalities, assuming that the inner worlds of people in the past are inaccessible to us now, unlike their external worlds of actions and words.[35]

life is well-worth examining, since she provides a useful array of diverse voices to consider when exploring Anglo-American family life in the seventeenth and eighteenth and early nineteenth centuries. See: Linda A. Pollock, *Forgotten Children: Parent-Child Relations from 1500 to 1900* (New York, 1983) and *A Lasting Relationship: Parents and Children Over Three Centuries* (Hanover, N.H., 1987).

33   Philip Greven, *The Protestant Temperament: Patterns of Child-Rearing, Religious Experience, and the Self in Early America* (New York, 1977).

34   For a recent interpretation of early American childhood, see Karin Calvert, *Children in the House: The Material Culture of Early Childhood, 1600-1900* (Boston, 1992).

35   Because of the assumption that childhood provided the basis for adulthood, my book was dismissed by Charles Cohen in the introduction to his study of *God's Caress: The Psychology of Puritan Religious Experience* (New York, 1986), because "a flawed research design dooms the attempt."(18) He believes that historians cannot use modern psychological theory to analyze seventeenth-century Puritans, and that we cannot connect childhood experiences with adults because the sources are all written by adults, not by children. As a result, his own study of Puritan psyches in the first generation in New England stays close

One major exception to this assertion, however, is to be found in John Demos's *Entertaining Satan*, which is one of the most probing psychological analyses of seventeenth-century New Englanders ever done.[36] His book is one of the most remarkable achievements of the past decade in terms of its exploration of the emotional life of early New Englanders. He demonstrates persuasively the centrality of anger, aggression, fear and hostility in the lives of ordinary folk in various communities. He makes brilliant use of psychoanalytic theories by Heinz Kohut and others to tease out the implications of childhood experiences in relation to adult personality conflicts. Methodologically, his book is light-years ahead of most of the field, but its daring exploration of the psyches of people fearful of witches appears to be too speculative for many historians. Speculation, however, has never seemed to be a problem for either John Demos or myself, since both of us have written books that pushed the boundaries of historical scholarship beyond the limits that most scholars find comfortable.

Before concluding, I want to offer some further speculations and thoughts for consideration by historians of a region that had intimate connections with

to the texts without seeming to impose much analysis upon their experiences. Of course, he missed so much by doing this.

Any psychotherapist today could confirm that adults need not know anything about their childhoods to be profoundly influenced by experiences in their formative years. Even though nearly all of the texts and documents from the seventeenth and eighteenth centuries were written by adults, every adult once was an infant and a child and a youth. Thus they had a personal history that ought not to be ignored when trying to understand the religious experiences and beliefs of any individuals or groups, be they first-generation New England Puritans or evangelical New Lights during the Great Awakening of the 1740s or Arminian Old Lights who bitterly opposed them or any other sort of religious type, then or now.

What Cohen failed to understand is that religious conversions provide mirrors of the complete life-experiences of anyone who undergoes such a transforming event. But to grasp the complexity of such experiences, historians need to pay heed to aspects of human life that most prefer to ignore — most especially those that take shape in childhood and form the basis for subsequent emotional life and psychic states that constitute the cores of human personality and character.

36 The other major recent exception is Kenneth A. Lockridge's *On the Sources of Patriarchal Rage: The Commonplace Books of William Byrd and Thomas Jefferson and the Gendering of Power in the Eighteenth Century* (New York, 1992), part of a series on "The History of Emotions" edited by Peter Stearns and Jan Lewis. Lockridge transforms our understanding of the powerful motives (often hidden from the men themselves) of rage, misogyny and envy that southern colonial males often obscured from themselves and their peers (as well as from subsequent generations of historians).

both Old and New England in the eighteenth century. The history of Nova Scotia and New Brunswick can be explored both in terms of the collective pasts of the immigrants from New England and elsewhere and the futures that they shaped as a result of their resettlement in these communities in Nova Scotia and New Brunswick. But these histories also can be explored by making use of questions and issues that hitherto have been overlooked or ignored by most scholars, but which — as a result of my own work for the past decade on the disciplining and the abuse of children — might alter our perspectives upon the historical experiences of people in the past, as it has for our understanding of the present.

The fields of family and community studies can provide models, both positive and negative, for Canadian Maritime history if they are read not for content but for design. Take the community studies first: I believe that we need to ask ourselves basic questions about the complex ways in which people organized their lives in new situations, drawing upon prior experiences and beliefs, customs, traditions and cultures, and then adjusting to the realities of entirely different contexts. We need to explore the issues of family structure, kinship and neighbourliness, to grasp the human dimensions of community and to perceive the ways in which things changed or stayed much the same over the course of time. We also need to ask ourselves questions about the nature of order and disorder in the context of both families and communities, sensitive now to issues around aggression, violence and abuse, both domestic and public, as well as to the ways in which people protected themselves from such experiences and created collective modes of order and civility even in new communities. Values, attitudes and beliefs all played a critical role in shaping people's lives and actions, and these, too, need to be assessed, making use of all that we have now learned about New Englanders' experiences over the course of a century and a half prior to their exodus to the Maritime colonies in the mid- to late-eighteenth centuries.

There are other issues that also matter but which historians are more likely to neglect or dismiss altogether, because they seem more elusive, more problematic, more unsettling. These are issues related to people's sense of self, their personalities, their innermost states of being, their psyches.[37] No better way exists to fathom such issues than to ask questions about their religious experiences and beliefs. Surely *The Protestant Temperament* demonstrates compellingly and in rich detail how profoundly different people throughout the colonies were in terms of the most central aspects of selfhood and beliefs. I explored three basic modes of temperament and religious experience, but obviously there were

---

37   See, for example: David Leverenz, *The Language of Puritan Feeling: An Exploration in Literature, Psychology, and Social History* (New Brunswick, N.J., 1980); John Owen King III, *The Iron of Melancholy: Structures of Spiritual Conversion in America from the Puritan Conscience to Victorian Neurosis*

many more present besides the ones I wrote about. Still, the immigrants to Nova Scotia and New Brunswick in the second half of the eighteenth century — both those who came voluntarily before the revolution and those who fled involuntarily during the revolution — brought very different temperaments and personalities as well as very different sets of religious experiences and beliefs with them, ranging from ardent New Light evangelicals to tepid Old Light moderates to self-assured but religiously indifferent genteel ladies and gentlemen.[38]

But, before concluding, there is something else that I now must add as a result of another decade of research and reflection following the publication of *The Protestant Temperament.* I also urge anyone who seeks to understand families and communities in eighteenth- and nineteenth-century Nova Scotia and New Brunswick to be sensitive to issues around the disciplining and rearing of children. I am aware now, as I was not altogether clear earlier, that physical punishments have profoundly damaging consequences for many people, consequences that persist from childhood throughout the entire life of an individual. My subsequent book, *Spare the Child,* explores some of the complex ways in which violence against children misshapes the psyches and sense of selfhood of those who were victimized by painful assaults by parents and other adults in the name of discipline.[39] This was no less true in the seventeenth and eighteenth centuries than it is today. But historians rarely take this issue with the seriousness that it merits.

Certainly I know from research I did many years ago on families such as the Belcher and the Byles families, some of whom immigrated to Nova Scotia during the revolution while others remained behind in Massachusetts, that attitudes toward children among New Englanders ranged from intensely punitive to intensely devoted. The Mather Byles family were of the latter sort, utterly

---

(Middletown, Ct., 1983); John Stachniewski, *The Persecutory Imagination: English Puritanism and the Literature of Religious Despair* (Oxford, 1991); Julius H. Rubin, *Religious Melancholy and Protestant Experience in America* (New York, 1994).

38 See, for example, the brilliant analysis by Rhys Isaac: *The Transformation of Virginia, 1740-1790: Community, Religion, and Authority* (Chapel Hill, 1982).

39 Philip Greven, *Spare the Child: The Religious Roots of Punishment and the Psychological Impact of Physical Abuse* (New York, 1991). Also see my study of the Reverend Michael Wigglesworth, the seventeenth-century New England poet of *The Day of Doom*: "'Some Root of Bitterness': Corporal Punishment, Child Abuse, and the Apocalyptic Impulse in Michael Wigglesworth," in James A. Henretta, Michael Kammen and Stanley N. Katz, eds., *The Transformation of Early American History: Society, Authority, and Ideology* (New York, 1991), 93-122.

captivated by their children and adoring of them. By examining their papers in detail to see how their attitudes and values were mirrors of their life-histories and beliefs, I am sure that we would discover a close correlation between these aspects of their being and behaviour. We also, by contrast, would be able to see why and how they differed from their new neighbours in Halifax and elsewhere in Nova Scotia. The New Lights of this era had entirely different values and attitudes toward children, as they did toward religion. My books help explain why this was so.

Historians have a rare opportunity to expand our understanding of the ways in which prior generations of human beings have taken shape and lived their lives. We can focus on their external lives, reconstructing their actions in detail and exploring their written words at length, and there is much to be said for doing so. But we also have an opportunity to do something even more daring, if we choose: We can focus upon their innermost being, their sense of self, their feelings and fantasies and thoughts, their personalities, their characters and their temperaments. If we do this, we will enhance our understanding of the ways in which successive generations of people sustain or transform the ways in which prior generations experienced themselves and their lives.

The past is never truly past. Just as within ourselves, our individual pasts live on, encoded in our memories and our bodies, so too our collective past persists, even when we least notice it. That is why being a historian is such a challenge. To understand people whose lives have been completed enriches our knowledge of ourselves and others. Surely no one could seek to do more. But it does entail asking the right questions if the answers are to prove useful and valuable to us now and in the future. That is why we are gathered together here: to ask new questions and to find some answers. This conference is both a culmination and a new beginning, as we reflect upon the past and look ahead to the future.

Widowhood and Canadian Family History

Bettina Bradbury
Professor of History
York University

Introduction

When figures dressed in black appear in the pages of Canadian history texts, they are more likely to be Jesuits or other "black robed" men than widows in their mourning clothes. Widowers, their male counterparts, have been even more shady characters in the works of social and family history. Yet, widows and widowers have historically constituted a much greater proportion of the population than priests or the nuns who were often so important in offering support to grief- and poverty- stricken men and women whose spouses had died. In this article, I examine how it is that widowhood has received such scant attention in the literature written about the family and communities in pre-twentieth-century Canada.[1] I start by drawing on major works in Canadian family history to demonstrate the numerical importance of widowhood. In the following sections, I argue that the methodologies and conceptual approaches of family history, particularly the study of family structures, historical demography, the family economy and inheritance have too often only allowed us tantalizing glimpses of this important part of the life cycle of those who married and outlived their partners. In the final section, I examine whether works by historians in Canadian women's or gender history have avoided some of these problems, offering a more comprehensive picture of widowhood in the past and suggest that to date they have not. I do not intend to survey every Canadian work dealing with the period before the twentieth century that mentions widowhood. Rather, my goal is to use some of the major works in family history and women's history to assess how useful their approaches have been in helping us to see widowhood as an important element of the history of families in the past.

---

1   I draw largely on Canadian literature here, and especially on published monographs and articles rather than theses. My comments would apply also to much family history written in the United States and in Europe until the last few years. This gap in the literature has begun to receive attention in several survey articles. Especially useful are: Ida Blom, "The History of Widowhood: A Bibliographic Overview," *Journal of Family History*, 16, 2 (April 1991), 191-210; Yves Aubry, "Pour une étude du veuvage féminin à l'époque modern," *Histoire, économie, et société*, 8, 2 (1989), 223-36; Alexander Keyssar, "Widowhood in Eighteenth-Century Massachusetts: A Problem in the History of the Family," *Perspectives in American History*, 8 (1974), 81-119. Ida Blom suggests that this stage of the life cycle may have received such scant attention compared to other stages because of its association with the histories of old age and death, "fairly

The Numerical Significance of Widowhood

Widowhood was the experience of one partner in all marriages except those where the spouses died at the same time. It was a normal phase in the family life cycle. In contrast to the more usual situation today where most deaths occur when the spouses are elderly, in the past higher death rates at all ages meant a man or woman could lose their spouse at any time across their married life. The impact of death on families in the past, then, was closer to that of divorce today.

Even when the historian's interest in widowhood is minimal, studies of specific communities demonstrate the numerical importance of widows and widowers. Some studies reveal the numbers of widowed people in the population at specific points in time — usually when the census was taken. Those drawing on more demographic sources measure the timing of widowhood within populations across time. In either case, we get some sense of the impact of death on pre-twentieth-century populations, and of the gender differences in mortality and remarriage rates.

Widowhood was widespread in New France and was certainly not limited to the elderly. Danielle Gauvreau's recent study of Quebec City prior to the conquest shows that some 20 percent of these urban women became widows before they reached 30 years of age, and around the same proportion of men were widowed before the age of 35. Around two-thirds of all women whose history she could trace with certainty were widowed before they reached 50. Proportions were slightly lower for the men.[2]

Clearly, rates of widowhood vary across time depending on the impact of disease, war and accidents as well as the risks of childbirth for women. Whether men or women remained widowed or remarried has also varied, depending on local sex ratios, the prevailing ages of death, and other options available to widows and widowers. In Quebec City prior to the conquest, men were widowed younger as the numbers of apparently tough and healthy young women immigrating from France who had formed the early cohorts of wives

---

new fields," or because of the negative stereotyping of old women historically. I think the reasons are more closely linked to the development of family history, and to the obsession of early family historians with questions of family structure and of demographers with "completed" families. Sheva Medjuck outlines some of the reasons early historians of the family ignored women in "Women's Response to Economic and Social Change in the Nineteenth Century: Moncton Parish, 1851-1871," *Atlantis,* 11, 1 (Fall 1985), 7-8.

2   Danielle Gauvreau, *Québec: Une ville et sa population au temps de la Nouvelle France* (Québec, 1991), 119.

diminished and more wives were drawn from the expanding local population.[3] In the seventeenth century when women were in short supply, remarriage rates were high among young widows in Quebec City, as they were in Montreal. Over the eighteenth century, remarriage rates began to resemble the more usual historical pattern elsewhere, with men much more likely to remarry than women, confirming, as Gauvreau suggests, men's need to "re-establish the equilibrium made necessary by the sexual division of labour within the household."[4] Allan Greer suggests that, as late as the mid-eighteenth century in the small town of Sorel, widows were still "more likely to find a second mate who had never previously married" than were local widowers. By the early decades of the nineteenth century, however, men there, too, were more likely to remarry.[5]

In rural and urban nineteenth-century Canada, widowhood was still widespread, widows outnumbered widowers by as much as three to one, and men were much more likely to remarry than women. David Gagan found that in Peel County, Canada West, one out of five women died during her childbearing years. For their survivors in this largely rural county, widowhood was a temporary state. Of the men who were permanent householders and under the age of 35 in 1852, one out of five became widowers over the next two decades, but nine out of ten of them remarried. Men five or ten years older were equally likely to lose a wife, but less likely to remarry. These findings led him to conclude that "family completion was as urgent a priority" for the men as was "family formation." Although he reports that one out of five women was widowed while still the mother of young offspring, he does not discuss remarriage among widows, leaving readers assuming that the clauses men wrote in their wills cutting their wives off from support should they remarry determined behaviour.[6] He does report that in 1871 "some 175 of every 1,000 of the ever-married women in Peel were widows," and gives details on their household status to which I shall return shortly.

---

3   On the longer life expectancy of immigrants and its implication for the unfolding of family life cycles see Yves Landry et Jacques Légaré, "Le cycle de vie familiale en Nouvelle-France: méthodologie et application à un échantillon," *Histoire sociale/ Social History,* XVII, 33 (May 1984); Gauvreau, *Québec,* 118.

4   Gauvreau, *Québec,* 126, 136; Louise Dechêne, *Habitants and Merchants in Seventeenth Century Montreal* (Montreal and Kingston, 1992), 53.

5   Allan Greer, *Peasant Lord and Merchant: Rural Society in Three Quebec Parishes, 1740-1840* (Toronto, 1985), 53.

6   David Gagan, *Hopeful Travellers: Families, Land, and Social Change in Mid-Victorian Peel County, Canada West* (Toronto, 1981) 89, 93.

While many rural widows would have remained on their farms, provided for by sons and daughters-in-law and sometimes running them themselves, some moved into nearby villages and towns where a greater array of services were available.[7] Larger cities like Montreal, Toronto, Hamilton and Ottawa may well have attracted disproportionate numbers of poor widows, in particular, because of the greater array of charities and work opportunities.[8] Certainly Michael Katz appears to have been struck by the extent of widowhood in Hamilton between the 1850s and 1870s.[9] In 1871 around one-third of all women in their fifties were widows, three-fifths were once they passed sixty. He reports that the total number of widows shot up by 133 percent in the decade between 1851 and 1861, increasing the percentage of all adult women who were widows from eight to 13. He does not investigate why, and by focusing on those resident in the city in both decades "to eliminate the possibly distorting effects of transiency," he effectively cuts off analysis of the possibility that widows came to Hamilton from other areas because it offered specific advantages to them. Even among those remaining in the city between 1851 and 1861, the impact of death is clear. One-third of women aged 50 to 59 lost a spouse in that decade, were compared to only 15 percent of men. Husbands of the predominantly poor, Irish Catholic women were much more likely to die than those of the "Canadian-born Protestant women, the most well-to-do."[10] In Montreal, the numbers of widows increased from around 3,000 in 1861 to over 7,000 in 1891, while widowers numbered only 1,000 and 2,000 respectively. In 1891 nearly one-quarter of women in their fifties were widows; in their seventies two-thirds were, compared to only one-third of men in the latter age group.[11]

---

7   There are hints of this pattern in Bruce Elliott's *Irish Migrants in the Canadas: A New Approach* (Kingston and Montreal, 1988), 174, 176. Danielle Gauvreau reports there were disproportionate numbers of widows in Quebec city in the censuses of 1716 and 1744. *Québec*, 92.

8   Bettina Bradbury, "Mourir chrétiennement. La vie et la mort dans les établissments catholiques pour personnes âgées à Montréal au XIXe siècle," *Revue d'histoire de L'Amérique française*, 46, 1 (été, 1992), 155.

9   Michael Katz, *The People of Hamilton, Canada West: Family and Class in a Mid-Nineteenth-Century City* (Cambridge, Mass., 1975), 254; Katz, *et al.*, *The Social Organization of Early Industrial Capitalism* (Cambridge, Mass, 1982), 100. Katz argues, in the first book, that the extent of widowhood should not be underestimated, in the second, that it should not be "minimized."

10 Katz, *The People*, 58-59, 254-55.

11 Bettina Bradbury, *Working Families: Age, Gender and Daily Survival in Industrializing Montreal* (Toronto, 1993), 184.

Wherever we look, then, widowhood was clearly the experience of a substantial minority of the adult population, of a majority of older women at any one point in time, and the experience of many more at some point in their adult lives. Age gaps between husbands and wives meant that women were likely to survive their husbands. This only partially explains the vast discrepancies in the numbers of widows and widowers in most populations. With the exception of the years in New France when men outnumbered women dramatically, it was a state women tended to stay in and men to get out of through remarriage, though the likelihood of remarriage decreased for both men and women with age.

In examining periods prior to the twentieth century, when death could hit at all ages because of disease, war and accidents, this dissolution of families by death needs to be conceptualized in as comprehensive a way as possible, taking into account the nature of the community, the economy, the period, legal structures and meanings of gender. Yet many of the methods and approaches we have used to study family history in Canada — few of which could be seen as intrinsically Canadian — have tended to mute rather than highlight widowhood. I do not want to suggest that widows, or even widowers, are absent from such works. Widows, in particular, flit through their pages, dark figures in black, occasionally coming close to life, but usually in some stereotypical form — as victims of patriarchy or poverty and occasionally as heroic exercisers of power. The dissolution of the family by death, and what this meant for the remaining partner and children, however, is usually inadequately analyzed.

Family Structures

Canadian historians have not escaped the obsession with family structures that characterized the early phases of family history in the 1970s and gave primacy to the question of whether industrialization had brought about the rise of the nuclear family. This was especially so in England, and to a lesser extent in the United States.[12] In borrowing both this major question and ways of categorizing family structures from the work of Peter Laslett and the Cambridge Population Studies group, Canadian historians adopted methodologies and typologies in which measurement of how many families were nuclear or extended was likely to take precedence over, what seem to me now, more interesting, and politically and historically relevant, questions. In particular, the focus on the question of whether extended or nuclear household structures had predominated in the past tended to hide the prevalence of single-parent families. In most of the analyses, widows and widowers heading their own households

---

12 The pioneer in this work was Peter Laslett. See especially Peter Laslett with Richard Wall, *Household and Family in Past Time* (Cambridge, England, 1972); Richard Sennett, *Families against the City: Middle Class Homes in Industrial Chicago* (Cambridge, Mass, 1970); Michael Anderson, *Family Structure in Nineteenth-Century Lancashire* (Cambridge, England, 1971).

were mentioned briefly, then included in following discussions that aimed to show that nuclear or "simple" families have always predominated. Any who did not head their households were lost within various categories of extended and multiple family households.[13]

This focus is particularly obvious in two early Canadian studies in the field of family history — Michael Katz on Hamilton between 1851 and 1871 and David Gagan on Peel County in the decades leading up to 1871. In Michael Katz's earliest work, *The People of Hamilton: Family and Class in a Mid-Nineteenth-Century City,* he appears to dismiss, in his introduction, the whole question of the existence of extended families in the past as "meaningless," a myth or as a tired issue.[14] Yet, he sticks with the question. Hamilton families were, he tells us, "overwhelmingly nuclear" — "in the vast majority of instances they formed nuclear families." Certainly his figures seem to prove this, and overall he is no doubt correct. One of the two main tables dealing with this question, and the one in which he gets the closest to considering it by focusing on the family life cycle, shows that in both 1851 and 1861 some two-thirds of households were a simple family when the head was aged under 30; this rose to over 80 percent among 50-59 year olds, then fell somewhat for the elderly. There are three problems with using such a table as a way to understand family structures at that time, and especially to assess the extent of widowhood. I focus on these problems in some detail because they are common to other works. Firstly, he only uses those families with a male head — we do not see any families headed by widows in this particular table. Secondly, even those headed by widowers are collapsed in the category of simple family. Thirdly, any widows or widowers living in extended or multiple families other than as heads are lost.[15]

In one other table Katz allows us to determine how important widow-headed households were in the city, and the proportions seem significant.[16] In 1861 around six percent of all households were headed by a widower with a child, and a similar proportion were headed by widows. Twelve percent of all households, then, at that time, were headed by a single parent — a point not mentioned in the text. In virtually all other discussions of family structure, these single-parent families are absorbed, collapsed and lost in the broader category of nuclear family.

---

13   The typology developed by Peter Laslett and his colleagues is set out in *Household and Family,* 31.

14   Katz, *The People,* 9.

15   Katz, *The People,* 35, 40, 251, Table 5.12.

16   Katz, *The People,* 223, Table 5.2.

David Gagan's work is equally difficult to use to determine the importance of widow- or widower-headed families. His category for simple family households completely hides any such families either as household heads or as parts of subsequent conjugal units within a household. Elderly widows or widowers living within the household disappear among relatives, boarders or visitors, despite his insistence in other parts of the book on the intricate main- tenance agreements made for widows in men's wills.[17] We do learn that, in 1871, 175 of every 1,000 ever-married women in Peel Country were widows, and that only 42 percent of them were mistresses of their own households, an in- crease from a decade earlier when only 35 percent were not dependents of the heads of the households in which they lived.[18] Because he carefully read and analyzed the wills made in this part of Ontario, he is able to spell out more about the lives that they might expect as widows in these households.

Katz's study does allow us to see the importance of taking in boarders for widows, 75 percent of whom did not list an employment themselves. Over three-quarters had boarders in 1851, some two-fifths a decade later. We get a hint of the impact of industrialization in his suggestion that by 1871 "the expan- sion of employment opportunity close to home for themselves and their children" meant that widows might be better "able to make ends meet on their own." Certainly this was true in industrializing Montreal where the average number of offspring working in widows' families increased between 1861 and 1881, then apparently began to decline.[19] Because such studies draw on the manuscripts of the censuses, the authors are able to describe how many widows had jobs and what they were.

The primary focus on male-headed households in these studies, and the par- ticular categorizations of family structures used, have tended to hide those men and women whose way of dealing with widowhood was to return to their parents, share households with other widowed men or women, or board with others. Furthermore, the discussions of widows or widowers in these works tend to pop up here and there, tied into other questions, rather than as an important phenomenon, or important phase in the family life cycle. The research does sug- gest that widows in cities like Hamilton or Montreal were more likely to maintain autonomous households than were those in rural areas like Peel Coun-

---

17 He makes no mention of whether widowed mothers living on a farm apparently run by their sons were ever listed as household heads. This seemed to be the practice in Moncton Parish where Sheva Medjuck reports that enumerators did list widows as heads of households in which their sons were clearly doing the farming. "Women's Response," 19.

18 Gagan, *Hopeful Travellers*, Table 17, 64; 54-55; 89.

19 Katz, *The People*, 59-60; Bradbury, *Working Families*, 203-6.

ty, where the arrangements husbands made in their wills shifted their dependence from their dead partner to the inheritor of the family farm.[20]

Historical Demography

Has the approach of historical demographers, with their methods of family
reconstitution and meticulous methodologies for measuring death rates, marriage and remarriage, migration and fertility, offered a better way of grasping the
significance of widowhood among past families? It has when demographers
carefully measure the extent of the phenomenon — the proportions of men and
women in specific cohorts and periods who ended their lives as widows or
widowers, or who lived as widows or widowers for a time and then remarried.
This is the case when demographers use a life-cycle approach to analyse their
data rather than simply measuring rates of marriage and death within populations. Longitudinal studies based on family reconstitution and analyses of
population patterns of whole regions like the studies of New France being pursued by demographers and historians at the Université de Montréal, and of the
Saguenay by historians, geneologists and others at the Université du Québec à
Chicoutimi also successfully demonstrate the extent of widowhood.[21] In other
methods that are widely used by historical demographers, the experience of
widows and widowers are frequently cast aside, swallowed up in demographic
conventions drawn from twentieth-century demography that hide the realities of
past family life by focusing only on families where both spouses live to the end
of childbearing and by eliminating what are called "uncompleted families" from
analysis. At other times technical terminology can obscure our understanding of
the processes involved.

The significance of widowhood in the past is obscured, for example, in all
demographic analyses that attempt to determine historical patterns of fertility by

20   In Montreal 60 to 70 percent of widows living in Sainte Anne and Saint Jacques
wards headed their own households between 1861 and 1891. Bradbury, *Working
Families*, 206.

21   For a recent description of the work of the Université de Montréal demographers
see Jacques Légaré, "A Population Register for Canada under the French
Régime: Context, Scope, Content and Applications," *Canadian Studies in
Population* 15, 1 (1988) and Hubert Charbonneau, Bertrand Desjardins, André
Guillemette, Yves Landry and Françoise Nault, *Naissance d'une population: Les
Français établis au Canada au XVIIe siècle* (Paris and Montreal, 1988). On the
Saguenay studies see, for example, Gérard Bouchard, "Introduction à l'étude de
la société saguenayenne aux XIXe et XXe siècles," *Revue d'histoire de
l'Amérique française*, 31, 1 (juin 1978); Christian Pouyez et al., *Les
Saguenayens: Introduction à l'histoire des populations du Saguenay, XVIe-Xxe
siècles* (Québec, 1983); Gérard Bouchard, "Donation entre vifs et inégalités sociales au Saguenay. Sur la reproduction familiale en contexte de satruation de
l'espace agraire," *Revue d'histoire de l'Amérique française, 46, 3 (hiver, 1993)*.

focusing only on completed families. When the childbearing history of a family is interrupted by the death of a spouse, it is usual practice to eliminate these "incomplete families" from the analysis. Given the high rates of widowhood in the past, this is a misleading way of presenting past demographic patterns. For example, when Gagan discussed fertility, he calculated the average number of children in "completed" families, the number of children under 10 per 1,000 married women, and the number of children per married women of specific ages. Only after the discussion of fertility does he point out that many women did not survive their childbearing years and that others became widows. Yet their fertility is not discussed.[22]

Some recent works by demographers influenced by studies of the life course, and (less frequently) by feminist historiography, have treated widowhood more seriously, making it the focus of their studies rather than an annoying variable to be controlled for. Danielle Gauvreau and Mario Bourque make "the formation and rupture of unions" central in their study of couples married in the Saguenay prior to 1930, and go beyond traditional demographic analyses by acknowledging that because of the sexual division of labour within families the death of a spouse meant very different things for men and women.[23] Since they can draw on the data base of the Saguenay population that includes all births, deaths, marriages and remarriages recorded in parish registers, they are able to follow couples from marriage to the death of the first spouse, know who remarried and when the second spouse died. In this area of colonisation where the tasks of husband and wife were equally vital to survival, one in five marriages was broken by death before the other partner reached fifty. As in the settlement of New France, unbalanced sex ratios during the early period of colonisation led to rapid remarriage among widows. Subsequently, although remarriage rates for both men and women seem higher than in urban areas, widowers remarried faster than widows and more of them did so.[24]

Clearly, access to constituted population databases facilitates measuring the extent of widowhood. Drawing on the database of *Programme de recherche en démographie historique* at the Université de Montréal, Yves Landry has been able to follow the *filles du roi* from their arrival in New France, through marriage to the dissolution of those marriages at death. The results that he reports in his *Les filles du roi au XVIIe siècle* show how useful such databases can be. Two-thirds of these women ended up widows, in large part because most were

---

22 Gagan, *Hopeful Travellers*, 72, 73, 77, 89.

23 Danielle Gauvreau and Mario Bourque, "'Jusqu'à ce que la mort nous sépare': Le destin des femmes et des hommes mariés au Saguenay avant 1930," *Canadian Historical Review*, LXXI, 4 (1990), 442.

24 Gauvreau and Bourque, "'Jusqu'à ce que la mort nous sépare,'" 456-60.

much younger than their husbands. Nearly one-quarter became widows between the ages of 30 and 45, when they were most likely to have young children to care for. On average, however, women were not widowed until they reached 51, men nearly three years older. Relegated to footnotes are odd glimpses of the people behind the statistics. Marie Hatanville, for example, was widowed three times. When her third husband died in 1685 she had 11 surviving children under 15 years of age. She remarried again several months later to a widower who already had seven youngsters![25] Here one might celebrate the famed Quebec fertility, but underlining the advantages of such a relatively complete database seems equally important.

Tracing large numbers of couples from marriage to death as well as to censuses is fraught with challenges and difficulties. Danielle Gauvreau spells these out very carefully in her study of the population of Quebec City before the Conquest and offers some solutions to those doing similar studies.[26] Despite the methodological difficulties, Gauvreau carefully examines widowhood as an experience differing for men and women and dedicates a chapter to the rupture of marriages and the importance of remarriage, showing how widespread it was. In the cases where she knows the date of death of both partners her findings correspond to those of other Quebec demographers — more marriages were broken by the death of the husband than the wife (57 percent versus 43 percent), so that women were more likely to be widows than men widowers, in large part because of age disparities. One of her most important contributions is to consider widowhood by the occupation of the husbands. She found that the wives of merchants and artisans in construction were more likely to become widows early than those of military or civil officers or other artisans, among whom it appears from her tables that the women were more likely to die first. The causes were different — merchants tended to be much older than their wives, and therefore more likely to die first, whereas artisans in construction were in a dangerous occupation.[27] Such consideration of the differential impact of death by occupation seems important in establishing the demography of widowhood and thinking about how class made a difference to the experiences of women as widows.

Work by historical demographers that follows couples from marriage formation to its dissolution by death, then, can be very useful in giving us an understanding of the extent of widowhood and of its timing. Yet, often we see little of the social or emotional side of it. The techniques of historical demography and family reconstitution can only take us so far. Widowhood was much

---

25   Yves Landry, *Les Filles du roi au XVIIe siècle: Orphelines en France, pionnières au Canada* (Montréal, 1992), 247-48.

26   Gauvreau, *Québec,* 66-70, 113-15, 122.

27   Danielle Gauvreau, *Québec,* 116.

more than a demographic event. It involved emotional reactions ranging from despair to relief, re-adjustment of family relations, and usually some kind of restructuring of the family economy.

The Family Economy

Historians focussing on the concept of the family economy have also ignored widowhood, largely because they treat sex roles within the family as complementary. Chad Gaffield, for example, stresses the importance of the role of each family member in the family economies of the people he studies in Prescott and Russell counties between 1851 and 1871. Despite discussions of family formation and family size, there is no hint that death might hit, let alone of what this might have meant for the surviving partner and children. Nor, when he discusses household structures, is there the slightest indication that at the moment the census was taken some of his "single, conjugal-family units" may have been headed by one, rather than two, parents.[28]

Allan Greer, like Chad Gaffield, draws on Chayanov's concept of peasant families to discuss the family economy of French-Canadians in the Lower Richelieu Valley between the 1740s and 1840s. There, he argues, "much more than in most rural societies, the family household was the fundamental unit of agricultural production."[29] The very notion of the family economy, with its division of labour by sex and age seems to make it likely that those families that temporarily or permanently had only one parent would be ignored. Greer avoids this problem because he draws on a variety of notarial documents, combined with some work in parish registers, that allow him to follow the marriage and remarriage histories of specific families. Thus we do see widows and widowers in his book, not just as statistical entities, but as social actors. The widow of Nicolas Thibault, for example, went to see her notary in 1760, and, by deed of gift, gave her portion of the family farm to her son Toussaint. In what Greer argues was a fairly typical pension arrangement for the period, Toussaint agreed to allow her "to live in the house for the rest of her life and to provide heat, light, and clothing, plus sixteen minots of flour, a quarter minot of salt, and 120 pounds of salt pork every year."[30]

Marjorie Cohen does not ignore widows in her study of *Women's Work: Markets and Economic Development in Nineteenth Century Ontario* because she uses a feminist analysis to determine women's role and power within the

---

28   Chad Gaffield, *Language, Schooling, and Cultural Conflict: The Origins of the French-Language Controversy in Ontario* (Montreal and Kingston, 1987), 56.

29   Greer, *Peasant*, 25.

30   Greer, *Peasant*, 34.

family and, like Gagan, examines wills that deal with widowhood.[31] We need more studies building on those of David Gagan, Allan Greer and Marjorie Cohen that would enrich our understanding of the family economy of rural widows. Systematic examination of maintenance agreements, like those used selectively by Greer, of wills drawn up in different areas, or of the residential situation of widows in agricultural areas and villages might give us a better idea of the diversity of widows' experiences. Historians need to examine other types of provisions made for widows as well as to determine what women actually received and what they did with it. Here the more genealogical approach taken by Bruce Elliot might be used to advantage. He was able, for example, to show that the small percentage of Ottawa Valley widows who received cash or an annuity from their husbands were able to use it to live independently.[32]

Interest in the family economy, then, like most of these approaches, has tended to preclude consideration of how families headed by a woman or man on their own operated, although this is not necessary. Several recent articles have examined how widows managed in nineteenth-century cities, looking at the jobs they held and some other ways of getting by.[33] These studies are limited, however, by their reliance on the census as a major source. Manuscript censuses show when a widow reported an occupation, and can demonstrate a widow's reliance on her children's earnings or her use of a garden or livestock to make ends meet. They do not, unfortunately, allow historians to see other resources she might have received such as her dower or inheritance.

Inheritance and the Law

Historians studying wills, other documents involving the transmission of land, and laws regarding inheritance have usually paid attention to widowhood. This stage of the family life cycle was hard to ignore because the documents were made by men or women who had set out to explain what should happen to their spouse, children and property when they died. It is his research in various notarial documents involving transmission of land that gave Alan Greer many of the examples of widows and other individuals that help to make his book such a lively read. The fact that the community of property created upon marriage in Quebec had to be inventoried when a spouse died to dissolve the first marriage

---

31   Marjorie Cohen, *Women's Work: Markets and Economic Development in Nineteenth-Century Ontario* (Toronto, 1988).

32   Elliott, *Irish Migrants*, 198-99.

33   Lorna McLean, "Single Again: Widow's Work in the Urban Family Economy, Ottawa, 1871," *Ontario History*, LXXXIII, 2 (June 1991), 127-50; Bettina Bradbury, "Surviving as a Widow in 19th Century Montreal," *Urban History Review*, 17, 3 (1989), 148-60; Bradbury, *Working Families*.

community has filled notarial archives with information about the material contents of people's houses, itemizing what a widow might lay claim to in her new civil status, although this has not been the way such documents have generally been used.

Similarly, studying wills enabled David Gagan to go beyond the question of household structure and begin to see how men provided for their wives. The picture he presents is bleak. Most wives, he suggests, "became the dependents of their sons, grandsons, sons-in-law or their husbands' executors, their standard of living and even their future conduct prescribed or proscribed literally from the grave." Over one-fifth of the husbands forbade them to remarry or cohabit as a condition of inheritance, with penalties ranging from loss of income or rights of domicile to loss of guardianship over their own children. Reading these wills shapes his whole treatment of widowhood for women. It was "a calamity the consequences of which clearly troubled even the stoutest hearts."[34] Ignoring the 40 percent he has said headed their own households, and the diversity of provisions made in wills, Gagan offers no hints of the diversity of their lived experience. Widows are written solidly in as victims: "the quality of their lives clearly depended on the nature of the contractual arrangements which deceased partners had made with their heirs, and on the strength of sentimental attachments within the family." Unable to resist this vision of victimization, he adds that few would have suffered the fate of one unfortunate grandmother who was reported to have died "like a hog up in the garret" in Toronto Township.[35]

Marjorie Cohen and Nanciellen Davis paint a similar picture of the exercise of 'Patriarchy from the Grave' and of the dependence of widows on their children following a husband's death.[36] Widows emerge as strongly as victims of patriarchy in their analyses as they do in Gagan's, with only the occasional one standing out as remarkable because a husband did indeed leave her some property or measure of autonomy. Both Gagan and Cohen imply that most rural widows lived out their lives dependent on sons for their support, often "little more than a drudge," in Susanna Moodie's words.[37] Bruce Elliott, in contrast, argues that Irish Protestant husbands from Tipperary who settled in the Ottawa Valley "allowed the women as much freedom and control as was possible without endangering the principle that the farm must revert to a male heir of the late husband after her death." The majority of men in the 52 wills he studied

---

34 Gagan, *Hopeful Travellers*, 55-56, 89.

35 Gagan, *Hopeful Travellers*, 89-90.

36 Nanciellen Davis, "'Patriarchy from the Grave': Family Relations in 19th Century New Brunswick Wills," *Acadiensis*, XIII, 2 (Spring 1984), 91-100; Cohen, *Women's Work*.

37 Cohen, *Women's Work*, 52-53.

gave their widows control over the homestead for life or until remarriage "even though this often meant denying the inheriting son title for decades." Others received a house or specified rooms, as well as maintenance provisions. Only one in ten received some kind of cash or annuity that might have allowed them to live independently.[38]

These fragments of information about provisions made for widows in different communities suggest there is much more to learn about the variety of experiences of rural widows. A systematic examination of men's wills in different areas of Canada in combination with other sources that could show where widows lived, with whom, and how they managed economically and socially might well reveal specific regional and ethnic traditions. American historian Lisa Wilson compared the estates that women in two areas of Pennsylvania received between the mid-eighteenth and nineteenth centuries and their own estates at the time of their death. The majority appear to have spent most of what they received, but a minority managed to increase their estates substantially. It clearly was not only in New France, or in the early colonial period, that women were able to profit from widowhood.[39]

Comparisons of provisions made for rural and urban widows in different periods would be useful and would help reveal how the changing bases of wealth in Canadian society made a difference to inheritance decisions and the fate of wives whose husbands died.[40] No Canadian studies that I have found

---

38 Elliott, *Irish Migrants*, 198-99. American historian Lisa Wilson's analysis is closer to Elliott's. In discussing the legacies given to widows in Chester County, Pennsylvania, between 1750 and 1805, she points out that the family farm was both a farm and a business; she suggests these rather typical rural legacies for widows were a "common sense response" in realizing family goals. Lisa Wilson, *Life After Death: Widows in Pennsylvania, 1750-1850* (Philadelphia, 1992), 107.

39 Lisa Wilson, *Life*, 122-31; Jan Noel, "New France: Les femmes favorisées," most recently republished in Veronica Strong-Boag and Anita Clair Fellman, eds., *Rethinking Canada: The Promise of Women's History* (2nd ed., Toronto, 1991); 28-50; Lilianne Plamondon, "Une femme d'affaires en Nouvelle-France: Marie-Anne Barbe, veuve Fornel," *Revue d'histoire de l'Amérique français, 31, 2 (septembre 1977), translated as "A Businesswoman in New France: Marie-Anne Barbel, the Widow Fornel,"* in *Rethinking Canada: The Promise of Women's History* (1st ed., Toronto, 1986), 45-68.

40 Lisa Wilson, *Life After Death*; Carol Shammas, Marylynn Salmon and Michel Dahlin, *Inheritance in America From Colonial Times to the Present* (New Brunswick, N.J., 1987), 7, 208. Julian Gwyn and Fazley Siddiq demonstrate the marked shift away from land to cash and other financial assets between 1851 and 1871 in "Wealth Distribution in Nova Scotia during the Confederation Era, 1851 and 1871," *Canadian Historical Review*, LXXIII, 4 (December 1992), 448-49.

look specifically at wills that widows made.[41] Studies elsewhere suggest that women made very different kinds of decisions about what to do with their property than men did.[42] Pictou County widow, Elizabeth Grant, seems to fit this pattern. Her will, made in 1897, and probated after her death two years later gave her whole estate to various bible societies, churches and other institutions.[43]

We will not understand the resources that different widows could command, however, if we limit our investigations to what was said in wills. We certainly need to know more about what those who did receive property or an annuity did with it. Yet, to fully understand the resources available to widows it is essential to consider some of the other ways widows might be provided for. A large proportion of the population never made a will. Further research on changes in women's dower rights and intestacy laws across Canada — what the law said she should receive as a widow — would clarify what a widow might expect when her husband did not make a will.[44] The workings of benevolent societies and company run benefit schemes, the shift to life insurance policies and the emergence of various kinds of pension schemes also warrant investigation. In Quebec, in particular, provisions for widows cannot be understood solely by examining wills. It was when a marriage was beginning and a marriage contract

41 Women's wealth is mentioned in one table but not discussed in Julian Gwyn and Fazley Siddiq, "Wealth Distribution in Nova Scotia," 449. Here is an example of a study where thinking about the evolution of the family life cycle, of which partner died first might have been useful. One of their groups includes all those people whose occupation they could not identify, most of whom were widowed and single women. In considering the distribution of wealth it seems relevant that widows may already have received wealth when their husband died. Thinking of wealth as attached to individuals rather than families may skew our understanding of the processes of transmission.

42 Suzanne Lebsock, *The Free Women of Petersburg: Status and Culture in a Southern Town, 1784-1860* (New York, 1984).

43 Fazley K. Siddiq, "Nineteenth-Century Wealth Transfers in Nova Scotia: The Administration of Probate," *Nova Scotia Historical Review*, 9, 2 (1989), 41. This is a useful article for understanding the probate process. There is, however, some misleading information regarding property in marriage. On page 37 he suggests that prior to 1898 whatever property a single woman possessed at marriage was transferred to her husband unless some other arrangement was made. Real property was only administered by the husband, it did not become his.

44 See, especially, Margaret McCallum, "Prairie Women and the Struggle for a Dower Law, 1905-1920," *Prairie Forum*, 18, 1 (Spring 1983), 19-34, Gagan, *Hopeful Travellers*, 54. Fazley K. Siddiq sets out some of the procedures surrounding death, dower, probate and intestacy in "Nineteenth-Century Wealth Transfers." Alan B. Sprague, in "Some American Influences on the Law and Lawcourts of Nova Scotia, 1749-1853," *Nova Scotia Historical Review*, 12, 2

was signed that couples set out provisions for a dower or its alternative. Those not making a contract were covered by the provisions of the Custom of Paris and changes made in legislation.[45]

In the common-law provinces the resources a woman might command would have changed after the passage of the Married Women's Property Act. Those who had brought real or personal property into the marriage or purchased it as their own separate property during the marriage would be better off than previously when all but real property fell to the husband on marriage.[46] Furthermore, in many provinces these acts gave married women the right to make wills for the first time. Yet, the majority of women who had ceased to work outside the home after marriage and been dependent on their husbands would have had little separate property. They remained dependent on what their husbands left them and their wits.

Women's History

To what extent is this minimizing of the importance of widowhood, its writing out of much family history, or its crystallisation to simplistic metaphors, the result of a lack of gender consciousness among practitioners of family history?

(1992), 1-31, suggests that the American legal influence led Nova Scotia legislators to pass an Act in 1771 that effectively made it very simple for couples wanting to sell land to bar a women's dower rights. On the growing tendency to bar dower in England see Susan Staves, *Married Women's Separate Property in England, 1660-1833* (Cambridge and London, 1990). A very useful survey of the laws in different American states is provided in Carole Shammas, *et. al., Inheritance.*

45 In contrast to common-law provisions for widows which set their dower at the right to use one third of their husband's real property for the period of their widowhood, the dower under the civil code in Quebec was the right to use "one half of the moveable property which the husband had at the time of his marriage, and half of any he acquired by lineal inheritance during the marriage." Alternative provisions could be made in a marriage contract as they could in a pre-nuptial agreement under the common-law. James Armstrong, *A Treatise on the Law Relating to Marriages in Lower Canada* (Montreal, 1857), 36.

46 On these Acts see Constance B. Backhouse, "Married Women's Property Law in Nineteenth-Century Canada," *Law and History Review* (Fall 1988), 211-57; Philip Girard, "Married Women's Property, Chancery Abolition, and Insolvency Law: Law Reform in Nova Scotia, 1820-1867," in Philip Girard and Jim Phillips, eds., *Essays in the History of Canadian Law, III, Nova Scotia* (Toronto, 1990), 80-127. There are hints about the effects on women's ability to control wealth, although they are few and far between. See, for example, Livio di Matteo and Peter George, "Canadian Wealth Inequality in the Late Nineteenth Century: A Study of Wentworth County, Ontario, 1872-1902," *Canadian Historical Review*, LXXIII, 4 (December 1992), 453-83.

If they had been looking at the world with gendered glasses that alerted them to sexual divisions of labour, patriarchy, or how meanings of gender and identity were made in the past, would widows and perhaps widowers too have been more visible?

Although we do see some widows much more clearly in works of women's history, here too, the approaches of the discipline have tended to constrain analysis. Widows often appear either as heroically autonomous actors or as victims of either patriarchy or poverty. Women's history has certainly tossed us a few widows as heroines, most notably Marie-Anne Barbel, the widow Fornel, studied by Lilianne Plamondon in 1977 and made accessible to a cohort of women's history students in the first edition of *Rethinking Canada*. This enterprising woman, when widowed at 41, with five living children to support, extended her husband's entrepreneurial activities, land purchases, finance and commerce. The economic activities of widows like her, combined with what were seen as the more advantageous provisions of the civil code, led Jan Noel to argue that women in New France occupied a favoured position compared to the later eighteenth, and especially the nineteenth, century.[47] It is important to look more carefully at subsequent periods to determine whether widows did face fewer opportunities and to better explain the forces changing their options.

Wars invariably create more widows than widowers, and are one of the few occasions when the state generally acknowledges some form of responsibility to assist dependents of those who die. Thus, periods following wars are one of the times when more voices of widows are audible than at other times. Janice Potter has shown the numerical importance of widows among the Loyalists settling in Ontario as well as women's strength and bravery during the American Revolution.[48] Once in Upper Canada, or Nova Scotia, however, wives and widows alike appear to have been expected to act submissively. They certainly were well aware of the need to frame their claims as widows for compensation and assistance in terms of feminine frailty and dependence, building their case on the merits of their husbands exploits rather than their own.[49] Petitions must be read

47 Noel, "New France: Les femmes favorisées." See the critiques of this article by Micheline Dumont, "Les femmes de la Nouvelle-France: Etaient-elles favorisées?" *Atlantis: A Women's Studies Journal*, 8, 1 (Fall 1982), 118-24 and Jan Noel, "Women in New France: Further Reflections," *Ibid.*

48 The significance of widows among Loyalist immigrants suggests the importance of looking more carefully not just at the gender composition of the various immigration movements that have peopled Canada, but especially after wars, and of paying attention to marital status as well. How did widows or widowers manage on arriving in a new land?

49 Janice MacKinnon-Potter, *While the Women Only Wept: Loyalist Refugee Women in Eastern Ontario* (Montreal and Kingston, 1992) and Janice Potter, "Patriarchy and Paternalism: The Case of the Eastern Ontario Loyalist Women," in Strong Boag and Fellman, eds., *Rethinking Canada*, 69-70. Beatrice Ross

with care, dissecting the conventions and postures of the age and critically evaluating the process of framing such a claim. Looking at petitions made by widows of veterans of the revolutionary war decades later, Gail Campbell argues convincingly that most of those claiming their right to an annual pension did so not in a begging way, but as "capable and competent women claiming, and if necessary, persisting in claiming pensions as their right." That right was, however, based on "services their husbands had rendered."[50]

Widows in nineteenth-century Montreal who claimed assistance from employers if their husbands died on the job, or benefits from benevolent associations, faced similar constraints — their right to any benefit was only through their husband.[51] Widows of men who died during the Boer War and sought help from the Canadian Patriotic Fund and those of men killed during the First World War who sought assistance under the new Pensions Act also found that any help they received was tied into their husband's performance. He had to have "died during war service or ... (as) a direct result of war service." Like a widow's dower, these pensions could be cut off if the Board of Pension Commissioners discovered that a female pensioner "entered into a sexual relationship with a man" or became a prostitute. In contrast, if they married, mothers and widows received one year's pension as a dowry.[52]

A husband's power over his wife's body thus extended beyond his death. The common law notion that when a husband and wife married they became one — the husband — continued after his death. Indeed, in many ways, a woman donning her widow's weeds became a symbol of her departed husband. Sometimes this was by stepping into his shoes — running his business or workshop. For middle class women it involved maintaining a respectable image. And, at times it involved representing him in other ways after his death. In his memories of his childhood, Robert de Roquebrune describes the widow and daughter of patriot De Lorimier who had been condemned to death in 1838. These women were

---

Buszek appears to read these petitions less critically in her "'By fortune wounded': Loyalist Women in Nova Scotia," *The Nova Scotia Historical Review,* 7, 2 (1987), 45-62.

50   Gail G. Campbell, "Disenfranchised but not Quiescent: Women Petitioners in New Brunswick in the Mid-Nineteenth Century," *Acadiensis,* 18, 2 (Spring 1989), 27-29. By the 1840s and 1850s women's sense of entitlement would have been shaped by changes in legislation and by the fact that many of their husbands had long been receiving pensions before their death.

51   Bradbury, *Working Families,* 187-8.

52   Margaret McCallum, "Assistance to Veterans and their Dependants: Steps on the Way to the Administrative State, 1914-1929," in W. Wesley Pue and Barry Wright, eds., *Canadian Perspectives on Law and Society: Issues in Legal History* (Ottawa, 1988), 163, 167.

still wearing "deep mourning; black dresses and black veils" a half-century later. The widow's funeral was a "patriotic manifestation of sorts at which the grim events of the Rebellion of 1837 were recalled."[53] Here patriarchy and nationalism combined to turn this woman's widowhood into lived symbolism.

Ancient patriarchal notions about family and men and women's rights were encoded in the common law and civil code that regulated the rights of husbands and wives and of widows and widowers in the colonies of British North America. While feminist historians in Canada have begun to pay some attention to changes in the legal rights of married women, few have looked at those of widows.[54] The Collectif Clio have examined some of the changes made to widows' rights in Lower Canada in the period immediately following the rebellions and see them as part of the defeat of women's traditional rights, that included limitations on widow's rights to their dower and the elimination of women's right to vote.[55] "The conflict between dower rights and the principle of land registration ended in defeat for the traditional rights of women, ironically, when a woman, Queen Victoria, was sitting on the British throne."[56] Whereas, prior to 1841, a married woman in Quebec could expect to receive the right to use one-half of the real property her husband had when he married or acquired thereafter as an inheritance from his parents, after that date such dower rights only existed if the dower was registered at a Registry Office. This curtailing of dower rights was a trend well underway in England and the United States by this period, and under discussion in the other colonies. Ideas about how widows should be provided for were changing as the basis of wealth shifted from land to other forms of property.[57] We need to know more about what this meant for widows in Canada. Receiving a cash settlement may have been better for many women than dower rights which offered the use, but not the ownership, of real property, usually did not attach to other assets, and were meaningless for the growing proportion of families with no land.

53 Robert de Roquebrune, *Testament of My Childhood* (Toronto, 1972) 22.

54 Exceptions include Margaret McCallum, "Prairie Women"; and parts of the Collectif Clio, *Quebec Women: A History* (Quebec, 1987).

55 For more on women who voted, a vast majority of whom were widows, see Nathalie Picard, "Les femmes et la question du vote, Bas-Canada, 1800-1850," M.A. thesis, Université de Montréal, 1992.

56 Collective Clio, *Quebec Women*, 123-4.

57 On Upper Canada/Ontario, see Jane Ursel, *Private Lives, Public Policy: 100 Years of State Intervention in the Family* (Toronto, 1992), 263, 327. On England, see Staves, *Married Women's Separate Property* and on the United States, Shammas *et al.*, *Inheritance*; Marylynn Salmon, *Women and the Law of Property in Early America* (Chapel Hill, 1986).

These examples of the constraints placed on widows' rights to benefits suggest the importance of thinking about widowhood for women in ways that go beyond the rather simple dichotomies that prevail. Some widows, like the Veuve Fornel, clearly were able to take advantage of the legal emancipation they experienced as widows freed from the legal fetters the law placed on all married women. Others lived what we would see as the lives of victims — dependent on charity or controlled by the provisions of their husbands' wills. Many, no doubt, carved out small domains for themselves within the particular economy and patriarchy of their region, family and time. Feminist historians in Canada have begun to reveal a little about the nature of widowhood, but we need more careful investigation of how economic, legal and social changes expanded or minimized their margins of manoeuvre.

Conclusion

Each of these different approaches, then, allows us to grasp some aspect of widowhood, more often for women than for men, but leaves much unsaid. None of these approaches needs to downplay or simplify widowhood, yet in the hands of most, though not all practitioners, they generally have. To be fair, it is important to point out that none of the people I have cited set out to make widowhood a main focus of their work. That they did not treat it more seriously is, I argue, a result of the conceptual and methodological approaches they used. I certainly do not want to suggest that all historians of communities and families should make widowhood their exclusive focus. There are, however, some lessons that those studying communities, families and individual genealogies can learn from this attempt to see how certain approaches within family history have downplayed the importance of widowhood historically.

It is essential to reflect on what gets hidden when we borrow typologies of household structures, or methods of measuring demographic phenomena. We need to be conscious that decisions about how to collect or code data can hide certain kinds of families, especially those headed by widows, widowers or other parents managing on their own, but not heading their own household. This is important not just because such single parents were significant numerically in past families, but also because if we do not do this, non historians reading about the predominance of nuclear families in the past tend to assume such families included both parents. This feeds into current fears about the disintegration of "the family," reinforces ahistorical ideas about the traditional family, and robs us of an understanding of similarities and differences in the challenges, strategies and lived realities facing single parents in the past and today.[58]

---

58   Stephanie Coontz cuts through such myths in the United States in *The Way We Never Were: American Families and the Nostalgia Trap* (New York, 1992), summarized in "The way we wish we were," in Arlene S. Skolnick and Jerome H. Skolnick, eds., *Family in Transition* (New York, 1994), 71-82.

Community studies could be enriched by integrating consideration of widowhood, most directly by including demographic analysis of the impact of death, and of the rates of remarriage, as well as consideration of provisions made in wills and other legal documents. However, it seems important to go further. Thinking about how men and women managed in specific communities when a spouse died can take us to the heart of meanings of gender, family and community in the past. Looking at how members of the wider family, of the community or local church leaders stepped in to help or to censure can reveal much about local patterns of mutual aid and community dynamics.

If widowhood was as important as I am trying to suggest, does it make sense for some historians to focus explicitly on widowhood? There certainly are more and more books appearing outside Canada, especially on medieval Europe, but also in more recent American history, that study widows within specific communities or regions.[59] Some of the most exciting work on widowhood is tied into a broader feminist legal historiography that studies transformations in the rights of married women over the nineteenth century and, in some cases, earlier. The best of these works study not only the law surrounding property and widowhood, but how women used it.[60] Here are areas we could fruitfully explore in more detail in Canada and which I am currently attempting to research in nineteenth-century Quebec.

Yet before plunging headlong into widowhood as a subject of study, it is important to think carefully about whether widows or widowers really constitute a category worthy of focused study. What did widows and widowers have in common? — nothing else than that they had married and that their spouse had been the first partner to die. Is this sufficient commonality to form the basis of a study? Katz, for example, found that female household heads in Hamilton, who averaged around 45 years of age in 1851 and 46 in 1861 had little else in common — they were "thoroughly representative of all religions and birthplaces, although slightly more Irish among them than in the population as a whole."[61] If we lump these people together because of their widowhood are we artificially imposing a meaning on their lives that might not have been terribly important for them?

---

59 For example, Wilson, *Life After Death*; Arlene Scadron, *On their Own: Widows and Widowhood in the American Southwest, 1848-1939* (Chicago, 1988).

60 Norma Basch, *In the Eyes of the Law: Women, Marriage and Property in Nineteenth Century New York* (Ithaca, N.Y., 1982); Salmon, *Women and the Law of Property*; Lebsock, *The Free Women of Petersburg*; Staves, *Married Women's Separate Property*; Shammas *et al.*, *Inheritance*.

61 Katz, *The People*, 59.

I do not think so, at least not if we do it carefully. Widowhood, it seems to me, is an ideal way to look at how class and gender, prescription and reality, and legal and religious discourses and family traditions played out in real people's lives in the past. This may be done by placing widows and widowers in specific historical contexts — carefully in their times and in their communities. It may also be done by examining how their married lives prior to widowhood influenced the life they lived later. Such research will not be very illuminating if gender, what it meant to be a man left without a woman, or a woman left without a man, is not made central.[62]

It also seems crucial to tie in questions of property, wealth and class, and see what a spouse's death meant for the life style and standard of living of the remaining spouse. This may mean drawing on all the approaches I have discussed and integrating material drawn from parish registers and censuses with legal documents like wills, maintenance agreements, other property transfers and court cases. It means searching in the records of hospitals, charities and even prisons to see how they ended their lives. And it means searching for biographies, letters and the other family documents that let us begin to get at how people reacted to, felt about and made meaning of being a widow or widower.[63] For many such men and women religion was a crucial solace and deserves to be treated more seriously.[64] If we draw on a variety of different sources, and break out of the constraints that some methodological and conceptual

---

62   Lisa Wilson argues that "focusing on issues of gender clouds" an understanding of the importance of mutuality and family centred values that were crucial well into the nineteenth century. She suggests that "the death of a married man created a new kind of family...who managed the best they could. This meant sacrifices for every family member to promote the good of the whole." *Life After Death*, 133, 167. Certainly historians have to try to understand the different notions of individuality, collectivity and mutuality that governed much family life prior to the twentieth century. Throwing out gender as a category of analysis does not, however, seem a good solution. An interesting attempt to deal with families as collectivities without jettisoning gender can be found in Tessie P. Liu, "Le Patrimoine Magique: Reassessing the Power of Women in Peasant Households in Nineteenth-Century France," *Gender and History*, 6, 1 (April, 1994), 13-36.

63   Here Margaret Conrad's research in women's diaries is very important. "'Sundays Always Make Me Think of Home': Time and Place in Canadian Women's History," in Strong-Boag and Fellman, *Rethinking Canada*, 97-112. Lorna Hutchinson describes one woman who was much happier as a widow than when she remarried in "'God Help Me for No One Else Can': The Diary of Annie Waltham, 1869-1881," *Acadiensis*, XXI, 2 (Spring, 1992), 72-89.

64   Bradbury, "Mourier chrétiennement." Serge Gagnon's *Mariage et Famille au temps de Papineau* (Sainte-Foy, 1993), 218-21, says little about widowhood

approaches have imposed widowers may also emerge, caught perhaps in that fleeting moment of demographic and historical time between dealing with death and remarriage, or as elderly men deprived of a wife's care. Widows will no longer materialize only as cardboard characters — victims of poverty in Katz's Hamilton, victims of patriarchal family inheritance strategies in Gagan's or Marjorie Cohen's rural Ontario or liberated hard-headed businesswomen. Rather, the diversity of their situations will demonstrate the different challenges and possibilities they faced, depending on their previous experiences and history, the ways class, gender and the law framed limits and opened doors to real people in specific periods. This kind of research can be done best in smaller communities, like those of the Planters of the Maritimes.

and very little about the role of religion at such a time. Of the four pages in the section entitled "La mort du conjoint, épreuve ou libération," fully two are dedicated to situations where one spouse killed the other.

The Family in Exile: Loyalist Social Values After the Revolution

Ann Gorman Condon
Department of History
University of New Brunswick

"All happy families are alike but an unhappy family is unhappy after its own fashion." Thus begins Leo Tolstoy's *Anna Karenina*, that extraordinary fictional journey into the private lives of the Russian aristocracy in the nineteenth century.[1] While modern anthropologists might gasp at Tolstoy's willingness to make such sweeping generalizations about the family, no one can deny his success in creating a vivid world of intimacy and intrigue, devotion and deceit, noble suffering and base humiliation, climaxing, of course, in the necessary self-destruction of its flawed heroine, followed by a ringing affirmation of traditional, and very Christian, family values.

Culturally, Tsarist Russia was a far different place than colonial Canada, but they did, for a short while, have one thing in common: an official ruling class. Until the mid-nineteenth century, the British North American provinces were ruled by a group of privileged officers who held their powers independently of the people they governed and reinforced their authority by elaborate social codes and extensive family connections. Indeed, so powerful and so notorious were these sets of provincial oligarchs that they are known pejoratively even to this day in the former colony of Upper Canada, now Ontario, as "The Family Compact."

Alas, thus far Canada's period of gentry rule has inspired no Tolstoyan masterpiece, no insider account of the intimate life, passions and pairings of this select group. In fact, it is both remarkable and regrettable that, for all the many treatises on the political operations of the Family Compact, we have so few accounts of its internal dynamics: its elaborate network of filiations and obligations, its shared aspirations and anxieties, and the mechanisms by which it ensured the transmission not only of property and power from generation to generation, but of a distinctive code of values.[2]

Using the new methodologies developed by family historians and the wealth of personal letters left by prominent Loyalist families (which extend in some cases through four generations), I have begun a research project aimed at

---

1 Leo Tolstoy, *Anna Karenina* (Rosemary Edmunds, tr., London, 1954), 13.

2 The *Jalna* series of Mazo de la Roche is, I believe, the closest fictional attempt to recreate the private life of Ontario's landed gentry but, unlike Tolstoy's novel, the *Jalna* novels are set in the period after the gentry's fall from political power and are essentially a romantic rejection of modern industrial Canada, not a depiction of the gentry in its years of power. More salient are several recent

discovering the personal bonds and ideals which united these people over such a long stretch of time. Eventually, I will include representative family writings from five of the British North American colonies, spread over three generations. I have started with the Maritime provinces because the Loyalist style of cultural leadership was established here so very quickly after their arrival in the 1780s and is so well chronicled in their letters to each other.

This essay represents the "first fruits" of my work, my first attempt to identify patterns and figures in this very complex material, based mainly on the Jarvis Papers and Robinson Papers in the New Brunswick Museum and the Bliss Papers in the Public Archives of Nova Scotia. Unfortunately editorial constraints will not permit me to explore the wealth of material in these letters fully, but let me at least hint at the tone and atmosphere of family life among the Loyalist grandees by quoting three sets of love letters from prominent Loyalists to their wives.

My first example is a letter from Edward Winslow, the unfailingly gallant, but perpetually impoverished, Massachusetts Loyalist, to his wife Mary. The two had married before the revolutionary war and she accompanied him on his circuitous flight pattern after 1775 — from Boston, to Halifax, to New York City, to Annapolis, Nova Scotia, and finally, ten years later, to their permanent abode in Kingsclear, New Brunswick. Throughout this long hegira, Mary managed the family household which at times included the first eight of their 11 children, Edward's elderly parents and his two spinster sisters. The letter I quote was written in 1784, while Edward was in Halifax, looking, as always, for a profitable job, and apparently aware that his lonely, overburdened wife could use some cheering up. Winslow starts off with trumpets blaring:

scholarly studies of Loyalist women. Especially noteworthy are Katherine Mc-Kenna, "Options for Elite Women in Early Upper Canadian Society: The Case of the Powell Family," in J.K. Johnson and Bruce G. Wilson, eds., *Historical Essays on Upper Canada; New Perspectives* (Ottawa, 1989), 401-24 and her recently published book, *A Life of Propriety: Anne Murray Powell and Her Family* (Kingston and Montreal, 1994), as well as Janice Potter-MacKinnon, *While Women Only Wept: Loyalist Refugee Women in Eastern Ontario* (Montreal and Kingston, 1993). Also valuable are three doctoral studies: Robin Burns, "The First Elite of Toronto: An Examination of the Genesis, Consolidation, and Duration of Power in an Emerging Colonial Society," Ph.D. thesis, University of Western Ontario, 1975; Robert L. Fraser, "Like Eden in Her Summer Dress: Gentry, Economy and Society, Upper Canada, 1812-1840," Ph.D. thesis, University of Toronto, 1979; Beatrice Spence Ross, "Adaptation in Exile; Loyalist Women in Nova Scotia after the American Revolution," Ph.D. thesis, Cornell University, 1981. My study, *The Envy of the American States: The Loyalist Dream for New Brunswick* (Fredericton, 1984) deals briefly with family life.

what do I care whether it's the fashion for men to write long letters to their wives or not .... In matters where my own feelings are concerned I will not be shackled by any of the rules which bind the generality of mankind .... I cannot enjoy a pleasure equal to that of writing to you, and that's sufficient for writing. If other men do not experience the same sensation they have not the same degree of affection.

He then launches into a hilarious description of the fashionable ladies of Halifax and, with mock pity, bemoans the fact that the

"immensity of False-Tops False Curls, monstrous Caps. Grease, Filth of various kinds, Jewels, painted paper and trinkets, hide and deform heads of Hair that in their natural state are really beautiful. Rouge & other dirt cover cheeks and faces that without would be tolerable, whilst the unfortunate neck and breasts remain open to the inclemency of the weather & the view of the World ...."

But his Mary, he notes, is the exact opposite: "From 16 years old to the present time you have literally set your Cap at no creature on earth but me. Regardless of Fashion you have only endeavoured by uniform cleanliness to make yourself desirable in my eyes." After declaring his continuing love for her, Winslow closes by saying he still hopes that she will be able once more to enter the world of fashion and elegance.[3]

My second example is a series of letters from Beverley Robinson, the dashing young military officer from New York. Beverley had married Nancy Barclay during the war, and he proved, in New Brunswick, to be a bit of a martinet. Even though Nancy had abandoned a comfortable home in New York City for a refugee farm on the Nashwaaksis River, and had borne 11 children during their marriage, Beverley cannot resist chastising her for "laziness" and negligence. In one 1799 letter, he gave her elaborate instructions on the proper way to cool down and curry horses, and then proceeded to remind her to wrap his doughnuts securely so they will remain moist. The last batch were so dry he could not eat them![4]

Yet the petty irritations of married life did not undermine Beverley's devotion to his wife. For example, when he heard that Nancy was worried about losing her attractiveness now that she was forced to wear spectacles, Robinson rushed to reassure her with this stunning declaration:

---

3   Edward Winslow to his Wife, W.O. Raymond, ed., *The Winslow Papers* (Saint John, N.B., 1901), 225-27.

4   Beverley Robinson to Nancy Robinson, 21 November 1799, Robinson Family Papers, New Brunswick Museum.

... my present feelings have nothing to do with the respectability of your appearance, no madam my imagination is not confined to the age of 45 but wanders back to those days of yore when you was all youth and beauty I all ardour and affection ... you are and shall be my beloved and adored mistress and as such only I will cherish the recollection of you ....[5]

A year later on their twenty-second wedding anniversary Beverley acknowledged, with exquisite sensitivity, that although many changes had taken place since "the day that gave my Nancy to me, I can truly say that she is dearer to me now than when I received her with the rapture of a Bridegroom ....[6]

My final example concerns Jonathan Bliss. A crusty, 47-year-old bachelor when he came to New Brunswick, Bliss had spent the revolutionary war in England, enjoying, to the full, the pleasures of London and Bristol. He came to New Brunswick for sake of a job, but candidly admitted that he was too old, too spoiled by England to appreciate such a new country, however promising.[7] Bliss performed his duties as Attorney General in a minimal sort of way and amused himself by writing political poetry. In 1789, after much deliberation, he decided to take a wife. He returned to his American home in Massachusetts and married the daughter of the richest man in Worcester County. She was Mary Worthington, a woman in her late 20s, and thus a full 20 years younger than Bliss. Her letters to her husband make it clear that she embodied the ideal of female grace and submissiveness so cherished by people in the eighteenth century.[8]

Unexpectedly, passionately, Jonathan Bliss fell in love with his young wife. She and the four sons she bore became the enchanted centre of his life. In his letters to Mary, this aging, cynical lawyer resorted to baby talk. He confessed to her that she had made him the "happiest man in New Brunswick" — but ruined him for living alone. Mary was more deferential and demur in her responses to this older man, but she did assure Bliss that his companionship supplied all the love and support she once drew from family and friends. When Mary died in 1799 delivering their fifth child, Bliss was crushed. He would never remarry,

---

5 *Ibid.*, 11 November 1799.

6 *Ibid.*, 20 January 1800.

7 Jonathan Bliss to S.S. Blowers, 19 September 1786, Bliss Family Papers, Public Archives of Nova Scotia, [PANS].

8 Phillip Buckner, "Jonathan Bliss," *Dictionary of Canadian Biography*, VI (Toronto, 1987), 74-6. Thomas Vincent, "The Image and Function of Women in the Poetry of Affection in Eighteenth Century Maritime Canada," in Margaret Conrad, ed., *Making Adjustments: Change and Continuity in Planter Nova Scotia, 1759-1800* (Fredericton, 1991), 234-46.

and for both Jonathan and their sons, her memory would profoundly shape their ideals of womanhood and of happiness.[9]

It seems to me that, on the surface at least, these are remarkable letters — delicate, witty, warmly demonstrative. They suggest deep mutual concern and enduring affection, the ideal of "companionate marriage" which Lawrence Stone has described so forcefully for the English gentry of the eighteenth century and which Bernard Bailyn finds so powerfully at work within the family of Thomas Hutchinson in colonial Massachusetts. It is an ideal, according to Richard Sennett, which calls for detachment and careful control in public roles, but a warm, expressive, supportive behaviour among one's intimates.[10]

Yet how are we, citizens of the late twentieth century, living as we do in the "Age of Deconstruction," to interpret these letters? Do we take them at face value? Or do we look for evasions, masks and ambiguities, which subvert and undermine the highly polished surface? These are some of the questions I am pursuing through the thousands of Loyalist family letters still available in our public archives. My goal is to uncover the inner workings of power and intimacy among the people known universally in Canadian history as The Family Compact. As for the all-important question of interpretation, my strategy is to pursue a dual track: to try to appreciate at full value the depth of feeling and mutual dependency radiating through these letters, and at the same time to recognize that these statements were also calculated performances, survival measures and personal defences against an undeserved fate and a relentlessly cruel world.[11]

9   Jno. Bliss to Mary Bliss, 4 June 1792 and Mary Bliss to Jno. Bliss, 23 July 1792, Bliss Papers, PANS. The story of the devotion of the Bliss men to Mary Worthington Bliss has never been written, but can be traced through the family papers.

10   Lawrence Stone, *The Family, Sex and Marriage in England 1500-1800* (New York, 1977); Bernard Bailyn, *The Ordeal of Thomas Hutchinson* (Cambridge Mass., 1974); Richard Sennett, *The Fall of Public Man* (New York, 1977), 98-107. For a fine survey of recent scholarship on the family in Europe and North America, see Tamara K. Hareven, "The History of the Family and the Complexity of Social Change," *American Historical Review*, 96 (1991), 95-124.

11   In developing my interpretive approach I have been especially influenced by the work of the French philosopher Paul Ricouer. For an explanation of this methodology see my "The Celestial World of Jonathan Odell: Symbolic Unities within a Disparate Artifact Collection," in Gerald L. Pocius, ed., *Living in a Material World: Canadian and American Approaches to Material Culture* (St. John's, 1992), 192-226. I find the recent effort by Edward Said to develop a "contrapuntal" approach to historical experience an equally rich, if less sys-

Rather than digress into methodology, I would like to use the balance of this essay to describe the three major conclusions which I have reached at this stage in my research. I hope this will provide a concrete sense of the richness of the material contained in these Loyalists letters, as well as practical examples of my interpretive strategy.

First, it seems abundantly clear from the written sources that, for the Loyalist refugees, the family was the most important institution in their lives. Despite occasional attempts by historians (including myself) to embroider Loyalist life during their years in the Maritime provinces, the fact remains that these colonial gentry found their new physical environment forbidding and its public life totally lacking in beauty or grandeur. Even those Loyalists who came with money, servants and prestigious public posts found their new homes strange and alienating.[12]

Since there was little hope of returning to America, and neither their Christian beliefs nor their self-respect would permit them to give in to despair, these displaced people threw their energies into their immediate families — the one area of life they could control and also the one area capable of positive response. Within the day-to-day life of their families, within the houses so carefully constructed and tastefully furnished, they could reenact their days of glory. They could organize little entertainments for friends according to the remembered standards of colonial Boston and New York; they could dress in silks and velvets and dancing shoes; they could exchange gossip and wit and observe the courtesies of a world far removed from the frontier. In such ways, private life became far more important than the crude tedium of public affairs.

Second, the fact that the Loyalists were exiles, not simply immigrants, had important psychological repercussions. The mentality of exile has been described many times by novelists and essayists in our century. Indeed, exile has come to be the salient fact of modern existence. Put simply, exiles are rootless, mutilated people, who live two lives simultaneously: first, their ordinary life which they find dull, even repulsive; and second, their imagined life — their dreams, memories and feelings of nostalgia which are full of warmth, vitality and success. In a remarkable essay, "The Mind of Winter," the literary critic, Edward Said, notes how many outstanding chess players, novelists, poets and

---

tematic attempt to capture both the pure and impure elements of literary texts within a single conceptual framework. See *Culture and Imperialism* (New York, 1993).

12 Neil MacKinnon captures this estrangement especially well in *This Unfriendly Soil: The Loyalist Experience in Nova Scotia, 1783-1791* (Kingston, 1986).

adventurers in the twentieth century are exiles — people to whom the imaginary life is much more important than the real world.[13] The personal letters of the Loyalists provide multiple diverse glimpses into the imaginary world which they cherished during long exile in the Maritimes. And what were its contents? The answer is obvious: it was filled with remembered moments of glory and power in colonial America! It was the world painted so magnificently by John Singleton Copley and described most recently by Richard Bushman.[14] It was a world of refinement, taste and elegance — a world where men were so confident of their authority in both society and the family that they chose to display the feminine side of their nature in their portraits. Hence the silk stockings, ruffled shirts and velvet suits worn by Copley's subjects. Hence the private, domestic backdrops of sinuously carved furniture and bookcases full of the bound books which signified a man of taste. Their wives' appearance complemented the men's. Although their dresses and jewels were dazzling, their faces were those of the hostess — gentle, attentive, welcoming. Despite their elaborate garb, there was nothing worldly about these women. They were domestic creatures — decorative, dependent, nurturing of husbands and guests. Their pride came from domestic accomplishment — a piece of needlework, a fine table, an appealing bowl of fruit. Their personal world did not extend beyond the front door.[15]

These prescribed male and female roles were reenacted in their letters as they doubtless were in the actual homes of the Loyalists. In fact, the extraordinary charm and grace of the Loyalist letters were quite deliberate, expressing affirmations of their cultural ideals. Although fewer in number, the women's letters were as lively and extroverted as the men's. And they were cheerful, often deliberately so, for it was clearly against the common code for either men or women to complain about their fate. Unfortunately, we have no extant letters written by Edward Winslow's wife Mary. We do know that she was very upset when her husband decided to send their son Murray, aged 12, to military school in England. This could suggest that she had already experienced too many separations in her life. Otherwise, she seems to have borne her fate bravely and silently.[16]

13   Edward Said, "The Mind of Winter: Reflections on Life in Exile," *Harper's*, 269 (1984), 49-55. For a subtle exploration of the imaginary worlds of exiled writers Joseph Conrad and Vladimir Nabokov, amongst others, see Michael Seidel, *Exile and the Narrative Imagination* (New Haven, 1987).

14   Richard L. Bushman, *The Refinement of America: Persons, Houses, Cities* (New York, 1992).

15   Margaret Doody, "Vibrations," *London Review of Books*, 5 August 1993, 13-14.

16   Edward Winslow to his wife Mary, 15 September 84, *Winslow Papers*.

Few letters from Beverley Robinson's wife Nancy have survived, but from her husband's comments it seems that she fell into a depression after moving with her 11 children to the howling wilderness. The fascinating response to her melancholy was that several members of her family — not only her husband, but her mother, her son and her brother — began writing letters urging Nancy to carry on and bear her burdens stoically.[17]

Jonathan's Bliss's wife Mary wrote letters regularly to her family and her husband, many of which survive. They are marked by delicate sensitivity and a humorous vein of self-mockery. Clearly, Mary, too, went through a difficult emotional period during at least one New Brunswick winter. After admitting to her sister that she felt a certain loneliness while her husband was away on business, Mary blamed herself for her low spirits — not her four young children, nor her absent husband, nor the piercing cold. She ended this confessional letter by telling her sister not to worry, for she had just written out two pages of resolutions to improve herself and now felt much better![18]

It is notable that all letters from Loyalist women to men contained an apology for the "stupidity" of their letters, ascribed usually either to their allegedly poor handwriting or to the scattered nature of their thoughts. Although the letters themselves do not bear out this harsh judgment, it seems to have been an unwritten rule among these Loyalists that women must openly and repeatedly acknowledge their inferiority to men. Some historians call this trait "learned helplessness," but I find it more significant. Although they were encouraged to tease and flirt with the men of their circle, like other eighteenth-century women, Loyalist women did defer to male superiority — men's education and worldly knowledge. This seems to have been fundamental to the marriage bargain, an essential part of the reciprocal, complementary roles they performed as husband and wife. In accepting this deference, men implicitly agreed to protect and cherish such "stupid" but lovable creatures.

Third, the letters suggest that Loyalist children were deeply affected by their parents' history, and the most talented devoted a significant portion of their lives to redeeming their parents' fate by achieving great distinction in their professional lives. The impact of Loyalist values on their *redeemer children* is without doubt the most important finding of my research thus far. These children were raised with enormous affection and care, but also with firm discipline and fond expectations. Children were expected to carry the torch — maintain the

---

17 Beverley Robinson, Jr. to Anna Robinson, 29 October [1799?] and Thomas Barclay to Beverley Robinson, 1 November 1799, Robinson Papers.

18 Mary Bliss to Frances Ames, 13 February 1797, Bliss Papers, PANS.

codes of manner and dress and use their talents to bring honour to family.[19] Among the numerous examples available, consider the case of Henry Bliss. Perhaps the most talented of all the Loyalist sons, Bliss was educated at King's College, Nova Scotia, and the Inner Temple in London. He emerged laden with academic prizes, good looks and acclaimed charm. Bliss chose to settle in London where he painstakingly established a reputation as a distinguished lawyer, ran for Parliament, and, in his private moments wrote at least seven historical dramas in iambic pentameter, exalting Loyalist principles. Although he considered these verse plays to be the most important aspect of his productive life, they were anachronistic to English tastes and failed utterly to win Bliss any notice, much less any commercial success. Admittedly discouraged, Bliss nonetheless continued writing such plays to the end of his life, in order to affirm the parental code and his own unrealized sense of destiny.[20]

The lives of Edward and Maria Jarvis illustrate a similar pattern of frustrated idealism. He was the English-educated son of Loyalist merchant Munson Jarvis and she, the daughter of a prominent medical man in Saint John. Soon after their marriage they lived for four years in the British colony of Malta, where Edward held an appointment as a law officer, and they both enjoyed the elaborate social life of the colony's rulers. Eventually, Edward's appointment as Chief Justice of Prince Edward Island permitted the Jarvises and their growing family to return to North America. They were dismayed, however, by the dull, "bumpkin" life on the Island. In consequence, the two expended both their health and their limited fortune building a grand house — "Mount Edward" — near Charlottetown and giving heroic entertainments in order to expose the local population to the best British standards. Maria's exertions produced a heart condition, and she died soon after the house was finished. The disconsolate Edward remained heavily in debt for the rest of his life, and confessed to his brother that he was so short of funds he felt he could not comment on his children's choice of marriage

---

19 The best book on parent-child relations for this period is Philip G. Greven, *The Protestant Temperament: Patterns of Child-Rearing, Religious Experience and the Self in Early America* (New York, 1977). Equally insightful is a three-generation study of Virginia families within almost the same time frame as this essay on Loyalist families: Jan Lewis, *The Pursuit of Happiness: Family and Values in Jefferson's Virginia* (New York, 1985).

20 Bertis Sutton, "The Expression of Second-Generation Loyalist Sentiment in the Verse Dramas of Henry Bliss," *Nova Scotia Historical Review*, 13, 1 (1993), 43-77.

21 Anna Maria Jarvis to Caroline Boyd, 6 March 1832; E.J. Jarvis to William Jarvis, 4 August 1835 and 30 January 1837; E.J. Jarvis to Mrs. William Jarvis, 21 September 1849, Jarvis Papers, New Brunswick Museum. J.M. Bumsted and

partners, even though he disapproved! Such were the links between financial power and patriarchal authority.[21]

A variation on second-generation experience was that of William Bliss, son of Jonathan and brother to Henry. After English legal training, William returned to Halifax to marry the richest bride in that city, Sarah Ann Armstrong, the adopted daughter of his father's childhood friend, Loyalist Sampson Salter Blowers. Within a decade William's connections enabled him to get appointed to the Nova Scotia Supreme Court. But despite this great honour, his very comfortable life, and apparently happy family, William worried ceaselessly in his letters to his brothers that he had sold out, taken the easy road, instead of seeking fame by pursuing the law in London or risking his all on a literary career.[22]

The preoccupation of these Loyalist children with their parents' world — their lifelong efforts to redeem and vindicate the parental sacrifice — meant that they, too, lived a great deal of their existence in the "floating world" of the imagination. Unlike the sons of ordinary immigrants, they had difficulty sinking roots in the local Canadian soil, committing themselves to the realities of time and place. In 1825 Henry Bliss recognized the disadvantages of this outlook and told William that he was considering returning to New Brunswick and marrying a local beauty:

> To marry a local girl will give me come connexion in the country, some friends. I mean some common interests with others; and I shall find somebody to sympathize with me, or seem to do it. That is just what our family has always wanted. We have been alone and unconnected with all the society in which we lived; and had any of us stumbled how the world would have trod on us! But then our situation...had its advantages —for when their daughters whored, or their sons got drunk, it touched not us .... I sometimes regret that Father did not take a different side, or that the side he did take was not more successful in the American Revolution. We should now have been great Yankees at Boston — full of money and self conceit .... But then I might never have seen Kean ... nor the inside of the Louvre ... nor the Pont du Gard, nor so much of this beautiful Earth. No I am well content with my destiny. How can people doubt that God is good.[23]

H.T. Holman, "Edward James Jarvis," *Dictionary of Canadian Biography*, VIII (Toronto, 1985), 428-30.

22 William Bliss to Henry Bliss, 18 May 1828, Bliss Papers, PANS.

23 Henry Bliss to William Bliss, Marseilles, 7 January 1825, Bliss Papers, PANS.

This introspective, ambivalent letter, written at the age of 27, perfectly captures the dilemma of second generation Loyalists — their cosmopolitan outlook, coupled with a severe, often crippling detachment from ordinary life. Only with the third generation do we find Loyalist heirs rooting themselves in the local soil, identifying with its landscape and people, including even the Protestant dissenting sects who once represented the antithesis of all the Loyalist gentry stood for.[24] Moreover, their obsession with Loyalist sacrifice lessened. It is true that genealogy became a hobby with the third generation, as did commemorating their ancestors in local churches and cemeteries, but such activities were not an unpaid debt, haunting their waking hours. As well, obsession with family life diminished. Relations between husbands and wives of the third generation were far more relaxed and informal, but also more separate. Husbands spent much of their leisure time in clubs or hunting camps or militia musters. This apparent preference for the exclusive company of males was a new development, an assertion of a type of "rugged" masculine identity which their grandfathers deliberately avoided.[25] Likewise, the third generation of Loyalist wives and mothers became more civic minded, more involved in such reform movements as temperance, public health and religious education. Their children were increasingly sent off early to boarding school where the girls were permitted to study an academic curriculum and even aspire to university by the end of the century, while the boys' training emphasized military drill from school days onward.[26]

As an inevitable part of this evolution, Loyalist elegance, Loyalist exclusivity and Loyalist intensity gradually dissolved. Although their grandchildren certainly respected their ancestors, they themselves had become Canadians and Victorians. In the words of the great conservative historian William L. Morton, grace had been transformed into respectability.[27]

Thus the special Loyalist culture — the special circumstances produced by the exile experience — seems to have lasted two generations at most. What we

---

24   See for example, Ann Gorman Condon, ed., "'The Young Robin Hood Society': A Political Satire by Edward Winslow," *Acadiensis*, XV (1986), 120-43.

25   W.L. Morton, "Victorian Canada," in W. L. Morton, ed., *The Shield of Achilles: Aspects of Canada in the Victorian Age* (Toronto, 1968), 311-33. For the equivalent development in the United States, see E. Anthony Rotundo, *American Manhood: Transformations in Masculinity from the Revolution to the Modern Era* (New York, 1993).

26   These impressionistic findings are based on my reading of the letters of William Jarvis, Jr. and his two wives and children in the 1860s and 1870s, Jarvis Papers.

27   Morton, "Victorian Canada."

need to define is how it shaped, and perhaps even transformed English Canada in general and Planter society in particular. It is a striking fact that the rampant individualism that seized American culture in the nineteenth century — the exaltation of success, of the loner, the wilderness and even of violence — never took hold of nineteenth-century Canadian culture.[28] On the contrary, group loyalties to the community and the family, a cordial acceptance of the complementarity of the sexes, a strong emphasis on public duty as well as an equal insistence on the sheer joy of human companionship: all were values which the Loyalists brought with them from colonial America and kept vividly alive through most of the nineteenth century. Philosophically, these exiles were Aristotelians rather than Platonists, Arcadians rather than Utopians. Surely their dominance for 75 years left a residue which requires definition. Indeed, it seems singularly unfortunate that the ruling historical metaphor for the Loyalist contribution to Canadian culture is Northrup Frye's "the garrison mentality." Without denying the elements of arrogance and paranoia in the Loyalist personality, we must also recognize the social virtues of wit, learning, style and profound human solidarity. Sustained exploration of their private papers may bring both the positive and negative aspects of the Loyalist legacy into proper balance.

---

28 Alexis de Toqueville was the first to recognize these traits in volume II of his *Democracy in America* (New York, 1957). For modern interpretations, see Richard Slotkin's trilogy: *Regeneration through Violence: The Mythology of the American Frontier, 1600-1860* (New York, 1973); *The Fatal Environment: The Myth of the Frontier in the Age of Industrialization, 1800-1890* (New York, 1985), and *Gunfighter Nation: The Mythology of the Frontier in Twentieth Century America* (New York, 1992). For the Canadian comparison, see Marcia B. Kline, *Beyond the Land Itself: Views of Nature in Canada and the United States* (Cambridge, Mass., 1970).

Connectional History:
A Gender-Related Approach to Genealogy

Althea Douglas
Ottawa

The profession of genealogy with all those quaintly named Heralds and Kings of Arms grew out of a need for a feudal society to keep track of who held land, and therefore who was obliged to fight for the king. Daughters did not fight, so it was the man they married who mattered. Those days are long past but patriarchal and feudal traditions persist.

Beginners in family history are advised to present their findings in one of the standard formats. Among the most familiar is that devised and used by Burke's Peerage Limited. As well, the New England Historic Genealogical Society has established a format that is used by many genealogists.[1] Both formats follow the male lines, sometimes mentioning the children, but rarely the grandchildren of daughters. After all, unless there is an abeyant Barony or large estate in dispute, why trace daughter's daughters?

Are the female connections important? To the genealogical purist, probably not. In academic circles, however, the way that women view the world is starting to matter. Lately, I have been both amused and delighted to find "what every woman knows" being dressed in academic jargon, garnished with footnotes, and set out in print for the scholarly world to quote. Gender-related studies are questioning stereotypical views of "women's place," and scholars in the field are developing new approaches and revising old ideas, changing the way we think about women's influence on history, sociology, anthropology, as well as technology,[2] and even archaeology.[3]

My academic career began too early to be fashionably gender-related. It revolved around a novelist who just happened to be a woman. I spent some 25 years working with Professor Joyce Hemlow, cataloguing the Burney Papers and editing Fanny Burney's later letters and journals. Thus I became a genealogist, or more properly, a "connectional historian," because our concerns were less with pedigrees and lines of descent and more with community links

---

1   Both formats are briefly and clearly explained by Terrence M. Punch, *Genealogical Research in Nova Scotia* (3rd ed., Halifax, 1983), 111-15.

2   Joan Rothschild, ed., *Machina Ex Dea, Feminist Perspectives on Technology* (New York, 1983). These essays on women's contributions to technology include Autumn Stanley, "Women Hold Up Two Thirds of the Sky: Notes for a Revised History of Technology," 5-22.

3   Margaret Purser, "'Several Paradise Ladies Are Visiting In Town': Gender Strategies in the Early Industrial West," *Historical Archaeology: Journal of the Society For Historical Archaeology*, 25, 4 (1991), 6-16.

and family relationships. Annotating Fanny's letters required not only full names, titles and the vital dates of the people she encountered, but usually some explanation of their place in society. That might mean both their family structure and how it fitted into the world around them.

We most certainly used the male-line pedigrees found in Burke, Cocayne, Chambers and occasionally Debretts, but we learned very quickly to look to the female lines if we wanted to know why people turned up at the same party. In eighteenth-century society, where young unmarried women were normally chaperoned, we found women moved about in family groups. When Lady Smith, Mrs. White and the Misses Jones came to call, they would usually turn out to be some combination of mother, aunt, daughter, sisters or sisters-in-law.

Fanny Burney's England and the Planter communities in Nova Scotia, though geographically distant, almost overlap in time. At Acadia University, I am close in geographic space, but how do I connect with that Planter community across time? Not at all if you look at my male-line descent that determines my racial origin when I answer the census taker. My father's grandfather came from Ireland to Saint John, married the daughter of another Irish immigrant, had sons, who had sons, one of whom had me. Officially, I am of Irish descent! Actually, three-quarters of me is not. My father's mother was descended from some of the first English-speaking settlers on the Miramichi. Two were Davidson settlers from Scotland, but it is also through her that I can claim to be a United Empire Loyalist (so important if you live in "Upper Canada") and through her I am probably related to the Mi'kmaq.

My mother was a descendant of the Yorkshire immigrant William Chapman through his son John who married Sarah Black and settled at Dorchester. The Yorkshire blood was diluted by a Weldon-Killam marriage that linked the family with the earlier New England Planter settlers in Chignecto. Mother's mother was a Cleveland, descended from Lemuel Cleveland, another Planter, who worked for Simonds and White at the mouth of the St. John River.

Grandmother's mother was a Cochran, born in St. Martins, New Brunswick. Her Cochran father came from Nova Scotia, as did her mother, the thrice married Lydia Smith Fownes Cochran Moran. Lydia, to whom we will return later, was descended from the Planter family of Vaughans who settled first at Chester. Have I made my point? Following the female lines often shows how a family fits into the wider community.

So often it is the women in a family who cherish heirlooms, recount family legends and preserve traditions, letters, documents and artifacts. I have an 1880s autograph album from St. Martins and a child's book with the maiden name of my great-grandmother. These, together with a sampler, worked by great-grandmother's sister that lists all the family and their birth dates (now treasured in Tacoma, Washington, where a daughter took it when she and her husband went West) are the artifacts that helped me trace my roots back to

Lydia, and through her to Planter Nova Scotia. Knowledge of family networks can aid in finding treasures from the past.

Fanny (Burney) d'Arblay left her papers to her niece, Charlotte (Francis) Barrett, who passed them on to her daughter Julia (Barrett) Thomas Maitland, and so to Julia (Maitland) Wauchope and the Wauchope children. It took a woman from Nova Scotia to follow that female line and unearth the treasured papers from under Miss Ann Julia Wauchope's bed.[4]

Useful knowledge as well as family treasures pass from mother to daughter. As a child growing up in Toronto, I listened to mother and her friends talk as they played bridge or sewed for the Red Cross. Almost every person they mentioned was identified by a place, then by two or three family connections. "She was a Teed from Dorchester, a sister married one of the Tennants from Amherst — or was it a McLeod? His mother was a Reid from Halifax." The links they spoke of might be blood or marriage. A few were simply "they lived next door and we grew up together" — though this situation often meant a marriage in the next generation. I visualized a great spider web that connected everyone in the Maritimes, with anchor lines stretching off to Montreal and Toronto, down to Boston, and west to the Pacific coast.

Looking back I can recognize the purpose of that conversational pattern. It reinforced knowledge of the wider community. Father, son, uncle, brother, all have the same surname so the connections are obvious; it is the women who change their name on marriage who must be kept track of. The place name associated with a family served not only to distinguish the Yarmouth Killams from the family of the Westmorland County Member of Parliament, but also as a way to remind an out-migrating younger generation of where people's roots were, and where "connections" might remain.

For my mother's generation, growing up in the first quarter of this century, a total familiarity with the intricacies of the Maritime network smoothed life's paths. The problem might be to find a reliable housekeeper for a widowed father or to establish a social life in a new community when a banker or railroader husband was moved there.

I learned by osmosis. I still link certain families with specific places as most Maritimers, wherever they may live, can, and do. Later I learned that both the Eastern Townships in Quebec and the Ottawa Valley were similar, compact regions, long-settled with inter-related families. Township and Valley people also know who each other's grandmothers are. British genealogist Stella Colwell found the same pattern in the Lake District where she grew up:

---

4   The most vivid account of her entry "into Eldorado" is given by Dr. Hemlow in the Introduction to *A Catalogue of the Burney Family Correspondence 1749 - 1878*, comp. Joyce Hemlow, Jeanne M. Burgess and Althea Douglas (New York, Montreal, London, 1971), xiv-xv.

The effective kinship network of living relatives ... offered financial support, help in obtaining work and accommodation, and provided contacts for relatives working away from home, material support for the elderly and newly married, a child minding service, assistance and wholesale attendance at family events and a host of other supportive acts. They also split into factions carrying grievances along the family network ....[5]

When anthropologists and political scientists talk about a "kin group" or "survival group," this can mean a typical band of primates or tribe of humans who instinctively co-operate with others having the same genes to ensure those genes are passed on to as many in future generations as possible. The natural size of such a kin group is between 50 and 200;[6] the tally of many people's Christmas card list, or a small Planter settlement.

In Rhode Island or Yorkshire, when a husband suggested the family move to Nova Scotia, "where there is good land and a better chance for the boys," you can imagine the woman's questions: "Who else is going?" "Who do we know already there?" "Is there a church? a meeting house? What day is market day?" No church? No market? Was there even a pedlar with needles and pins? For the Yorkshire women the culture shock must have been overwhelming and some did not live long in the new land. The Yankees did better, but even knowing what you were up against, it could never have been easy.

Until well into this century, family historians expect to find a married woman having a baby every two or three years. If a wife lived to age 50, she could expect to bear 10 to 12 children. Moreover, in the isolated pioneer communities, most of the children survived to grow up.[7]

A man looking at famiiles of this size is likely to think "Ah, six sons to carry on the name," and more practically, "more hands to help with haying, chores and clearing the land." A woman looking at the same family tree will think, "Oh dear! Six boys to feed and keep in clothes; lucky she had daughters to help." Considering the meals to cook, the wool to spin and weave, the colic and croup, most women will also wonder about the wife's support network. Did she have family nearby, her mother, sisters, or in-laws to help in an emergency?

---

5   Stella Colwell, "Family History into Community History," *Genealogists' Magazine*, 24, 6 (June 1993), 247.

6   Roger D. Masters, *The Nature of Politics* (New Haven & London, 1989), discussing the survival of the "fittest," defined "fitness" as the capacity to transmit genes to succeeding generations (6). Various authorities and opinions on the numbers in a kinship group are given (219).

7   Naomi Griffith in *The Contexts of Acadian History, 1686-1784* (Kingston and Montreal, 1992), 17, points out that in Acadia "the people were fertile and the children lived. ... In common with the experience of much of New England, in

If the first settlers had little support, the next generation was far better off. Take a conservative estimate of eight children per family and assume six of those children married, each into another eight-child family. That is a lot of in-laws and, in an emergency, even a sister-in-law's in-laws, might be called upon for help. Move to the third generation; even if those six couples averaged only five children each, each child would have 25 cousins on the father's side, 25 more on the mother's. Most of the 50 cousins would marry, and though divorce was rare, death in childbirth, or at sea, or in the woods, meant there were almost as many second and even third marriages as today. The cousins, their spouses and children, make a large "kin group." A newcomer marrying into such a family would have to make quite an effort to learn the ins and outs. There would be rich cousins to be cultivated — and n'er-do-wells to avoid, a few who went back to New or Old England, and some who "went west" and lost touch. That is what "connectional history" is all about, and why mothers taught daughters about connections.

Take the specific example of three inter-connected Planter families: Stephen Smith, from Chatham, Massachusetts, was a Proprietor of Liverpool. He and his wife Mehitable Eldridge had at least 10 children.[8] Ebenezer and Rebecca (Spencer) Harrington who came from Rhode Island to New Dublin, had nine, perhaps 10 offspring. Three of the Smith children married Harringtons, while another Harrington daughter, Lydia, married Daniel Vaughan. Daniel was one of three brothers (from a family of 13 siblings) who came to Nova Scotia. Thus the Vaughans and the Smiths were both Harrington in-laws. Daniel and Lydia had 11 children who, through their marriages, brought the Crandall, Brown, Bailey and Dimock families into the kinship group.

That is why D.G. Bell, describes the Vaughan family "an instructive example of how important 'connectional' history can be in understanding the Newlight and Baptist network. Scholars in other fields are also becoming connectional historians, expert at tracing family and social networks."[9] Esther Clark Wright and A. Gregg Finley have both noted the important links between a younger generation of this same Vaughan family and the Morans of St. Martins, two families that kept their profitable ship-building and ship-owning firms well

---

fant mortality was low." Recent work by Yves Landry at the Université de Montréal indicates the same situation in the St. Lawrence River valley before 1730 (interview reported in *The Gazette*, Montreal, 31 July 1993, A4). This seems to apply as well to the early years of Planter settlement.

8 Elizabeth Pearson White, C.G. "Nova Scotia Settlers from Chatham, Massachusetts, 1759 - 1760," *National Genealogical Society Quarterly*, 62, 2 (June 1974), 96-117.

9 D.G. Bell, ed., *Newlight Baptist Journals of James Manning and James Innis* (Saint John, 1984), 283.

within the control of the extended family.[10] The effectiveness of such an extended family network is probably limited only by the data the human brain's computer can process. Luckily, our internal computers are very good at handling such data, much of which may be "fuzzy" and context related.

Consider the much-married Lydia Smith - Fownes - Cochran - Moran, a granddaughter of Daniel and Lydia (Harrington) Vaughan. Her daughter by her first husband married James H. Moran, the ship builder of St. Martins. A daughter of her second marriage became James H. Moran's second wife. Then Lydia married James H. Moran's father. Explaining this singular relationship to his half-brother, young William H. Moran noted that Lydia was their father's mother-in-law twice, as well as his stepmother. "She was three times my grandmother, viz: She was my mother's mother, my step-mother's mother and my father's stepmother".[11] You can puzzle it out at leisure in "From Mother to Daughter ..." in the *Nova Scotia Historical Review*.[12]

Lydia is an extreme example of connectional history out of control. And as one descendant ruefully commented: "It's rather like having a plate of spaghetti for a family tree!" No wonder many genealogists prefer to stay with relatively straightforward male-line pedigrees. They compute relatively easily on software specially designed for such genealogies. But there is other software in other fields. To display all of Lydia and her daughter's convoluted family ties at one time, perhaps you could try a livestock breeding program. Researchers in agriculture care very much about the connectional history of pure-bred milk cows.

For some years now historians have been looking at family structure and such basic matters as the size of families, the ages at which people married and the mobility of the population, but this work is not always widely known outside of academic circles. Even within those circles, one profession is not always aware of how other disciplines are developing, much less of where useful research is published, often in very specialized journals where family historians in particular will hardly ever find it.

In the field of medicine, connectional history is called "genetics." Back in the 1970s the Department of "Neurogenetics" at the Montreal Neurological Institute were tracing neurological disorders in extended families in Quebec.

---

10 Esther Clark Wright, *The Ships of St. Martins* (Saint John, reprinted 1978), 7; A. Gregg Finley, "The Morans of St. Martins, N.B., 1850-1880," in Lewis R. Fischer and Eric W. Sager, eds., *The Enterprising Canadians* (St. John's, 1979), 37-54.

11 Provincial Archives of New Brunswick, Moran Family Papers, typescript "Family History," by William Moran (1849-1945), 12-13.

12 Althea Douglas, "From Mother to Daughter: Some Maritime Planter Family Links," *Nova Scotia Historical Review*, 13, 1 (June 1993), 139-56.

AUGUSTANA UNIVERSITY COLLEGE
LIBRARY

They were already developing a computer program to analyze their family data. As medical interest in linking specific genes with diseases grows, we can expect to see new and more sophisticated software to analyze family connections and, it is hoped, the funding to collect and enter the data.

Counting cousins is also an important facet of historiography as Esther Clarke Wright's studies demonstrate. At the Université de Montréal, demographers have secured funding to compile a database using the parish registers that have been kept in that province since the first settlements. Women's maiden names are given regularly in most entries. The tabulations are now in print and widely available.[13]

As more and more records are microfilmed, indexed on computers, and widely distributed in soft or hard copy, it becomes far easier to document individuals from the past; so we find more well researched genealogies published every year. Computers then make it easier to tie such works together. The sources used for "From Mother to Daughter" included several published, but unrelated, male-line pedigrees. The data they contained was linked by looking at wives, daughters and the female lines that connected families from New England, across western Nova Scotia and into New Brunswick. As we develop such data bases, the work of editors, sociologists, medical researchers, historians and even museum curators, it is hoped will come together as it is doing at this conference.

Yet names, dates and relationships do not make a community. I will leave the last words to Stella Colwell who would see connectional history take an additional step. She suggests that since many of the challenges in the hunt for ancestors have been removed by the ever increasing quantity of published records and indexes, family historians should widen their studies:

> ... The community is the sum of its parts, and the families of which it is made up all have their special histories .... The family historian is often accused of a blinkered and self-centred approach to history, seeing only the time road along which his own forebears travelled, to the exclusion of the communities in which they lived and interacted ... he sifts through the same documentary material as the local historian ... and is exposed to a wealth of evidence about his family's neighbours, friends and

13 René Jetté, *Dictionnaire généalogique des Familles du Québec* (Montreal, 1983), and *Répertoire des actes de baptême, mariage, sépulture et des recensements du Québec ancien,* Programme de recherche en démographie historique [P.R.D.H.], Université de Montréal (Montreal, 1982-1990), 48 vols.. This index of all Catholic B.M.D. Confirmations and census returns from the beginning up to 1765 is arranged by chronological periods with indexes at the end of each period.

fellow-workers, future in-laws and established kinsfolk, if only he would pause to take account of them.

... A family cannot be understood in isolation from the community, nor that community in isolation from its neighbours.[14]

It could offer a "most exciting prospect" for family historians to connect their family into its community environment — then compare its experience with that of other families, both in other communities — and in other eras. What I have heard at this conference suggests that on this side of the Atlantic we are already well on the way to doing just that.

14 Colwell, "Family History into Community History," 248-49.

Planter Genealogical Data Bases at the Old Kings Courthouse Museum, Kentville, Nova Scotia

Ron Illsley
Volunteer with the Kings Historical Society,
and Old Kings Courthouse Museum, Kentville, Nova Scotia

Genealogy, or "Family History" as some prefer to call it, has been my hobby for many years. Now that I am retired and can spend more time on it, it is more of a passion. I will be concentrating here on how we at the Kings Historical Society use the computer to record, organize and present the Family History of the Planters. Most of my examples are based on Kings County families because the largest number of Planters came to this area and, of course, we are a Kings County organization. But the basics of recording Planter families in the computer is the same wherever they are.

Sources for this information are varied. When the Planters arrived they kept Township Books for areas such as Cornwallis, Horton and Aylesford. In these books the births, marriages, deaths and other information relating to Planter life were recorded. Soon, other primary sources developed; registries of deeds, probate records and many more. In time, people began to write histories of their families. In the late nineteenth and early twentieth centuries there were several published genealogies for this area.[1] Over the years there have been many publications of this type, as well as personal manuscripts and notes that families had in their possession. Also, many of the Planter families' histories had been recorded in locations in New England.

The accumulation of all this material in so many different places has given researchers a real challenge. Preparing a family history becomes a big puzzle with many pieces missing or lost altogether. Then came the personal computer. It was not long before researchers discovered that the computer would make their lives much easier and more fun. Computers can serve a number of different functions: word processors, graphics, databases, spreadsheets and communications. I will only deal with word processors and data bases.

The word processor is really a glorified typewriter on which you can write documents, but it has the ability to do much more. Most of you are aware of the many advantages the modern word processor has, including ease of making corrections, moving text around, spell checking and more. A data base is a program that stores data in records and fields, which can be sorted, rearranged and displayed in many different ways. In my work in genealogy I first used the word processor to record my findings. I developed formats for families; I also

---

1　See for example, A.W.H. Eaton *The History of Kings County* (Belleville, Ont., 1972) and William Chute *Genealogy of the Chute Families in America* (Salem, Mass., 1894).

developed data bases to keep track of notes, and thought I did not need a "Genealogical Program." A "Genealogical Program" is a data base primarily designed to record family history. It has the ability to link families together and show relationships. Information on an individual has to be entered in the "Genealogical Program" only once; after that the person will show up in pedigree charts, ancestor charts and descendants lists. The information on that person allows the genealogist to create family groups for the individual listed in the program and his or her children.

I finally purchased a Genealogical Program and started entering my families. I now have almost 20,000 persons entered, each linked in one way or another. There are many of these programs available, each with its own advantages and shortcomings. Programs range in price from $35 to several hundred dollars. I use the PAF (Personal Ancestral File) developed by the Mormons and sold at a subsided price of $35 U.S. It is not only the least expensive, but, in my opinion, the most flexible. It offers the ability to transfer data from computer to computer via floppy disk or modem (telephone lines) and can translate to and from other types of programs.

However, the Genealogical Program is not the end all. We, at The Kings Historical Society Family History Committee, have developed data bases to organize our Planter families, record cemeteries, and provide other functions as well. Those of you who have computers will understand the advantage of their use, and those of you who have not yet been converted will see the advantages and likely rush out and purchase one immediately. Here are some of our programs:

1. The PAF (Personal Ancestral File). The Family History Committee of The Kings Historical Society will eventually have a PAF program solely containing Planters and their ancestors and descendants. Because I have already so many entries in my PAF, containing most of the Planters of this area, we have used it as the basis of a Planter file. One of the advantages of a Genealogical program is that it will generate pedigree and descendants charts from the data entered. After we have data entered, relationships show up and become an additional source of information in researching other families.

2. "Planter Families" Data Base. This is a data base developed by the Kings Historical Society Family History Committee. We have entered all of the New England Planters who came to Kings County, as listed in the book *Planters and Pioneers*, by Esther Clark Wright,[2] with additions of our own. Each record has the following fields: surname, given names,

---

2   Esther Clark Wright, *Planters and Pioneers* (Hantsport, N.S., 1978).

parents, spouse, community, township, PAF number, source, notes and children. (It notes the existence of entries in PAST, *Planter Archive SysTem*) which will be covered later). Our Planter Family data base is only an index or reference, because basic records on the Planters are entered in the PAF program not in this data base program. This data base will be expanded to contain all known Planters; in fact, I have some of this data ready to enter on Planters outside of Kings County. We have a "Planter Binder" which contains the print outs of this data base. This binder includes the general index and family sheets and in some cases pedigree charts of the Planters on record.

3. "PAST" or Planter Archive SysTem. It was compiled by Judith Norton for the Planters Studies Centre at Acadia University in 1991. It contains a bibliography of Primary Sources of New England Planters in the Maritime Provinces of Canada, 1759-1800. Unfortunately, it is not easily converted to other computers, but we now have a copy in our computer. It lists primary sources and a brief summary of items to be found in many places in the Maritimes and New England. It does not contain much genealogy as such, but is valuable for family research. This data base is on the main frame computer at Acadia, accessible through Internet and is also now available in printed form.

4. Cemeteries of Kings County. In the early 1980s the Family History Committee, under the leadership of Ed Brownell, recorded most of the 100 cemeteries in Kings County. The recorded information was stored in binders and files in the Old Kings Courthouse Museum Archives and has proved very useful for family research. In late 1992 we decided to enter the data into the computer, which meant typing all of the data, about 34,000 names, with inscriptions, into the computer. Five members started doing this work, some on their home computer, others on the Society computer at the museum. We updated some of the cemeteries as we went and plan to update all of them eventually. We plan to print a master index and have the computer printout of each cemetery in binders. The data base gives us the ability to print out all of the recorded burials of a given family name with the places of burial. We also have records of many burials that have no stones. These have been supplied to us by individuals, cemetery records and other sources.

In addition to databases, we are working on a number of other projects. Our volunteer Family History Committee Archivist, Katy Boudreau, has made an index of Kings County names in the recently released 1901 census. The information has been printed and can be found in a binder in our archives. She is also working on an index of probate records, 1785-1942, a summary of obituaries from the Halifax paper for 1993, and some births, marriages and deaths in Digby County.

One other project for which we use our computer is to produce and maintain a binder called "QUICKFIND." QUICKFIND is a user friendly finding aid for the entire archives of the Kings Historical Society Family History Committee. This binder contains over 1000 names of the families that are researched to some degree, and can be found in various files and publications in the archives. Our Committee also keeps a file of over 900 families that our 170 members are researching. We publish this list along with the membership list once a year in our newsletter, and copies are kept in the "QUICKFIND" binder in the archives.

We are also starting a new project called "My New England Ancestry." Our brochure includes a form for New England Planter descendants to fill out their lineage to a New England Planter. These forms are to be returned to us where they will be checked and the data entered in our computer. If every visitor to the museum does this we will end up with a tremendous amount of Planter information which will be useful for all of our future research endeavours.

The Kings Historical Society and the Old Kings Courthouse Museum in Kentville now have a permanent Planter display sponsored and developed by Parks Canada. The official opening was Friday, 1 October 1993. It offers a permanent exposure to our New England Planter heritage, and will tie in with the efforts of the Planter Conference to preserve the history of our Planter ancestors. On the bottom floor of the Museum is housed the Archives of the Kings Historical Society Family History Committee. Our collection is growing daily with more than 130 microfilm; over 300 family files, many books, charts and other research material. We encourage you to visit our Museum and Archives located at 37 Cornwallis Street in Kentville, Nova Scotia.

Before They Were Planters:
Economic Conditions in Eastern Connecticut, 1740-1760

Patricia A. Norred
Kutztown University
Fulbright Scholar, Acadia University 1993-94

In eighteenth-century New England, the city on a hill had become the city on the make. Traditional Puritan ideas of community and religion clashed with new values of self-interest and freedom of conscience. Some historians have attributed this shift to the impact of the Great Awakening, a series of revivals which began in New England in the 1730s.[1] Although religious revivalism undoubtedly contributed to breaking down Puritan views of social and ecclesiastical authority and hastened the transformation that was already underway, the Great Awakening may have been as much a manifestation of this transformation as its cause. New Englanders had committed themselves to an active role in the British imperial system before they overthrew the Dominion of New England in 1689, and new churches were just as likely to be the product of community expansion as religious differences.[2] Moreover, the response of individual communities to changing conditions varied considerably. Some New England towns appeared to adjust rather easily while others endured profound societal instability as a result of economic and ecclesiastical uncertainty. The men and women from Connecticut who would become Planters — with hometowns like New London, Norwich, Lebanon, Colchester, Lyme and East Haddam — were not exempt from the winds of change sweeping across New England, nor were they exempt from the diversity which characterized the response to their changing world.

Connecticut formed part of the most diverse regional economy in British North America, but the elements of diversity were not fully developed within the colony itself. John J. McCusker and Russell R. Menard, in their economic study of the colonies, list three strategies that New Englanders developed in the late seventeenth century to secure their economic future. First, they initiated domestic manufacturing to produce some goods they would otherwise have to import. Second, they sought trade with areas other than England. This trade, which concentrated on the West Indies, allowed New Englanders to sell goods not in demand in England and receive, in return, goods or bills of exchange valued in the parent country. Finally, they developed the carrying trade,

1 Richard L. Bushman, *From Puritan to Yankee: Character and the Social Order in Connecticut, 1690-1765* (New York, 1970), 267-88.

2 Richard R. Johnson, *Adjustment to Empire: The New England Colonies, 1675-1715* (Rutgers, 1981), xi, 413-21.

becoming "the Dutch of England's empire."[3] McCusker and Menard's analysis holds true only if one considers Boston as the whole of New England. Connecticut, by its own admission in 1762, had comparatively little manufacturing capability, preferring to buy what it needed from Boston merchants. Such manufactured goods as did exist were traded largely within a local network and on a small scale. Connecticut merchants tended to rely on exports to the West Indies, primarily because European markets tended not to value what Connecticut farmers could produce. Of the three strategies, this one was the most developed. Finally, ships owned by Connecticut merchants were part of the Atlantic carrying trade, but Boston still controlled the bulk of the trade.[4]

For much of the eighteenth century, Connecticut struggled to compete with its larger neighbours. Although New London was the major entrepot for goods travelling in and out of Connecticut, its significance paled in comparison with Boston and New York. New London became the official customs port for Connecticut in 1752, but even ten years later, colonial officials reported tax income from custom duties as "inconsiderable."[5] A sampling of recorded entrances into the port of New London between 1758 and 1760 indicates that twice as many ships came to Connecticut via Boston or New York than from all other ports combined.[6]

The most comprehensive work on economic conditions in colonial Connecticut is Jackson Turner Main's *Society and Economy in Colonial Connecticut*. He argues that four economic cycles affected the colony before 1775. From 1700 to 1730, the colony experienced gradual economic growth that reached its apex in the 1720s. The 1730s ushered in two decades of depression. A gradual recovery began in the 1750s and, by 1763, economic activity had returned to the level of the 1720s. A postwar recession began in 1765 and lasted until the eve of the American Revolution.[7]

3   John J. McCusker and Russell R. Menard, *The Economy of British America, 1607-1789* (Chapel Hill, 1985), 91.

4   Answers Returned to the Queries Sent to the Governor and Company of Connecticut, by the Lords Commissioners of Trade and Plantations, 1762. MSL. Massachusetts Historical Society. It would not have been unusual had Connecticut officials deliberately underestimated the actual amount of manufacturing done in the colony since imperial law prohibited the colonies from engaging in domestic manufacturing that might compete with Great Britain's products.

5   *Ibid.*, Connecticut Archives, Trade and Maritime Affairs, Ser. 2, I:20.

6   *New London Summary or Weekly Advertiser, 1758-1760.* Connecticut State Library.

7   Jackson Turner Main, *Society and Economy in Colonial Connecticut* (Princeton, 1985), 115.

Although by 1775 Connecticut had not experienced any significant decrease in wealth compared to 1720 levels, it is misleading to argue for widespread economic growth because of mitigating factors that slowed the recovery of the 1750s. Population growth skyrocketed from 65,000 to 100,000 in the 1740s and continued to increase until the American Revolution, albeit at a much reduced rate.[8] Colonial officials estimated the population in 1756 as 128, 212 whites and 3587 blacks. In 1762, in spite of emigration, population figures had risen to 141,000 whites and 4590 blacks.[9]

One reason for the stunning population growth, other than the fecundity of Connecticutters, may lie in their willingness to accept immigrants. When British officials in Nova Scotia began the systematic expulsion of the Acadians in 1755, many were deported to other English colonies. Massachusetts accepted the refugees only reluctantly, but Connecticut was somewhat more welcoming. New London selectmen worked to insure that lodging and employment was secured for all the refugee men.[10] The nineteenth-century historian Frances Manwaring Caulkins interpreted this event as evidence of the nonconformity of New Londoners. It is far more likely, however, that outmigration had left the community with a temporary labour shortage, and a seaport with a large transient population usually had an abundance of low wage jobs. Although most Acadians eventually settled elsewhere, their presence in Connecticut before and during the Planter migration cannot be dismissed. Many Connecticutters saw Nova Scotia first hand during military service, but some may have gained additional information from the previous residents of the Minas Basin during the Acadians' stay in New London.

In the mid-eighteenth century, New London was a major urban centre in Connecticut and was more diversified in both population and occupation than the surrounding communities. Caulkins noted that her birthplace was not a favourite place in Connecticut. "Unlike others, ... it frequently voted wrong: harbored foreigners; was often boisterous and contentious; manners were too free; actions too impulsive; in short, it had less of the Puritan stamp than any other place in Connecticut."[11] Approximately 11-12 percent of its residents were merchants or involved in the carrying trade. Artisans comprised 25 percent of the population, and only one-third were exclusively farmers. The rest were

---

8   *Ibid.*, 14.

9   Answers Returned to the Queries..., 1762.

10   Frances Manwaring Caulkins, *The History of New London, Connecticut from the First Survey of the Coast in 1612 to 1852* (New London, 1852), 469-70.

11   *Ibid.*, 469.

labourers. The wealthiest 10 percent controlled almost 50 percent of the wealth, a percentage which lends itself to economic inequality, but one that was far lower than other colonial cities. Upward mobility, at least statistically, seemed a probability for most residents.[12] These statistics may not reflect as rosy a reality as they seem. While most men, age 40 and over, would be considered as living above mere self-sufficiency, the population of the colony in 1760 was getting older. Young, unmarried men or those with young families, those most likely to bring down the averages of wealth, were leaving in large numbers. The family structure of many Planters would suggest, however, that even men with well-established property holdings and older children had acquired as much wealth and land as was possible in Connecticut.

Farmers in eastern Connecticut produced for the market, and in examining motives for emigration, one must keep in mind that the status of a self-sufficient yeoman farmer was not the goal of most New England men. While that idea may appeal to traditions of rugged individualism, it is more likely that the "self-sufficiency" that occurred in some areas was more of an inconvenience than a luxury. It was a step through which young farmers hoped to pass on their way to a more comfortable and secure status. The statistical third who were classified as farmers diversified as much as possible. Land advertisements in the *New London Summary or Weekly Advertiser* stressed those improvements that would allow the new owner to take best advantage of the market and to provide additional income during winter or in case of crop failures. For example, the presence of a grist mill or a tannery usually raised the price of land, and noting that the land was "on the Hartford Road" was more than just a geographical denotation. It provided the owner with direct and unencumbered access to two of the largest markets in Connecticut.

Greater economic security, however, required available land at an affordable price. A larger population puts a greater strain on resources, especially land. Land prices in New London had steadily increased since 1700, but the increase became more pronounced between 1730 and 1760. Good meadowland that sold for £2 per acre at the turn of the century sold for as high as £6 per acre by 1760.[13] Advertisements in the *New London Summary or Weekly Advertiser* suggest that improved and unimproved land was available, but not at readily affordable prices.[14] In one of the less informative advertisements, Stephen Beckwith sought to sell land of "several sizes in Colchester on the Hartford

---

12 Main, *Society and Economy in Colonial Connecticut*, 132.

13 Main, *Society and Economy in Colonial Connecticut*, 119-20.

14 *New London Summary or Weekly Advertiser,* 1758-1761. Main, *Society and Economy in Colonial Connecticut,* 59.

Road."[15] Others were more specific. In September of 1758, John Bishop advertised a 75-acre farm with a good house and saw mill timber. Ten acres were fenced and the property was located only 1/4 mile from the grist mill. As evidence of the growing divisions in religion, Bishop also notes that the farm is five miles from the New London North Parish meeting house and only 1 1/2 miles from the Separatist meeting house.[16] The size of farms being sold is significant. From the mid-1750s to the early 1760s, no farm advertised for sale in the *Summary* was larger than 200 acres, and many were only 50 to 75 acres.[17] Even admitting the fact that New England farms tended to be smaller than farms in other areas, the significant absence of larger properties for sale suggests that men of wealth had less desire or need to leave Connecticut. Those with more to gain, and conversely, less to lose, appeared to be seeking opportunity elsewhere.

Those who purchased land in the first third of the century and were able to hold on to it were the fortunate ones. The availability of land had diminished significantly in the 1730s, and although land prices were high, so were the prices of everything else, diluting many benefits of a seller's market. The market remained shaky in the late 1750s, at least in New London and Norwich. In 1759, New London selectmen promoted a public lottery to raise money for the city's coffers. The winner would receive land once owned by Mathew Stewart. The selectmen were forced to postpone the drawing because not enough tickets had been sold.[18] Unlike most eighteenth-century lotteries in which the participants received the lot designated on the ticket they drew, the New London lottery operated on a winner-take-all basis as its primary purpose was to raise money, not to provide land for all who chose to participate. Hard economic times and the absence of a reliable currency apparently forced many residents to conclude that the risk was simply too great, even if the possible reward was land ownership.

Price fluctuations and the change from old to new tenor in the 1740s also contributed to economic uncertainty. Prices in "country pay," based on local opinion of worth, were usually higher than those in "cash" or currency based on the Spanish silver dollar. Specie, however, was rarely available. Attempts to

---

15 *New London Summary,* October 1758. Stephen Beckwith did not migrate to Nova Scotia, but three cousins did. Benjamin settled in Horton in 1761. John and his brother, Samuel both settled in Cornwallis, John in 1761 and Samuel in 1764.

16 *New London Summary,* 29 September 1758. Bishop was not selling all his holdings. In 1758, he was living two miles away on another property. He was probably selling the land as executor of a relative's estate.

17 *New London Summary,* 1755-1762.

18 *New London Summary,* 3 August 1759, 1758-1762.

regulate monetary values, while mitigating the problem temporarily, could not stem the general inflation that came with Connecticut's participation in two colonial wars between 1740 and 1760. For example, in 1700, oxen cost £11 in country pay. In 1754, the price was £84. By comparison, the same oxen were worth £6.14 in cash in 1700 and £7.10 in 1755.[19]

In order to determine economic status within a community, it is necessary to define the amount of property needed to be considered comfortable or middle class. Main has argued that an adult male with assessed property between £30 and £99 could be considered as comfortable. Those with property assessed at over £100 were well-off, but those below £30 ranged from basic self-sufficiency to poverty.[20] In 1748, the property holdings for 132 members of Lyme's Congregational parishes averaged £56, also the average for those families with established Planter connections. If the number of families averaged is expanded to include those individuals who possibly may have been related in some way, the average rises to £60 total wealth.[21] The assessments themselves range from a low of £1 to a high of £422, with only 13 men with property worth over £100. Taken alone, these figures indicate that the Lyme Planters were indeed from the vast middling sort who maintained a comfortable living but were seeking to improve their status, and that of their sons, in Nova Scotia.

Defining middle class so broadly, however, leaves a great deal of room for interpretation. The age and number of children and the amount of outstanding debts could make a major difference in determining if these families were comfortable or merely self-sufficient. The future Planter Benjamin Beckwith, with a young family and assessed property of £38.07.09, was much less financially secure than Thomas Lord (father of Barnabus Tuthill Lord), who had £97.18.06. Lord, however, had an older family with sons.[22] Lord would need to provide for his children sooner than Beckwith, but they could help their cause by contributing to the household. Benjamin Beckwith, Jr. was only nine years old in 1748 and several years away from mature productive labour. Moreover, assessed property values did not take into account any debts the family may have accrued. Although he was wealthier, Lord may have incurred a debt load

19 Main, *Society and Economy in Colonial Connecticut*, 43. The monetary regulation that helped stabilize the price of oxen lasted only a few months. By 1756, prices had begun to rise again.

20 Main, *Society and Economy in Colonial Connecticut*, 116-17.

21 Connecticut Archives, Ecclesiastical Affairs, Ser. 1, IV: 158-159b. Connecticut State Library. Main estimates the total per capita income in 1756 for all adult males over 21 at £54.14. Main, *Society and Economy in Colonial Connecticut*, 115.

22 *Ibid.*

that could wipe out his security if his business fortunes spiralled downward. Likewise, Beckwith could have been one or two bad crops away from debtors' prison.

If Beckwith and Lord were merely uneasy about the future prospects for providing for their families, Benjamin Peck was positively desperate. In 1748, Peck owned property assessed at £14.02.06 and was supporting a wife and five or six children, all under the age of 11.[23] If Peck was an artisan, his financial status might not have been as bleak since he would not have been required to own livestock or farmland to earn a living. With such a large family and one with no children old enough to contribute productive labour, however, he was likely on the cusp of destitution. With the economic upturn of the 1750s, he probably improved his status somewhat, but the price of good land was still high and, in all likelihood, beyond his reach.

The Planters represented a cross-section of eastern Connecticut society. Some, like the Lothrop family of Norwich, were shopkeepers and importers. Lebbeus Harris was an innkeeper who hosted the meetings of the proprietors before they left Connecticut, and Charles Dickson was a merchant and subscription agent for the *New London Summary*.[24] Still others were tradesmen who sold almost everything they owned to finance their new start in Nova Scotia. While it may be impossible to learn precisely why individual Planters came to Nova Scotia, some clues exist in the type of property they owned and how they proposed to sell it.

Christopher Miner was a shoemaker, owning his own house and shop on the post road a mile outside New London. In addition to his house, he owned a large garden, a good well, and 50 rods of unimproved land with available water. Miner was not destitute and the location of his cobbler's shop on the post road gave him access to the business of passersby as well as townfolk. The land he owned, however, was not sufficient to insure a decent living, and would be woefully inadequate as he added to his household. Before he moved, he advertised his willingness to sell all as cheaply as possible. But he could only accept cash or very short credit terms.[25] Obviously, he needed money, probably to pay off debts before he left Connecticut, and he probably took a below market value price for his land. Miner was not a prominent landowner in Horton. In 1765, his portion of the county assessment totalled £0.2.2, the lowest amount

---

23   The Pecks' sixth child was born in June of 1748.

24   *New London Summary,* 3 April 1761.

25   *New London Summary*, October 1760.

listed.[26] In 1770 or shortly thereafter he apparently sold his land and moved elsewhere.[27]

John Copp of New London was more successful. Before leaving for Nova Scotia, he owned 200 acres, 130 acres of which were improved and well-watered. His possessions included a large house, a barn and two orchards with enough fruit to make 100 barrels of cider yearly. He would accept terms of part cash and part credit. In April of 1761, Copp was still living on the premises and appeared willing to wait for the right price. His name does not appear on the 1764 assessment to build the courthouse in Horton, but he was assessed £0.6.6 in 1765 to pay for various county improvements.[28] Copp apparently had the luxury of a considered move for self-improvement.

As the Connecticut Planters prepared to leave the colony, there was no glut of farms and businesses on the open market, perhaps the best indication that good land was scarce and snatched up quickly. Some, obviously, had no land to sell; others perhaps sold their land to family or friends. Still others, like the Lothrops, had family remaining behind in Connecticut and the emigrants tended not to be the primary owners of the business. Daniel and Joshua Lothrop owned a shop in Norwich specializing in goods "just imported ... from London and Bristol."[29] They remained in Connecticut, but Elisha, Elijah, Isaac and Thaddeus Lothrop received grants in Horton between 1761 and 1764.[30] Although records do not clearly indicate if all the grantees actually settled, it appears that they hoped to establish business links between the two colonies. They were not alone. Samuel Witter, a tailor and clothier in New London, was also an example of this latter group.

In April of 1761, Witter owned a fulling mill and clothier's tools and three small tracts of land, ranging in size from 13 to 74 acres to which he had made no significant improvements. He was prosperous enough to employ another tailor, George Hill, who would remain with the business until Witter sold it. Witter, however, was willing to lease his clothing mill if he could not find a buyer, some evidence that he planned to continue ties with New London.[31] Almost immediately after arriving in Nova Scotia, Witter became involved in the carrying trade between New London and Horton. With his partner, Jonathan

26   Chipman Papers, Public Archives of Nova Scotia, [PANS], MG 1, Vol. 181, #81.

27   Map of Horton Township, c. 1770. V7/230, PANS.

28   Chipman Papers, PANS, MG 1, Vol. 181, #183-184a. *New London Summary*, October 1760.

29   *New London Summary*, 3 July 1761.

30   A.W.H. Eaton, *The History of Kings County* (Belleville, Ont., 1972), 73.

31   *New London Summary*, 3 April 1761.

Rockwell of New London, Witter leased a ship to carry provisions to the new settlements. The ship was to sail in early March 1762 after taking on provisions at New London and Norwich. He charged 4s.2d per barrel for freight and shipping costs. Those shipping goods would either have to pay Rockwell when the provisions were put on ship or Witter would collect the price in Spanish dollars when the ship arrived in Horton.[32] I could find no evidence that Witter had participated in the carrying trade before he left New London, other than purchasing materials for his clothing business. The tailor perhaps saw migration to Nova Scotia as his chance to enter into the merchant/importer class, and he hoped to make a fortune reintegrating the Planters into the consumer economy they left behind.

In communities along the seaboard, the stress of change manifested itself in different ways. In Norwich, Lyme, Lebanon and East Haddam, the economic consequences of church schism seemed to attract most attention. Because the Congregational Church was established in Connecticut, colonial law required that all residents pay taxes to support the Congregationalist minister and the ministry of the church. Anglicans and Baptists were the only exceptions. As legal dissenters, they were allowed to pay taxes to their own congregations. Prior to the Great Awakening, church splits were more related to expansion than to religious differences. Connecticut law allowed the creation of new parishes if the petitioners to the General Assembly could prove they lived too far from the established church to attend services and that a separation would not seriously affect the financial stability of the parent congregation. The new congregations were then allowed to collect taxes for the support of the new church.[33]

In 1722, Robert Denison petitioned the Assembly to allow the taxing of vacant lands in the north parish of New London in order to support a minister. This area, later called Montville, was a product of New London's expansion. Denison's petition was granted, and he and Jonathan Copp (father of Planters John and Samuel) surveyed and laid out the land and ensured that all taxes from the unimproved land were directed to the parish. Copp, a parish deacon, also collected taxes for the construction of the meeting house.[34] By contrast, members of the Fourth Society of Lebanon had to petition twice before being

32   *New London Summary,* 12 February 1762.

33   See, for example, the proposed church separations in East Haddam in 1727 and East Lyme in 1718. Ct. Archives, Ecclesiastical Affairs, Ser. 1, II: 294; Ser. 2, III: 25a. For additional information on the relations between church and state in early Connecticut and on attitudes toward township government, see Thomas W. Jodziewicz, "Vox Populi: Fairfield and Early Connecticut's Dual Localism," *New England Quarterly,* LVIII (December 1985), 578-97.

34   Ct. Archives, Ecclesiastical Affairs, Ser. 1, II: 255-64.

allowed to separate. The Goshen Society of Lebanon was allowed to form only after the Assembly was convinced that the parent society could survive with fewer members being taxed.[35]

By the 1730s, the number of petitions for new churches prompted the Connecticut Assembly to devise firmer regulations for allowing separation. Societies were to mark their boundaries with the obvious aim of taxing any non-dissenter who lived within those boundaries. Since Anglicans and Baptists were the only legally defined dissenters, Separates could be prohibited from establishing churches within the boundaries of another Congregational society. Moreover, boundaries would ensure that churches split equally and built new meeting houses near the centre of any congregation.[36]

In 1747, thirty members of the First Society in Norwich formed a separate society, without legislative consent, and ordained Jedidiah Hide as their minister. While they refused to pay taxes to benefit the older congregation, the Separatists insisted on voting on church matters, which usually consisted of voting against any proposal made by or supporting Benjamin Lord, minister of the First Society. In response, the remaining members of the First Society voted overwhelmingly to prohibit the Separatists from voting on church matters. The Separatists, in turn, petitioned the Connecticut General Assembly, asking to be excused from paying taxes. The General Assembly was reluctant to set a precedent. It refused to exempt the Separatists from paying church taxes, but remained silent on the question of voting privileges.[37]

The Assembly's 1747 ruling had economic as well as social consequences. Congregational churches depended on consensus, not simple majorities, in deciding church affairs. The Separatists could always be outvoted, but they formed a significant and disruptive minority. Moreover, Norwich had no mechanism for forcing the Separatists to pay taxes, and indeed most of them did not. Nor it appears did all of the remaining members of the First Society. For much of the 1730s and 40s, assessments continued to rise as contributions fell, and the absence of consistent collection of church taxes threatened to produce disastrous results for the civic economy. Church taxes supported the school and paid the schoolmaster, maintained the meeting house, still used as much for civic purposes as for religious services, paid the minister's salary, and no doubt aided in the relief of the community's poor.

Not surprisingly, less than a year after the 1747 ruling, the problems of the First Society were again before the General Assembly. On 18 October 1748, the First Society sent a desperate plea to the Assembly for a tax collector. In the

35 Ct. Archives, Ecclesiastical Affairs, Ser. 2, IV: 111a.

36 Ct. Archives, Ecclesiastical Affairs, Ser. 2, IV: 48a, 57; V: 149. Bushman, 223-24.

37 Ct. Archives, Ecclesiastical Affairs, Ser. I, XI: 35-37.

past, it seems, the job had rotated among the men of the community. Now, men were openly refusing the responsibility. Collections had fallen to such an extent that the congregation feared it could not live up to its obligations without going into debt. Norwich got its tax collector, and the citizens of Norwich continued to avoid him.[38] The affairs of the First Society apparently drifted along for almost a decade until the appeal of Benjamin Lord again brought the economic problems of the First Society to public attention.

Benjamin Lord was called to the pastorate of the First Society in 1717. The church voted that his salary would be £100 a year and continued to vote for that sum even as schisms rocked the congregation. Voting for his salary and paying him, however, proved to be two different things. In 1742, the society noted that they already owed Lord more than £1400 (old tenor) and vowed to increase collections to absolve the debt. Once again, the society found it easier to talk about raising money than to collect it, and in 1757, Lord finally took his case to the General Assembly. Recognizing that church separations had limited the society's ability to pay, Lord nevertheless complained that he was in severe financial distress. The Assembly ordered the inhabitants of Norwich to appear to explain themselves and present some justification to show why Lord should not be paid. Moreover, they appointed a committee to ensure that taxes were collected and the minister compensated for his labours.[39]

The trials and tribulations of the First Society of Norwich are illustrative of more than just an obstinate determination not to pay the bills. Separatists may have regarded Lord's request for money as simple greed, and evidence, in their minds, of the minister's unregenerate status. But behind the theological controversy lurked the possibility of real economic hardship. Granted, colonists tended not to pay their debts until forced, but Puritans had always supported their churches and the revivalism of the Great Awakening should have made tax collection easier, if for no other reason than the determination of the Old-Light factions not to be outdone by the enthusiasts. Yet, the problems of the First Society suggest that even those who agreed with the church's stance would not or could not support it with their tax dollars and this reluctance continued into the 1750s when the rest of Connecticut was experiencing an economic upturn. Moreover, the inability of the Norwich church to find a tax collector might suggest the reluctance of neighbours to dun neighbours for money at a time when money was scarce. It could also suggest that tax collectors feared violent reprisals from the Separatists if they tried to collect from them.

One area of Connecticut society as it related to the Planters that requires much more study is the impact of church schism on individual families. Several

38   Ct. Archives, Ecclesiastical Affairs, Ser. I, XI: 37.

39   Ct. Archives, Ecclesiastical Affairs, Ser. I, XI: 52-53.

Huntleys are listed on Lyme's tax list in 1748, but the Planter Daniel Huntley, also from Lyme, was a Baptist. Huntley's wife was Susanna Beckwith, and numerous Beckwiths were also Lyme Congregationalists. Robert Denison was a respected member of New London's North Parish, a standing order Congregationalist church, but members of his wife's family, the Griswolds, were among the Separatists fighting Benjamin Lord in Norwich.[40] Patient research in probate and church records might yield evidence of family estrangement, of sons or daughters being disinherited because of religious differences. Such estrangements would add nuance to the established argument that religion provided a reason for taking up land in Nova Scotia.

The Planters came from a rapidly changing society. The tradition of close-knit, well-ordered communities was being tested throughout eastern Connecticut. Certainly the Great Awakening, with its accompanying church schisms, helped redefine the social hierarchy. Greater participation in the market economy helped lessen barriers to economic prosperity, but it did not erase them entirely. Connecticut was changing, but perhaps it was not changing fast enough for the Planters. Stymied in their quest for land acquisition by high prices and scarcity, it is not surprising that many first moved to Nova Scotia, then deviated from the neatly ordered township maps drawn up for them. The Planters' conception of community had very little in common with the structured Puritan township of the seventeenth century, with its single church serving as the focus of religious and civic life. They demanded the right to control their own affairs, not just to recreate a New England ideal of self-government, but to ensure that their interests would always be served. The Planters were after the main chance, and that perhaps marks them as more Yankee than those they left behind.

---

40 Ct. Archives, Ecclesiastical. Affairs, Ser. 1, IV: 158-159b; XI: 35-37.

Growing Up in Granville Township, 1760-1800

Barry Moody
Professor of History
Acadia University

In the summer of 1805 Sarah (Woodward) Foster lay dying at her home in Granville, Nova Scotia. If she had had time to consider anything but the state of her immortal soul, she might well have contemplated with some satisfaction her impact on the development of Nova Scotia. Not that she would, one suspects, have seen it in those terms. Almost certainly she would have viewed the results of her life in terms of family relationships. For at the advanced age of 104 Sarah Foster was the matriarch of the sprawling Foster-Chute-Wheelock "tribe," which, by the turn of the century, had grown to impressive dimensions and social significance in Annapolis County.

The widow Foster and her immediate descendants in many respects exemplify some of the important characteristics of family in the first several generations of Granville Planters. A study of her family and those of her neighbours can provide a number of insights into what it meant to grow up in a Planter community, and the forces that moulded and shaped the lives of this first generation of Yankee Nova Scotians. This information, in turn, sheds much light on how the Nova Scotia experience of the Planters was similar to and different from that of New England.

Bernard Bailyn, in his important study *The Peopling of British North America*, determined that British migration to North America just prior to the American Revolution was overwhelmingly youthful and male. Only one-third of the immigrants, he found, travelled in family groups.[1] The full impact of this youthful, male, and often indentured, immigrant group was to be found in the southern colonies, much more than in New York or New England. In the northern colonies, the male/female ratio was closer (1.6/1.0), and family units moved to the New World essentially intact. These were primarily farming families, still in the process of growth.[2]

David Fischer, in *Albion's Seed*, described a similar pattern for the settling of New England in the mid-seventeenth century. Fully 94 percent of the immigrants came as part of family units, the highest percentage in the history of early American immigration. The pattern of age distribution was equally unusual. Except for the absence of significant numbers in the over 60 category, the distribution of ages was remarkably similar to that of the population of

---

1 Bernard Bailyn, *The Peopling of British North America* (New York, 1986), 10-11.

2 Bailyn, *Peopling of BNA,* 12.

England. As with Bailyn's later arrivals, the male/female ratio was very close (1.5/1.0).[3]

Throughout its colonial history, New England, more than other areas of British North America, was characterized and influenced by the early and powerful presence of family. It was a place where "normal family life was not the exception but the rule." As Fischer pointed out, "From the start, this exceptionally high level of family integration set Massachusetts apart from other American colonies."[4]

The situation for Nova Scotia's Granville Township in the 1760s was very similar. Sarah Foster was a widow when she came to Nova Scotia from New Hampshire, at age 59, with all of her six children, in 1760. Unlike most of her contemporaries, she did not remarry on the death of her husband of 34 years, but remained a widow for the remaining 46 years of her life. Four of her children were already married, with young families, before the migration, and two others married shortly after their arrival in Granville. Three generations of the same family were thus represented in the move to Nova Scotia, and this pattern seems to have been repeated in other families which settled in the township.[5]

This was not a migration, then, of young couples and children only, nor does one find many examples of single men of marriageable age arriving without parents and siblings. The multigenerational family was present in Granville from the very beginning, with ages ranging from the mid-80s to the newborn. Thus was transplanted in Nova Scotia the norm of rural life in New England, providing a sense of both stability and continuity that was an important factor in the development of a Planter community.

The move to Nova Scotia represented a continuation not merely of the traditional form of family to be found in New England towns and villages, but of the very way of migrating that was so characteristic of that region's past. The youth of Granville Township would, from the beginning, grow to maturity in a society that was remarkably similar to that of New England, and even old England before it, in terms of age distribution, gender ratios and the presence of kin. It would thus be, in many respects, a familiar society that was being recreated on the banks of the Annapolis River.

---

3   David Hackett Fischer, *Albion's Seed: Four British Folkways in America* (New York, 1989), 25-26.

4   Fischer, *Albion's Seed*, 26.

5   The Foster family has been reconstituted using William E. Chute, *A Genealogy and History of the Chute Family in America with some account of the Family in Great Britain and Ireland* (Salem, Mass., 1894) and W.A. Calnek and A.W. Savary, *History of the County of Annapolis* (Toronto, 1897).

For the New England emigrants of the 1760s, the claims of family and kin were clearly not confined to the nuclear family alone. John Adams and Alice Kasakoff, in their study of migration patterns within colonial New England, concluded that "there is little evidence for the importance of kin beyond the nuclear family."[6] Even a preliminary survey of the Granville settlers would appear to show considerable evidence to the contrary. While some apparently came to Nova Scotia with no relatives,[7] others arrived as part of an extended and intricate web of kin, a network which appears to have transcended and at times even replaced the primacy of the nuclear family itself.

The Farnsworth-Longley network serves as a good example of the way in which "family" was frequently refashioned and redefined as part of the process of migration. William Longley came to Granville in 1760 with his wife, Mary Parker, and only one of his twelve children, Israel, then aged 15. William's sister, Lydia and her husband, Amos Farnsworth, were included in the migration to Granville. With them came at least six of their ten children; the rest remained in New England. Amos's brother Jonas, his wife Thankful Ward, and five of their nine children made the trip to Nova Scotia, as did a nephew of Amos and Jonas, Solomon Farnsworth. In addition to being related by marriage, this generation of the Longleys and Farnsworths were tied by blood; Lydia and William were first cousins of Jonas and Amos. William Longley would eventually return to New England to be near the rest of his family, leaving his then-grown son, Israel, in Granville with his own wife and children, his aunt and uncle and assorted first cousins, second cousins and first cousins once removed.[8] For Israel Longley and his children, this Nova Scotia extended network of relatives, who were also neighbours, was bound to play a more significant, and immediate, role in their lives than would the more distant members of Israel's original nuclear family.[9]

6   John W. Adams and Alice Bee Kasakoff, "Migration and the Family in Colonial New England: The View from Genealogies," *Journal of Family History*, IX, 9 (Spring 1984), 34.

7   The intricacies of the New England family relationships of many of these immigrants has not been fully explored. Further research may well show even more extensive kinship than has already been determined.

8   Calnek and Savary, *History of Annapolis County*, 507-08, 540-41; *Joseph S. Longley, His Life and Family*, compiled by Richmond W. Longley (n.p., 1951), 7-9; *Joseph S. Longley, His Life and Family — A Supplement*, compiled by Richmond W. Longley (n.p., 1977), 8-10.

9   The surviving letters of the Farnsworth family from the 1770s and 1780s reveal, if not first-rate spellers, at least genuine desire to maintain the ties of family even if separated by considerable distance. Public Archives of Nova Scotia, Halifax, N.S. [PANS], Manuscript Group, MG 100, Vol. 140, Farnsworth Family Papers.

In a similar (if not quite as complicated) manner, three of the sons of Obadiah and Martha Wheelock settled in Granville and married there, as did their second cousin, Abel Wheelock.[10] As already noted, the Fosters came to Granville as an extended family — Sarah, her three married sons with their families, a daughter with her husband and children, and two daughters of marriageable age.[11] These, as well as other examples, would suggest that, at least in the case of those who settled Granville, the ties of extended kinship played a more significant role in their lives than some New England historians have claimed.

The ties of family clearly extended beyond the mere move to Nova Scotia. Having drawn their lots, and sometimes finding themselves widely scattered in the sprawling township of Granville, family members began to trade or sell, in order to settle close to kin.[12] Most of the family units were able, in this way, to establish themselves within a few miles of their closest relatives, and, given the comparatively easy transportation provided by the river on which all of the lots fronted, access to these family members could be fairly frequent for most of the year. Sarah Foster's two sons, for example, occupied adjoining lots 104 and 105, while their sister, Judith Chute, lived about three miles away on lot 123. Sisters Sarah Wheelock and Elizabeth LeCain were within easy travelling distance of the rest of the family, across the river in Annapolis Township. Only brother Jeremiah was missing; he had moved back to New England, possibly to Maine.[13] The ties of kinship from the beginning thus encompassed not merely the parent-child relationship, but, for many families, extended to include aunts and uncles, grandparents and cousins of various degrees.

Ties were also maintained with relatives left behind in New England. Letters, occasional visits and business trips helped maintain the link with "home." In addition, some of those who settled in Granville moved on after a few years, many back to New England, thus reinforcing that tie, and extending the network of family back and forth across the water. The American Revolution

---

10 Calnek and Savary, *History of Annapolis County*, 623-24.

11 Calnek and Savary, History of Annapolis County, 491, 510-12; Chute, *A Genealogy and History of the Chute Family*, liv, lv, lvi, 20; PANS, MG 4, No. 185, Granville Township Book, 9.

12 See Barry Moody, "Land, Kinship and Inheritance in Granville Township, 1760-1800," in Margaret Conrad, ed., *Making Adjustments: Change and Continuity in Planter Nova Scotia 1759-1800* (Fredericton, 1991), 166; PANS, Record Group, RG 20, Series C, Vol. 85 #225, list of Granville Proprietors.

13 *Ibid.*; Calnek and Savary, *History of Annapolis County*, 511, 537, 623-24.

and the resulting division of North America might have slowed this process, but certainly did not stop it. About 1786, 14-year-old Joanna, 12-year-old Crocker and 8-year-old George Washington, three of the 13 children of Sarah Foster's grandson John Chute, moved with their Crocker grandparents back to the United States, where they were naturalized the following year. When it came time for Crocker Chute to choose a wife, he returned to Granville to marry 15-year-old Cynthia Dodge and take her back to Lunenburg, Massachusetts.[14] Forty years later, their younger brother Joseph Fowler Chute, who had not even been born when they had left home, joined his older siblings in Massachusetts.[15] In such ways was the fabric of family continually being reknit, and reinforced.

The ties of family that existed before the move to Granville in 1760 were obviously of considerable significance in the creation of the atmosphere in which the youth of the township developed. However, as strong as the familial ties were which bound them to their original homes, and as comforting as those close relationships were in their new ones, none of the Planters could ultimately escape the consequences of the fact that Granville was not New England. Merely by coming here they had thrust themselves into a very different context, with significant results for their children and grandchildren. Although the majority of those who settled in Granville were from New England, a significant minority were not, and, however closely it might draw its relatives about it like an encircling cloak, no Planter family in the township could protect itself from the influences of the "strangers" who had settled in their midst. The Shafners and Boltzors from Germany, the McKenzies and Armstrongs from Scotland, Neilys, McBrides and Reaghs from Ireland, Clarks, Mills, Gilliatts and Baths from Yorkshire were suddenly next-door-neighbours.[16] The end of the American Revolution brought Dutch Bogarts, Coverts and Bohakers from New York, and German mercenaries such as the Jewish Calneks.[17] Across the river in nearby Annapolis Township, there were even more "foreigners." Unlike the towns of New England, the proprietors of the Nova Scotia townships did not control the

14   Calnek and Savary, *History of Annapolis County*, 491-2; Chute, *History of Chute Family*, 29, 49-51.

15   Chute, *History of Chute Family*, 53.

16   Calnek and Savary, *History of Annapolis County*, 465-66, 470-71, 475, 482-83, 485-86, 493-97, 516-17, 545, 547-48, 551, 556-57, 568; PANS, RG 20, Series C, Vol. 85, #225, list of Granville Proprietors; Fort Anne National Historic Park, Annapolis Royal, Nova Scotia, original grant, Township of Granville, 30 October 1765. The large number of deeds for the township give the best indication of the distribution of settlers. See Registry of Deeds, Lawrencetown, Nova Scotia, Vols. 1-10.

17   Calnek and Savary, *History of Annapolis County*, 482-83, 485-87, 495-96.

distribution of the land (this was done from Halifax), and had no means of determining who settled in their communities.

Thus, from the first day of arrival, the New Englanders were confronted with a radically altered environment, and the first generation of Granville children would grow up in a very different context from that of their parents. The children on the next farm might well speak with a different accent, or even a different language, come from a different culture, worship God in a different way. The extent to which Planter parents attempted to protect their children from such foreign influences, and thus to perpetuate the purity of the New England Way, tells us much about both the nature of these Planters and the experience of growing up in such a township.

In the numerous studies of colonial New England communities, much has been made of the homogenous nature of these towns and villages, and the way in which, generation after generation, New Englanders deliberately excluded those who did not conform in terms of religious, ethnic or national origins.[18] If Michael Zuckerman is correct in his assessment, what he calls "ethnic exclusivity" was widely practised before the American Revolution, with pluralism seldom prevailing during these years.[19] Homogeneity, and the harmony that it was believed it could bring to a community, were still the objectives of the average New Englander. And yet, for this first generation of Granville children, ethnic exclusivity was not even a possibility. If this close contact with "strangers" disturbed these Planter parents, there is little indication of it for most of the families. It is possible that it may explain why some stayed only a short time in pluralistic Granville before returning to more familiar, and safe, New England. Those more conservative elements, unwilling to face the changes that the proximity of such a diverse population threatened, may well have dealt with it by simple removal. But for the rest, the mere fact of remaining indicates that the fear of the consequences of having their children grow up next to families who would not be allowed to settle in many New England towns, if it existed at all, was, at best, second to other considerations.

One measure of the Planter acceptance of such diversity is to be found in the choice of marriage partners by that first generation of New Englanders to come of age in Granville. A few families showed a hesitation to integrate, or at least a desire to continue their family tradition, by marrying extensively with first and second cousins, mostly Nova Scotian. This is especially striking in the

---

18 See for example Philip J. Greven, Jr., *Four Generations: Population, Land, and Family in Colonial Andover, Massachusetts* (Ithaca, N.Y., 1970); Kenneth A. Lockridge, *A New England Town The First Hundred Years: Dedham, Massachusetts, 1636-1736* (New York, 1985); Michael Zuckerman, *Peaceable Kingdoms: New England Towns in the Eighteenth Century* (New York, 1972).

19 Zuckerman, *Peaceable Kingdoms*, 108.

Foster-Chute family, where this practice lasted well into the mid-nineteenth century. But even here, in this most conservative of Granville families, the exclusion of "outsiders" was never complete. As early as 1761, Elizabeth Foster (Sarah's daughter) married Francis LeCain, of an old Annapolis Royal family of Huguenot origin. She was, however, the only one in her family of that generation to marry a non-Planter. Sixteen years later, her niece, Sarah Chute, married Thomas Hicks, admittedly a New Englander by birth, but a member of the Society of Friends. In spite of the family's strong preference for marrying those like themselves, Sarah Foster, before her death in 1805, would witness the union of grandchildren and great-grandchildren with Granville neighbours of Irish, Scottish, German, Yorkshire and Loyalist origin. Even for the Fosters, New England purity could not be maintained in the face of the dramatically different context in which they found themselves after their move to Granville in 1760.[20]

Most Planter families in the township do not seem to have had even the reservations shown in the marriage patterns of the Fosters. Different cultural and even linguistic groups quickly merged. Equally noticeable is the remarkable lack of marriage ties back to New England. Although most of the home communities were less than a week's travel away, and intimate ties had been retained by visits and letters, there is little indication of parents reaching back to the old network of kin and friends in search of a suitable bride or groom for their son or daughter. From the first, most young Granvillites married those with whom they had grown up, a common Granville experience apparently considered more important than a shared cultural or even religious background.[21]

The effects of such intermarriage for succeeding generations is significant. Like the Planters, other cultural groups had usually arrived as family units, rather than as single men who might more easily have been absorbed into the prevailing Planter ethos. The women, especially, are often viewed as powerful conveyors of tradition and folkways, and long before the revolution the mothers of many new Planter Granvillites were women from Yorkshire, Ireland, Germany or Scotland. They must have crooned lullabies, cooked foods, related

20   Calnek and Savary, *History of Annapolis County*, 491-93, 510-13, 537-39; 623-24; Chute, *History of Chute Family*.

21   Calnek and Savary, *History of Annapolis County*, 465-640; Chute, *History of Chute Family; Joseph S. Longley: His Life and Family*, 7-10; Leone B. Cousins, "The Fellows Family of Granville, Nova Scotia." *The Nova Scotia Historical Quarterly*, 8, 1 (March 1978), 81-91; *Pedegree of Troop (Troup) Family*, Canada, compiled by J.D. Eric Troop (Newmarket, Ont., 1974); William I. Morse, *Genealogiae or Data Concerning the Families of Morse, Chipman, Phinney, Ensign and Whiting* (Boston, 1925); PANS, Granville Township Book.

tales, taught skills, and conveyed a whole body of knowledge and belief that was either quite or entirely foreign to their staunch New England spouses. The houses which those husbands built to shelter their families might well reflect the feel of the New England countryside, but what went on inside those homes must, on occasion, have been radically different.[22]

Long before the end of the eighteenth century, the process of change and cultural amalgamation was well underway. That this should be considered acceptable by that first generation of Granville Planters tells us much about the nature of that group, and reveals the gap that already separated them from their New England origins. From the moment they first settled in Granville, the Planters, and more significantly their children, would be exposed to an environment, and moulded by a context, that was radically different from that which they had left behind in New England. Without enforced homogeneity, the Puritan ideal could not flourish in Nova Scotia, and the rising generation would be shaped by other forces; *Nova Scotians*, not transplanted New Englanders, would begin to appear. The New England close communal life, what Conrad Arnseberg has termed a "dense collective experience,"[23] had no chance of survival in increasingly diverse Granville Township.

Zuckerman has claimed that, "Under the auspices of the monolithic ideal, fundamental differences in values were rarely admitted within a town, while differences of race, nationality, and culture almost never appeared east of the Hudson River before the Revolution." That such a statement does not apply to the settlement of Nova Scotia in the 1760s is a fact of profound significance for the evolution of the colony. The emphasis on uniformity and conformity that had characterized the evolution of New England would be muted and diluted in Granville. With the disappearance of this ideal of community went most of the Puritan concept of the social order, allowing, indeed forcing, the development of a new sense of community and a new definition of the individual in emerging Nova Scotian communities such as Granville. As Fischer has pointed out, "The homogeneity of New England's population was not an historical accident; it arose from the religious purposes and social values of a regional culture."[24] Without that homogeneity, the first generation of Nova Scotian-born Granvillites grew up in a community that lacked the focus, the sense of united purpose, and exclusivity that had characterized the New England towns and villages of their parents' childhood. The lives of this first generation, and the nature of the evolving community, were much marked by this fact.

---

22 Very little has been done to examine the transmission of folkway in English-speaking Nova Scotia. In particular, the role of women in this important process has been largely overlooked. For a good model, see Fischer, *Albion's Seed.*

23 Quoted in Zuckerman, *Peaceable Kingdoms*, 48.

24 Fischer, *Albion's Seed*, 811.

One of the important physical characteristics of the township tended to reinforce the early breakdown of the New England ideal in Granville. With the exception of the important marsh lots, all of the land granted to a proprietor was in one lot, fronting on the Annapolis River and stretching northward in long, narrow strips to the Bay of Fundy. It was the deliberate choice of the proprietors to create a township that did not possess a settled centre where the majority of the inhabitants would live. Although the river provided a convenient means of transportation and travel, settlers at one end of the township were still 25 miles away from those at the other extreme, adding to the difficulty of creating a community of consensus, and placing more importance on the role of the family.

Michael Zuckerman has pointed out that "an isolated settlement pattern is often connected with substantial self-reliance, but 'closely packed' settlement forms are likelier to be linked to a high evaluation of 'responsibility to the group.'"[25] Such "closely packed settlement" demanded conformity and unity, for without them harmony and peace would not be possible. Writing further, he stated:

> Pursuit of private ends never was approved in provincial Massachusetts. Subordination of the individual to the group began with the first Puritan, and it remained constant to the very eve of the Revolution. Assertion of the self against the community was considered conducive to contention; selfish interests were assumed to be opposed to the public interest, and the public interest was primary .... Children who grew up in provincial Massachusetts grew up in a society which insisted on concord and consensus; as they grew they became, subtly, almost irresistibly, people who could live in such a society.[26]

Those New England parents for whom the collective ideal remained important would not have chosen to raise their children in pluralist, diverse Granville. Both the presence of other cultural groups and the demography of the township made the replication of the aims and ideals of rural New England impossible in nearby Nova Scotia. Pressures on the children to conform, to suppress the self in the interest of the good of the community, were not present in Granville to the extent that one would find them in Massachusetts or Connecticut, and freer reign was thus given the growth of the individual.

Granville differed in another significant way from the communities from which most of these Planters had come. The studies of individual communities that have provided so much insight into the development of rural New England have chronicled the growing problems of land acquisition, and the resulting

25   Zuckerman, *Peaceable Kingdoms*, 48.

26   Zuckerman, *Peaceable Kingdoms*, 70, 72.

difficulties that this scarcity posed for the family. Most New England farmers never possessed large amounts of land in the beginning, and long before the mid-eighteenth century, in many areas, the division and redivision of the family lands among many sons had reduced farm sizes to the minimum.[27] In such areas, it was no longer possible to leave land to more than one son, without endangering the land's ability to support those dependent on it. The resulting internal family tensions, the impact on the patriarchal family system and the pressure on non-inheriting sons to seek livelihoods in non-agricultural occupations have been extensively examined by the historians of colonial New England.[28]

Granville, and, one suspects, many other agricultural townships of Nova Scotia, presented a new beginning in many respects, and the mere taking up of land in this colony acted as a major disjuncture with the New England past for many of those who chose to settle here. Land in the Annapolis Valley was, for the first several generations, both plentiful and relatively cheap, providing for settlers that great commodity of the frontier: room for expansion. Each of the proprietors of Granville in the 1760s received 500 acres of land, a combination of dyked marshland, uncleared valley land and mountain woodlots. In addition, the early securing of grants for underage sons, the very minimal price of undeveloped land, at least until the arrival of the Loyalists, and the availability of additional lands in nearby Wilmot township, meant that the average Granville family could have at its disposal more land than could be dreamed of by the residents of the older-settled areas of New England.[29] If historians such as Kenneth Lockridge are correct in their calculations of the amount of land available to a mid-eighteenth-century New England family, and their assessment of the resulting strains that such scarcity imposed on community and family, the move to Nova Scotia, or the backwoods of New Hampshire, for example, must have had dramatic and significant repercussions for those daring enough to migrate out of the region. Lockridge has claimed that, by the eve of the

27 See Jackson T. Main, "The Economic Class Structure of the North," in Gary B. Nash, ed., *Class and Society in Early America* (Englewood Cliffs, N.J., 1970), 102; Kenneth Lockridge, "Land, Population, and the Evolution of New England Society, 1630-12790," in Nash, *Class and Society*, 153-55; Greven, *Four Generations*, 128-29.

28 Linda Auwers, "Fathers, Sons, and Wealth in Colonial Windsor, Connecticut," *Journal of Family History*, 3, 2 (Summer 1978), 136-49; John Waters, "Family, Inheritance, and Migration in Colonial New England: The Evidence from Guilford, Connecticut," *William and Mary Quarterly*, 39, 1 (January, 1982), 64-86; Greven, *Four Generations*, 131-54.

29 See Moody, "Land, Kinship and Inheritance," for a discussion of land in Granville Township.

American Revolution, "Instead of being the land of opportunity, this part of America [New England] was rapidly becoming more and more an old world society; old world in the sense of the size of farms, old world in the sense of an increasingly wide and articulated social hierarchy, old world in that 'the poor' were ever present and in increasing numbers."[30] In more than one respect, Granville constituted a new beginning, separating the township's inhabitants from some of the social pressures which were mounting in nearby New England.

The move to Nova Scotia, and the resulting availability of land, must have somewhat dissipated certain internal family tensions. There was no longer the necessity of a father choosing which of his several sons would inherit the land, there now being enough for all. Thus rivalry between sons, and tensions between parent and child, would be lessened, although probably not obliterated completely. As an earlier study of land distribution and inheritance in Granville has shown,[31] it was often possible for a father to provide all of his sons, and sometimes his sons-in-law as well, with farms of substantial size. This could, and often would, be done well before the death of the father, without jeopardizing his own livelihood.

In this way, for the male youth of Granville Township, the necessity of leaving the land and seeking a livelihood in a non-agricultural occupation was much reduced. Since the young men of the next several generations were not forced to choose between abandoning agriculture or abandoning the area, the trend in Granville Township would appear to have been the reverse of that which obtained in parts of New England. The occupational list of the first generation is much more likely to contain such professions as mariner, carpenter, chairmaker, wheelwright, cordwainer, blacksmith and housewright than a similar list for the second or third generation, where yeoman, husbandman or farmer is to be found much more frequently. The first generation of males continued to practise the skills learned in New England, if only on a part-time basis, with farming quickly constituting their primary source of livelihood. With plenty of land for all, the majority of their sons would see farming as their chief occupation.[32] The creation of largely landless classes of labourers and craftsmen occurred slowly, and the evolution of towns in the area would be even slower.[33] The crisis of space and occupation, so crucial in the

---

30   Lockridge, "Land, Population," 166.

31   Moody, "Land, Kin and Inheritance," 170-71.

32   See the listing of occupations in the more than 800 deeds drawn up for Granville Township between 1760 and 1800. Registry of Deeds, Lawrencetown, Nova Scotia, Vols. 1-11.

33   In fact, only one small town evolved in the entire township, and that in the latter part of the nineteenth century. See Elizabeth Ruggles Coward, *Bridgetown Nova Scotia: Its History to 1900* (Kentville, N.S., 1955).

shaping of the rising generation, would not occur in Granville until after the first one hundred years, and by then both the North American context and the available options had altered considerably.

If the community context in which the child of Granville matured differed from the New England home of his or her parents, so too did the very nature of the family in which that child was nurtured. Fairly good records of births and deaths are available for Granville Township during this early period, and from this information much can be learned about the nature of the Granville families. Of 225 known families begun before 1800, data sufficient to determine family size is available on 167. Of these, 145 families were primarily or solely of New England origin, and these produced 1322 children, giving an average of 9.12 children per family. Three couples produced no children, while two families numbered 16 offspring. The handful of German families averaged 11 children, while families of British origin produced only 7.3 children each.[34]

Such figures reveal much about the eighteenth-century Granville family. Greven, in his study of colonial Andover, Massachusetts, noted a steady decline in the birthrate after 1710, reaching its lowest level of 3.0 births per marriage in the period 1785-1794.[35] The 9.12 births per marriage in Granville stand in sharp contrast to the Andover figures, which, if typical for Massachusetts in general, reveal that a dramatic increase in the birthrate accompanied the move to Nova Scotia. More work remains to be done, but it would appear from preliminary figures that the immigrants themselves came from larger than average New England families, although falling considerably short of the 9.12 average of the families of their children and grandchildren.

This dramatic increase in the birthrate cannot be attributed solely to a significant decline in the age at marriage of the Granvillites. Data on available marriages would indicate that Planters who married in New England did so at age 24.35 for males, and 23.1 for females. These figures vary only slightly from those of Greven's Andover for the same period: 25.3 for males, 23.2 for females.[36] From 1760 to 1800, the age at marriage of Granvillite males appears to have risen, to 24.87, while that of females declined to 20.12. The fact that land was more readily available to second and third generation Planter males than might be the case in many New England communities does not appear to have affected the average age at marriage. The lowering of the average age at marriage for women could account for some of the increase in family size, but certainly not the amount reflected in the figures. Possibly, greater economic

---

34 The information for this analysis was obtained from the numerous genealogies listed in earlier footnotes, and was used to reconstitute all of the families about which any data was available.

35 Greven, *Four Generations*, 183.

36 Greven, *Four Generations*, 206.

security, associated with the more extensive, cheaper and more readily available amounts of land, freed the settlers from some of the constraints imposed by the developing situation in New England during the first three-quarters of the eighteenth century.

Whatever the reasons for the larger families, the implications for the members of those units were extensive. Children who grew up in a family with eight, nine or even 15 siblings were part of a unit whose dynamics were quite different from one with only three or four children. Given the size of these nuclear families, it would be quite wrong to view them as a single entity. "Family" could mean very different things to its various members. The large nuclear family was not a well-defined, static unit, but one which was in an almost constant state of flux, creating a complex, multiple and diverse set of relationships. Children grew to adulthood, married and left the home while younger siblings were still being born into the family. By the time younger children reached maturity and were ready for marriage, older brothers and sisters might already be grandparents. Many children might know older brothers and sisters far less well than cousins or even neighbours of their own age. A sense of obligation, duty, a feeling of "family," might well bind siblings separated by 20 or even 30 years, but the sense of intimacy that comes from growing up together would be largely, or entirely, absent. Children nearer the middle in such large families would experience a different sense of family than their siblings at the two extremes, having more intimate relations with both. For parents and children alike, the family was a constantly changing entity, constituting an almost infinite variety of relationships and experiences.

The larger number of children, and the longer period of child bearing, had important implications for the parents as well as the children. The years between marriage in the early 20s and the mid-60s were filled with child-bearing and child-rearing. For many, it was a life-long occupation. Joshua Banks and his wife Dorothea Craft produced 12 children between the years 1778 and 1800; child-rearing took up at least 42 years of their lives. Samuel and Rachel (Ray) Bent began their family in 1765; the youngest of their 12 children was married 46 years later. Benjamin and Elizabeth (Richardson) Foster's 13 children were produced over a 26 year period, resulting in children in the home for nearly 50 years. Sybil Marshall, married to Thomas Chute at age 16, bore the last of her 16 children 32 years later, with child-rearing taking up the last 50 years of her life. For many of these parents, the birth and rearing of their younger children coincided with the arrival and raising of their older children's children. In such situations, uncles and aunts, nephews and nieces might well be of similar ages, and be reared more like cousins, or even siblings. Such occurrences tended to complicate, and expand, the definition and meaning of the term "family."

Given the large number of children in the average Granville family, there was considerable scope to continue the naming strategies that were so prevalent in New England. David Fischer, in his book *Albion's Seed*, explores what he terms the "nuclear naming strategy" of colonial Massachusetts families. He found that two-thirds of the first born in that colony were named after one of the parents, a pattern which set it apart from the other colonies.[37] The largely Massachusetts-born Planter community in Granville, while following this strategy to some extent, did not adhere to it as rigidly as had their ancestors. In 76 percent of the families examined, one of the sons was named after his father, but rarely was it the eldest. For daughters the proportion was somewhat lower, with the mother's name reappearing in the next generation in 68 percent of the cases. Like many other practices, the naming strategy of New England was somewhat muted in the migration process.

The presence in Granville of these large families would, one might expect, increase the likelihood of young children experiencing the death of at least one parent. Sufficient data is available to examine in detail 68 Granville families begun in the period 1760-1800. In 26 cases (38.2 percent), the death of at least one of the parents occurred before all of the children reached the age of 20. In 13 families, all of the children were under that age. Taken together, in the 26 families, 67.5 percent of the children were raised at least partially by only one of their natural parents. These children were more likely to lose their father than their mother. Of the 26 families affected by parental death, in 15 cases it was the male who died prematurely. By projection, parental death was experienced by approximately one-quarter of the young children of the township. Preliminary research indicates that this figure is somewhat lower than that which pertains for the same area during the first half of the nineteenth century, when epidemics were much more prevalent.[38]

The emotional trauma, as well as the physical difficulties attendant upon the death of a parent were only part of the experience. In virtually all of the cases cited above, death of one parent was very shortly followed by the remarriage of the surviving one. Adjustment to a step-parent, often step-siblings, and very quickly half-brothers and sisters, must also be dealt with by the young child. New relationships, often-complex new families were rewoven in the process, sometimes to the detriment of the children involved.

Given the uncertainty of life, one might expect to find careful planning for all eventualities, especially by the fathers. Surviving documentation, however, indicates that few young or even middle aged men gave much thought to the care of their children in the event of their own premature death. Most of the men in their 20s through 40s who died suddenly (e.g., by drowning) had made no

---

37 Fischer, *Albion's Seed*, 95-97.

38 These figures are drawn from the family reconstructions based on the genealogical material already cited in this paper, supplemented by the cemetery records for the township, Archives of Historic Restoration Society, Annapolis Royal, Nova Scotia.

legal provision for their families, leaving behind a tangled web of problems which often required years to resolve. On 22 November 1786, Samuel Chute was drowned while crossing the Annapolis River; he was 39. The youngest of his nine children, Rachel, was not yet a year old, while the eldest, Elizabeth, was 17.[39] The inventory of the estate, taken two months later, listed land, with "Buildens," cattle, household goods, and blacksmith and silversmith tools, valued at £574.7.5.[40] No will appears to have been drawn, leaving affairs in disarray, and the children in a vulnerable position. Within a year, the widow, Sarah, was back in probate court, seeking protection for her young children:

> The humble petition of Sarah Lynam, late widow of Samuel Chute deceas'd
> Most Respectfully Sheweth!
>
> That your Petitioner with a View of bettering her Situation lately Married Dr. James Lynam, & as the Affairs of the Estate were in a very Confused Train found herself necessitated to Empower her present Husband to Act, & Settle the Accts of Said Est. in her Stead, But by the late Visible & Glaring Acts of Mismanagement, & Squandering, Committed by the said Dr. Lynam, She has the Strongest Reason to fear her large Family's being soon reduced to poverty & Want, Unless proper methods, are speedily taken to prevent the Consequences of his Irregularities.
>
> Your Petitioner therefore humbly begs that Your Worship would please to Interfere, and prevent the Ruin of her large Family ....[41]

A petition, signed by a number of relatives and neighbours, supported Sarah's request, recommending speedy action as "the large family within Mentioned, will Shortly become a parish Charge, unless timely & Effectual Methods are taken to prevent the Ruin of said Estate."[42] Brothers of Samuel Chute were appointed guardians of the children, and some order was brought to the affairs of the estate.[43] However, the family itself remained in a state of chaos, furthered by

39   Calnek and Savary, *History of Annapolis County*, 491-92.

40   Inventory of estate of Samuel Chute, 1 January 1787, Registry of Probate, Annapolis Royal, Nova Scotia.

41   Registry of Probate, Samuel Chute Estate Papers, Sarah Lynam to Joseph Winniett, Registrar of Probate, n.d. [1787].

42   Registry of Probate, Samuel Chute Estate Papers, John Chute, Benjamin Chute, Spencer Barns, Benjamin Foster, George Troop and Sarah Lynam to Joseph Winniett, 9 January 1788.

43   Registry of Probate, Samuel Chute Estate Papers, Petition of Benjamin Chute and John Chute Jr., 10 April 1788.

Sarah Lynam's early death in 1799, having borne two children to her second marriage. Dr. Lynam returned to England the following year, leaving behind both his stepchildren and his only surviving son, presumably in the care of relatives.[44] The estate of Samuel Chute was not finally settled, and the property divided, until 1802, 15 years after his death.[45] For this family, the emotional upheaval of parental death was greatly exacerbated by the years of financial chaos which followed, due, at least partially, to the failure of the father to make any legal provision for his children in the event of his death. Awareness of the uncertainty of life and the problems associated with intestate estates did not influence the father to attempt to ensure the future of his children by the simple act of drawing up a will.

Scottish-born Henry Munro, the largest landowner in the township at his sudden death in 1781, likewise failed to make provision for his Planter wife, Sarah Hooper, and their seven children ranging in ages from 13 to one.[46] The widow's remarriage less than two years later to George Newton, "who has turned out a Very profligate & Abandoned Character ...," in the words of his new wife, led eventually to fears that "Great Waste & Destruction is Like to Happen to the Said Munroe's Estate." Sarah (Munro) Newton had to petition for the appointment of a new administrator, fearing that there would soon be nothing left for her children.[47] Henry Munro's failure to plan for his children's future caused a delay of over twenty years in the settling of his estate, much to the detriment of his heirs.[48]

Planter Abijah Parker's early death in 1780 left seven children under the age of 15,[49] with no provision for their future. It was not until 1801 that the estate was settled and the property divided among his heirs.[50] In this case, fortunately, widow Miriam Parker proved a most able administrator of the estate and protector of the family's future. Abednego Ricketson left 10 under-age children, and a considerable estate, but no will, on his death in 1778. Even the problems

---

44 Chute, *History of Chute Family*, 28-29.

45 Registry of Probate, Samuel Chute Estate Papers, Order of Joseph Winniett, 25 July 1802.

46 Calnek and Savary, *History of Annapolis County*, 331-32, 555-56.

47 Registry of Probate, Henry Munro's Estate Papers, petition of Sarah Newton to Joseph Winniett, n.d.

48 Registry of Probate, Henry Munro's Estate Papers, division of lands of Henry Munro, January 1803.

49 Calnek and Savary, *History of Annapolis County*, 560-61.

50 Registry of Probate, Abijah Parker's Estate Papers, order of William Winniett, 29 April 1801.

associated with dealing with her husband's estate did not encourage widow
Phebe Ricketson to draw up a will to provide for the property in her own name;
she died intestate in 1795, leaving two minor children. The estate of the two,
then valued at £1050, was not settled until 1802.[51]

Only a few Granville fathers attempted, through their wills, to plan for the
orderly disposition of their estates and the security of their children's future in
the event of their premature deaths. At least some of these Granvillites were able
to plan for the future because their deaths were preceded by periods of illness.[52]
The wills of these individuals reveal varying concerns about the welfare of their
families, and of their property. Andrew White, drawing a will three-and-a-half
months before his death in 1787, said little about the raising of his children,
leaving a living from the farm to his wife "as Long as She Stays at home and
takes Care of the Family and Remains my Widow." Minor sums of money were
provided for his five young daughters when they came of age, with the real
estate divided among his sons. White was clearly concerned about keeping the
land together, making his dispositions on the condition that none of the sons
should sell or mortgage the property "to any stranger, or to any other person out
of the Family." Nothing was said about keeping the family together.[53] The only
other Granville Planter to make testamentary provision for minor children was
Valentine Troop who, in a will drawn in 1775, and amended 10 days before his
death in 1776, provided that all of his estate go to his wife Cattee for her
lifetime, on the condition that she bring up his [and her!] children. It was
Troop's wish that all his minor sons should be put out to proper masters to learn
a lawful trade.[54]

The non-Planter Granvillites appear to have been more concerned for the
provision of minor children. British-born John Litch, writing in 1781, carefully
planned for each of his children, and provided his wife with the financial
resources to care for them during their minority. He even named his wife
guardian of their six children (something most fathers did not bother to do), and
provided that "my Said Wife be solely benefited by their labour during their
minority unless she see fit to bind some, or any of them out as apprentices, to
some master or masters, to learn a trade, or to receive such Donations from their

51   Calnek and Savary, *History of Annapolis County,* 572-73; Registry of Probate,
     Abednego Ricketson's Estate Papers. Phebe Ricketson's estate papers are in-
     cluded with those of her husband.

52   See, for example the wills of Andrew White, 1787, John Parsons, 1777 and
     Richard Clark, 1783. Registry of Probate, Annapolis Royal, Nova Scotia.

53   Registry of Probate, Will of Andrew White, 5 May 1787.

54   Registry of Probate, Will of Valentine Troop, 3 August 1775.

Said Master, or Masters as is customary in such cases."[55] Yorkshiremen Thomas Brown and Richard Clark, in their wills, were more concerned with keeping their families together, under the care of their wives.[56]

Different concerns and strategies for family survival and care of minors are revealed in the extant wills of the period, but clearly such concerns were not equally present among all Granvillites. In spite of the uncertainties of life, and the glaring problems associated with inadequate legal provision for one's family, it would appear that most residents of the township were not concerned enough with the future of their minor children to take the step of drawing a will, at least until they were sick or elderly.

The migration of New Englanders to Nova Scotia in the 1760s meant leaving behind a number of institutions and amenities, among them the schools which played such an important part in the intellectual growth of the youth of that region. The early evolution of education, both formal and informal, in the township of Granville remains rather vague and unclear. In 1765, John Morrison, an Irishman, was granted a licence "to keep a School at Granville for teaching Writing Arithmetick Bookkeeping Navigation English & Latin." The licence was to continue during pleasure, Morrison "having taken the Oaths of Allegiance Supremacy & Abjuration ...."[57] Although Morrison remained in the township for the rest of his life, it is not known how long his school operated, nor if other "teachers" arrived in the township to open schools. However, given the lack of a physical focal point for the township, and the resulting scatted nature of the settlement, easy access to schools for most of the youth of the region was impossible. Probably most of the teaching of the basics of reading and writing occurred in the home, at least until the end of the century.

With the scarcity of schools, the lack of a community consensus or ideal, and teaching on occasion in the hands of non-New Englanders, education could not serve the same function as it still did in many New England towns of the period. It was not consistent or focused enough to be an essential part of the socialization of the youth, the moulding of the child to fit the community ideal, the suppression of the individual in the interest of the collective.[58] Education would remain an important concept in the minds of future Granvillites, but more as a utilitarian service for the individual than as an agent of social control. As with so many other aspects of the New England heritage, the very purpose and shape of the learning process could not be transferred intact to Nova Scotia.

55 Registry of Probate, Will of John Litch, 21 March 1781.

56 Registry of Probate, Wills of Thomas Brown, 5 August 1777, and Richard Clark, 13 May 1783.

57 PANS, RG 1, Vol. 165, 386, License by Montague Wilmot, 1 August 1765.

58 Zuckerman, *Peaceable Kingdoms*, 49, 74-75.

The scattered nature of the pioneer settlement and the diversity of the population of the township assured that the church would not play the same role in shaping the Granville youth that it did in nearby New England. Anglican priests were active in the area on an irregular basis,[59] and only one Congregational minister, Arzaralah Morse, served his fellow New Englanders — rather unsatisfactorily, it would appear — for at least part of the time under review.[60] Henry Alline and his New Light followers made many converts among the settlers of Granville, appealing to New Englander, Scot and German alike. Before the end of the eighteenth century, two New Light (later Baptist) preachers had settled in the area, James Manning serving the lower part of the township, and Thomas Handley Chipman the upper.[61] The revivalism of the New Lights almost certainly played a significant role in the shaping of many Granville youths of the period, but once again the community lacked cohesion in this matter; diversity, not unity, remained the rule.

In the end, to view Granville Township as a transplantation of New England society in the wilds of Nova Scotia would be a serious misreading of the situation, for it was infinitely more complex than that. Many vital New England attitudes and practices would not survive even the short two day voyage to Granville. The context for development had changed, and those Planters who ultimately decided to remain in the township, to a greater or lesser extent, came to terms with those changes, and made the necessary adjustments, subtle as well as more dramatic, that such recognition demanded. Some of the Planters even enthusiastically embraced these changes, helping to create the very differences which would separate them from the New England of their past, shaping a new society in which their children and grandchildren would be raised.

We have long been conditioned to think of the entire region of the Maritimes as "New England's Outpost" and to see its citizens as Nova Scotia's Yankees.[62] In the case of Granville, at least, this is both more, and less, than the truth, for while there was much that is identifiably Yankee in the township, long before 1800 there was much that was completely foreign to New England as well, and

59   Calnek and Savary, *History of Annapolis County*, 297-98.

60   Calnek and Savary, *History of Annapolis County*, 297-98.

61   David Bell, ed., *Newlight Baptist Journals of James Manning and James Innis* (Hantsport, N.S., 1984), 2-96; James Beverley and Barry Moody, eds., *The Journal of Henry Alline* (Hantsport, N.S., 1982), 192-93.

62   These are concepts and terms first used by historian John Barlettt Brebner, writing in the 1920s and 1930s. His work has remained the conceptual framework within which this entire period is still largely viewed. See his *New England's Outpost: Acadia before the Conquest of Canada* (New York, 1927) and *The Neutral Yankees of Nova Scotia: A Marginal Colony during the Revolutionary Years* (New York, 1937).

this is to be seen in the lives of the several generations which had grown to adulthood since the migration. *If* the historians who have examined the villages of New England in the eighteenth century are correct in their view of that society, Granville Township does not fit the pattern. However, the values, attitudes and practices observable among the first generation of Granvillites, and passed on to their children, might well suggest that another look be taken at the extent to which homogeneity had survived into the mid-eighteenth century even in New England itself.

Neither does the Granville of these settlers quite fit the evolving picture of the expanding New England frontier that has been drawn by recent American historians. The rawness, the absence of authority, and the threats from large land speculators and aboriginal peoples which characterized white America's push westward were largely or wholly absent as moulding factors in the lives of the first two generations of Granvillites who came of age after 1760. Granville Township in the late eighteenth century was neither a duplicate of settled New England, nor a replication of the experiences of the New England frontier by those who chose to move east rather than west. The youth of the township were shaped by different forces, and ultimately would evolve in different ways.

And so, as my great, great, great, great, great, great, grandmother, Sarah Foster, lay dying that summer day in 1805, she might well have reviewed in her mind the successive births of hundreds of grandchildren, great-grandchildren, and finally even great-great-grandchildren, born since that long-ago landing in Granville. She would have seen this process largely or entirely in terms of the extension of family, the projection of the past into the future, the continuation of the lives of herself and her long-dead husband. What she had witnessed, however, and participated in, was the emergence of a different society, certainly strongly New England in many of its aspects, but also the creature of the new context in which the people now found themselves, and the inheritor of the many diverse elements that had haphazardly collected together in Granville Township in the first 40 years of its existence. To grow up in Granville Township was not the same as growing up in New England, or even on New England's frontier, and it should not really be surprising to see substantial differences beginning to emerge long before the death of that first generation.

Joseph Pernette:
A Foreign Protestant in a Planter Township

Joan Dawson
Research Associate, Nova Scotia Museum

Dublin, or New Dublin as it was generally called, was one of the townships originally established under the terms of Governor Lawrence's 1759 proclamation. Although it would have appeared at the outset to be a potentially successful area for settlement, it seems to have had a slower start than other designated "Planter" townships. Extending from the LaHave River to Port Medway, and some miles inland, it encompassed the agricultural land at Petite Riviere that was first cleared and farmed by Isaac de Razilly's French colonists. It included relatively fertile drumlin soil, good stands of timber and access to prolific fishing grounds, with the LaHave River providing both a natural harbour and a means of communication. Like other South Shore townships, New Dublin could support a mixed economy of fishing and farming. In the early 1760s two groups of settlers, one consisting partly of New Englanders, and another brought from Ireland by Alexander McNutt, made only feeble attempts to develop their grants before most of them moved on to what they hoped might be greener pastures.

The township of Dublin was established on 21 May 1760, and granted to "Robert Sloan and sundry others" on terms similar to those governing other Planter townships. One-third was to be settled by 31 May 1761; another third by the same date in 1762, and the rest a year later.[1] It was to be a "double" township consisting of two parishes, and was expected to be settled primarily by families from Connecticut, for whom 351 shares were set aside. A "list of persons for the settlement of LaHave," made at this time, however, includes only five from Connecticut, together with seven from Massachusetts, 23 from Halifax and 11 from Lunenburg, as well as 18 "half-shares." Among the Halifax names was that of Joseph Pernette.[2]

The chief grantee within the township in the early days was Robert Sloan, named above, who also received "a Grant of One Thousand Acres of Land in the Township of Dublin on Petite Riviere Including the Long Beach and two small Islands contiguous" (Crescent Beach and Bell and Bush Islands) in August of 1761.[3] Sloan claimed, in a memorial written in Halifax in December 1762, to act

---

1   Public Archives of Nova Scotia, [PANS], MG 100, Vol. 195 #32 A. The terms of the grant were not unusual; neither was it unusual that they were not strictly adhered to, but the deficiency in this township seems to have been particularly notable.

2   PANS, MG 100, Vol. 195, #32M.

3   PANS, MG 100, Vol. 195, #32B.

as agent for the settlers.[4] The document was written from Halifax, and there appears to be no record of Robert Sloan's actually living in New Dublin.

Early plans and documents indicate that the first lots to be developed were along the shore in the vicinity of Fort Point, westward towards Petite Riviere, and on the Petite itself.[5] The town plot was to be established just north of Fort Point, at the site of the centre of the present settlement of LaHave.[6] There is no indication that town lots were actually laid out or generally allocated in the early 1760s, although we find that on 6 October 1761 a "Town Lott at New Dublin" was to be given to Mordow McCleod, who was also granted permission, on 17 November 1761, to occupy land about a mile from the Old French Fort for a fishery, "until a division shall be made for the Township."7 Other shares and half rights in the township were given sporadically during the early 1760s to various individuals, but few of the originally designated settlers from Connecticut came to, or remained in, the area. In January 1762, Charles Morris, who had been largely responsible for the organisation of Planter settlements throughout the province, reported that "This Township ... was granted in 1760 to two hundred and sixty proprietors in the Colony of Connecticutt, very few have attempted to settle, and those without ability to support themselves, these few resided there about Nine months and then quitted it, it remains at present without inhabitants."[8] Clearly, the terms of the grant had not been met, and so the area was available for redistribution.

During the years 1762-63, a handful of individual shares or grants were allotted, mostly to people from Lunenburg.[9] Moreover, on 17 August 1762, approval was given for the laying out of "Two Hundred Lotts ... in the Township of Dublin, adjoining the River and Harbour of LaHave, Bay of Petite Riviere and Port Mettois, not exceeding Two hundred acres each, to be drawn for as settlers shall arrive ...."[10]

4   PANS, MG 100, Vol. 195, #32N.

5   Anon., "Map of Lunenburg and New Dublin Townships," PANS V7/230 c1767, and other contemporary plans.

6   Anon., "The Plott of New Dublin Town Surveyed Jany. 1763," PANS, RG 20, Series C, Vol. 90A, #3.

7   PANS, MG 100, Vol. 195, #32C, G.

8   PANS, RG 1, Vol. 37, Governors to the Board of Trade, doc. 13 3/4.

9   PANS, MG 100, Vol. 195, #32J.

10 PANS, MG 100, Vol. 195, #32L.

These expected settlers were part of a group brought to Nova Scotia from Ulster by Alexander McNutt.[11] By 29 October 1763 Morris would again report on the state of New Dublin:

> Dublin has about 30 families mostly protestants from Ireland. They have been settled only since last Winter, are very Industrious but poore [sic] having no stock nor clear improveable Lands. They have caught Fish sufficient for their Support, but are in want of Bread Corn. A Justice of the Peace is wanting here also.[12]

One of those who accompanied the prospective settlers to New Dublin was Henry Ferguson,[13] not a newly-arrived Irish immigrant, but one of those named in the original 1760 grant as a resident of Lunenburg. He applied for, and eventually received, a grant of an island (now known as Mosher's Island, but identified on contemporary plans as Ferguson's Island) on which he set up a fishery. Many of the Irish, however, were as reluctant as the Connecticut proprietors to remain in the area, and moved to other townships such as Truro and Onslow where some of their fellow countrymen were already established. They left only a small group of fishermen and farmers scattered between Fort Point and Petite Riviere, on approximately the site of the old French colony.

Meanwhile, Mordow McCleod and Henry Ferguson retained their lands for fisheries, and a number of other shore lots were occupied, mostly by people from Lunenburg. A handful of settlers developed farm lots along the Petite, but nowhere near the 407 families projected in 1760, nor even the 200 for whom lots were to be laid out in 1762, took up residence in New Dublin. The early proprietors' inability to settle was compensated for by the appearance on the scene of Joseph Pernette and a group of associates. Pernette's activities have been described first by Mather Byles DesBrisay,[14] and again, with some corrections regarding his military record by Winthrop Bell.[15] DesBrisay, writing only a little over 60 years after Pernette's death, probably relied on local oral tradition for part of his information. He paints a picture of a local folk hero and his family which is supported to some extent by documentary evidence. Bell's

---

11   John B. Brebner, *The Neutral Yankees of Nova Scotia* (New York, 1937), 40.

12   PANS *Report*, 31 December 1933, App. B.

13   PANS, MG 100, Vol. 195, #32O.

14   M.B. DesBrisay, *History of the County of Lunenburg* (2nd ed., Toronto, 1895), 181-84.

15   W. P. Bell, *The "Foreign Protestants" and the Settlement of Nova Scotia* (Toronto, 1961, repr. Sackville, N.B., 1990), 544-55n and elsewhere.

statements are more firmly based on material in the Public Archives of Nova Scotia. Pernette appears from time to time in his study of the Foreign Protestants' settlement, both as a participant in public affairs and as a private citizen. A more complete picture of him emerges from a further look at the limited evidence available, including supplementary material in the Public Archives, and information contributed by his descendants,[16] particularly a memorandum by Pernette himself written 18 years after his arrival at LaHave.[17]

Pernette was born in Strasbourg in 1726, and had a varied military career both in Europe and in North America. Among the records in the Public Archives is a certificate issued in 1748 attesting to his honourable service in the Breton Volunteers' Regiment.[18] We next find him in 1751, at the age of 25, coming to Nova Scotia on board the *Murdoch* as a "Foreign Protestant." He was entrusted with the care of his fellow passengers by the agent John Dick, and was personally recommended by Dick to Governor Cornwallis for his capabilities.[19] He continued his military career in Nova Scotia, serving as second lieutenant in Proctor's Rangers from 1752, then as lieutenant in Gorham's Rangers from 1755.[20] He was involved in the Expulsion of the Acadians, and supervised the transportation of some of their cattle to Lunenburg.[21] As a member of Gorham's Rangers, he may have taken part in the capture of Québec in 1759, as claimed by DesBrisay, but Bell could find no evidence of his presence there.[22]

Pernette was also an entrepreneur: by his own account, he operated a successful business in Halifax before moving to LaHave.[23] In 1754, he had married Frederica Augusta Erad, daughter of a Lunenburg surgeon,[24] and in the mid- 1750s he invested some money in his father-in-law's mercantile business in

---

16   Some information was received orally from Mr. Harry Pernette of West LaHave, and Mrs. Margaret (Miller) McKee of Vancouver and West LaHave, in the summer of 1993.

17   [J. Pernette] "Memorandum of Sundry Matters Relating to my settlement on Lahave River" [*ca* 1783], [Pernette "Memorandum"] communicated by Mrs. Margaret McKee, a descendant of Joseph Pernette.

18   Certificate, 1748, PANS, MG 100, Vol. 25, #17.

19   Dick to Cornwallis, 23 June 1751; quoted by Bell, *Foreign Protestants,* 184.

20   Bell, 545n.

21   Bell, 488n.

22   Bell, 545n.

23   Pernette "Memorandum," [1].

24   Bell, 414n.

Lunenburg.[25] In 1757, he made a proposal for the construction of a portion of the proposed road from Halifax to Lunenburg, which won approval by the Lords of Trade but seems not to have been proceeded with immediately.[26] Since he had come to Nova Scotia as a "Foreign Protestant," it is perhaps not surprising that both Pernette's personal and his public interests were frequently linked with the Lunenburg settlement.

His connection with New Dublin began as early as 1760 when his name appeared on the "list of persons for the settlement of LaHave" as a resident of Halifax.[27] The following year he was elected to the Legislative Assembly as one of the members for Lunenburg County, which of course included New Dublin Township.[28] In 1763, Pernette joined with Michael Francklin and Joseph Frederick Wallet DesBarres to form a colonising syndicate which proposed to bring another hundred Protestant families from Germany to form a new township. The members of the syndicate were prepared to invest a considerable sum of money to transport and equip the settlers, but the scheme came to nothing.[29] Pernette, however, continued to interest himself in the settlement of Nova Scotia, and particularly of his Lunenburg County constituency. DesBrisay tells us that he had initially drawn a grant of land in the Wallace area; the tradition among his descendants, however, is that his original grant was in the Minas Basin or at Annapolis. In any event, in DesBrisay's words,

> in going through the woods to Liverpool, with an Indian as a guide, he was so struck with the beauty of the LaHave, that he decided, if possible, to effect an exchange of grants with a brother officer, which he succeeded in doing, and established his home at West LaHave Ferry.

In 1764 he applied for, and the following year received, a grant of 22,400 acres of land in New Dublin — 20,000 for himself, and 200 acre lots for each of twelve associates.[30] This new phase of settlement began a period of development, much of which was directly due to Pernette, his associates and his descendants.

Pernette's grant lay within the boundaries of Dublin township, extending from the falls just above the present town of Bridgewater almost to the proposed

---

25 Bell, 443n.

26 Bell, 529.

27 PANS, MG 100, Vol. 193, #32M.

28 Bell, *Foreign Protestants*, 542.

29 Bell, 112.

30 DesBrisay, *County of Lunenburg*, 181-82.

"town plot" of New Dublin, which existed at that time only on paper at the site of the present village of LaHave.[31] The terms of his grant included the establishment, over ten years, of one settler for each 200 acres — a more realistic aim than some earlier grants had specified. It was further provided that five acres of land should be devoted to growing hemp.[32] (In those days, hemp was seen as a valuable crop for making cordage for ships, rather than as a source of illicit enjoyment!) After a few years, in 1770, he acquired an additional grant of land in the area of Fort Point.[33]

Pernette immediately established the first sawmill in the township on the brook near his home, followed by a grist mill.[34] He carried on a considerable business, shipping some of his lumber to England as well as to Halifax.[35] He built the first ship on the LaHave, and brought in an English shipwright named Cleversy to take charge of its completion.[36] He farmed the land in the vicinity of his home, clearing the fields and using the rocks to build massive field walls, some of which are still extant. He thus provided employment for a number of the settlers in the area.

The Pernette homestead stood in an enviable location near the mouth of a brook still bearing his name which runs into the LaHave.[37] It was, to begin with, extremely isolated, so Pernette proceeded, at his own expense, to construct a road from the east side of the LaHave to Lunenburg. To encourage settlement on that side of the river, in the Township of Lunenburg, he bought or exchanged for lots there, which he then sold "upon Trust to Such People as ingaged to Settle on

31 "The Plott of New Dublin Town," RG 20, Series C, Vol. 90A, #3, PANS.

32 DesBrisay, *County of Lunenburg*, 182.

33 Grant to Joseph Pernette, 1770, in private hands; copy at Fort Point Museum, LaHave.

34 Pernette "Memorandum," [1]. They stood near where Highway 331 crosses Pernette's Brook today.

35 DesBrisay, *County of Lunenburg*, 183.

36 A man named Cleversy, from the Naval Dockyard on the Thames, to whom Pernette gave a lot just above the sawmill. His brother also joined him in New Dublin. One of the brothers was drowned in the LaHave, but the other remained in the area and their descendants are still to be found there. J. Arthur Miller, "Foretime Tales," PANS, MG 100, Vol. 221, #21.

37 Mr. Harry Pernette of West LaHave remembers the foundations of the old house, which overlooked the cove in the area of the present Yacht Club. It was a big, double house; the Pernettes were a large family, and the household also included a number of servants. Some of the furniture from the original house is still in use in the homes of his descendants. Stones from the foundation of the house now

them immediately, in which Mr. Pernette Succeeded So far that there is now [1783] Thirteen Farm Houses in Sight ...."[38]

In public life, Pernette made good use of his military experience: in 1766 he was appointed Captain of the Militia for the area.[39] In his seventies, he still held the rank of Lieutenant Colonel of the New Dublin Company of Militia, though no doubt Lieutenant John Pernette, his son, was more active in its administration. Only shortly before his death did he relinquish his command of the militia in favour of John on the grounds that "being far advanced in years and infirm, [he] finds he can no longer attend to the duties of a militia officer."[40]

In 1767 he was made a Justice of the Inferior Court of Common Pleas for Lunenburg County;[41] he served as a JP for the district for many years. He was responsible for conducting a census, drawing up "A Return for the Township of New Dublin, 1770,"[42] which records 154 settlers in the township — still a far cry from the 407 initially expected to arrive in the first three years after 1760. Pernette's own household in 1770 consisted of 30 persons, including himself, his wife, and seven of their 15 children. (Two daughters died in early childhood; the younger children were not yet born.) At the beginning of the American Revolution, there were 72 persons on Pernette's estate.[43]

During the revolution, Pernette's settlement on the LaHave was threatened by privateers, and he was obliged to call out the local militia in its defence. To make matters worse, there were "disaffected people" in New Dublin who sympathised with the rebels, and some members of Pernette's own militia mutinied. He was informed:

> That Ebenezer Harrington one of those who had been at the head of the Mutiny, had offered to the Captain of one of the Enemie's Privateers to pilot him up to Mr. Pernette's House where besides securing said Pernette he would find very good plunder.

For some time the Pernette household lived under this threat, mounting a four-man guard every night, but eventually,

---

38   Pernette "Memorandum," [1].

39   PANS, RG 1, Vol. 167, #30.

40   PANS, MG 1, Vol. 684.

41   PANS, RG 1, Vol. 167, #57.

42   PANS, MG 100, Vol. 195, #32 (P).

43   Pernette "Memorandum," 4.

being at last Tired of living in Constant Alarm with his Numerous Family and Finding the Number of Privateers increasing every day, the harbor blocked up, The Coast lined with them so as to put an end to all business with Halifax, Mr. Pernette to his great loss and detriment Retired with his Family to Lunenburg and soon after to Windsor, but on the first appearance of Peace Returned to his Lands at LaHave ....[44]

Pernette seems to have brought to Nova Scotia money with which to support the enterprises in which he took part.[45] His financial interest in his father-in-law's business in the 1750s, his readiness to invest in the colonising syndicate of 1763, his ability to sponsor indentured servants among the Foreign Protestants,[46] are examples of his access to capital with which he established himself in Nova Scotia. He had had what he described as "a very profitable business in which he was engaged" before taking up his grant on the LaHave. He admitted that earlier settlers had left in search of better lands:

Everybody looked upon the Lands on both Sides of the River to be so Wild, Barren and Rocky as not to be worth Cultivating, and it was the general Opinion of the People, that Mr. Pernette was in a fair way of Ruining himself in attempting to make improvements and force a Settlement on such Bad Lands. Which indeed he has since found by Experience and to his great loss and sorrow to be the case, and what is now most discouraging and distressing is to find that after Eighteen years of the most assiduous Industry and Toil, spending not only all the Money he acquired whilst he was in Business, but his whole fortune and the prime of his life besides, in Endeavouring to make a Settlement and provide for his Numerous Family...[sentence incomplete].[47]

The events of the American Revolution when the LaHave was under enemy blockade added to his difficulties. In 1790, Pernette borrowed a sum of money from some London businessmen, but his payments of interest and principal were regular, and he does not appear to have been in desperate straits.[48] He advanced £150 each (a considerable sum in those days) to two of his sons-in-law, providing in his Will that the same amount be given to each of his other children

44   Pernette "Memorandum," 3.

45   Bell, *Foreign Protestants*, 545n.

46   Bell, 144.

47   Pernette "Memorandum," [1].

48   Bond to Brook Watson *et al*, PANS, MG 100, Vol. 205, #6.

before the residue of his estate was divided.[49] The sums he had invested in his establishment at West LaHave did not, clearly, produce the immediate profit Pernette may have hoped for, but they created what in modern terms may be called an infrastructure on which later development depended.

Joseph Pernette built two houses at West LaHave, the first of which he gave to his son John, while the other, just down the river, was given to his daughter Catherine and her husband Garrett Miller.[50] He did not remain permanently in New Dublin Township. After some years, DesBrisay tells us, he spent more time in Halifax, having become "tired of country life,"[51] but he clearly maintained his interest in his West LaHave property and his command of the New Dublin Militia. DesBrisay says that he spent his latter years in Lunenburg, but his descendants believe that he lived with his daughter Catherine at West LaHave and Halifax. He died on 10 October 1807 and was buried at St. Paul's in Halifax. Mrs. Pernette, who died at LaHave in 1813, presumably continued to live with their daughter after her husband's death. Charles Pernette, Joseph's oldest son, died at an early age while studying for the ministry.[52] Joseph junior also died young, leaving John Pernette, Joseph's third son, to carry on the family interests at West LaHave. John, born in 1769, lived in the family homestead near Pernette's Brook, where he and his wife, Jane Bolman, raised eleven children. Joseph Pernette's will had directed that all his real estate was to be sold and the proceeds divided among his wife and family. John seems to have bought back a large lot around the house, as a contemporary plan of the area identifies the property of "John Pernette by Purchase 2000 acres."[53] As well as maintaining both the grist mill and sawmill, John ran a ferry service across the LaHave River. This ferry was a vital link on the road from Lunenburg to Liverpool for many years, before the construction of a bridge some 10 miles up the river. From time to time, John petitioned for government subsidies for this service, which was difficult and dangerous to maintain in bad weather.[54] The heavy row boat carried horses and waggons as well as passengers; in 1830 John applied for assistance to purchase "an additional gondola for the conveyance of horses." He complained on several occasions that he was obliged to carry the postman and

49   PANS, MG 100, Vol. 205, 318-18v.

50   DesBrisay, *County of Lunenburg*, 183.

51   *Ibid.*, 183.

52   This and subsequent genealogical information, unless otherwise attributed, is based on Canon Harris's Notes, Lunenburg County, Vol. VII. PANS, MG 4, Vol. 100, #12.

53   "Plan of Lands for Sale at LeHave," n.d. PANS, RG 20, Series C, Vol.90, #26.

54   PANS, RG 5, Series P, Vol. 57, #95, 131, 147, 160, 174.

his waggon and horse for nothing. John's son, Joseph, later took over the operation of the ferry.

John Pernette was, as we have seen, an officer in the New Dublin Militia. He was also a deputy land surveyor; in this capacity, on 6 May 1827, he made a report to John Spry Morris, Assistant Surveyor General (and, incidentally, the son of his sister Charlotte) on the potential for further settlement of the district. Its final paragraph nicely evokes the problems of surveying in early summer in Nova Scotia (and, indeed, of clearing the land for settlement):

> Perhaps it would prevent much inconvenience to mention a difficulty there is in exploring this country at the present period and until about the tenth of July, during which time the flies are so numerous and harassing neither man nor beast can endure them.[55]

Michael Pernette, Joseph's next son, did not remain at West LaHave; he moved to Halifax, and, following the military tradition established by his father, became an officer in the King's Royal Regiment.[56] But Michael's son, Charles Russel Pernette, although born in Halifax, returned to the LaHave area to run a tavern at Middle LaHave, on the east side of the river.[57] He assumed the public office of Deputy Registrar of Marriages, Deaths and Births.[58] He also established a second ferry, a little farther down the river, carrying passengers and the mail.[59] This ferry was a further source of annoyance to John Pernette, Charles' uncle, who considered — probably quite correctly — that the new ferry cut into his profits.[60]

The other member of the Pernette family keeping close ties to the West LaHave area was Catherine, Joseph's third surviving daughter. She married Garrett Miller, whose family owned considerable property in Halifax. The Millers lived in the second of Joseph's two houses, down river from the first, and overlooking the small cove above Miller's Point. In 1818, Garrett Miller

---

55   PANS, RG 20, Series C, Vol. 90, #100.

56   DesBrisay, *County of Lunenburg*, 184.

57   Anon., "Plan and Profile of a Proposed Improvement of the Main Road from Lunenburg to LaHave River," [n.d., ca 1830?] PANS.

58   He was appointed on 9 July 1864. PANS, RG 3, Vol. 1, #203.

59   In 1856, Charles was petitioning for further remuneration for ferrying mail across the river. PANS, RG 5, Series P, Vol. 59, #42.

60   PANS, RG 5, Series P, Vol. 57, #174.

gave a piece of this land for the establishment of St. Peter's Church and cemetery. Until then there had been no church in New Dublin: Joseph Pernette is buried at St. Paul's, Halifax; his eldest son lies in St. John's, Lunenburg. Two daughters who died in early childhood were buried in the old French cemetery at Fort Point.[61] By 1821, Miller was writing to the Reverend John Inglis that the church was almost complete, but that funds were running low, and he hoped that some money might be available from the Society for the Propagation of the Gospel. The cost had exceeded £850; the members of the congregation were poor and could raise only £250. "The remainder the Trustees will have to pay," he wrote. "I myself have paid two-thirds of the remainder. The ground for church and burial lot 250 square feet I have given. I have also offered, which will be accepted, to give ground for a parsonage house."[62] The church was completed, but has since been removed to a new site on Highway 331. The old foundations remain visible in St. Peter's cemetery, where several members of the Miller and Pernette families are buried.

Some descendants of the Pernettes and the Millers stayed in the West LaHave area; others scattered throughout the province and beyond. Most of his daughters married into respectable establishment families. Elizabeth Pernette, wife of a Lunenburg doctor, had several daughters married to officers in the army and navy, and sons who were also military officers. Mary's husband, Edmund Hickey, was a language teacher in Lunenburg. Sophia married a clergymen, while Catherine, as we have seen, married into the well-to-do Miller family of Halifax. Garrett Trafalgar Nelson Miller, son of Catherine and Garrett, was born in October 1805 and named for the British naval victory and its hero. He married Maria Morris, daughter of the superintendent of Sable Island, who became a well-known painter, illustrator and teacher of art. Charlotte Pernette's husband, Charles Morris III, army and militia officer, MLA and Council Member, JP, of Halifax, was succeeded in his office of Surveyor General by their son, John Spry Morris. Lucy Pernette and her husband, Joshua Newton, the Customs Collector for Liverpool, were among that town's leading citizens, entertaining the Lieutenant Governor, Lord Dalhousie, during his tour of the province.[63] Frances Pernette married Isaac Wolkins, whose brother was a judge. Joseph Pernette's "numerous family" and their offspring followed his example of participation in many aspects of Nova Scotian life.

Why did the Pernette settlement achieve permanence where earlier attempts to establish the township had failed? The would-be settlers from Connecticut knew nothing of the region; most of them seem to have made little effort, and to

61 PANS, MG 4, Vol. 100, #12.

62 PANS, MG 100, Vol. 195, #33.

63 Marjory Whitelaw. ed., *The Dalhousie Journals*, Vol. I (Ottawa, 1978), 40, 41.

have been without the necessary resources to undertake any kind of development. They were also without strong leadership; Robert Sloan, who acted as "sole agent" for those who remained, represented their — and his own — interests from the relative comfort of Halifax.[64] The lack of leadership was even more true of "McNutt's penniless Irish" as Bell describes them.[65] Henry Ferguson, who accompanied them to New Dublin, does not appear to have done so in any official capacity, and their ostensible sponsor, Alexander McNutt, whose speculative interests were spread thinly around the province, was conspicuous by his absence.

Joseph Pernette, by contrast, gave up his business in Halifax to be present in the settlement while it was getting established, organising the local Militia Company, conducting marriages and resolving disputes in his capacity as a JP, bringing up his family in the growing community, working his land and developing his business endeavours. It was probably largely Pernette's willingness to invest capital in the area that distinguished the settlement for which he was responsible from previous abortive attempts. But it was also a matter of character, ability and determination. DesBrisay's romantic account of Pernette's journey through the woods is only part of the story of his attachment to New Dublin. He made a personal as well as a financial commitment to the area; despite his complaints of hardships in raising his large family, and lack of monetary rewards, he left a legacy of cleared land, industry and roads. His participation in the affairs of the community was continued by his descendants. Most of the huge Pernette grant has passed into other hands, but the old site by the brook, after more than 200 years, is still farmed by his descendants, and a cluster of houses nearby are still inhabited by members of the Pernette family.

64   PANS, MG 100, Vol. 195, #32 (N).

65   Bell, *Foreign Protestants*, 547n.

Land, Family and Inheritance in Lunenburg Township, Nova Scotia: 1760-1800

Kenneth S. Paulsen
Department of History
University of Maine

In an agricultural community such as Lunenburg, land holdings are a determinant of wealth and form the basis of family wealth, as well as the wealth structure of the community. While land is a permanent feature, the people who occupy it are not, and the intergenerational transfer of landed wealth becomes an important strategy for ensuring the survival of a family. The means and timing of transfer are influenced by the land, demography and cultural traditions. For historians the first avenue of approach to the intergenerational transfer of wealth is inheritance. In Lunenburg the nature of inheritance reflected the settlers' European traditions and the impact of settling on new land.

Lunenburg was founded in 1753 by crown initiative and settled by Foreign Protestants from the German States, Switzerland and the Principality of Montbéliard. The town plot for Lunenburg was laid out on the neck of a peninsula which separates Mahone Bay from Merliguesh, or Lunenburg Bay. The forested township stretched approximately 16 kilometres inland from the town site and was bounded by the LaHave and Martin's rivers. Unlike the Acadian lands on the Bay of Fundy, occupied by New Englanders in the 1760s, Lunenburg was unimproved in 1753, but as the land was cleared, the settlers would discover good agriculture land.

Enough land was surveyed in 1753 so that each head of household could be given a 30-acre farm lot. Several ranges of lots were laid out inland and immediately adjacent to the town site along the shore. These farm lots were distributed by lottery to 516 individuals which represented every head of household present in the township in 1753.[1]

In 1753 every settler had equal access to land. By 1760 when the settlers registered their farm lots, distinctive patterns of land ownership and wealth stratification had begun to emerge. Some settlers had left the township, freeing up land for those who remained. The 1760 registry of farm lots shows 396 individuals in possession of 498 of the 655 surveyed parcels in the township.[2] Some settlers acquired more land than others. In the early 1760s access to land was expanded when a series of 300-acre lots were surveyed and granted by lottery. As with the 1753 division, everyone had access to a parcel, but this time

---

1 "Farm Lotts in the Township of Lunenburg [1754]," Public Archives of Nova Scotia [PANS], RG 20, Series C, Vol. 90A, # 1.

2 "Lunenburg: The Registry of the Thirty Acre [Farm] Lotts, finished 12th Day of June 1760," Ms., PANS: Micro: Places: Lunenburg: Lunenburg Allotment Books.

settlers were required to pay the surveyor's fee to participate in the lottery.[3] A total of 306 lots were surveyed and granted between 1763 and 1767.[4] By 1767, theoretically, all heads of household had access to at least 330 acres of land which would form the basis of family wealth and legacy. Sons who had come of age before 1767 also had access to a 300-acre lot.

In 1784 Lunenburg finally received its township grant giving legal ownership of the land to the settlers and listing the proprietors with the acreage that each person held. The grant provides a good snapshot of the landed wealth structure of the community 30 years after its foundation. The spread in acreage among the 216 listed land owners is quite wide; the largest land owner was the sawmiller Heinrich Koch from the Grafschaft Sayn with 2000 acres, while the smallest land owner was the cooper Georg Koch from the Electorate of the Pfalz with two acres. While land was still available within the township, not everyone had equal access or ownership compared to 1753 when the initial playing field was level. The range among landowners in the number of acres owned indicates that stratification had occurred within the township over the preceding 30-year period.

Lunenburg was settled by 1453 people of which 516 were heads of household or singlemen, based upon the 1753 lottery.[5] Due to out-migration and wandering to and from Halifax in the early years of settlement, the population of Lunenburg fell to 1042 in June 1755 and recovered by natural increase and returns from Halifax to 1374 by January 1758.[6] As a result, the 1770 census presents a picture which more accurately reflects Lunenburg's long-term demographic make-up. The community had a population of 1493 Protestant settlers dispersed among 294 households, scattered throughout the township, with an average family size of 5.1 persons.[7] The dispersed nature of settlement in the township broke with European settlement patterns of a centralized village and outlying fields. Despite Lunenburg's location on the coast, the sex ratio did not reflect the demographic characteristics of imbalanced sex ratios common in many active port towns. Thus, Lunenburg was demographically characteristic of

3   Winthrop Pickard Bell, *The "Foreign Protestants" and the Settlement of Nova Scotia* (Toronto, 1961), 572.

4   "The Registry of Three Hundred Acre Farm Lotts, 1767," PANS: Micro: Places: Lunenburg: Lunenburg Allotment Books.

5   "A Return of the Settlers at Lunenburg With the Alterations from 28th. May 1753 being the Time of Imbarcation to the 22th. January 1758 as viz:-" PANS, RG 1, Vol 382, #31.

6   *Ibid.*

7   "A Return of the State of the Township of Lunenburg the First of January 1770," PANS, RG 1, Vol 443, #19-21, 23.

an agricultural community but in its arrangement of physical space reflected North American rather than European standards.

In its Nova Scotian context, Lunenburg was unique because of its ethnic composition. Lunenburg was essentially a German community with a sizeable French-speaking minority from the Principality of Montbéliard. The Germans came primarily from the Pfalz, Württemberg, Baden, Hessen-Darmstadt, and the small states of southwestern Germany. Based upon the 1753 lottery and the 1784 township grant, the German-speaking element comprised 80 percent of the population.[8] The Montbéliardian settlers were a declining segment of Lunenburg's population with 18 percent in 1753, 13 percent in 1784 and 10 percent in 1793, the last based upon the poll tax of that year.[9] Scattered among, but included primarily with, the Germans were a number of Swiss. The remaining population were English. Due to its size and relative isolation from the communities settled by New Englanders (with the exception of Chester across Mahone Bay), Lunenburgers were able to retain a cultural awareness and create institutions to serve their community. European traditions tended to influence formal interactions and transactions such as inheritance and other means of transferring wealth.

For the purpose of analysing wealth transfer in Lunenburg, it is important to recognize that these Germans had access to much greater amounts of landed wealth than they probably would have had in Germany. Access to land in Europe was much more restricted due to higher population densities. Most available land in the German States and other jurisdictions was under cultivation or improved in some manner. Another consideration regarding landed wealth is the relatively unimproved nature of the land in Lunenburg compared to Europe. By 1800 much of land in the hands of the settlers was still unimproved, making it difficult to compare landed wealth in Lunenburg with that of Europe.

The intergenerational transfer of landed wealth is best examined through the probate records, which, for Lunenburg, began in 1762. The period of examination, 1762 to 1800, includes wills written before 1800 and probated by 1806. This period produced 83 wills in the will books,[10] 24 of which were

---

8   "Farm Lotts in the Township of Lunenburg [1754]," PANS, RG 20, Series C, Vol. 90A, No. 1; "Grant Township of Lunenburg [30 June 1784]," PANS, O/S: #243.

9   "Farm Lotts in the Township of Lunenburg [1754]," PANS, RG 20, Series C, Vol. 90A, #1; "Grant Township of Lunenburg [30 June 1784]," PANS, O/S: #243; "Census of Nova Scotia Poll Taxes 1793, Assessment on the Inhabitants of the Township of Lunenburg, 1793," PANS, RG 1, Vol. 444 1/2, #2-6.

10 Wills in the books are generally transcriptions of the originals which probably no longer exist.

written in German and none in French. Although it is a small number in relation to Lunenburg's total population, it is a complete sampling of extant wills and provides a reasonably good cross-section of the community in terms of ethnicity, religion, family size and wealth. Of the 83 wills written before or during the year 1800, Palatines wrote 28 of them; Montbéliardians six; Swiss five; Englishmen, including a Barbadian, three; North Germans three; French Protestants two; and Southwest and Rhenish Germans the remaining 32.[11] They account for 79 wills, with second generation Lunenburgers writing the remaining four. The distribution of the wills based upon origins and ethnicity approximates the percentage of each group within the community.

The demographic break-down of testators by age reveals interesting characteristics of life expectancy in eighteenth-century Lunenburg. The majority of people who wrote wills lived beyond age 60. They represent 52 wills or 63 percent of all testators. This sampling would suggest that many Lunenburgers were living long enough to transfer property and wealth to mature or adult children and, in some cases, to grandchildren; in short, that Lunenburgers were living to see their families mature. Within this group of 52 testators, seven lived past the age of 80, with the eldest reaching age 95. In contrast to the elderly testators, the remaining 28, for whom ages can be determined, were between ages 31 and 60 (Table 1). Sixteen were over age 50 and had complete families but not all children had necessarily reached adulthood. The ages for three of the

Table 1
Testators of Lunenburg Wills by Age Group

Age	Number	Percentage
Unknown	3	3.5
31-40	4	4.8
41-50	8	9.6
51-60	16	19.3
61-70	16	19.3
71-80	28	33.8
81-90	7	8.4
91-100	1	1.2
Total	83	100.0

11 The North German states are Pomerania, Hannover, and Waldeck. The Southwestern and Rhenish German states are Baden-Durlach, Erbach, Hessen-Darmstadt, Isenburg, Königstein, Leiningen, Löwenstein-Wertheim, Nassau-Weilburg and Württemberg.

testators can not be determined, but the information in their wills indicates that two had mature families while the third had a young family.[12]

The vast majority of these wills were written by men. Only two women wrote wills. In 1769 Elisabeth Dahn, a widow for 13 years, died at age 39. Although she died young, Elisabeth Dahn had three children approaching majority who received her real and personal estate in equal shares.[13] In contrast, Dorothy Gourdon (who was the widow and heir of John Mange,[14] and had no natural heirs by either her first husband or by her second husband, Louis Gourdon, for whom no will is recorded), left her real and personal estate to David Langille who was unrelated.[15]

Inheritance in eighteenth-century Lunenburg was overwhelmingly partible, generally reflecting German and probably Montbéliardian tradition. In the German States, partible inheritance was the norm. The few wills of the Montbéliardian settlers would suggest that in the principality, partible inheritance was also the norm. The Swiss were also among those who apparently practised partible inheritance of which Jacob Mosher is a good example. He arrived in Lunenburg in 1753 with a young family of six children. He received his initial 30-acre farm lot in 1753 at LaHave Range lot B-1, but by 1760 had traded it for a lot at Königsburg.[16] In 1762 he received an 100-acre grant also at Königsburg.[17] His last grant was a 300-acre lot in the Second

---

12 St. John's Anglican Church Records, PANS, MG 4, Vol. 91; Zion Lutheran Church records, PANS, MG 4, Vol. 88; Dutch Reformed Church records, PANS, MG 4, Vol. 86; "Kirchenbuch," Evangelische Gemeinde, Klein-Heubach, Germany; "Kirchenbuch," Evangelisches Pfarramt, Zwingenberg, Germany; "Kirchenbuch von Mutterstadt," Evangelische Kirche der Pfalz, Landeskirchenrat, Speyer, Germany; Esther Clark Wright, *Planters and Pioneers* (Hantsport, N.S., 1982).

13 "Will of Elisabeth Dahn, written 12 February 1769, probated 14 March 1769," PANS RG 48, Reel 19832, Lunenburg Will Book, Vol. 1, #2

14 "Will of John Manche, written 15 December 1762, probated 10 May 1762," PANS RG 48, Reel 19832, Lunenburg Will Book, Vol. 1, #1. The name Manche is more correctly spelled Mange.

15 "Will of Dorothy Gourdon, 17 August 1784," PANS RG 48, Reel 19832, Lunenburg Will Book, Vol. 1, #34. .

16 "Farm Lotts in the Township of Lunenburg [1754]," PANS, RG 20, Series C, Vol. 90A, #1; "Lunenburg: The Registry of the Thirty Acre [Farm] Lotts, finished 12th Day of June 1760," PANS: Micro: Places: Lunenburg: Lunenburg Allotment Books. Königsburg was originally designated Deep Cove in 1753.

17 "Lunenburg: The Registry of the Thirty Acre [Farm] Lotts, finished 12th Day of June 1760," PANS: Micro: Places: Lunenburg: Lunenburg Allotment Books.

Division Range B, lot 8.[18] Jacob Mosher was buried on 2 March 1779 at age 68[19] and his will, written in German, was probated on 27 July 1779. It provides for all his children on the basis of partible inheritance. The land was divided among his four sons Samuel, Jacob, Heinrich and Matheus. His youngest son Matheus was to be given, upon his mother's death, the 30-acre farm and family homestead at Königsburg. Although the shares in terms of acreage are not stated, the remaining property was divided among the four brothers,[20] and thereby Jacob was ensuring that each of his sons would have access to landed wealth. Although Jacob, Jr. was included in the will, he had already acquired his own lot at Indian Point which gave him and his family a secure legacy without having to wait for his inheritance.[21] The division of the property, although not necessarily a true reflection of the property accounted in the will, can be seen in the 1784 township grant which states that Jacob owned 420 acres, Heinrich 62 acres and Samuel 249 acres.[22] Matheus does not appear at all in the grant. Jacob Mosher stipulated that the personal estate be divided in equal shares among his wife and six children. It included all household goods, farm equipment, cattle and clothing. Despite these provisions, Jacob then set aside one cow with a calf, one bed, and clothing for his daughter Judith who was to be maintained by either his wife or Matheus who was to receive two oxen, one horse, a plow and a wagon.[23]

The heirs of Peter Wambolt, who died at age 65, were in a similar position to those of Jacob Mosher. The families of Johann Peter Wambolt and his brother Johann Adam Wambolt came from the town of Zwingenberg in the Pfalz. Most of Peter Wambolt's children were born in Lunenburg after his second marriage. At the time of his death, Peter's will, which was written on 20 November 1785 and proved on 29 December 1786, mentions two 30-acre farm lots, one of which he acquired in 1753. The will does not mention his 300-acre lot, which, according to the 1784 township grant, he owned.[24] There is no record in the deed

---

18 "The Registry of Three Hundred Acre Farm Lotts, 1767," PANS: Micro: Places: Lunenburg: Lunenburg Allotment Books.

19 Dutch Reformed Church records, PANS, MG 4, Vol. 86.

20 "Will of Jacob Mosher, written 5 April 1768, probated 27 July 1779," PANS, RG 48, Reel 19832, Lunenburg Will Book, Vol. 1, #15.

21 Lunenburg Registry of Deeds, Book 1, No. 717, Michael Schaffet to Jacob Mosher, 12 February 1768.

22 "Grant Township of Lunenburg [30 June 1784]," PANS, O/S: #243.

23 "Will of Jacob Mosher, written 5 April 1768, probated 27 July 1779," PANS, RG 48, Reel 19832, Lunenburg Will Book, Vol. 1, #15.

24 "Will of Peter Wambolt, written 20 November 1785, probated 29 December 1786," PANS, RG 48, Reel 19832, Lunenburg Will Book, Vol. 1, #38.

books indicating that the 300-acre lot was sold. The will stipulated that son Peter was to receive First Peninsula lot B-8 and had to maintain his mother who had use of a cow. Peter's other sons, John and Leonard, were to split First Peninsula lot A-6. Despite this division of the property, Peter's wife Catherine had final say over the division of the land and could divide it into three equal shares if she desired. There were two daughters who, by 1784, were married and received a cash legacy of £30 each, part of which had been received in life. Unlike Jacob Mosher, Peter Wambolt made no specific mention of the division of the personal estate other than the provision that his wife, as long as she remained a widow, would have use of one cow which was to be kept by their son Peter.[25]

The foreign Protestants, as illustrated by the wills of Jacob Mosher of Switzerland and Johann Peter Wambolt of Zwingenberg, Pfalz, practised partible inheritance, the norm in the German States, especially in the Pfalz, Württemberg, Baden, Hessen, and the other states of the Rheinland region which form the core of states that provided Lunenburg with the vast majority of its settlers. In a study of Neckarhausen in Württemberg, David Sabean states that partible inheritance was common in areas of viniculture and proto-industry.[26] The Rheinland, Württemberg and neighbouring territories were such areas, while Lunenburg was strictly an agricultural settlement. In contrast to the German practice of inheritance in Lunenburg was the New England experience. Unlike Germany where land was seen as a security for the family future, New Englanders tended to look at landed wealth as an investment. While inheritance in Lunenburg was generally partible, in Horton and other Planter townships the tendency was to impartible inheritance despite the abundance of land. This type of inheritance was influenced by conditions in New England where land and population pressures led to a shift away from partible to impartible inheritance, with the idea of keeping a viable family legacy.[27]

David Sabean found that, in Württemberg, parents made land accessible to children, both sons and daughters, upon marriage. Title to this *Heiratsgut* was often not transferred until the death of the father.[28] It did, however, encourage a tradition of partible division of family land before and at death. In Lunenburg

---

25 *Ibid.*

26 David Warren Sabean, *Property, Production, and Family in Neckarhausen, 1700-1870* (Cambridge, England, 1990), 13.

27 Debra A. McNabb, "Land and Settlement in Horton Township, N.S. 1760-1830," M.A. Thesis, University of British Columbia, 1986, 96-97.

28 Sabean, *Property, Production and Family*, 185-86. The Heiratsgut is translated as marriage portion or marriage endowment. It was not strictly a dowry in the English sense but one's fixed portion of the parents' estate which could be given in life or in death. The Heiratsgut could be amended in life to reflect changing circumstances.

the practice of partible inheritance had a strong tendency to include daughters in the division of real property. Women received property in 31 of 83 wills or 37 percent. Many of the wills include all of the daughters while others include one or two of them in the division of landed wealth. In regard to women receiving property, it is keeping with German custom which allowed female ownership of property even after marriage. Whereas Sabean states that female inclusion in the partibility of landed wealth was unique to Württemberg, the evidence in Lunenburg suggests that it may have been common in other German states. In Lunenburg not all Württembergers included their daughters in the division of real property while many non-Württembergers did.

The inclusion of women in the division of real property in Lunenburg set the Germans apart from the New Englanders. In many cases Lunenburg women (usually daughters and sometimes wives) received real property through inheritance and without stated restrictions. Yankee women in Nova Scotia townships generally did not receive ownership of real property through inheritance, although wives held considerable power over their late husbands' estates as long as they remained alive or widowed, as seen in Granville Township studies by Barry Moody.[29] While women in Granville Township had greater room to manoeuvre with inherited real estate, women in Horton, as indicated by Debra McNabb, generally received dower rights to the homestead, but little or no control over real property.[30] The nature of female inheritance in Horton and Granville was characteristic of the situation in New England, where Toby Ditz, in her study of Connecticut communities, found that daughters (and wives) were generally excluded from the inheritance of real estate, while receiving a larger share of the personal estate.[31] Women in Lunenburg also retained dower rights which were comparable to those in the New England-settled townships, as reflected in some of the Lunenburg wills. What remains unclear is to what extent English common law traditions affected the nature of partibility and dower rights in the German community of Lunenburg.

The clearest example of a testator dividing his property among all his children is that of Johann Jacob Kraus. He came from the Pfalz in 1752. He was a weaver by trade but at Lunenburg became a farmer. Jacob received his 30-acre farm allotment at First Peninsula B-17 in 1753 and seems not to have

---

29 Barry Moody, "Land, Kinship and Inheritance in Granville Township, 1760-1800", in Margaret Conrad, ed., *Making Adjustments: Change and Continuity in Planter Nova Scotia, 1759-1800* (Fredericton, 1991).

30 McNabb, "Land and Settlement in Horton Township, N.S. 1760-1830."

31 Toby L. Ditz, *Property and Kingship: Inheritance in Early Connecticut, 1750-1820* (Princeton, 1986).

participated in the 300-acre lotteries since no lot was registered to him in 1767.[32] He later acquired two 300-acre lots in South Division. He bought lot no. 1 for £15.10 in 1774[33] and then, for £80, in 1786, lot no. 2,[34] which, when compared with other lots, would suggest that the parcel may have been improved. In 1779 Jacob Kraus acquired a second 30-acre lot at Centre Range, lot no. A-23.[35] In his will, dated 9 June 1792 and probated 10 March 1794, Jacob Kraus, who died at age 67 on 17 December 1793,[36] divided his property among four sons who each received a 50-acre share in either South Division lot no. 1 or 2; his four married daughters who received a 40-acre share in either South no. 1 or 2; his three unmarried daughters, two of whom received a 35-acre share each in South no. 2 and the third who received a 30-acre share in South no. 2; and a grandson by the unmarried daughter Judith who received a 30-acre share at South no. 2. The two 30-acre lots and all the personal estate went to his wife with no mention of restrictions on the future disposition of the property, a common feature in most wills when the wife received property. Additionally, she received a 30-acre share at South no. 1.[37] The will accounts for only 550 acres of the combined 600 acres of lots no. 1 and 2. It is interesting to note that son Philip bought a 50-acre share of South no. 2 for £14 on 8 June 1792, the day before Jacob wrote his will.[38]

The mother, Maria Clara Kraus, retained the land on which the house was built as well as the additional farm lot and 50-acre share. The will mentioned that the 50-acre parcels that Johannes and Leonard received were the lands on which they built their houses. Jacob, by dividing his property as he did, was ensuring that each of his children received their *Heiratsgut,* or legacy. Although it was not divided in equal shares in terms of acreage, each child received a tract of land. Variations in land values, as seen in prices of the two 300-acre lots

32 "Farm Lotts in the Township of Lunenburg [1754]," PANS, RG 20, Series C, Vol. 90A, #1; "The Registry of Three Hundred Acre Farm Lotts, 1767," PANS: Micro: Places: Lunenburg: Lunenburg Allotment Books.

33 Lunenburg Registry of Deeds, Book 2, #17, Casper Heckman to Jacob Kraus, 7 May 1774.

34 Lunenburg Registry of Deeds, Book 3, #350, John Christian Fehr to Jacob Kraus, 9 January 1786.

35 Lunenburg Registry of Deeds, Book 2, #366, Christian Kuhn to Jacob Kraus, 26 July 1779.

36 Zion Lutheran Church records, PANS, MG 4, Vol. 88.

37 "Will of Jacob Kraus, written 9 June 1792, probated 10 March 1794," PANS, RG 48, Reel 19832, Lunenburg Will Book, Vol. 1, #62.

38 Lunenburg Registry of Deeds, Book 3, #817, Jacob Kraus to Philip Kraus, 8 June 1792.

owned by Jacob Kraus and as reflected in the deeds for the township may provide hints as to which land may have been improved, unimproved or marginal. It is reasonable to say that the mother, Maria Clara, received improved land on at least the original farm lot while the sons who had houses also had some improved land.

While the Kraus will states specifically who received what property, the will of Hans Adam Eisenhauer does not clearly state how his estate was to be divided, although the daughters are included. The Eisenhauer family came to Nova Scotia from Wilhelmsfeld, Pfalz in 1752. He received his 30-acre farm lot at Mahone Bay C-13 in 1753, but by 1760 had ownership of a 30-acre lot at Second Peninsula B-9.[39] The 1767 registry of 300-acre lots records that Eisenhauer owned Second Division lot D-1. The 330 acres formed the basis of his landed wealth and the legacy to his children. On 11 June 1763 Hans Adam Eisenhauer wrote his will. He was 84 years old when he died on 16 February 1781,[40] leaving a family of adult children. In the will which was probated on 18 July 1781, Hans Adam stipulated that the property at Second Peninsula would be left to his youngest son Johann Nicolaus while all the other property would be divided equally among all his children. Nicolaus was required to pay £24 in equal shares to his siblings and was to retain half the cattle with the remaining cattle to be divided equally among the remaining siblings. Hans Adam made extensive provisions in his will for the yearly maintenance of his wife. She was to receive seven bushels of rye and/or wheat; four of barley; three each of buckwheat and oats; one gallon of flax seed; one gill of turnip seed; half a bushel of peas; six quarts of *Lindzen*;[41] and one cow for life. The provisions which Eisenhauer made for his wife were common among the foreign Protestants and are a common feature of wills in Horton. These types of specific provisions for the widow reflect both Anglo and German traditions. Not all the wills make provisions for the widow as did Adam Eisenhauer's, but, of those that did, few are as detailed in terms of the manner in which the widow is to be maintained.

The Eisenhauer will also shows a case in which sons began to develop their own land base rather than wait for their share through inheritance. Lunenburg, unlike Europe, had abundant land, and sons were not necessarily tied to their families as in Europe. However, sons were probably dependent upon their parents for financial help to allow them to acquire their own land (which would

---

39 "Farm Lotts in the Township of Lunenburg [1754]," PANS, RG 20, Series C, Vol. 90A, #1; "Lunenburg: The Registry of the Thirty Acre [Farm] Lotts, finished 12th Day of June 1760," PANS: Micro: Places: Lunenburg: Lunenburg Allotment Books.

40 Dutch Reformed Church records, PANS, MG 4, Vol. 86.

41 This may be the German word for lentils.

not be an option in Germany where all the available land was occupied in one manner or another). Two of Eisenhauer's sons acquired property in the 1750s: Johannes at Northwest A-23 and Johann Georg at Indian Point no. 5.[42] By 1784 Johannes owned 530 acres and Georg 145 acres,[43] some of which may have been their respective shares of their inheritance. When Hans Adam wrote his will in 1763, Nicolaus did not own a 30-acre farm lot as his brothers did which may explain why he was given his father's lot at Second Peninsula. Yet, after writing his will, Hans Adam received his 300-acre lot at Third Division A-6 during the lotteries of the mid-1760s.[44] The Eisenhauer family demonstrated a strategy taken by many families in Lunenburg when given the opportunity to acquire more land other than that owned by the testator.

While the Eisenhauer, Kraus and other families provided for their daughters through land, the quality of the property cannot be determined. The Kraus family divided two 300-acre lots among its heirs, but to what extent was the land improved? The same may be asked for any family dividing landed-wealth among their sons and daughters. Given the unimproved nature of property in early Lunenburg, it is difficult to determine who got the unimproved and who the improved land. The value of land in terms of its productivity and the nature of its improvements would be factors in the division of landed wealth. Compared with Germany where most land was improved in one manner or another, Lunenburg was largely unimproved land even in 1800.

Keeping in mind that only 83 wills were written in the pre-1800 period, much of Lunenburg's landed-wealth should have passed hands either as pre-death transfers or intestate transfers. Some of these pre-death transfers are among Lunenburgers who wrote wills. Jacob Kraus is a good example of this phenomenon in that a small portion of his estate was passed to a son. Johann Friedrich Heyson, who died on 11 June 1792 at age 83,[45] left a will disposing his 300-acre lot in equal shares to his grandson Johann Friedrich Heyson and his son-in-law Heinrich Koch who was a sawmiller.[46] He had given his 30-acre farm lot at Mahone Bay C-10 by deed of gift to his son in 1782.[47]

42 "Lunenburg: The Registry of the Thirty Acre [Farm] Lotts, finished 12th Day of June 1760," PANS: Micro: Places: Lunenburg: Lunenburg Allotment Books.

43 "Grant Township of Lunenburg [30 June 1784]," PANS, O/S: #243.

44 "The Registry of Three Hundred Acre Farm Lotts, 1767," PANS: Micro: Places: Lunenburg: Lunenburg Allotment Books.

45 Dutch Reformed Church records, PANS, MG 4, Vol. 86.

46 "Will of Friedrich Heison, written 11 April 1789, probated 3 June 1793," PANS, RG 48, Reel 19832, Lunenburg Will Book, Vol. 1, #58. The name Heyson was also spelled Heison and Heÿson. Today in North America it is Hyson while in Germany it is Heuson.

47 Lunenburg Registry of Deeds, Book 3, #19, Friedrich Heyson to Philip Heyson, 10 August 1782.

The 1784 township grant provides evidence that there was intergenerational transfers of wealth that are not found in traditional sources. By 1784 there were a significant number of second generation property owners. Some of these people, like Peter Zwicker Jr., were old enough to have acquired land by the 1760 registry of 30-acre farm lots or the 1767 registry of 300-acre lots. Peter Zwicker and his brother-in-law were able to obtain a grant to farm adjacent to Oakland lot no. 13.[48] Both of them appear on the 1784 grant with significantly larger amounts of land. Many of the second-generation land owners acquired land either in life from their fathers or with the help of their fathers. In either case the accumulation of landed wealth appears to have been a family enterprise rather than an individual effort. The 1784 grant may be viewed as a confirmation of this dynamic of intergenerational transfer of wealth.

While the transfer of wealth from generation to generation is important for any community, Lunenburg offers a case which differs from Anglo-Nova Scotia. Lunenburgers came from a German tradition in respect to their inheritance practices. They tended to retain the concept of partible inheritance even with respect to female inheritance of property. The nature of partibility in Lunenburg was a strategy to give sons and daughters the ability to have some measure of security in their futures. In the German tradition, land would be divided among the heirs but reconstituted in different configurations as both parties in a marriage brought their portions together. This did not happen in Lunenburg as it did in Germany, but Lunenburgers had more land available to them to create larger legacies for their heirs. A son was able to obtain land without necessarily having to think about his wife's share as in Germany. In this respect Lunenburg reflected some similarity to the New England townships where the sons normally received land while the daughters received personal estate items or cash which formed the basis of their dowries. Overall, Lunenburgers' approach to the intergenerational transfer of wealth reinforced the community's uniqueness as a German cultural island in eighteenth-century Nova Scotia.

---

48 "Lunenburg: The Registry of the Thirty Acre [Farm] Lotts, finished 12th Day of June 1760," PANS: Micro: Places: Lunenburg: Lunenburg Allotment Books.

Oliver Lyman:
Deputy Surveyor of Horton Township,
1755 - 1814

Taunya Dawson
Independent Researcher, Halifax, Nova Scotia

Oliver Lyman, a Deputy Surveyor of Horton Township at the beginning of the nineteenth century, was a Loyalist, who moved to the Horton area in 1786. His significance to Planter studies lies in his work within the township of Horton, and in his assimilation into the Planter community. As the Deputy Surveyor, Lyman would have left his mark on the community; he would have been involved in the building of roads, the maintenance of the dykes and the allocation of land. He was one of a succession of surveyors who gave shape to the area in the ongoing reassessment of the existing lands in Horton, and in the development of the smaller communities that grew up as the second generation of Planters required more land.

This paper cannot paint a full picture of either Oliver Lyman or of Horton Township; both community and genealogical records are incomplete. While admirable research has been done on Horton, there are gaps in the primary documentation that may never be filled. It is the intention here to present "work in progress;" it is hoped to add more pieces to this jigsaw puzzle over time. The aim of this paper is to discuss Oliver Lyman: a Loyalist who moved to a Planter township, married a Planter woman and participated in the affairs of a Planter community. This "assimilation" — for his descendants are as much Planter as they are Loyalist — was part of the evolution of both a family and a community. This interweaving with other peoples has been a part of the social evolution of all of Nova Scotia's cultural groups, and is, indeed, the inevitable result of time and geography. It is interesting to examine this process at a relatively early stage in both Planter and Loyalist community development. Finally, it is intended to describe some of the principal sources available to researchers involved in either genealogical or general research concerning the Horton Township area. Although far from complete, the material available is both fascinating and valuable.

A fifth generation American, Oliver Lyman was a descendant of Richard Lyman who emigrated to America in 1631.[1] Lyman himself was born on 22 January 1755 to Phineas and Eleanor Lyman of Suffield, Connecticut. Major-General Phineas Lyman was Commander-in-Chief of the Connecticut forces for the British during the Seven Years' War. He had participated in the

---

1   Dumas Malone ed., *Dictionary of American Biography*, Vol. XI (New York, 1933), 517.

victory over the French in the battle of Lake George, and in 1762 was in command of the Colonial forces employed against the French at Havana. He also had a civil career as a lawyer and a representative of the Connecticut Assembly.[2] It is perhaps not surprising that his son became a Loyalist during the revolution.

Major-General Lyman was one of the group of British officers and soldiers called the "Military Adventurers," who petitioned the British Government for grants of land on the Mississippi and Yazoo Rivers. After eleven years of petitioning in England, he received his grant of 20,000 acres in Natchez, West Florida, on the banks of the Mississippi River.[3] There is evidence to suggest that Oliver attended Yale, but there is no record of his having graduated.[4] He and his remaining brothers and sisters inherited the Florida land in 1776, following the deaths of his father, mother and elder brother. At some point, he became the Deputy Surveyor for Natchez,[5] practising the same skills that would later be brought to Horton Township.

The American Revolution and its aftermath forced Oliver to flee Natchez, and eventually to move to Nova Scotia as a Loyalist. While in Halifax, he was hired to be an assistant to Benjamin Marston, the Deputy Surveyor for Port Roseway, soon to be christened Shelburne.[6] It is likely that his education and practical experience secured him the position, as there is no evidence of his having any technical qualifications. Charles Morris II, the Chief Surveyor of Nova Scotia, would probably have welcomed any expertise at the time because experienced surveyors were rare. Since Marston himself had no previous experience, Oliver's training would have been useful. His tenure in Shelburne was not an easy one; the government was not prepared for the large influx of Loyalist settlers. There was also a lack of leadership, abuses of the land lottery,

---

2 Lyman Coleman, D.D., *Genealogy of the Lyman Family in Great Britain and America; the Ancestors and Descendants of Richard Lyman from High Ongar in England, 1631* (Albany, 1872), 204-207.

3 Malone ed., *Dictionary of American Biography*, Vol. XI, 517.

4 L. Sabine, *Biographical Sketches of Loyalists of the American Revolution*, Vol. 11 (Boston, 1864), 35-39.

5 Oliver Lyman's claim, 24 December 1785, Public Record Office of Great Britain, AO13\26\240-244. In Lyman's claim he requested compensation for the loss of a theodolite, chain and mathematical instruments, as well as the loss of time as deputy surveyor of land.

6 Letter from Charles Morris II to Oliver Lyman, 4 September 1784, Public Archives of Nova Scotia [PANS] RG 1, Vol. 395, 16.

and a lack of effort on the part of the settlers whose labour was needed in the preparation of town lots.[7]

During this time, Oliver's most significant achievement was the surveying of a road from Shelburne to Annapolis. A map of the Shelburne area dated 1783 indicates the proposed new road leading off from the North end of the town.[8] The road was an important one since it would provide the settlement with access to valuable farm land. In 1786 he was granted a town lot in Shelburne and 200 acres along the same road he had surveyed.[9]

Lyman was married in Horton in 1786, suggesting that he was either resident there or was about to be. He married Deborah Allen, daughter of John Allen, a Horton Township Planter.[10] It is uncertain as to when Lyman left Shelburne; he was in Halifax in 1785, when he petitioned George III. We can conclude that at some point he gave up his land in Shelburne and moved to Horton; whether he met Deborah Allen there, or whether she was his reason for moving is a matter for romantic speculation. The Horton Township Book does not provide information regarding their religious denominations or the type of marriage ceremony they had. From the available evidence it appears that Oliver's family was Congregationalist.[11] Deborah's family was probably the same, as many of the Planters were Congregationist, but church records do not reveal this information.

John Allen was a well-established farmer, and his daughter may therefore have come with a healthy dowry; Lyman would not have been the only Loyalist to have made a fortunate marriage with a well-off Planter. In any case, the farmland around Horton would have compared favourably with that around Shelburne, for a man accustomed to Connecticut or the banks of the Mississippi.

Concrete evidence of Oliver Lyman as a member of the Horton community emerges in the Horton Township book on 30 June 1788, when Oliver registered the birth of his first born son, Phineas, and in 1792 with the record of the birth of

7   For a more in depth study of the Loyalist settlement of Shelburne see M. Robertson, *King's Bounty a History of Early Shelburne* (Halifax, 1983).

8   J. Dawson, *The Mapmaker's Eye* (Halifax, 1988), 123. This map was likely Lyman's as it fits the description of his map of Brewer's Location, Roseway River East, Shelburne Co., located in the Shelburne County Court House. This map was drafted to indicate the allotment of land along the road to Annapolis.

9   Map of Brewer's Location Roseway River East, Shelburne Co, PANS.

10 See Horton, Kings Co. Township Book, Register of Marriages, Births and Deaths, 1751-1889, PANS, Micro: Places, 36; D. Eagles, *A Genealogical History of Long Island* (North Grand Pré), King's Co. (Sarnia, 1977), 53.

11 See C. Cuningham, *Timothy Dwight 1752-1817: A Biography* (New York, 1942).

his first daughter, Eleanor. Further confirmation of his presence continued in the Horton Township book with him registering the births of four more children from 1796 - 1801.[12] Evidence of his presence is also found in the ledgers of a local merchant, Edward Dewolf. On 20 August 1794 Lyman made some purchases and charged them to his Dewolf account. The amount was added to previous charges, confirming that Lyman was established in the area prior to 1794.[13]

In 1799, he and other members of the Allen family sold four acres of land in the Grand Pré area. From the deed, the land appears to have been a part of the Allen estate, and sold for £42, a significant sum for the period.[14] It is not clear how much land Lyman acquired in the Horton area, as many of the contemporary deeds are missing; however, there is evidence to suggest that he was earning a decent living for himself and his family. In 1798 he purchased 100 acres on the main road from Partridge Island (close to Parrsboro) to Cumberland County, together with a share in a sawmill, presumably to process the extensive lumber resources of that area. This joint venture is interesting, as it suggests business activity by Horton residents 25 kilometres across the Minas Basin, in another area settled by both Loyalists and Planters. It is easy to forget that the Minas Basin was once as much a focus of economic activity as it is now a natural obstacle.[15]

By 1800, Lyman evidently had access to at least enough land in Horton to raise a significant number of cattle, requiring the assignment of a cattle earmark.[16] Five years later Oliver's eldest son, Phineas, had his own cattle earmark recorded.[17] The second generation of Loyalist-Planter hybrids was establishing itself in the community.

The exact date of Lyman's appointment to the position of Deputy Surveyor is unknown; presumably upon the appointment of his predecessor, Colonel John Bishop Jr., to the bench. Lyman's 1806 copy of Charles Morris I's original survey of Horton Township suggests that he was actively surveying by that time.[18] Lyman's appointment as Deputy Surveyor suggests that he had the trust

---

12 Horton, Kings Co., Township Book, Register of Marriages, Births and Deaths, 1751 - 1889, 36.

13 E. Dewolf Registers, 1773 - 1784. PANS, MG 3, Vol. 1233.

14 Deeds, Kings Co., PANS, RG 47 Vol. 2, 1799.

15 D. Eagles, *Eagles of North America* (Sarnia, 1982), 40.

16 Horton, Kings Co., Township Book, PANS, Micro: Places, Reel 2, cattlemarks, 29.

17 *Ibid.*, 29.

18 D. Eagles, *A History of Horton Township* (Sarnia, 1975), 15.

and respect of the township, to whose committee he would be required to report regularly. The Surveyor General for the Province would have the final say about who was entrusted with the position; however, the recommendations of the county magistrates would be seriously considered. In Horton, as in any community, land was important, and the man who surveyed the land would have to be both competent and trusted. Debra McNabb states in her thesis "Land and Families in Horton Township, N.S., 1760-1830" that:

> ... despite the relevant abundance of land in the new settlement, local landholding practices led to restricted access almost immediately. This had a profound effect on the fortunes of Horton families and the development of agriculture and community .... In 1791 two thirds made their living as wage labourers .... To farm they had to rent land.[19]

The land survey function was very important to the development of pioneer communities in the eighteenth century. Ownership of new land required measurement and record-keeping — the application of order to raw nature, in the spirit of the Age of Reason. "Surveying" in a broader sense also involved the process of assessing the available natural resources and the specialized process of building and maintaining the infrastructure required to extract them. Thus, we find reference in 1788 to Surveyors of Lines and Boundaries, performing land surveys, but also to Surveyors of Lumber, Fish and Highways. The Surveyors of Lumber would presumably perform such forest management tasks as identifying potentially suitable masts for His Majesty's ships; Surveyors of Fish would identify and chart the fishing grounds; and Surveyors of Highways would supervise the repair of roads, bridges and streets.

Every township in Nova Scotia was required to appoint two surveyors of lines and boundaries and four surveyors of highways.[20] By 1788, Horton Township had ten surveyors of lines and boundaries, twelve surveyors of highways, four surveyors of fish and four surveyors of lumber, for a total of thirty surveyors.[21] Given a relatively small total population, this number serves to indicate the importance of all sorts of surveying as secondary tasks within a pioneer community. Holders of these offices would be paid a fee for the days worked, as well as perhaps gaining some status and power within the community. Such appointments would be highly prized, and possibly the subject

---

19 Debra A. McNabb, "Land and Families in Horton Township, N.S., 1760-1830," MA Thesis, University of British Columbia, 1986, iv, 82.

20 *Nova Scotia Acts*, 1765, George III, Chapter 1, Section 4.

21 Chipman Papers, Horton Town Officers, June 1788. PANS, MG 1, Vol. 184, 137.

of some patronage. This high number of appointments of surveying officers continued well into the nineteenth century.

The Deputy Surveyor appears to have been specifically involved in the lines and boundaries aspect of surveying; in Lyman's case this also appears to have included the assessment of dykes in the area. While not a full-time career, the appointment required a fair amount of time. According to the 1765 act for " ... the Choice of Town Officers and the Regulating of Townships," the boundary lines of every township were to be renewed every three years and the boundaries of privately owned lands were to be reassessed every two.[22] There were strict regulations as to how these duties were to be carried out. The town officers who assisted the deputy surveyor were required to take an oath of affiliation in the presence of a Justice of the Peace. If a Justice of the Peace was not available within two miles of the location where the survey was to be made, the Deputy Surveyor was authorized to swear in his chainbearers.[23]

It is unfortunate that more of Lyman's work is not available for study. There are two possibilities to explain the absence of primary documentation. Township surveys often came into the possession of private owners rather than the government.[24] Perhaps more of Lyman's work is owned by private individuals than by the Province of Nova Scotia. A less optimistic explanation is offered by Don Thompson in *Men and Meridians*: "For any lot surveys whether farm or town, the surveyor was responsible, not to the government, but the Township Committee. For this reason, plans and field notes of those early surveys were, more often than not, burned or lost."[25] Although poor archival practices are probably to blame in many instances, it is not difficult to imagine other reasons why survey records might conveniently be "burned or lost."

While there is little primary documentation of Lyman's surveying available, what does exist at least offers a sampling of the type of work a deputy surveyor was expected to perform. The known examples of Lyman's work include the following:

1. An Allotment Book for the township, undated; many names appear in it that do not appear on the original 1760 township map, including Lyman's, which suggests that it dates from after 1786. The writing appears to the untrained eye to be his, but the evidence is speculative. As the surveyor was presumably also responsible for recording the names of

---

22 *Ibid.*

23 *Nova Scotia Acts*, 1793, George III, Chapter 8.

24 Lyman's plan of the Horton Town Plot, 1807, for example, was in the ownership of Mrs. Graham Harvey, Grand Pré in 1975.

25 D.W. Thompson, *Men and Meridans* (Ottawa, 1966), 120.

those who owned the land he was surveying, this book was probably drawn up by Lyman.[26]

2. Lyman's copy of Charles Morris I's surveyed plan for the Town Plot of Horton, found in the home of a Horton resident by Douglas Eagles. Morris evidently drew up the plan in 1797 and Lyman made a copy in 1807.[27]

3. A copy of the original township plan, also by Charles Morris I, made by Lyman in 1806. The copy is believed to be an 1840 reproduction, copied exactly to replace Lyman's original copy which was presumably showing signs of age.[28]

4. The testimony of Lyman and others in a lengthy appeal court case between George Bishop *et al.* and Jonathan Crane *et al.* of Horton, which took place from 1813 to 1814.[29]

The court case between Bishop and Crane appears to have dealt with work performed on the dykes in the area, and the assessment of taxes charged for their upkeep. There is no evidence of an earlier court case; in this context, the term "appeal" court appears to be a court convened at Cornwallis to hear appeals of tax assessments. It is the evidence recorded from 53 deponents that provides our insight into this case, which is easily the subject for paper in itself. Lyman was involved in his capacity as the Deputy Surveyor, as an "expert witness" assessing the damages involved in the case. The dykes in question enclosed some 800 acres of the "West Marsh" between Grand Pré and Wolfville (then known as Mud Creek). Crane refers to one of the dykes as the "New Dyke."[30]

Much of the controversy in this case deals with the *abbateaux* in the dyke around the West Marsh. These *abbateaux* had originally been put in place by the Acadians when the dykes were constructed; a trap-door valve that let the fresh water out from the ditches and streams in the reclaimed farmland, while preventing the same culverts from flooding the land with salt water every high

---

26   Index to the Horton Township Allotment Book, no date, PANS, MG 100, Vol. 165, 2.

27   Eagles, *History of Horton Township*, 15.

28   Plan of the Township of Horton, true copy of the original plan drawn by Oliver Lyman, 29 March 1806, PANS, R\230\1806.

29   Examination of 53 inhabitants of Horton witnesses in the case of George Bishop *et al*, appellants vs. Jonathan Crane *et al.*, PANS, RG 20, Series C, Kings Co., Vol. 179.

30   *Ibid.*

tide. Maintenance of these *abbateaux* was the responsibility of those who owned land adjoining the dyke, and taxes and labour were exacted in a similar manner to the system of road taxes. This maintenance was obviously vital for the use of the reclaimed dykeland, and neglect of an *abbateau* could affect more than one landowner. Jonathan Crane was a Commissioner of Sewers, and therefore responsible for maintaining the *abbateau* that controlled the water flow to and from Bishop's land. The case suggests that Crane's maintenance was faulty; the *abbateau* in question had required rebuilding several times.[31] Presumably, when it was not working, it irrigated the land with salt water twice daily, which would have made farming difficult for Bishop and his neighbours.

The appellants in this case claimed that the taxes that were paid on the land were too high, and based on inaccurate surveying of the land. Elihu Woodworth's testimony states that a subsequent survey by Lyman revealed significant errors in the original survey work.[32] This original work was presumably performed by either Charles Morris I or John Bishop, and represented in Lyman's copy of the plan signed by Morris. (It would not have been uncommon for the Deputy Surveyor to draft a plan for the signature of the Chief Surveyor). These errors were not noticed in Lyman's first survey which was based on the plan, which, in Woodworth's words was "the guide and standard for the Commissioners in making up the Rate-bill or Assessment."[33] The bi-annual survey of private lands was presumably a matter of confirming the locations of boundary markers; original errors, if left unchallenged, would simply be perpetuated. Woodworth also participated in a resurvey conducted by John Bishop, which confirmed the existence of inaccuracies. This would have been after Bishop's appointment as a Justice of the Peace, at which point Lyman took over the duties of Deputy Surveyor; Bishop however seems to have remained active in the area.[34]

Jonathan Crane's defence suggests that the improprieties in tax assessment were the work of two other Commissioners for Sewers, David Harris and George Johnson. It was alleged by Crane that the survey was carried out without the landowners concerned being present; he refers to:

> ... the survey of the lands ... without the owners in general being present (as Oliver Lyman the Surveyor acquainted me was the case ...), and he confessed at the time [that] the work ought to be redone over again to be correct .... Simon Fitch Esq., one of the appraisers, confessed to me

31 *Ibid.*

32 *Ibid.*

33 *Ibid.*

34 *Ibid.*

(since seeing many of the bounds of said Lots) he should not have consented to tax lands and water &c., moreover he said it was done at an improper time as snow was over the ground, he also said that David Harris [was] sworn as [an] assessor who is not a Magistrate in this County .... I know Samuel Harris to be a proprietor in said West Marsh who was one of the appraisers of damage. [He] tells me he acquainted said Johnson and Harris so before he entered into office which is contrary to law. James Hamilton was also one of the appraisers of damage, and they both told me they did not know when the damage was done, and were only sworn to appraise such damage as should be shown to them by the Commissioners.[35]

Crane's deposition alleges that the Commissioners, Johnson and Harris, by failing to point out the boundaries to the assessors, caused Bishop *et al.* to be wrongly taxed in excess of £100, and that by not pointing out damage (to the *abbateaux* and dykes), they prevented compensation being paid. From Crane's evidence, Lyman apparently admitted that the entire West Marsh needed to be resurveyed, after having checked several lots. Crane states that Lyman later resurveyed the marsh in the presence of himself, Elihu Woodworth (who was later appointed Deputy Surveyor of Horton in 1814), and other town officers and interested landowners. Lyman's own testimony suggests that the Commissioners of Sewers were not at fault for the lack of maintenance. He suggests that the problem lay in a shortage of labour from the community — presumably Bishop *et al.* — which was equally necessary to maintain and repair the *abbateaux.*[36]

Unfortunately, any record of the outcome of this case appears to have been lost. Crane's deposition suggests a certain amount of improper procedure, including the appointment of a local landowner to assess damages — an apparent conflict of interest. The inconsistencies between surveys apparently involved areas of up to 16 acres that were unaccounted for, and he states, having accompanied Lyman on his resurvey of about a third of the land involved, that "not one lot I have examined appears to be correct." At best, there appears to have been incompetence, at worst, outright corruption. It is not, however, the intent of this paper to assign blame, or to attempt to second-guess the actual outcome of the case; this is a subject for some speculation and probably another paper.

This case merits our attention as it appears, from the surviving evidence alone, to have been a fairly major one. It lasted for more than a year, involved many of the major members of the Horton community, and, most importantly,

35 *Ibid.*

36 *Ibid.*

provides a fascinating insight into the politics and life of Horton Township. For Lyman, it provides a record of some of his work as Deputy Surveyor, and what he did — or possibly did not do — in discharging his duties. It highlights the importance of surveyors and of survey work in the development of this Planter community, in which land ownership was an important key to wealth and social status. The dykelands, originally cultivated by the Acadians, were the oldest significant piece of arable land in the province, and are arguably still among the best; their ownership, maintenance and taxation could be expected to generate litigation.

Lyman himself died in April 1815, while he was still the Deputy Surveyor. A letter from the Township Committee to Charles Morris II dated 10 April 1815 requests the appointment of "one or more Deputy Surveyors, resident in this township." The successor appointed was James Noble Crane, presumably a relative of the Jonathan Crane mentioned earlier.[37]

During his career, Lyman undoubtedly had a effect on the development of the area of Horton Township. While his contribution was not necessarily an extraordinary one, it was a part of the evolutionary development of the community, building on the works of John Bishop, and preparing the way for subsequent generations of surveyors. His activity in the court case described above appears to have resolved some issues of land ownership and taxation, which, in turn, allowed for the continued exploitation of the valuable farmland. His role in the survey of the surrounding communities is not well documented, but they were surveyed and developed during his tenure as Deputy Surveyor. The family tradition in surveying continued after Lyman's death. His eldest son, Phineas, was a Surveyor of Highways in 1822, and his second son, Oliver, was a Deputy Surveyor in Kings County until his death in 1877.

Oliver Lyman's importance as a Loyalist living in a Planter community can best be described as symbolic. He was not the only Loyalist to settle in the area, or to marry a Planter; he was, however, among the first, and can be seen as symptomatic of the gradual blending of both cultures in their gradual transition from pioneers to a settled agricultural society. His descendants, who still live in the Annapolis Valley and throughout Nova Scotia, form a part of this area's combined Planter and Loyalist heritage.

---

37 Magistrates of Horton Township to Charles Morris II, 10 April 1815, PANS, RG 20, Series C, Kings Co., Vol. 89, 24.

Gendered Responses: The Seccombe Diaries

Gwendolyn Davies
Department of English
Acadia University

On 2 November 1762, 19-year-old Mercy Seccombe of Harvard, Massachusetts, noted in her diary: "Father & Mother went Westtown & Medford."[1] The entry is instructive for biographers of her father, the Reverend John Seccombe, for nowhere in his journal, written the year before in Halifax and Chester, Nova Scotia, is there any mention of his wife and children, of his having left them behind in Massachusetts when he joined the Planter exodus to Nova Scotia, or of his planning to return to New England to facilitate the removal of his family to their new home. Whereas Mercy records the activities of parents, grandparents, her sister Hannah and her friends throughout the diary, including references to personal health and the state of the weather, her father avoids intimacy. Public events, journeys of exploration, people whom he sees, and the sermons that he preaches all inform his daily entries. More important a subject than any of these, however, are his meals. Like Winnie the Pooh, the Reverend John Seccombe constantly feels that it is "Time for a little something,"[2] and he dwells upon the event. Thus his daily diary meticulously records what he ate, where he acquired his main course, and whether it was boiled, fried or fricasseed. Typically, on 6 October 1761, he notes of a trip to visit parishioners:

> Tuesday: Cloudy weather & a little rain. I went with Mrs. Bridge to Mrs. Goreham's point. We Saild it in 2 hours & qur. Mrs. Bridge Sea Sick — Din'd with Mrs. Clap & Mrs. Craton on Boild Bacon & Pork & Cariots, Parsneps. Turneps/Squash Good Wines & Spruce Beer — Cheese & Cake. Revd. Mr. Robt. Vincent & Esqr. Craton came to us just in ye Evening — we had Coffee/Current Jelly — Boild Bacon etc. Cake & Cheese. Wind. Lodged there — Boild & rost Corn & app. roasted & milk.[3]

---

1   Memoranda of leading events by a member of the Seccombe family. Harvard & Chester, Nova Scotia/1755 to 1770. No. 78. by Miss Seccombe daughter of Rev. John Seccombe, Family Papers: Seccombe, Public Archives of Nova Scotia [PANS], MG1, Vol. 797C, #2, 3. All references are to this edition.

2   A.A. Milne, *Winnie-the-Pooh* (Toronto, 1925), 77.

3   [John Seccombe], "Journal," Family Papers: Seccombe, PANS, MG1, Vol. 797C, #1, 13. All references are to this edition.

The result of such graphic detail is that the Reverend John Seccombe's diary emerges as one of our best records of culinary taste, dietary standards and food distribution in eighteenth century Nova Scotia. It also, in its focus on his private stomach and public life, draws attention to the differences in voice — the gender differences — in the diaries written under the Seccombe domestic roof. While the father writes nothing more dramatic after dinner than "an Extraordinary good baked Indian Pudding," (13) his 27-year-old daughter emotionally confides to her journal: "A sorrowful secret revealed" (June 16, 1769) (4), "very awful & unexpected news" (April 4, 1770) (10), "heart Brakeing News" (April 14, 1770) (11), and "accused of many things falsely; A Sad day: for disputes" (July 17, 1770) (14). It would seem from such revelations, so different in tone from her father's, that Mercy Seccombe turned to her diary — as other eighteenth-century women did — to have what Felicity Nussbaum has described as a "place" where women could "speak the unthought, unsaid, and under-valued."[4] Yet a closer reading of Mercy's confessions — such as "accused of many things falsely; A Sad day; for disputes" — suggests that she was able to gain little comfort from her act of writing. The reader never learns what the awful and unexpected news is for the simple reason that Mercy seems locked in silence rather than liberated into speech, even in that most private of moments, the writing of her journal. We know nothing of the conditions under which she made her intermittent diary entries from 1753 to 1770, except that in 1769-70, a year of regular entries, she was living in Chester with her parents and siblings. Throughout 1769-70, the year before her sister Hannah married Ebenezer Fitch, she and Hannah shared one of the two small upper bedrooms in a classic Cape designed house. On 25 October 1769, Mercy records: "Moved our bed room down below" (7) and on 2 January 1770, as a "Smart Storm of rain with very high East Winds" (8) lashed the house, she notes: "Hannah and I was obliged to Lodge in the best bed room" (8). It seems highly likely, therefore, that Mercy had little privacy in which to write her diary, and even less possibility of maintaining its confidentiality. This may explain her reluctance to break silence and go beyond initial protestations of emotion to explain the nature of the events that have so upset her, particularly if they in any way involved her sister. While the details of relationships will never be known, it is interesting to note in Mercy's diary for 1769-70 how often she mentions the comings and goings of Eben Fitch, the man her sister eventually marries. Beginning with 6 February 1769, she notes that Eben is "very much hurt by the fall of a tree" and, two days later, his mother arrives to nurse him. On 24 April, Eben goes home with his father, returning on May 1st "to visit us again." On the 4th, he returned home "at

---

4   Felicity A. Nussbaum, "Eighteenth-Century Women's Autobiographical Commonplaces," in Shari Benstock, ed., *The Private Self: Theory and Practice of Women's Autobiographical Writings* (Chapel Hill, 1988), 154.

night," but on the 10th, "Eben came from Vaughns Sleep here." On the 14th, "Eben came to live with us again." Mercy continues to record his activities in this vein. Then, on October 25, the night that she, and presumably Hannah, "moved our bed down below," she becomes upset by the discussion that follows in the new bedroom: "Spent Part of the Night in conversation & Plainly Saw mine own familiar friend in whom I trusted had lifted/up his heel against me." Who is this he? What has Hannah confided to her? The answer lies in the realm of Mercy's silences in her journal. All we know is that she ends her diary for the year 1769 with the entry: "the most awfull & Melancholy year l ever felt. —" (8)

In the following months, Mercy's entries include "very awful & unexpected news"(April 4) and "heart Brakeing News" (April 14). On 28 October 1770, she notes: "Eben Fitch publiced to H_____h Seccombe." Two weeks later, after the oxen have been killed, she records that on Sunday, 18 November, "in the Evening Eben Fitch was Married to Hannah Seccombe; I was very Ill." Two more days pass and she makes the entry: "Eben Fitch & Wife visited Mrs. Houghton." There is no further mention of the newly married couple until a month later when Mercy makes her last entry in her diary. Years later on 24 October 1781, her father records in his book of baptisms: "Son of Ebenezer & Hannah Fitch call'd John."[5]

It is difficult to construct meaning from the silences between Mercy Seccombe's words and dangerous to give them a substance that they may not have. But there is no doubt that the character of Mercy's diary is very different from that of her father both in content and sensibility. Margo Culley has commented on the fact that eighteenth-century women's journals in America were often a "chronicle of who visited, who was ill, who was born, and who died, with events, traditionally considered 'historical'... very much in the background." Their fractured, fragmentary sentences added to the sense that women's journals were meant to be a family or community record, notes Culley, as if it were one of the duties of the female writer to be a family historian rather than to write subjectively of the self.[6] Mercy Seccombe's journal in many respects conforms to this pattern. Mercy's world is narrow, extending beyond the Seccombe house only as far as the village of Chester. Within the confines of the home, she refers to brewing diet tea (presumably medicinal tea) (5),

---

5   "Record of Baptisms, Marriages & Sermons of Rev. John Seccombe Congregational & Presbyterian Minister of the First Church in Chester, N.S.," "Marriages Under Chester," Seccombe Papers, PANS, MG 1, Vol. 797C, #3, p. 15; #128, 1781, p. 19.

6   Margo Culley, "'I Look at Me': Self as Subject in the Diaries of American Women," *Women's Studies Quarterly*, Vol. 17, No. 3 & 4 (Fall/Winter, 1989), 16-18.

receiving new shoes from Mr. Marshall (5), making soap (7), writing letters to New England (10), cutting her brother Thomas's hair (11), washing (12), finishing "Mother Shift, & Some Pocket Handkerchiefs" (14), painting butterflies (15), steeping "my wine & Raisons" (16), washing "our little chamber floor" (14), and "writing Letters for Father." (16) She clearly enjoys receiving visits and returns visits, but some of her happiest moments seem to be spent in singing psalms with others (4, 13) and in reading "With considerable pleasure in the Book of Martyrs." (15) There is little doubt that Mercy's devotional life is important to her but she is remarkably free of the Christian guilt and sense of unworthiness that inform the diaries of fellow Planters, Henry Alline and Mary Coy Bradley. Only once, on 15 July 1770, does she refer to "a very uncomfortable day to me for want of a christian Spirit to fear wrongs" (13-4), a remark that suggests self consciousness but not obsessiveness.

The narrowness of Mercy Seccombe's life is further emphasized by recurring references to illness and weather. As this 27-year-old unmarried woman dwells under her father's roof with few people to see and even fewer places to go, constant allusions to headaches (14), sleeping poorly (14), taking fits (16), having ulcers break in her stomach (16) and vomiting (11) alert the reader to a pattern of ill health that makes Mercy dependent on her family as well as on occasional drugs such as Ipecac (an emetic) (7). Her last entry on 23 December 1770 is, "I thought I had been adying," and her health was sufficiently a matter of family and neighbourly concern that the Reverend John Seccombe in writing to the Reverend Bruin Comingo on 28 May 1773, adds: "As to my Family we are in general, in a Usual State & Measure of health: Mercy, I think, no worse, Unless with regard to a Violent toothach with which She is greivously afflicted pretty often. She sends you thanks for the Sermon you Sent her last, & all kindnesses ...."[7] Perhaps because illness is such a pre-eminent part of Mercy's life, it features consistently in her diary, not just in terms of her own afflictions, but also those of the other women in her circle. Thus, running through the diary as a subtext is a sense of the physical vulnerability of women in colonial towns, whether birthing babies as does Mrs. Floyd in August 1769 (5), being blooded as is sister Hannah on 28 March 1770 (10), suffering from fits as does the Seccombe's black servant, Dinah, on 22 June and 8 August 1770 (12), or dying of dropsy as does Mrs. Negoos on 15 December 1770 (17). Sore throats, colds, sweats and headaches (12, 14) remind the reader that a life of Atlantic fog and rain in an eighteenth-century heating system was a challenge for all but the hardy. One senses that there is in the description of women's illnesses here what Felicity Nussbaum has called a commonplace theme in women's writing "in attempting to define women's

---

7   John Seccombe to "Revd. & dear Sir," Chester, 28 May 1773, "John Sec-
     combe," PANS, MG 100, Vol. 219, #9D.

difference — our physical bodies, life cycles, relationships to others, love, independence, power, passivity, madness" (152). Although illness is not a woman's preserve, in this diary it brings a gender consciousness that men's ailments do not, resonating with what Nussbaum calls "an authority of women's experience and imagination."

The most remarkable dimension of Mercy Seccombe's diary is its focus on weather, something that one might expect from a farmer or a mariner, not from a young woman still in the prime of life. But Mercy seems preoccupied with this universal topic and her entries go beyond the references to cold, wind or rain that one might expect because of adverse effects on her health. In one sense, the frequent references to weather act as a comment on the narrow sphere of her life. Confined to home, she has nowhere to look but out or up. High winds often seem to frighten her, eliciting such adjectives as "terrible" (6) and "shocking" (7) and causing her on nights such as 16 October 1769, to "Set up Cheif of the Night." On November 21st she is so disturbed by the force of the winds that she describes herself as being "extremly overcome with fear" (7), and her most descriptive writing is in response to weather conditions: "The Shockenest, highest & distresingest East winds in the Night that ever was known in these Parts before with rain; it blew down a vast many trees on the Point we all expected to be distroyed" (7). On 2 January 1770, she is disturbed by the "Terrible roaring of the Sea in the morning & again at Night," suggesting, as does her earlier reference to "the Point," that the Seccombes were living in 1770 not in the Cape house on Wake-up Hill usually ascribed to them, but on lot 69 on Pleasant Point, the lot and house that the Reverend John Seccombe leaves to Mercy in his will in case she should survive both he and his wife and remain unmarried.[8] Most revealing, however, are Mercy's descriptions of the skies above her. Here, in her response to the colours of rainbows or the northern lights, one glimpses the artistic sensibility that reinforces the one reference to the aesthetic in her life: painting butterflies. On 18 January 1770, she notes: "A Surprizeing Stream of bright red light in the Heavens reaching from the N-west to the East in the Evening from which Essued many bright Streams of a red, white, & yellow Coullor; Pointing towards the South then Suddenly the Skey Clouded over — "(9). Her lengthiest description appears on 29 June 1770 when she speaks of a "Strange Blur as large as a Gallon Bason" appearing around a

8   Will books, Lunenburg County Court of Probate, Vol. 1 (1762-1818), PANS, 113-14. The will, dated 20 November 1779 and probated 17 January 1793 says: "And as long as she [Mercy] remains Unmarried she shall have the priviledge of Occupying and improving the whole of my House Lot Number Sixty Nine (commonly called Pleasant Point) with all the buildings thereon, and all such livestock as shall remain Undisposed of in my wife's time." I wish to thank Lois York, Head, Manuscripts Division, PANS, for this information.

star. The domestic nature of this image — "as large as a Gallon Bason" — reinforces the gender vision in the journal. As an afterthought to her diary at the end of December 1770, Mercy recalls the comets of August 1769 and February 1770 that she has observed. Living in towns and cities in the twentieth century, as we do, with the brightness of the sky obscured by reflected illumination from office towers, street lamps and parking lots, we may forget how vast, bright and close the evening sky would have appeared to eighteenth-century viewers such as Mercy Seccombe. Pinpointed on her father's allotment in Chester, she clearly feels the magnificence of the sky and the stars at night even without the prompting of the eighteenth-century's interest in astronomy and science.

If the skies and the weather prevail as the dominant images in Mercy Seccombe's diary, and in a sense reinforce the gender base of her diary by situating her at home, so the food images that dominate her father's journal suggest, in this case, a male and more public gender base. Eating for the Reverend John Seccombe is not only a joy and a necessity but also a convivial pastime that he shares with visitors and the visited. In his role as clergyman and public man, he frequently dines with others, including his old Harvard classmate, Governor Belcher, when he goes to Halifax to preach at Mather's Meeting House. His references on 26 October 1761 to Entertainments and the illumination of houses in Halifax to celebrate the coronation of George III in London a month before; his description on 5 November 1761 of the Procession of the Devil and the Pope through the streets of Halifax (a New England re-enactment of Guy Fawkes Day); and his allusions from 20-23 December 1761 to comforting a deserter, James Morrison, before his military execution ("visited the prisoner"; "visited the prisoner"; "visited the poor prisoner"), all point to the range of experience that John Seccombe encountered beyond the confines of his Chester home. But interesting as his comments on drawing town lots, meeting native peoples, visiting St. Paul's cemetery in Halifax, or patching up patients after a fray prove to be in providing a glimpse of the rhythm and activities of Planter life, it is as a recorder of food that he excels. In this respect, his journal reminds one of that of a fellow clergyman of the eighteenth century, the Reverend James Woodforde (1740-1803) of Somerset and later Norfolk who, during many years of uneventful parish life in England, documented the foods that he ate, the people that he buried and the seasons that passed in his quiet life. Because Woodforde's life was "so tranquil and so obscure," argues John Beresford, his diary is "uniquely interesting. The ordinary life of ordinary men passes away like a shadow."[9] In a sense, this too could be said of the diary of John Seccombe. Written specifically, as he notes on the cover of the original manuscript, "for the use & inspection of my Family," Seccombe's diary is a

---

9   John Beresford, "Introduction" to James Woodforde, *The Diary of a Country Parson, 1758-1802* (Oxford, 1992), vi.

series of jottings — a record of whom he saw, where he went, and what transpired each day for the year 1761. It makes no mention of the family that he has left behind in New England as he gets settled in Planter Nova Scotia, but it may well have been written to provide his family with a record of his life while he was absent from them and to fill his leisure hours without his wife and five children.

A study of Parson Woodforde's English diary, notes Jennifer Stead in *Food And Cooking in 18th Century Britain*, reveals that "His diet is a heavy one with too much meat, too few vegetables, too many puddings, cakes and pies, so that he suffers from the common complaints of heartburn, colic, bleeding piles and gout."[10] Seccombe's references to taking purgatives suggest that he may have shared at least one physical ailment in common with Woodforde, but his daily diet, at least in summer, seems to have included cucumbers, potatoes, peas, turnip, beans, squash, parsnips and carrots (during the winter, he eats cabbage and root vegetables). In this sense, as in others, Seccombe may have enjoyed a better range of food than his contemporaries in England, for squash, corn and potatoes were not regular English staples at the time (though the potato was in Ireland), and Seccombe's choice of meat and fish is enhanced by his being brought moose, beaver, coot, salmon and trout by native peoples in Chester. Cod, mackerel, halibut, perch and cunner, along with chowder, become regular features of his meals, and he even talks of eating watermelon in Chester. When Seccombe goes to Halifax, however, his diet changes subtlety, becoming more like that which the middle class would have enjoyed in London. Thus, when he dines with Governor Belcher or merchants such as Mr. Fairbanks, he relishes anchovies (the paste had just begun to become popular in England), celery (a great luxury), nuts, roast goose (along with duck, expensive in towns), rabbit, squab, quince, mince pie and sausage. The richness of the Halifax fare, along with the good wines Seccombe encountered there, would have sent a lesser man on the road to gout rather quickly, but, in 1761 at least, Seccombe seems to have been a man of remarkably good health and vigour. His specific reference to enjoying a good Frotenac wine while dining at the governor's may well reflect the political tenor of the time, for "because of the troubles with France which started in the late seventeenth century," notes Stead,[11] "French wines and brandy became scarce and expensive (and widely smuggled) and Portuguese and Spanish wines were drunk instead. However, the government, in the hopes of reducing smuggling, encouraged the production of homemade wines," an undertaking that Mercy Seccombe embarks upon, according to her journal. As

---

10   Jennifer Stead, *Food and Cooking in 18th Century Britain: History and Recipes* (English Heritage, 1985), 26.

11   Stead, 25

well, Seccombe drinks quantities of "cyder," fresh lemon punch, coffee and chocolate.

Pudding, a starch filler in the English diet of the period, is in Seccombe's world as well. "Blessed Be He That Invented Pudding," Stead quotes one connoisseur of the day, "for it is a manna that hits the palates of all sorts of people .... (and they) are never weary of it."[12] Clearly Seccombe would have endorsed this sentiment as he cheerfully consumes whortle-berry pudding (16), buck-wheat hasty pudding (15), apple pudding (11) and bisket pudden (5) at various tables, remarking as well on the pleasures of cranberry pie (12), apple pie (9) and Goose Berry Tart (3). Following the British pattern of the time of having his main meal at midday and supper at night (the term still lingers in Nova Scotia for the evening meal), Seccombe typically enjoyed boiled pork and cabbage, moose stakes, fry'd veal, roast fowl or codfish in the evening. In England at the time, this was often a cold meal of meat pie or neat's tongue, so that Seccombe's hot meal seems to suggest, as does the rest of his diet, a much healthier basis of eating in eighteenth-century Nova Scotia than in England of the day.

"Traditional literary studies," as Helen Buss has observed, have "been based on the assumption of a separation of art and life." Recent efforts to broaden the literary canon in the wake of postmodernist reappraisals of critical bases of assumption have liberated the "word 'literature' from a capital 'L'," notes Buss, and have opened the way for a variety of texts — letters, memoirs, sermons, songs and diaries such as the Seccombe diaries — to be examined in new ways, to challenge "the limits of our imaginations."[13] The journals of Mercy Seccombe and her father have long lain in the archives as seemingly uninteresting and terse documentations of their daily lives over a short period of time in the eighteenth century. Yet beneath the cursory entries — and in the silences of what they do not say — lie revelations of our cultural past, of the texture of lived lives, and of distinctively different views on the world as father and daughter observe it through different gender lens. In a sense their diaries echo one of the closing stanzas of "Father Abdy's Will," that 1731 broadside poem that first escalated the Reverend John Seccombe to fame in New England. These journals, in the words of the poem, have been their "store":

I have no more,
I heartily do give it,

---

12 Stead, 20

13 Helen Buss, "'The Dear Domestic Circle': Frameworks for the Literary Study of Women's Personal Narratives in Archival Collections," *Studies in Canadian Literature*, Vol. 14, No. 1 (1989), 1.

My years are spun,
My days are done,

And so I think to leave it.[14]

The Seccombe diaries are, in this sense, their final signatures.

14 [John Seccombe], "Father Ab__y's Will," (Cambridge, Mass., 1731), Xerox of Goodspeed I (original in Massachusetts Historical Society), American Antiquarian Society, Worcester.

Civilian Everyday Clothing of Adult Planters, 1759-1783

Clary Croft and Sharon Croft
Halifax, Nova Scotia

We know much about the politics, religious persuasions and built heritage of the Planters, but we know very little about their personal appearance. It should not be surprising to find scant information about this most intimate, and yet ubiquitous, element of Planter material culture. Few contemporaries bothered to record descriptions about clothing styles which were part of daily life. Although manufacturers' records and mercantile reports are helpful, first hand descriptions of what the average person actually wore are frustratingly rare.

Clothing styles seen in eighteenth-century portraits rarely reflect everyday wear. Even today, we tend to dress up when our image is about to be captured for posterity. Generic clothing and textile descriptions do not reflect the influence of Mi'kmaq dress, residual Acadian styles, or even clothing styles influenced by religion or the military presence. The possibilities are seemingly endless and far too complex to be covered in so short a text. In this paper, we are concentrating on civilian everyday clothing which might have been worn by adult Planters in Nova Scotia between 1759 and 1783.

The Planters arrived in Nova Scotia with their basic dress code already established. That pattern of dress would change over the years, but not so rapidly as the fashion plates and journals of dress might lead us to believe. Our most detailed account of Planter attire comes from the description by John Robinson and Thomas Rispin after their 1774 journey through parts of Nova Scotia:

> The men wear their hair queu'd, and their clothing, except on Sundays, is generally home-made, with checked shirts; and, in winter, they wear linsey-woolsey shirts, also breeches, stockings and shoes; instead of which, in summer, they have long trowsers, that reach down to their feet. They dress exceedingly gay on a Sunday, and they wear the finest cloth and linen. Many of them wear ruffled shirts, who, during the rest of the week, go without their shoes and stockings; and there is so great a difference in their dress, that you would scarce know them to be the same people.
>
> The women, in general, (except on Sundays) wear woolseys both for petticoat and aprons; and instead of stays, they wear a loose jacket, like a bedgown. It is owing to the high price of stays, and not to any dislike they have to them, that they are not worn in common. The few that are used, are imported either from Old or New England, as they have not any staymakers amongst them. The women, in summer, in imitation of the men, usually go without stockings or shoes, and many without caps.

They take much pains with their hair, which they tie in their necks, and fix it to the crown of their heads. Nor are they on the Sabbath less gay than the men, dressing for the most part in silks and callicoes, with long ruffles; their hair dressed high, and many without caps. When at Church or Meeting, from the mistress to the scullion girl, they have all their fans. We ever thought, in the article of dress, they out did the good women of England.[1]

Aside from the obvious physical description of the garments worn, this account enlightens our costume knowledge in another important way. It shows that Planter dress for work and everyday was not a ragged or out of fashion version of contemporary styles, but different attire made specifically for daily wear. Costume historian, Claudia Kidwell, has broken this polarity of dress into two distinctions: difference in textiles and difference in clothing construction.[2]

Textiles were the single largest import into North America during the colonial period. Most people had some access to this selection of textiles which could range from high quality fashion fabric to lower grade homespun. However, access does not imply purchase. The investment of enough cotton print or silk for a dress would be substantial and, if made, would be expected to pay dividends over many years of wear.

Domestic production of clothing textiles in the North American colonies began to rise dramatically during the second quarter of the eighteenth century. Even so, this was still relegated to production of wool and linen fabrics. Lace making never progressed beyond production for personal consumption. Cotton was too expensive and had too many trade and manufacturing restrictions placed upon it by Great Britain to become a colonial homespun industry until later in the century.

Aside from the production of textiles for personal wear, Nova Scotia offered little in textile or clothing manufacturing. The "Report of the Present State and Condition of His Majesty's Province of Nova Scotia, 1773" stated: "In 1772 The [textile] Imports into Nova Scotia were as follows ... from Great Britain, Ireland, the Islands of Jersey and Gernsey: wollen and linnen drapery, hats, haberdashery, milinary ... There is no other manufacturing here than linnen cloth, which is made in some parts of the country by farming people and mostly for their own use."[3] The report lists no costume or textile entries from other

---

1   John Robinson and Thomas Rispin, *Journey Through Nova-Scotia Containing A Particular Account of the Country and its Inhabitants* (Sackville, 1981), 26-27.

2   Claudia Kidwell and Margaret C. Christman, *Suiting Everyone: The Democratization of Clothing in America*, (Washington, 1974), 21.

3   Public Archives of Nova Scotia [PANS], RG 1, Vol. 222, #46.

areas of normal trade including southern Europe, Africa, the Azores and West Indies or from several colonies. By 1776, sixteen years after the first Planters arrived, Michael Francklin reported two hatteries as the only clothing related manufacturers.[4] These reports suggest little or no trade with the colonies. However, John Brebner suggests that "... Nova Scotia received about half her imports from Great Britain, which makes it seem practically certain that more than half Nova Scotia's trade was with New England."[5]

Certainly, barter of goods is in evidence in many merchant's ledgers (see Appendix A), but such exchanges might not always show up on official records of commerce. In addition, smuggled goods reached Nova Scotia from the colonies on a regular basis. A 1776 letter from Whitehall shows an awareness of mercantile trade between Nova Scotia and colonial rebels and expresses concern over smuggling.[6]

Whatever the means of obtaining goods, it is certain that Nova Scotia Planters had access to a wide variety of clothing and textile items. Import lists and merchant ledgers attest to this range of fabrics and ready-made clothing recording: alamode, beaver cloth, broadcloth, breeches, buckram, buttons and button molds, calimanco, camleteen, cambric, checks, chintz, dowless, drab, duffel, felt hats, flax, flannel, fustian, garlick, gauze hoops, gingham, handkerchiefs, hose, irish, lasting, lawn, linsey-woolsey, muslin, osnaburg, plush breeches, russel, shalloon, silk, stuff, tammy, tape, twist, white corduroy and worsted stockings. Many times, these items were bartered for some aspect of in-kind labour or domestic production. (For a more complete listing refer list Appendix A and Glossary Appendix B)

Robinson and Rispin recorded domestic production of bleached linen and dyed woollen yarn. Their term "yarn," as opposed to cloth or wool, leads one to speculate that the spun wool may have been dyed before weaving. Unfortunately, they do not say whether the dyes used were local, natural dye stuffs or commercial dyes. Merchant accounts list indigo, which was the most common dye used in the eighteenth century.

Looms were common in many homes; they were fairly easy to assemble from ready materials. Among personal items listed in the estate papers of the late David Shaw of Falmouth, 31 May 1777 is a "loom, the weaving apparel of the deceased."[7] New Brunswick Planter, Margaret Coy, began weaving for barter after her husband's timber business suffered a poor market.[8] Most women

---

4   John Brebner, *The Neutral Yankees of Nova Scotia* (Toronto, 1969), 127.

5   *Ibid.*, 105.

6   PANS, RG 1, Vol. 32, #36.

7   PANS, MG 1, Vol. 806, #3.

8   See Margaret Conrad, "Mary Bradley's Reminiscences: A Domestic Life in Colonial New Brunswick," *Atlantis*, 7, 1 (Fall 1981), 92-101. Mary Coy was born in Gagetown New Brunswick in 1771 to Planter parents. She married

knew how to weave as well as spin and handweaving was an established trade for many men, as well.

Styles were slow to change for the majority of the population, and were similar all through the colonies. American social historian J.C. Furnas suggests, for example, "The clothes of the Colonial leaders who met in Albany in 1774 ... were probably ... much the same whichever Colony they hailed from ...."[9] There was appreciably more distinction in dress among various occupations and classes than we see today. The formal court dress was far removed from the average person's life. Most clothing was made at home, except that made by tailors and mantua makers who specialized in non-working class attire. "The housewife's tools were simply scissors, needle and iron. She cut out her garments using the age old system of cutting around the picked apart pieces of an existing item of apparel."[10]

Shoes, buckles, stockings, garters and handkerchiefs were basically the same for men as for women. Shoes, shoe leather and soles were common items in merchant accounts. Frequent distinction is made in these accounts referring to men's shoes, women's shoes or boy's shoes. Could these items of footwear be of a higher standard and therefore more gender oriented than common footwear? Perhaps the shoe leathers and soles offered for sale were intended for the more at-home manufacture of family footwear. Certainly, the distinction between right and left was seldom observed in eighteenth-century footwear; one wooden last acted as the mold for both feet.[11]

Buckles came in a variety of styles and sizes. For instance, a man may have worn as many as six buckles at a time: one at each knee of the breeches, one at the back vent of the breeches, one on each shoe, and one at the neck stock. This was the plainer style of buckle without a spring closure which did not appear until after 1784. Women's clothing had few buckles or buttons.

Everyday buttons of horn and bone were used on waistcoats and breeches. These buttons had two, four or five holes. Shanked buttons were used more for coats and better quality waistcoats. Examples found at Upper Falmouth are constructed of copper alloy, iron and bone.[12]

David Morris in 1793. She began weaving and took barter to make the payment easier for her customers. Although this happened later than the period we are covering, it indicates the possibility of in-kind weaving being carried on from a domestic perspective.

9   J.C. Furnas, *The Americans: A Social History of the United States* (New York, 1969), 130.

10   Kidwell, *Suiting Everyone*, 27.

11   Furnas, *The Americans*, 130.

12   Marc C. Lavoie, "Archaeological Evidence of Planter Material Culture in New Brunswick and Nova Scotia," in Margaret Conrad, ed., *Making Adjustments: Change and Continuity in Planter Nova Scotia 1759-1800* (Fredericton, 1991),

White silk hose were the most fashionable, but most people wore knitted homespun, leather or cloth stockings, saving the knitted worsted stockings for Sundays and special occasions. It was not uncommon for stockings to be re-footed to increase their lifespan. Stockings were fastened by garters or ribbons. Knee garters could be knitted, but were more commonly woven on tape looms.

The eighteenth-century handkerchief was most commonly worn around a woman's neck as a cross between a small shawl and collar. Many handkerchief fabrics were woven expressly for this use and could be a yard square.[13] Men sometimes wore handkerchiefs tied around their necks, as well.

It is doubtful whether many Planter men wore wigs on a regular basis. By 1770 wigs were out of fashion, but men's own hair continued to be powdered until the English tax on hair powder in 1795 made it prohibitive for many. However, some men likely retained the habit and employed wigs of human hair, horsehair, goat hair or hair from the tails of cows. Archaeological evidence, from eighteenth-century Halifax, shows the presence of clay wig rollers, which were a form of curler.[14] These could have also been used for women's wigs. On dress occasions women frequently wore pieces of false hair to give their hairstyles height. This may be the "hair dressed high" style which Robinson and Rispin reported.

For men of all classes the basic item of clothing was the shirt. Commonly made of linen, wool, or a combination of linen and cotton or linen and wool, this garment served as nightshirt and underclothes. Some men of all classes did wear underdrawers of wool or linen, but this does not appear to have been the norm. It was common for the long shirt tails to be tucked between the legs as protection from the coarser fabrics of the breeches. This is understandable given the fact that fine linen feels as soft and supple as silk. We should not underestimate the quality of linen available for purchase or barter, or the fineness of domestic linen manufacture. In fact, when Deacon Burpee of Maugerville died in 1781, he left behind several work shirts and one fine shirt.[15] Such a shirt could see several more generations of wear and be considered a

---

218-33. Examples found at Castle Frederick, Upper Falmouth; established around 1764.

13 PANS, MG 1, Vol. 181, #46, records a widow, Abigale Johnson, "hanging her self with a handkerchief that she tied about her neck ...," 1762.

14 Stephen A. Davis, Catherine Cottreau and Laird Niven, *Artifacts from Eighteenth Century Halifax* (Halifax, 1987), 119.

15 M.A. MacDonald, *Rebels and Royalists* (Fredericton, 1990), 34. Also listed as personal effects are: "Coats and jackets — blue, white and mix't color — a few westcot, several pairs of breeches, ... stockings, shoes, kneebuckles, a felt hat and a beaver hat."

valuable legacy. The shirt had a basic cut. It was frequently made from a length of linen folded at the shoulder, or two lengths joined at a shoulder seam with a hole cut slightly off centre for the head. Sleeves were sewn at right angles to the body. Gussets under the arms and at the neck edge aided ease to the fit. The centre front slit was frequently reinforced with a triangular or heart-shaped piece of fabric. Since the style of the body of the shirt remained the same well into the nineteenth century, alterations to the collar or cuffs were made to bring the item up to date.

Breeches could be made of leather or cloth, linen, homespun and a variety of other textiles. Some leather breeches were made without any opening flaps and were so full that the wearers ordinarily changed the rear to the front if any signs of wear appeared.[16] From c. 1750 on, the fly was replaced by falls, and the back of the breeches closed by lacing or a buckle.

In 1772 a tailor, Thomas White of Horton, was charged by Samuel Hamilton and Andrew Lisk, a weaver from Kings County, with embezzling cloth.[17] A variety of textile pieces and clothing were given to White for him to make garments. Perhaps he would be using the clothing items for patterns. We might speculate that the breeches were of fine enough quality to keep and risk prosecution. Unfortunately, we do not know if any of the cloth was of Hamilton's or Lisk's manufacture. However, what this record does tell us is that some breeches were tailored outside the home.

Robinson and Rispin tell us that the men wore trousers during the summer. This form of dress definitely sets the wearer apart from the upper classes. They were the common form of dress for seamen, farmers and apprentices. Kidwell writes that the wearing of trousers was so much a badge of the "lower orders" that Governor Bernard of Massachusetts noted that in order to conceal their participation in the Stamp Act violence of August 1765, "some fifty gentlemen actors were disguised with trowsers and jackets."[18] These trousers were cut in imitation of breeches, except for longer legs.

Men of all economic stations wore waistcoats. An example of a fine quality waistcoat which belonged to Colonel Joseph Morse (1721-1770) can be found at the New Brunswick Museum.[19] Waistcoats of various styles and fabric composition were worn; and sometimes more that one waistcoat was worn at the same time. Layering of clothing to combat cold and dampness was more common than literature suggests. Two different styles of under-waistcoats were

16 Elizabeth McClellan, *Historic Dress in America 1607-1870* (New York, 1977), 328.

17 PANS, MG 1, Vol. 182, #55, 56 and 60.

18 Kidwell, *Suiting Everyone*, 21.

19 See: MacDonald, 47, for photograph of Morse Waistcoat made of pale yellow silk. It appears to have been altered.

worn. A woollen waistcoat could be worn under the shirt. It would have sleeves and a centre front opening from neck to hem. The second type of under-waistcoat was of flannel faced with some kind of fashionable fabric and worn under an outer waistcoat. Thus, only the faced section of this insulating layer would be visible. Several styles of these waistcoats are documented in New England; some are interlined with old clothes, such as stockings, to provide extra warmth.[20]

Most men would have some sort of coat to complete their attire. Tailor-made coats would be set apart from the obvious home construction styles.[21] Kidwell suggests that "the very swing of a coat told who patronized a good tailor and who did not .... Most people in colonial America wore clothing made by amateurs."[22] A coat could set a man apart by the cut of the skirt.[23] In the eighteenth century, the term "skirt" was not used to designate the lower part of a woman's dress, but to identify those extensions of a man's coat or waistcoat which fall below the waist line. Upper class coat tails were stiffened and lower class coat tails hung limp. Between 1750 and 1760, fairly plain coats with closer fitting skirts became the norm. After 1750, except for court dress, the fashion of edging all seams with braid was relegated to military and livery suits.

The chemise was the standard undergarment for women. Usually made of linen, it was knee length or longer. There is little indication of women wearing any type of underdrawers. Robinson and Rispin comment on the lack of stays worn by Planter women for everyday wear. However, it may not have been uncommon for these same women to wear stays for dress occasions. When used, stays were made of linen and boned with cane or baleen. The lack of professional stay makers may not have meant a lack of stays. This may have been another example where the woman picked apart an existing garment, like stays, to get a pattern for a new pair.

The other item of dress understructure which would only have been worn for dress was hoops, again made with supports of cane or baleen, and frequently covered with fabric specially woven for this purpose. Even then, from 1777 on, hoops were less worn by all classes.[24]

---

20   Linda Baumgarten, "Under Waistcoats and Drawers," *Dress*, 19 (1992), 8.

21   See, PANS, MG 1, Vol. 182, #55, 56 and 60 for examples of locally ordered tailor-made coat.

22   Kidwell, *Suiting Everyone*, 25.

23   Phillis Cunnington and Catherine Lucas, *Occupational Costume in England*, (London, 1967), 39.

24   Elizabeth Ewing, *Dress and Undress: A History of Women's Underwear* (New York, 1978), 4; "pannier" is a term adopted in the Victorian era.

Women's dresses frequently consisted of two parts: the petticoat and the bodice with attached skirt. Fabrics were luxurious and frequently pinked with special chisel-like implements to add decorative edgings. Extant merchant records from Nova Scotia show a wide variety of these high quality fabrics available. [see Appendix A] The petticoat is the one section of the dress which would be common to both classes. Naturally, in the upper classes it would be silk or some other fine fabric, and quilted with elaborate designs based on images from nature. The working class would also wear a petticoat, but frequently made of homespun fabric, and without the time consuming quilting. From 1730 onwards, the skirt of the petticoat was usually ankle length, especially for every day wear. It was fastened about the waist by drawstrings.

Perhaps the most common costume item for working class women was the short gown. Kidwell speculates that the terms short gown, bed gown, jacket and waistcoat refer to various styles and may have changed names with regions. "As yet, no one has found a garment with a firmly documented eighteenth-century note identifying the item as a 'short gown.'"[25] This paper will not attempt to explore the variant styles of mid-eighteenth-century dresses. It is sufficient to say that one popular style of construction, commonly known as the "sack back," was echoed in the plainer, everyday bodice, or short gown.

Robinson and Rispin's term "bedgown" would not imply an item of sleepwear, but was standard eighteenth-century nomenclature for the short or mid-length bodice worn by working class and country women in Britain and the colonies.[26] The most common fabrics for short gowns in North America were linen and combinations of linen and wool, but examples also survive which are made from printed cotton.[27]

The standard method of construction was first to assemble the individual pieces and sew in a lining (if used). The majority of extant examples of short gowns in America are unlined. Once assembled, the waist seams were curved and back pleats folded in. Sometimes this fullness was controlled by tapes at front or back, or both. The folding pattern of an inverted box pleat is present in the majority of extant garments. This fullness of short gowns could be adjusted to accommodate the wearer's figure through all stages of pregnancy and

---

25 Claudia Kidwell, "Short Gowns," *Dress*, 4 (1978), 31.

26 Anne Buck, "Variations in English Women's Dress in the 18th Century," *Folk Life*, 9 (1971), 18.

27 See: Kidwell, *Short Gowns*, 34. Several examples in Kidwell's study are made from cloth with three blue warp yarns in its selvages, each probably exported from England between 1774 and 1811. The blue threads fulfilled a regulation that cloths intended for export be woven this way if a refund of taxes levied on printed cloth was to be claimed.

28 *Ibid.*, 45.

lactation.[28] The full width of material was used whenever possible, even retaining the selvages. In all cases the sleeves were pieced to achieve the desired length.[29]

Many short gowns which were open at centre front were held closed by pins, or by an apron tied around the waist, or a combination of both. Straight pins were standard forms of closure for much of women's clothing during the eighteenth century.[30] Most straight pins were made of brass. Early pins were made in two parts; the head was of finer wire and attached to the shank. As many as 25 different steps were involved in their manufacture.[31] Kidwell's study has only one example of short gowns being closed with leather buttons.

Aprons were made of wool, or less frequently, linen or cotton. However, cotton was expensive and posed a hazard around open fires. One of the common ways of wearing an apron was to take one bottom edge and tuck it into the drawstring at the waist, forming a convenient carry-all for the busy wearer.[32]

Although men's and women's working class shoes were similar, if not identical, in manufacture, women were likely to have a more delicate style of footwear for dress and wear pattens to help keep their shoes clean. The *Nova Scotia Chronicle* of 1771 lists women's patten iron. Eighteenth-century patten fragments have been discovered in Halifax.[33]

Styles of headgear and hair fashion were varied, mainly depending upon class. When headgear was worn, it is likely most women adopted some sort of ubiquitous eighteenth-century mob cap. Until the 1780s, the small mob cap was popular, in imitation of the simple hairstyles which echoed the fashionable look of a small head. When worn, hats and bonnets were varied and numerous. Even when a dress could not be brought up to style, a piece of millinery would help give the wearer a more contemporary look. And frequently, it was the reverse; many women retained hair styles and forms of head dress long after they changed other styles of attire. The style known as "calashe" was popular before the 1770s and had numerous baleen stiffeners in the crown. A later variant of this style, the pumpkin hood, was made in a similar manner with wadding between ridges for cold weather.[34]

It is important to guard against romanticizing Planter clothing and only paying attention to the fancy, more flamboyant aspects of costume. For most

---

30 Edwin Tunis, *Colonial Craftsmen: And the Beginnings of American Industry* (New York, 1965), 143.

31 *Ibid.*

32 See: Cunnington and Lucas, *Occupational Costume in England,* Plate 10, for an example of a worker's apron being pinned to one side; from engraving "Haymakers" by G. Stubbs, 1785.

33 See: Davis, *Artifacts,* Plate 24, for patten fragments.

34 McClellan, *Historic Dress,* 222.

people in eighteenth-century Nova Scotia, clothing was a vital necessity, designed to protect the wearer from the harsh elements. Of course, the study of Planter clothing is just beginning. We may discover greater class and cultural variations in clothing style among Planter society than we suggest in the foregoing discussion. And, in this paper we have ignored the clothing worn by children. In short, there is still much work to do on this aspect of Planter society. But, by having the costume researcher work in tandem with the historian, we can develop a better understanding of Planter material cultural life.

Appendix A
Costume and Textile items from Daybooks and Account Books:

PANS, Micro: Biography Bishop Family. Account Book kept by Timothy Bishop of Horton 1775-1824.
— 1764 2 felt hats.
— 1766 Daybook — trade with Newburyport, lists: black russill, tammy, parsian, sewing silk, broad cloths, cambrick, spunyarn, lindsey, shalloons, bayers, part of cambric cloak, ticklenbury, iris, caps, dowless, cambleteen, button, ribbon, mitts, hose, cotton, linen, buckram, pinchback, buckles, camblet clouk, irish, oznabrigs, dowless, pair hair shag britches, jacket for Leonard, great coat, woolsey, hose grown holland, twist, callimanioc, knee garters, milled caps, pins, mink, muskrat, otter, tape, 8 yards galiix, bayer jacket, pair drawers, leather mitts, cambletune, yarn stockings, plushe breetches, handkerchiefs, black senett.
— 1769 breeches, 1 gingham gown.
— 1779 one pair of shuse, soul leather for one pare of shuse.
— 178[?] received of Samuel Gore for ... three handkerchiefs, cordage for britches, silk for cloke.

PANS, Micro Places: Granville, Annapolis County Businesses, Dodge, Benjamin. Account book 1778-1782 lists items sold or traded:
— leather for a pair of shoes, pair snowshoes, soals for women's shoes, shoes, cambrigs, silk handkerchief, pair of buckals, pair of moggasons, pair of worsted stockings, britches, trousers, pair of shirts, half brod cloth, silk, to making jackot and trousor, flannel, leather britches, making two shirts, butons and thread, pair thick mitens, stockings, garters, linen shirt, bever hat, toe cloth, linseywoolsy, linen, fuld cloth, wool.

PANS, MG 1, Vol. 181, #110. Chipman Papers, Horton 1764-65 daybook has entry for:
— shirts, lining, jacket.

PANS, MG 1, Vol. 182, #24. Nathan Dewolf Esquire account with John Avery, 1770:
— 2 oz, indigo delivered Elisha Fuller, [?] yads. check, 1 doz. needles, 1 pr. womens shoes.

PANS, MG 1, Vol. 182, #26.
— 4 1/4 yd. check, 2 1/2 yd calico.

PANS, MG 1, Vol. 752. Letter book of Simeon Perkins, Liverpool, March 22, 1765 to January 1, 1766.
— check flannel, yarn stockings, men and women's shoes, boys shoes, shoe buckles, hoops, brown thread, tow cloath, oznabrigs, check linen, stuffs, blue broad cloth, blue shalloon, blue buttons, scarlet buttons, shalloon and trimming, spun yarn, stripes swans[?]i[?]d, cotton thread, yarn stockings, riband, scarlet shalloon, 2 bags blue coat buttons, bluesilk, blue strou[?], red strou[?], scarlet broad cloth, blue broadcloth, worsted hose, striped camblet, white flannel, check linen sorted, 1 dozen cheap check shirts, blue shalloon, brown shalloon, black allamode, brad, blue shroud, yarn stockings, worsted stockings, 2 dozen mittens, cot[?] thread, silk twist.

PANS, MG 1, Vol. 2630, #123. 1764 Starr Family, Cornwallis, accounts:
— striped stuff, duffle, hose, cloth, linen, check shirts, pins, white shirt, needles, checks, [?]usha linen, stockings, silk handkerchief, caliminco.

PANS, MG 1, Vol. 2630, #143, November 16, 1774 Starr Family, Cornwallis, account of William Graham:
— ribed hose, beaver silk gloves, brown hunter, shalloon, buttons, small buttons, horn buttons, lasting, minding, stript tape, shirts linen, silk mitts, black lasting.

PANS, MG 1, Vol. 2630, #146. 1775 to 1778, Starr Family, Cornwallis, account of Ebenezer Thayer:
— twist, oznabridgs, check, binding, tape, linen, leather breeches, shoes, callico, kinsman, wool cards, cambrick, nankin, lawn, handkerchief, brod cloth, button, buck, dowlas, sheeting, drab, silk, black hose, button mould, ribbon, white thread, shoes, calliminco.

PANS, MG 1, Vol. 2630, #156. 1778 to 1780, Starr Family, Cornwallis, account of Whidden and Thayes:
— gause handkerchief, lace, woman's shoes, lawn, oznabridge, thread, buttons, dutch lace, striped linen, check, linen, pins, black handkerchief, hose, crud[?]l, buckram, silk, lasting, hatt, felt hatts, narrow ribbon, brown linen, green cloth, twist, cloth, silk binding, course linen, thred,

broadcloth, brown holland, silk twist, pensh be[?]coat buttons, wascot buttons, baze, muslin, buckskin gloves, fustain, holland, wilton, tammy, dowlas, thred and moulds, buckskin, white corderoy, gloves.

PANS, MG 1, Vol. 2630, #159. 1783, Starr Family, Cornwallis, bought of Robert Pagan:
— corduroy, silk twist, coating, buttons, striped holland, thread.

PANS, MG 1, Vol. 2630, #160. 1783, Major Samual Starr to Robert Pagan:
— woorsted stockings.

Appendix B
Selected Glossary of Eighteenth-Century Textile Terminology:

Alamode [allamode] — lightweight silk used in black of mourning
Baize — [baze] — coarse wool cloth.
Beaver cloth [bever] — a stout woollen cloth with a raised finish resembling beaver fur.
Binding — a tape or braid.
Broadcloth [brod cloth, broad cloths] — carded wool in plain weave and fulled after weaving.
Buckram — a stiff-finished heavily sized fabric of cotton or linen used for interlinings.
Buckskin — a fine woollen cloth with a milled and dressed finish showing a distinctive twill.
Calico [callico] — cotton cloth of many grades.
Calimanco [caliminco] — a worsted stuff with a fine gloss upon it.
Cambric [cambrick, cambrigs] — fine white linen cloth in plain weave.
Camlet [camblet] — made of goat hair, partly of silk or linen, and some entirely of wool, of plain weave.
Camleteen [cambleteen, cambletune] — stuff of mixed wool and goat hair, thread or cotton.
Chintz — usually glazed, printed cotton fabric.
Cloth — term for any woven fabric, but more specifically with reference to closely woven woollen material of fine quality.
Coating — thick heavy woollen cloth with a long nap.
Corduroy [corderoy] — cotton fabric with a plied surface like that of velvet, raised in cords, ridges or ribs.
Crape — light transparent stuff, similar to gauze, made of raw silk, gummed and twisted on the mill, wove without crossing and much used for mourning.

Dowlas [dowless] — coarse linen, commonly worn by lower classes.

Drab — thick, closely woven overcoating which was heavy and expensive; also an undyed cloth of gray-beige colour.

Duffel [duffle] — heavy, napped woollen cloth.

Duroy — lightweight worsted material generally used for men's clothing.

Everlasting [lasting] — stout, closely woven worsted stuff, dyed black and other colours, and much used for ladies shoes.

Flannel — made of woollen yarn.

Fustian — general term covering a large category of linen and cotton, or later, all cotton textiles.

Garlick [galiix] — coarse linen cloth.

Gauze [gause] — thin, transparent fabric woven in a crossed-warp technique.

Gingham — usually yarn-dyed cotton in plain weave.

Holland — linen cloth.

Lawn — a delicate linen.

Linsey-Woolsey [linseywoolsy] — coarse cloth made of linen warp and woollen weft.

Muslin — fine cotton.

Nankeen [nankin] — cotton cloth of plain weave.

Osnaburg [oznabrigs, oznabridgs, oznabridge] — coarse unbleached linen or hempen cloth.

Plainback — worsted, twilled face and plain back.

Plush [plushe] — wool velvet.

Russel [russill] — worsted damask woven in solid colours, two colours, or brocaded.

Sennit [senett] — possibly a straw or grass braid for hats.

Shalloon — cheap twilled worsted.

Stuff — a general term for worsted cloth.

Taffeta [taffety] — most European taffetas were plain woven silks.

Tabby — a fine silk with a watered or plain finish.

Tammy — strong, lightweight worsted of plain weave and open texture, often glazed.

Ticklenburg [tickleberg, ticklenbury] — coarse cloth made of hemp or linen.

Twist — thread formed of two or more strands spun hard together.

Wilton Cloth [wilton] — woollen cloth made in Wilton, Wiltshire.

Worsted [woorsted] — a smooth compact yarn from long wool fibres used especially for firm napless fabrics.

Bibliography

Baumgarten, Linda. "Under Waistcoats and Drawers." *Dress*, Vol. 19 (1992).

Brebner, John. *The Neutral Yankees of Nova Scotia*. 1937. Toronto: McClelland and Stewart, 1969.

Brooke, Iris and James Laver. *English Costume of the Eighteenth Century*. London: Adam and Charles Black, 1931.

Buck, Anne. "Variations in English Women's Dress in the 18th Century." *Folk Life*, Vol. 9 (1971).

Burnham, Dorothy. *Cut My Cote*. Toronto: Royal Ontario Museum, 1973.

Conrad, Margaret. "Mary Bradley's Reminiscences: A Domestic life in Colonial New Brunswick." *Atlantis*, Vol. 7, No. 1 (Fall 1981).

Clabburn, Pamela. *The Needleworker's Dictionary*. New York: William Morrow & Company, 1976.

Cunnington, Phillis and Catherine Lucas. *Occupational Costume in England*. London: Adam and Charles Black, 1967.

Davis, Stephen A., Catherine Cottreau and Laird Niven. *Artifacts from Eighteenth Century Halifax*. Halifax: Saint Mary's University Archaeology Laboratory, 1987.

Earle, Alice Morse. *Home Life in Colonial Days*. New York: MacMillan, 1953.

Ewing, Elizabeth. *Dress and Undress: A History of Women's Underwear*. New York: Drama Books, 1978.

Fennelly, Catherine. *The Garb of Country New Englanders*. Sturbridge: Old Sturbridge Village Booklet Series, 1966.

Furnas, J.C. *The Americans: A Social History of the United States*. New York: G.P. Putnam's Sons, 1969.

Gehret, Ellen J. *Rural Pennsylvania Clothing*. York, Penn.: Liberty Cap Books, 1976.

Glubok, Shirley, ed. *Home Life and Child Life in Colonial Days*. Toronto: The MacMillan Company, 1969. (Abridged from: *Home Life in Colonial Days and Child Life in Colonial Days*, by Alice Morse Earle).

Gordon, Joleen. *Handwoven Hats: A History of Straw, Wood and Rush Hats in Nova Scotia*. Halifax: Nova Scotia Museum, 1981.

Kidwell, Claudia. "Short Gowns." *Dress*, Vol. 4 (1978).

Kidwell, Claudia and Margaret C. Christman. *Suiting Everyone: The Democratization of Clothing in America*. Washington: Smithsonian Institution Press, 1974.

Lavoie, Marc C. "Archaeological Evidence of Planter Material Culture in New Brunswick and Nova Scotia." Ed. Margaret Conrad. *Making Changes: Change and Continuity in Planter Nova Scotia 1759-1800*. Fredericton: Acadiensis Press, 1991.

Lock, Carolyn. *Country Colors: A Guide to Natural Dyeing in Nova Scotia.* Halifax: Nova Scotia Museum, 1981.

McClellan, Elizabeth. *Historic Dress in America 1607-1870.* New York: Arno Press, 1977.

MacDonald, M.A. *Rebels and Royalists.* Fredericton: New Ireland Press, 1990.

Montgomery, Florence M. *Textiles in America 1650-1870.* New York: W.W. Norton and Company, 1984.

Northampton Museums and Art Gallery. *A History of Shoe Fashions.* Northampton, 1975.

Robinson, John and Thomas Rispin. *Journey through Nova-Scotia Containing A Particular Account of the Country and its Inhabitants.* 1774. Sackville: Ralph Pickard Bell Library, Mount Allison University, 1981.

Rothstein, Natalie, ed. *Four Hundred Years of Fashion.* London: Victoria and Albert Museum in association with William Collins, 1984.

Starobinski, Jean and Phillipe Duboy, Akiko Fukai, Jun I. Kanai, Toshio Horii, Janet Arnold, and Martin Kamer. *Revolution in Fashion 1715-1815.* New York: Abbeville Press, 1989.

Taylor, Lou. *Mourning Dress: A Costume and Social History.* London: George Allen and Unwin, 1983.

Tozer, Jane and Sarah Levitt. *Fabric of Society: A Century of People and their Clothes 1770-1870.* Wales: Laura Ashley Limited, 1983.

Tunis, Edwin. *Colonial Craftsmen: And the Beginnings of American Industry.* New York: World Publishing, 1965.

Ulrich, Laurel Thatcher. "Cloth, Clothing, and Early American Social History." *Dress*, Vol. 18 (1991).

Warwick, Edward and Henry C. Pitz and Alexander Wyckoff. *Early American Dress: The Colonial and Revolutionary Periods.* New York: Bonanza Books, 1965.

Waugh, Nora. *The Cut of Women's Clothes 1600-1930.* New York: Theatre Arts Books, 1968.

_____. *The Cut of Men's Clothes 1600-1900.* London: Faber & Faber, 1964.

Williams-Mitchess, Christobel. *Dressed for the Job: The Story of Occupational Costume.* Dorset: Blandford Press, 1982.

Wright, Merideth and Nancy Rexford. *Put On Thy Beautiful Garments: Rural New England Clothing 1783-1800.* East Montpelier, Vermont: The Clothes Press, 1990.

Regional Variations in Nova Scotia Planter Furniture

James Snowdon
Department of History
Acadia University

Rarely in the history of population migration was the process so easily facilitated as with that of the Planters. Motivated by the lure of free land and guarantees of political and religious freedom by the Proclamations of 1758 and 1759, the move to Nova Scotia was relatively free of many of the vexations commonly associated with mass movements. Geography certainly played a part. For most, Nova Scotia was merely a few days sail and often port to port — much easier than an arduous overland trek or a lengthy transoceanic voyage. Equally significant was the free passage on vessels chartered by the Nova Scotia authorities which allowed the migrants to bring large amounts of livestock, farming implements, personal effects and even houses. In short, free transport provided Planters the opportunity to transfer much of their material world to Nova Scotia.

It was this process, facilitated by geographic proximity and free transport, that rapidly transformed the rural landscape of the province to one exhibiting the traits and complexities of a highly developed New England material culture. It was this material culture — captured in their houses and buildings, tables and chests, clothing and decorations, implements of farm and fishery that comprises a vital link in our understanding of the Planter experience and thereby compliments the written record. The problem facing us is one of interpretation for, as Michael Conforti has argued " ... some of the most significant assumptions of culture are never verbalized." Artifacts, he suggests " ... can represent keys to cultural understanding; they are particular expressions of the perspectives and values of the society that generated their creation and their formal evolution."[1]

If one accepts Conforti's assumptions, then the "perspectives and values" of the Planter community were of a highly utilitarian and practical bent. Most of their possessions represented items of durable form and function and many had seen long service with several generations of New England ancestors before being brought to Nova Scotia. The Pilgrim-Century Hadley chest found in the Cornwallis district, for example, may be an example of colonial America's rarest forms of jointed furniture,[2] but for generations of anonymous owners it provided

---

1   Michael Conforti, "The Transfer and Adaption of European Culture in North America," in Francis J. Puig and Michael Conforti, eds., *The American Craftsman and the European Tradition, 1620-1820* (Hanover, N.H., 1989), xiv.

2   See Suzanne Flynt and Philip Zea, *Hadley Chests* (Deerfield, Mass., 1992).

durable utilitarian storage — long before and long after 1760. The probated estate inventory of Edward Church, taken on 12 January 1761, illustrates that, in his move to Nova Scotia during the spring of 1760, virtually everything of utilitarian or monetary value was shipped from Little Compton, Rhode Island, to his newly-constructed home in Falmouth; pewter plates and porringers; tea pots, coffee pots, iron pots, knives and forks; one great chair, a half dozen bannister back chairs, six flat back chairs and one little chair; one oval table, a tea table, tea cups, glass and earthenware. Even an old saddle, old iron and "cloth for one pair of britches" were included in an estate valued at £108 excluding real estate.[3]

The Church inventory provides a rare glimpse of the material world of a Planter shortly after arrival — a material world that was transferred virtually intact from New England. Other inventories reveal the accumulation of possessions after several years or decades in their new environment. But to the material historian such written records, limited both in the detail that they contain and in the information that they convey, are but one tool. Equally important is the artifact itself. Surviving examples of Planter-era furnishings do exist, such

1. Queen Anne Sidechair, c. 1720-30, Connecticut. This chair, brought to Cornwallis by John Newcomb, is characteristic of the many chairs brought by the Planters. (Courtesy of Randall House Museum, Wolfville, Nova Scotia)

3   Hants County Nova Scotia Probate Records, 1-A Edward Church, 12 January 1761.

as the Queen Anne Style chest with drawers brought to Cornwallis by Perry Borden and listed in his household inventory of 22 March 1805,[4] and the Hicks family oval drop leaf table brought first to Falmouth and then, in 1765, to Granville. Through the analysis of such documented pieces, or comparable anonymous items that have survived, we are better able to grasp the sense of aesthetics and form that made up the material culture of the Planter.

Collectively, these items are part of a larger colonial American material culture. In isolation they illustrate the reality of that culture — products of specific regions in which the people worked, traded, thought and even spoke alike.[5] In most instances they were the products of anonymous craftsmen working in the provincial towns or rural regions and so reflect these origins in their distinctive stylistic and technological interpretations. In detail, proportion and style as well as specific material usage and construction technology, they reveal their origins and the origins of their owners.[6] Thus, the artifacts of Essex County, Massachusetts, can be differentiated from those of the Connecticut coastal communities, and also from those of outport Newport and Boston.

2. Queen Anne Armchair, c. 1750, Connecticut. From the Granville Township area. Replaced seat and a repair to the top posts and crest rail. (Unless stated all pictures are from private collections)

4   Kings County Nova Scotia Probate Records, B-10 Perry Borden, 22 March 1805.

5   Philip Zea, "Rural Craftsmen and Design," in Brock Jobe and Myrna Kaye, *New England Furniture: The Colonial Era* (Boston, 1984), 49.

6   See, for example, Albert Sack, "Regionalism in Early American Tea Tables," *The Magazine Antiques* (January 1987), 248-63.

3. Country Chippendale Sidechair, c. 1760, probably Massachusetts. Retaining its original finish and rush seat. From the Sackville area.

4. Lowback Windsor Armchair, c. 1760. Attributed to Timothy Waterhouse, Newport, R.I. Original finish, legs shortened. Brought to Falmouth by the Wilson family.

A low-back Windsor armchair recently acquired in Falmouth, Nova Scotia, provides an apt example. The low-back was a rare form even in the eighteenth century when production was commonly associated with the chairmakers of Philadelphia. But this specimen did not share construction characteristics commonly associated with Philadelphia, and in design suggested an English influence — finely saddled seat, decoratively turned spindles, back treatment and cross-stretchers. Constructed entirely of maple and retaining its original worn green paint, it clearly had all the characteristics of the only other centre of North American production before the revolution, Newport, Rhode Island. Continued investigation revealed that it was, in fact, identical to one in the collection of the Museum of Art, Rhode Island School of Design, and similar to a set of twelve made for Newport's Redwood Library and Athenaeum in 1764, probably by Timothy Waterhouse, and still in their possession.[7] Joseph Wilson had brought the chair to Falmouth from Newport; it had remained with family descendants in that Nova Scotia community for over two hundred years. Other examples of Rhode Island-produced furnishings have come from Falmouth — a tripod base tea table and a chest, again suggesting the geographic and stylistic origins of that Township.

5. Lift Top Chest-With-Drawers, c. 1800. From the Berwick area. Original untouched condition, but missing the pulls.

7   Charles Santore, *The Windsor Style in America Vol. II: 1730-1840* (Philadelphia, 1987), 65.

6. Tap Table, c. 1730-40, New England, and found in Newport.

7. Queen Anne Oval Drop Leaf Table, c. 1740, Rhode Island. Brought to Nova Scotia by John Hicks. This table remains the property of a direct descendant.

While the furnishings of Falmouth exhibited this strong, but not exclusive, Rhode Island character, other communities relied on different regions of New England for their influences. Townships such as Cornwallis with its heavy concentration of Connecticut settlers, exhibited the characteristics of that region, while Massachusetts migrants brought the character of Ipswich, Rehoboth or Cape Cod to Maugerville, Sackville or Yarmouth. Indeed, the material legacy continues to identify the origins of the first Planter residents throughout the region.

As the Planters began to produce household objects in Nova Scotia this regional diversity in the way of "seeing things" would continue — often into the second and third generations. In some instances they reproduced forms and styles long out of fashion but with which they were comfortable. A simple bannister back chair dating from the late eighteenth century, yet incorporating design features out of fashion in Connecticut for fifty years, was found in Canning and constructed from memory or by using a surviving chair as a pattern. Like their houses, the locally constructed items usually incorporated the essence of proportion and design but were often stylistically scaled down — even from the provincial New England prototypes upon which they were based. Donald Blake Webster, in his discussion of English-Canadian furniture of the Georgian period, states:

> The best of Georgian-Canadian furniture is by any standard well-designed and skillfully constructed, but it is understated simplified, and generally unadorned.[8]

8. Chair Table, late eighteenth-century Cornwallis. In its original condition.

8   Donald Blake Webster, *English-Canadian Furniture of the Georgian Period* (Toronto, 1979), 11.

9. Tea Table, c. 1760, Newport, R.I. and brought to Falmouth by the Wilson family.

10. Hepplewhite Drop Leaf Table, c. 1790-1810. Made of birch and from the Round Hill-Tupperville area of Annapolis.

The rural nature of the region, the small population and the nascent economy were all factors which precluded the emergence of professional cabinetmakers, forcing the talented artisan to combine his craft with an array of other occupations, including house and boatbuilding as well as farming and fishing.[9]

Even with the arrival of prosperity during the American and French revolutionary eras, prosperous merchants and government officials reaffirmed their proud colonialism by importing much of their furnishings and accessories from London and other British cabinetshops rather than fostering vibrant indigenous industry through their patronage. The Scottish traveller Patrick Campbell commented, in 1792, that:

> ... so prevalent is custom, and the desire of emulation, the bane of all society, that many of the gentlemen here, who cannot well afford it, have mahogany furniture in abundance, and despise what can be got at their doors, and at no expense but the workmanship.[10]

11. Hepplewhite Games Table, c. 1790-1810. Made of birch and from the Round Hill-Tupperville area of Annapolis. Descended in the Chipman family.

9   On a rare printer paper label found intact on a Halifax gamestable, John Tulles listed his occupations as "Upholsterer, Cabinet-Maker and House Carpenter."

10   Patrick Campbell, *Travels in the Interior Inhabited Parts of North America in the Years 1791 and 1792* (Toronto, 1937), 251-52.

Production was necessarily limited, therefore, to fulfilling the requirements of an immediate community or district. An unknown artisan, probably working at the turn of the nineteenth century, produced furniture exhibiting a high degree of artistic finesse and technical competence in the Round Hill area of Annapolis Township. Both a games table and a drop leaf table, constructed from local birch in the Hepplewhite style, illustrate a command of design and construction in their simple, yet elegant, execution. In Maugerville, the output of David Burpee seems to have been limited to his own family's requirements — despite his obvious abilities. Within each township and district the work of many such artisans, most anonymous, have been found, all exhibiting some element of the New England sensibilities and coming together to produce a distinctive tradition within "old" Nova Scotia.

This material tradition is also elusive. Only a small percentage of items have survived the use and abuse of over two hundred years, and those that have are scattered far and wide — usually with no provenance or historical association. While antique dealers have long recognized Nova Scotia as one of the earliest areas of colonial American expansion and have continually sought out prime specimens since at least 1920, the result is that literally thousands of items have left the province and now form parts of private and public collections throughout North America — but without the Planter provenance. The Canadian museum community has had neither the inclination nor the resources to acquire and preserve representative collections. The student of material culture is primarily reliant on those private collectors whose foresight and dedication have saved a few specimens and who share their knowledge of the Planter era with others.

12. Looking Glass, c. 1750-60. Either England or New England. Characteristic of the looking glasses found in eighteenth-century Nova Scotia. From Granville.

At the Counter of the General Store:
Women and the Economy in Eighteenth-Century Horton, Nova Scotia

Elizabeth Mancke
Department of History
University of Akron[1]

We associate women in the North American rural economy with the household, with kitchens, looms, gardens, dairies and children. We associate men with the fields that produced grain, rice and tobacco, and the woods that yielded timber for homes, barns, boats and barrels. Scholars have debated the extent to which this economy was oriented to the subsistence needs of its constituent households or to the market pull of the Atlantic economy.[2] To the extent that farm families produced surpluses for the market economy, their market-oriented activities have been interpreted as gendered, with men producing the goods that they loaded onto carts for urban centers or into the holds of vessels bound to any of the many ports on the Atlantic littoral. Much evidence exists to support these general divisions; and considerable evidence provides qualifying examples of times when women did men's work or produced for the market.[3]

Four types of sources have been used to provide most of what we know about women in pre-industrial economies. Personal accounts in the form of diaries, letters or household journals have yielded vivid portrayals of women's

---

1 Acknowledgements: Research for this paper was made possible by a grant from the Canadian Government through the Canadian Embassy in Washington, D.C. I am grateful for the encouragement of Julian Gwyn and Rusty Bittermann, each of whom in their very different ways prodded me to continue. Margaret Conrad and Barry Moody are sentinels for many of us working on the eighteenth-century Maritimes and maintain the space for these papers to be aired. I am indebted to their vigilance.

2 Michael Merrill, "'Cash is Good to Eat': Self-Sufficiency and Exchange in the Rural Economy of the United States," *Radical History Review* (1977): 42-71; James A. Henretta, "Families and Farms: Mentalité in Pre-Industrial America," *William and Mary Quarterly* 3rd ser., 35, 4 (1978): 3-23; Winifred Rothenberg, "The Market and Massachusetts Farmers, 1750-1855," *Journal of Economic History,* 41 (1981): 283-314.

3 Joan M. Jensen, "Butter Making and Economic Development in Mid-Atlantic America from 1750 to 1850," *Signs: Journal of Women in Culture and Society,* 13, 4 (1988): 813-29, rpt. in Jensen, *Promise to the Land: Essays on Rural Women* (Albuquerque, 1991); Jensen, "Cloth, Butter, and Boarders: Women's Household Production for the Market," *The Review of Radical Political Economics,* 12 (1980): 14-24, rpt. in *Promise to the Land*; Marjorie Griffin

roles.[4] Wills and probate records tell us the lot of widows and female descendants when men bequeathed the household wealth. In aggregate, they suggest the social norms within which women and men accumulated and redistributed wealth. Court records, both civil and criminal, tell us how society judged women when social norms had been breached, or when a woman was involved in disputes involving property, contracts or children.[5] All three of these types of sources are focused on discrete persons and households and, while we can extrapolate social values from similar cases, we often lack related cases from the same time and place. Nineteenth-century censuses in which enumerators recorded the butter, cheese and cloth produced by the women in a household are the fourth type of source frequently used for studying women's economic activities.[6] Unfortunately, censuses from the eighteenth century are scarce and the extant ones often enumerate only some of the products of the rural economy and never those associated with women. The 1767 aggregate census for Nova Scotia did not preserve a record of the production of hay, potatoes or turnips, much less butter, cheese or cloth, all of which were important items produced and sold locally.

This study of women and the economy in late eighteenth-century Horton, Nova Scotia, begins, figuratively, in Edward Dewolf's general store at Horton Landing.[7] Established in 1773, Dewolf operated the business until his death in

Cohen, *Women's Work, Markets, and Economic Development in Nineteenth-Century Ontario* (Toronto, 1988), 59-92.

4   Laurel Thatcher Ulrich, *A Midwife's Tale: The Life of Martha Ballard, Based on Her Diary, 1785-1812* (New York, 1990); Ulrich, *Good Wives: Image and Reality in the Lives of Women in Northern New England, 1650-1750* (New York, 1982); Ulrich, "Martha Ballard and Her Girls: Women's Work in Eighteenth-Century Maine," in *Work and Labor in Early America*, ed. Stephen Innes (Chapel Hill, 1988), 70-105; Margaret Conrad, Toni Laidlaw, and Donna Smyth, eds., *No Place Like Home: Diaries and Letters of Nova Scotia Women, 1771-1938* (Halifax, 1988).

5   Toby L. Ditz, *Property and Kinship: Inheritance in Early Connecticut, 1750-1820* (Princeton, N.J., 1986); Ulrich, *Good Wives*, passim.

6   Janine Grant and Kris Inwood, "Gender and Organization in the Canadian Cloth Industry, 1870," in Peter Baskerville, ed., *Canadian Papers in Business History*, Vol. 1 (Victoria, 1989), 17-31; Kris Inwood and Phyllis Wagg, "The Survival of Handloom Weaving in Rural Canada Circa 1870," *The Journal of Economic History*, 53, 2 (1993): 346-58; and Joan M. Jensen, "Butter Making and Economic Development in Mid-Atlantic America from 1750 to 1850," 813-29.

7   See Debra Anne McNabb, "Land and Families in Horton Township, N.S., 1760-1830," M.A. thesis, University of British Columbia, 1986, for a study of early Horton.

1796. A perusal of his two surviving ledgers, one from 1773-1786 and the other from 1794-1796, and one daybook, from December 1793-September 1794, shows that the shop provided a place for the intersection of numerous individual household economies, the local economy of Horton, the provincial economy of Nova Scotia, and the Atlantic economy.[8] In Dewolf's general store, people exchanged butter for tea, a yoke of oxen for a poker and pan, flannel for calico, oats for iron, cheese for molasses, one's labour for a coat. Women were frequent customers, albeit not as often as men. Their large number in the account books, in comparison to their numbers in diaries, letters, wills and court records, underscores the importance of women to the eighteenth-century agrarian economy. Such evidence also exposes the considerable social and economic stratification among women and points to the variable economic niches they had.[9] And finally, the sharp distinctions scholars have drawn between subsistence and market economies blur significantly at the counter of a general store and suggest an intrinsically symbiotic relationship between production and consumption, not in the neo-classical sense that people produce more to consume more, but rather in the sense that access to many goods through the market made household production possible.

The extent to which market consumption made household production possible in colonial economies needs to be acknowledged if we are to understand the linkages between local economies and regional economies, between the individual household and distant staple production, between the labour of rural people and the labour of urban workers or plantation slaves. For example, women in Horton bought raw cotton and cotton carding brushes so they could spin cotton thread to weave cotton cloth to sew into shirts and petticoats to clothe their families. Dewolf's general store brought together the labour of an unknown and distant field hand who grew and harvested the cotton, the wares of an anonymous craftsman who made the carding brushes, and the women of Horton who carded, spun, wove and stitched the cotton into serviceable, if modest, homemade garments. Some of their families may have struggled by on a bare subsistence, but on their backs and in their work baskets was the residual labour of distant people exchanged over the counter of the general store.

If we look at the goods sold by Edward Dewolf between December 1793 and September 1794, when we can follow individual transactions in the daybook, we can begin to see the extent to which people consumed in the market to produce

8   The three account books in the Public Archives of Nova Scotia are MG 1, Vols. 223, 224, and 236 respectively (hereafter Ledger I, Ledger II, and Daybook). The daybook has no merchant's name on it, but internal evidence shows that it is one of the daybooks for the latter ledger.

9   See Gloria L. Main, "Gender, Work, and Wages in Colonial New England," *William and Mary Quarterly,* 3d ser., 51, 1 (1994): 39-66.

in the home. Appendix 1 indicates the variety of goods sold. While comprehensive in its general categories, it does not capture the various sizes of iron pots, the degree of fineness of the fabrics, the sizes of clothes, or the grade of nails. What it does show is how few finished goods were sold that did not require further labour inputs or that did not make further production possible. Field implements for hoeing, cutting and raking eased the planting, tending and harvesting of the crops whether in fields or kitchen gardens; nails sped the building of houses, barns, sheds and stores; adequate cookware enhanced and varied food preparation; food, with some exceptions, had to be cooked; cloth had to be sewn into garments, curtains, sheets and quilts. Many, if not most, of the goods Dewolf sold required the additional labour of women — whether sewing, cooking, carding, spinning, hoeing or cleaning — before they were "consumed." The items associated with men's production were fewer and largely hardware for farming, building and blacksmithing.

Among the finished items that did not require further labour for consumption were some ready-to-wear clothes, though, significantly, most were men's clothes. Some of the clothes sold at Dewolf's store had been produced locally, including handmade shoes and worsted mitts. A few luxuries were also available; a mirror could be hung to tempt a household's vanities, a glass decanter and cups and saucers graced a table setting, a silk bandanna symbolized one's affluence.[10] These items also suggest an economy that was shedding its "frontier" image, in contrast to the items that can be identified in the 1773-1784 ledger. Moccasins, leather and buckskins did not appear in the sales of the 1790s, while they had in the 1770s, and fewer men brought in furs to trade.

In contrast to the goods Dewolf sold, the goods he bought from local people indicate that rural men produced more goods that entered the commercial economy than did women. Appendix 2 is a list of goods produced locally. What is striking is how many are associated with men's labour and how few with women's. Butter, cheese, eggs, flannel, feathers, full cloth, linen and raspberries are normally associated with women. Both men and women sold their labour. Harvesting the apple crop and raking hay could be family endeavours.[11] And as the accounts of women heads of households show, they often raised and sold livestock, especially cows and pigs. But most of the goods are customarily considered the fruits of men's labour and claimed by men: barrels, boards, flour, fish, oats, potatoes, bricks, wheat and more.

---

10   See T.H. Breen, "'The Baubles of Britain': The American Consumer Revolutions of the Eighteenth Century," *Past and Present*, 119 (1988): 73-104, for an argument about luxuries in the Anglo-North American economies.

11   For some discussion of the role of daughters in the family economy, including haying, see the diary of Louisa Collins, 1815, in *No Place Like Home*, 61-78; and Main, "Gender, Work, and Wages," 53-55.

What becomes apparent from an analysis of the goods Dewolf sold and bought is that women consumed to produce and men produced to consume. The women of Horton, like women throughout the Anglo-American world, purchased imported goods to facilitate domestic production for themselves, their menfolk and their children. It is thus not surprising that during the import boycotts preceding the American Revolution, women were urged to make do with what they had at home and with what they could produce for themselves. And when commentators deplored a dependency on imported goods, they labelled it effeminate.[12] Women were not necessarily purchasing baubles and trinkets, as the list from Dewolf's store shows. Rather the day-to-day needs of a family, met by the labour of its women, necessitated purchases of imported goods. Men ostensibly paid for those purchases "for women" by raising corn and wheat, cutting clapboards and shingles, making wheelbarrows, and butchering livestock.

The commercial transactions in Dewolf's eighteenth-century general store were points of convergence for household production and the commercial world, for women's economic production geared to the demands of a household and men's economic world geared to the demands of the market. Within this commercial sphere, tangible differences between women and men existed, as the lists of goods bought and sold suggest. But those lists also suggest that the coupling of women's and men's economic worlds took place in the market, over the counter of a general store, as well as through the bonds of marriage and family formation. Women in eighteenth-century North America did not function apart from the market, but rather, they had a particular relationship to it. Men produced in the household economy for the market. Women purchased in the market to produce in and for the home, thus putting their enormous labour inputs, and seemingly women themselves, beyond the calculus of the market.

If most of the goods Edward Dewolf sold required the addition of women's labour before they could be consumed, men dominated the space itself, being the majority of customers, holding most of the accounts, and often quaffing a gill of rum during a visit.[13] Nancy Osterud has observed, though, that even if

---

12 Mary Beth Norton, *Liberty's Daughters: The Revolutionary Experience of American Women, 1750-1800* (Boston and Toronto, 1980), 156-63; Linda K. Kerber, *Women of the Republic: Intellect & Ideology in Revolutionary America* (Chapel Hill, N.C., 1980), 35-45; and James A. Henretta, "The War for Independence and American Economic Development," in *The Economy of Early America: The Revolutionary Period, 1763-1790*, eds. Ronald Hoffman, John J. McCusker, Russell R. Menard, and Peter J. Albert (Charlottesville, 1988), 58-68.

13 Daybook of Edward Dewolf, 1793-1794, PANS, MG 1, Vol. 236. A careful assessment of this daybook and others would yield much on the patterns of male sociability in general stores.

most work in an agrarian community was gendered, men and women crossed the boundaries that separated their spheres, much more so than in an urban setting.[14] Thus, we find a goodly number of women in Dewolf's store, some making purchases, some selling home produce, some collecting and spending the proceeds of the sale of their labour. Analysed in aggregate, we can begin to find patterns that describe the scope of women's exchanges, as well as gauge the parameters that constrained them and kept their commercial affairs gendered.

In the transactions recorded in the daybook from December 1793 to September 1794 women appeared most frequently when they made purchases on or applied credits to another person's account. Approximately 175 different women participated in hundreds of these kind of commercial exchanges, which, in all but eight cases, were on men's accounts. These women involved in third-party transactions can be divided into six groups by the type of relationship with the account holder (see Table 1).

Table 1
Third-Party Relationships of Women[15]

Wives	73
Daughters	21
Married Women	17
"Girls"	7
Single Women	40
Other	17
Total	175

The largest single category of women were the wives of 73 different men, identified in entries reading "Zebbediah Wickware by wife," "Nathan Kinne by wife," etc. Twenty-three wives had multiple transactions; Ezra Reed's wife shopped most often with purchases on nine different occasions. Fifty wives made purchases on their husbands' accounts once during this nine-month period from December to September. Twenty-one females were identified as daughters, e.g., "Joseph Williams by daughter." Seventeen were married women, e.g., "John Loveless by Mrs. Dodge." Forty women were probably single. They were identified by their first and last name, by their first name only, or by "Miss", e.g., "Josiah Wood by Betsy Whipple," "James Hamilton by Sarah," or "George

14   Nancy Grey Osterud, *Bonds of Community: The Lives of Farm Women in Nineteenth-Century New York* (Ithaca and New York, 1991), 139-58.

15   I have said the number is approximate because of possible duplication of names in counting or missing names. The count is accurate within ten.

Johnson by Miss Allan." Seven females were identified just as "girl," e.g., "John Davis by his Girl," a term, like its masculine equivalent "boy," used for servants. The occasional mother, sister or granddaughter made purchases, as did two African-Nova Scotian women identified as "Bilba" and "Black Henry's wife." Of these 175 women who purchased on accounts held in another's name, over 60 were not an immediate family member, in other words, not identified as a wife, daughter, mother, sister or granddaughter. They were very probably working for wages or selling services at the time they made the purchases. The seven females identified as "girl" were hired help. "Miss Allan" [Elizabeth Allen], who purchased a shawl, raw cotton, a handkerchief and thread on George Johnson's account, received a ten shilling credit from him on her ledger account, as well as credits from Asa Dewey, James Dewolf and Charles Steward.[16] Nancy Comstock, who made purchases on the accounts of Ann Crawford and William Bishop, 3rd, seemed to work for a number of people. Dewolf debited the ledger account of Hampton Stokes for the cost of a pair of shoes for Nancy Comstock, probably a form of payment or support. Mrs. Gilbert appeared to do sewing, dying and spinning for different families. On 19 December 1793 she purchased muslin and indigo on Daniel Harris's account; on 3 February 1794 she purchased six yards of cotton on Thomas Beckwith's account, which, Dewolf noted, "she has promised to pay if he does not"; that same day she charged Steadman Beckwith's account for two pounds of raw cotton. Similarly, Miss Lovelace acquired sewing notions and cloth charged to the account of David Harris. Mrs. Dean purchased chintz on the account of Mrs. Elisha Dewolf. In most of the cases in which women purchased fabrics and sewing notions on another's account, they probably were working for others.[17]

These 175 women who made transactions on another's account were, by the nature of the third-party transaction, subordinate to the account holder. The overwhelming prevalence of male account holders meant that the nature of the subordination was shaped by gender, as well as by conditions of service and family relationships.[18] The 73 wives, by the nature of the marriage contract, were legally subordinate to their husbands and identified by their husband's name. (Their individuality within their respective domestic spheres is not at

---

16 Daybook, 24 December 1793, fo. 4; Ledger II, fo. 184.

17 Edward Dewolf's Daybook, fos, 3, 4, 15, 22, 82, 121, 146, 160, and passim.

18 For a discussion of the cultural embeddedness of gender subordination, see Leonore Davidoff, "'Adam spoke first and named the orders of the World': Masculine and Feminine Domains in History and Sociology," in Helen Corr and Lynn Jamieson, eds., *Politics of Everyday Live: Continuity and Change in Work and Family* (New York, 1990), 230-34.

issue here and is a separate concern.)[19] Only five married women had ledger accounts separate from their husbands' accounts. Notably, in their own accounts they were still identified by the name of their husbands: Mrs. Perez Martin, Mrs. Thomas Miner, Mrs. John Coaldwell, Mrs. Samuel Reed and Mrs. David Scott. Mrs. Martin and Mrs. Coaldwell credited items of household production such as feathers, flannel, butter and pork to their accounts and purchased household goods against them. Mrs. Miner had three credits of ten shillings each applied to her account by Elizabeth Graham, John Dewolf and Green Randal; and Elisha Dewolf applied £1.18.6. It is possible that Mrs. Miner was a midwife or caregiver, the proceeds of which were often claimed by women. Mrs. Scott and Mrs. Reed worked for others.[20]

The relationship of fathers and their daughters in these documents is, to some extent, problematic. In many cases, daughters had gone to Dewolf's store to make purchases for the household. For example, Charles Palmeter's daughter bought tea one time, molasses another; Rebecca Harris, daughter of Daniel, purchased molasses; William Coaldwell's daughter bought cotton yardage; William Bishop's daughter went to Dewolf's store for cotton and knitting needles. Those times when these daughters purchased rum, tobacco or spirits, they were probably on errands expressly for their fathers. In other cases, their purchases may have been for themselves, but charged to a father's account.[21] In late adolescence and early adulthood and before they married, women often were given some autonomy, including some control over their labour. Many of the women who purchased in their own names and who held ledger accounts were single women.[22] Nonetheless, they still lived within their fathers' households and often were identified first as their fathers' daughters.

---

19 On the importance of domestic space to women see Margaret Conrad, "'Sundays Always Make Me Think of Home': Time and Place in Canadian Women's History," in Veronica Strong-Boag and Anita Clair Fellman, eds., *Rethinking Canada: The Promise of Women's History* (Toronto, 1991), 97-112.

20 Mrs. Perez Martin, Daybook, fos. 22, 23, 203, 211, 216, 219, 247, 253 and Ledger II, fo. 102; Mrs. David Scott, Daybook, fos. 15, 27, 66, 86, and Ledger II, fo. 58; Mrs. John Coaldwell, Daybook, fo. 185 and Ledger II, fo. 72; Mrs. Samuel Reed, Daybook, fos. 8, 28, 29, 44, 171 and Ledger II, fo. 72; and Mrs. Thomas Miner, Ledger II, fo. 49.

21 Daybook, fos. 27, 184, 195, 215. For other examples see, fos. 13, 27, 37, 47, 50, 103, 115, 116, 122, 133, 185, 214, 217, 219, 226, 227, 232, 233, 252.

22 For a study of single women in this period see, Lee Virginia Chambers-Schiller, *Liberty, a Better Husband, Single Women in America: The Generations of 1780-1840* (New Haven, Ct. and London, 1984).

The 60-plus women who are not related to the account holder were subordinated by a condition of service. Wages derived from service may suggest some possibility for the mitigation of subordination, perhaps through greater household power or discretionary consumption. It is analytically dangerous, though, to assume that through wages these women might have escaped social subordination itself. Not only were these women subordinated by service, they, like the married women, were subordinated by gender, and the latter brought with it certain kinds of legal and social constraints on the economic activities of women. And women seldom acquired the land that was a basic minimum for political recognition in eighteenth-century Anglo-America.[23]

Some women had commercial transactions with Dewolf in their own names. Eighty-four can be identified in the December 1793-September 1794 daybook and corresponding ledger from 1794-1796. These women's commercial activities provide markers for assessing the perimeter of women's economic range in eighteenth-century Horton. Probably the most significant marker for establishing the outside reaches are the standing ledger accounts some women had. These ledger accounts indicate which women had some socially acknowledged economic autonomy and credit-worthiness. In the mid-1790s only 16 women had standing accounts in Dewolf's ledger. Thus, while many women participated in the commercial economy, few were acknowledged to have the long-standing economic independence signalled by an account of one's own.

Of these 16 women, five were the married women mentioned above, who, through established and accepted control over household production and probably female-specific skills, had accounts separate from their husbands. The law, though, could hold husbands liable for their wives' debts, probably a major reason why the balance of debits and credits was kept close. Three women were widows, who, by the death of their husbands, had been accorded some economic autonomy. One was an elderly widow with no credits and another was a recent widow. Unlike some places where "widow" just replaced "wife" in a woman's public appellation, for example from "John Smith's wife" to "John Smith's widow," in Horton widows were referred to by their Christian names. Sylvanus Miner died on 8 May 1794 and his account became the account of Mrs. Lucy Miner, an acknowledgement that these women did have an identity separate from that of their husbands.[24] Three women were definitely single and five more were probably single. Most of the credits on these last eight women's accounts were from third parties, probably for services rendered. Only in the cases of Elizabeth Allen, who taught school, and Amey Miner, who did spinning, were

---

23 See McNabb, "Land and Families," passim, for the lack of female grantees, landowners, and inheritors in Horton.

24 Daybook, fos. 112, 133, 146, 151, 177; Ledger II, fo. 40.

the services identified.[25] These 16 women with their own accounts represented the most economic autonomy to which a woman in eighteenth-century Horton, in all but extraordinary circumstances, could aspire.

No one of these women's ledger accounts, however, exceeded ten pounds, and the largest two were held by married women; most accounts were under three pounds. That the two largest accounts were held by married women, Mrs. John Coaldwell and Mrs. Perez Martin, is significant because they probably controlled some household labour reflected in the items of household production, such as feathers, flannel, butter and pork, credited to their accounts. Economic advancement depended, in part, on being able to derive benefit from the labour of others. The evidence from eighteenth-century Horton is that few women could claim the proceeds of another's labour, and if they did it was usually a daughter or a woman working for wages. Only 22 times did a third-party purchase items for a woman, and in 10 cases the purchase was by another women. In four cases the man is identified as a family member of the woman. In eight cases the relationship of the third-party male purchaser to the woman is ambiguous. What is striking, though, are the very limited number of times that persons went to Dewolf's store for a woman compared to the hundreds of times that both women and men bought and sold for men.

Many women did sell their labour, far more than we might expect. Thirty-nine can be identified as having received third-party payment through Dewolf's general store between 1794 and 1796, though over 30 of those cases are in 1794. In seven cases one women received payment from another women. Seventeen women were married, one widowed and 21 single. For most of these women, it is not possible to say what services they sold; in four cases spinning or casting was entered as the task performed; one woman, Mrs. David Scott, worked a total of eight days on two occasions; and Elizabeth Allen taught school. Women who did weaving tended to sell the cloth which was the product of their labour rather than their labour directly; 11 sold cloth on their own account. Fifteen sold dairy products or yard produce. Of the 84 women who had transactions with Dewolf in their own names, only 16 had ledger accounts. Sixty-eight women did not have accounts of their own, suggesting that they paid for their purchases directly or received third-party payment immediately. Very possibly there were exchanges of cash or services which took place beyond the realm of Dewolf's store.

These cumulative numbers give us a sense of the significance of women's labour in Horton outside their own homes. We can identify the 39 who received third-party payment. Then there are the seven "girls" who made third-party purchases and are clearly working for room, board and/or wages. Of the 17 married women and 40 single women who made third-party purchases, some were

---

25   Ledger II, fos. 3, 29, 34, 38, 49, 58, 65, 72, 76, 82, 84, 102, 172, 180.

probably working for wages or exchanging some form of services or goods. And the 68 women who had transactions with Dewolf on their own behalf and in their own name had access to wealth that allowed them to act as purchasers in the commercial economy. Some of these women overlap, though how much is hard to say. The use of first names only in many third-party transactions makes cross-referencing names difficult. But it is not unreasonable to say that between 60 and 100 women sold their labour or goods in 1794.

What are we to conclude from these data, which are much more numerous than I had expected to find? First, subsistence economies in eighteenth-century Anglo-America detached from the commercial world did not exist, or existed in such limited numbers as to be far from the norm. Poor households, perhaps verging on destitution, surely existed, but even they depended on external markets and sale of their labour, often through the agency of a merchant. Second, women were intricately linked into the market, primarily through consumption of goods that made their household production possible, then through the sale of their labour, and finally through the goods that they sold back. Just because their linkage was not like a man's association with the market does not mean it did not exist. Third, a high percentage of women sold their labour, but that sale of labour varied according to their life-cycle and social condition, as well as what society would allow. It did not allow them to transform their subordinate social condition as women; indeed, it probably confirmed it with servitude and low wages. Finally, the pattern described for Horton no doubt has strong parallels in other agricultural towns in Nova Scotia, though it would probably be significantly variant in towns oriented to the sea and in Halifax.

Note on Methodology

The methodology for this paper is largely apparent from the text. I add this note because account books are, as Barry Moody noted during the conference proceedings, "a source that most of us had considered largely useless," and therefore discussing the basic methodology might be useful. For social historians, account books are remarkable historical documents because they are so tediously pedestrian, repetitive and detailed. They are also patterned, both explicitly in the accounting method employed and implicitly in the recording of day-to-day activities in a community. The task for the historian is to uncover and reconstruct the implicit or embedded patterns and within one account book they might be numerous.

For this paper I looked for patterns relating to women, a task which immediately required that I look past accounting patterns which are biased in favour of men, who held the vast majority of accounts. Most women did not have publicly legitimated economic identities that show up as ledger accounts in a merchant's records (or in tax records and censuses.) But within men's accounts women's names appeared frequently. Any and every mention of a woman's name became cause to make a record of it. I recreated these women as discrete economic actors by making a notecard for each one, noting in whose account they appeared and the nature of the transaction. Some women became repeat economic actors, appearing in more than one account, appearing as third-party purchasers, or appearing to purchase something for themselves. Soon the accumulation of pedestrian detail about many women began to yield patterns of its own.

This paper represents only some of the patterns that appeared from my winnowing of Dewolf's account books. What I have presented is the general argument that in eighteenth-century rural communities women were often economic actors beyond their homes and that even what they did in the home was dependent on the commercial economy. With hundreds of extant account books available, it is possible that, with numerous collections of detail, a more nuanced understanding of women's work in early Anglo-America will emerge.

Appendix 1
Goods Sold at Edward Dewolf's General Store,
Horton Landing, December 1793 —July 1794

Hardware
bag
barrel
bridle
brimestone
cabbage seeds
chalk
chest hinge
chest lock
clapboard
cod hooks
codline
cordage
crooper
cupboard lock
flies
flax seeds
gimblets
glass panes
hammer
hand irons
hardsaw
hay seed
horse whip
jack knife
lamp black
lead, hogs
lead, white
lime
linseed oil
molds
nails
oil
paint
putty
rack comb
rope
saddle, std
saddle, side
saddle cloth
sheet lead
shingles
shoe brushes
shot
shovel

shovel, tongs,
& poker
spurs
steel
stiliards, pr
sythe
tap borer
tape
vamps & bootleg
wire

Housewares
bees wax
blacking ball
bottle
bowls
brush, hearth
brush, buckle
brush, house
camphor
candle stick
candles
cannister
carding brushes
chamberpot
coffeepot
coffee pot, tin
comb
corks
cream pot
cruit
cup, tin
cups & saucers
decanter, glass
dish
frying pan
funnel
glasses
iron knife
knives & forks
milk pot
mirror
mug, qt
mustard pot
pasta board

patte pans
pitcher
plates, ceramic
plates, pewter
pot, iron
pot, tin
quart, tin
razor
salt cellar
scissors
shears
snuff box
soap
soup plates
spoons
starch
stone jar
tea kettle
tea pot
tumblers
wine glasses

Food
allspice
annis
butter
cake
cider
clove water
cloves
cod
coffee
cordials
corn
flour
gasperoes
hops
maple sugar
molasses
mustard
mutton
nutmeg
pepper
pork
raisins

rice
rum
salt
saltpeter
spirits
sugar
tea, Souchang
tea, Bohea
tea, green
wheat
wine

Cloth
baize
bed ticking
crepe
bombazine
broadcloth
brown Holland
buckram
calamanco
calico
cambric
cat gut
chintz
corduroy
ferret
flannel
fustian
India rommel
kersey
lawn
linen
mode
muslin
nankeen
oznabrig
ratteen
sarcenet
satin
shallon
shorn jane
tammy
thickset
ticking

Notions
binding
bobbins
buckles
buttons
utton molds
edging
elastic
fig blue
flax to spin
hair ribbon
hat pins
knee buckles
knitting needles
lace
lasting
needles
patterns
pins
silk, skein

shoe binding
soles & heels
tape
thimbles
thread
twist

Clothes
aprons
boots
cravat
gloves
handkerchief
hats
hose, cotton
hose, handmade
hose, wool
jaycoat
mitts, worsted
shawl
shoes

shoes, best
shoes, homemade
silk bandana
slippers
stockings, cotton
trousers
waistcoat
woolen garters

Miscellaneous
Anderson pills
Bible
cards, pack
fan
fur
ink powder
paper
pipes
pocket book
primer
rabbit skins

sealing was
snake root
snuff
spectacles
spelling book
tobacco, leaf
tobacco, roll

Appendix 2
Goods Sold to Edward Dewolf

From Daybook, 1793-94	Additional goods Ledger 1: 1773-1786	freighting goods
apples (b)		geese
barrels (m)	apple trees	gelding
boards (m)	ash	hats
butchering (m)	ax (blacksmith work)	honey
butter (f)	baize	house frame
cheese (f)	barn frame and boards	keeping livestock
clapboard (m)	barrel staves	lambs
cod (m)	baskets	mitts
corn (m)	beans	moose meat
cow (b)	beaver	mowing
eggs (f)	beef	oxen
feathers (f)	binding	parsnips
flannel (f)	blacksmith work	patridges
flax (m)	board & diet	pease
flour (m)	boots, mending	planks
full cloth (f)	bran	poles
furs (m)	breeches	rafting
gaspereaux (m)	bricks	rakes
hay (m)	bridle	ribbon
hog (m)	bucket	salt
hoops (m)	buckles	sashes
horse (m)	bulls	schooling
labour (b)	button molds	sledding
leather (m)	cabbages	soap
linen (f)	calf	spinning
maple sugar (m)	candles	stockings
mare (m)	carriage of goods	stone
mutton (m)	cart construction	tailoring
oats (m)	cart rental	thread
pork (m)	cattle	threshing
potatoes (m)	cellar, digging	ticking
rabbit (m)	chairs	tongs (blacksmith work)
raspberries (f)	cherries	turnips
salmon (m)	chickens	vinegar
shad (m)	cider	washing
sheep (m)	cider mill	weaving
sheep skins (m)	cloth	wool
shingles (m)	coating	
skins (m)	colt	
steer (b)	cordwood	
swine (b)	cucumbers	
veal (m)	dyke land	(b) both
wheat (m)	eels	(f) female
wheelbarrow (m)	ferrier work	(m) male

The Dark Side of Planter Life:
Reported Cases of Domestic Violence

Judith A. Norton
Truro, N.S.

"... on the ninth day of February Captain Edward Yorke of Falmouth in the County aforesaid, violently assaulted, beat and bruised him, this deponent [Nehemiah Wood] by kicking him on the hip, by throwing a frozen cow-dung at him which hit him on his side, and then by violently pushing him against a Fence; and at last pushed this deponent down a hill whereby he fell and was much hurt, and threatened that he would send said Deponent to hell. Nehemiah Wood. 9 February 1769."[1]

A survey of eighteenth and early nineteenth-century court records in the Planter townships of Nova Scotia and New Brunswick indicates that violence was not an uncommon factor in everyday life. Unfortunately, the surviving evidence regarding violence is found almost exclusively in the legal records; therefore, only those assault cases in which charges were laid can be identified. There are two ways of looking at this evidence. Either these are the exceptions that prove the rule of the peaceable Planter kingdom, or they are the tip of the iceberg, giving us a glimpse of the everyday lives of some of the Planters.

In the early records of most Nova Scotia counties, charges of assault are rare, and domestic assault almost nonexistent. Kings County, Nova Scotia, is the exception; almost 80 percent of the cases of assault on record occurred there. This cannot, however, be offered as evidence of the unusually violent personalities of the Kings County Planters, or of their extremely litigious natures, but results from the fact that Kings County is the only Planter county for which a relatively full set of Court of General Sessions records exist.[2]

Three levels of courts functioned in Nova Scotia in the eighteenth century: the Supreme Court, the Court of Common Pleas and the Court of General Sessions. The Supreme Court, which became a provincial circuit court in 1774, dealt with charges such as treason, which were laid by the Crown, and with matters referred to it by the lower courts. The Court of Common Pleas was a county court and, judging by the records which have survived, dealt primarily with charges of unpaid debts. The Court of General Sessions, which met quarterly in each county, was the basic unit of justice as well as the vehicle of county administration. It was comprised of magistrates and justices of the peace appointed by the provincial government, and grand and petit juries selected

---

1   Chipman Collection, Public Archives of Nova Scotia [PANS], MG 1, Vol. 181, #333-4.

2   These exist as part of the *Chipman Collection*, the collected papers of Handley Chipman, Kings County justice of the peace, PANS, MG 1, Vol. 181-85.

from residents who held freehold property. This court was responsible for the appointment of township officers, the support of the poor and the maintenance of such services as highways, bridges and jails. It was also the court at which charges such as assault, theft, blasphemy and Sabbath breaking were laid by individuals against other individuals.[3]

Generally, charges of assault do not seem to have been taken very seriously by the justice system in Planter Nova Scotia, and violence against women and servants was deemed to be of very little consequence. Many assault charges were dropped before they came to trial; others were dealt with summarily by the local justices of the peace — bonds of recognizance were required or a small fine imposed.

Reported cases of violence in Planter Nova Scotia fall into three general categories: 1) Family violence, between spouses or the abuse of a child by a parent, including cases of neglect or abandonment; 2) Abuse of a slave or indentured servant; 3) Assault charges laid as a result of confrontations between neighbours or extended family members (not living in the same household). The majority of assault charges fall into this last category.

Research for this paper identified 45 incidents of abuse or assault occurring in Planter townships during the first 50 years of settlement. While 20 of the victims were female, only five of the accused assailants were female. Four victims were servants or slaves; four were children; two were Natives; and three were constables in the course of their official duties. It is difficult to get any kind of comprehensive picture because the evidence is incomplete — almost certainly only a small percentage of cases were reported; and for those that do appear in the court records, 17 out of 45 were either discharged or the records are incomplete to the point that we do not know the verdict or sentence. Of the cases that were prosecuted and the assailant found guilty, only one person was retained in custody. Fourteen were fined amounts ranging from one shilling to 40 shillings; the average fine was 19 shillings.[4] To put these fines in perspective, in Horton Township in 1776 three gallons of rum could be purchased for one pound.

Aside from the legal aspect, a survey of the evidence presented provides information about the darker side of life within a Planter household. The available court records include three instances where a woman charged her husband with abuse. Two of those cases involve Robert and Lurana Roberts of Cornwallis Township. In 1772 Lurana came before the county magistrate and made oath that she was afraid that Robert Roberts, her husband, would beat,

---

3   J. Murray Beck, *The Government of Nova Scotia* (Toronto, 1957), 65-67.

4   The exception to this occurred in Horton Township in 1763 when John Arnold Hammond was convicted of assaulting a Mi'kmaq, Bartholemew Noucot. Arnold was fined three pounds, which amount was paid to Noucot.

wound, main or kill her as he had already threatened and "snapt his gun at her ...." He was arrested and ordered to appear before the Court of Quarter Sessions, but she went before the court and dropped the charges.[5] Two years later she charged him again. She and her son by a previous marriage, Jabez Eagells, both gave evidence that Roberts had beaten her, threatened her life and swore she should not live to see the light of another day. By the time this case came to trial she had left Roberts and was living with her son. Roberts confessed his guilt and the judge ordered that he provide bondsmen as sureties for his good behaviour. There is no record of any fine or punishment.[6]

The other instance of the abuse of a woman by her husband was brought before John Chipman, one of the justices of the peace for Cornwallis Township, in April 1773. The record reads that Mary Dewey appeared before Chipman and swore that her husband Elijah Dewey (who was a blacksmith) "has at sundry times beat, bruised and evil entreated her the said complainant, and she ... saith that her husband has a number of times threatened to kill her ... and one day within six weeks past the said Elijah Dewey did in a vile manner strike her ... with a stick and bruised and hurt her in such a manner that she ... saith she thought she should have been killed by him ... and ... being very weak and unable to keep out of the way of her said husband, she is afraid he ... will actually kill her or do her some bodily hurt, and therefore she prays that her said husband may be bound to keep the peace." A warrant was served for Dewey's arrest. He was brought before the justice and required to provide sureties to be bound with him for recognizance. He refused to do so and was placed in custody in the jail on 16 April 1773. On 20 April William Bishop and Reuben Cone agreed to act as sureties. The recognizance was discharged in court and Dewey was released.[7] There is no further record of any problem. However, the Cornwallis Township Book provides the information that six days later, on 26 April 1773, Mary Dewey died.[8] No cause of death is given; there was no inquest, no record of any inquiry into her death. Elijah remarried and two years later he and his second wife and Robben Robbens of Cornwallis were convicted of fighting and "breaking the peace."[9]

There are no cases where parents in Planter Nova Scotia were charged with abusing their own children. Apart from cases involving indentured servants, which will be addressed later, there are only three cases in the court records in which the victim of violence was a child. Alice Crossman beat Elizabeth Irish, a

5   Chipman Collection, Vol. 182, #95.

6   Chipman Collection, Vol. 182, #290.

7   Chipman Collection, Vol. 182, #115.

8   Cornwallis Township Book, PANS, MG 4, Vol. 18, D.

9   Chipman Collection, Vol. 182, #279.

girl of about ten years of age, with a large stick. The justices found Mrs. Crossman guilty and sentenced her to pay the court costs. In late May 1770 Ebenezer Vernom, cooper, "did beat and abuse Capt. Caleb Wheaton's son Joseph, a boy of about 14 years, and did heave him into the river, whereby he was wet all over and was in danger of drowning." The charges were dropped.

The third instance was actually an inquest into the death of a newborn baby. The mother, a young, unmarried woman, claimed that the child had been stillborn. The report of the coroner's inquest describes marks which had been seen on the body, "... the body is broke in the skin from the breast to the grind, also on one arm together with one to two blisters on it like a scald," indicating that the baby was either deformed or had been mutilated. The jury ruled that "the child was lost for want of means." No further explanation was given and no charges were laid.[10]

Cases of desertion were taken more seriously by the early Nova Scotia courts, because women and children who were abandoned might become chargeable to the overseers of the poor of the township. In these cases the overseers of the poor were given authority to confiscate all the "goods and chattels" belonging to the man so that they could provide for the woman and children.[11] Although a widow was often allowed to manage her late husband's estate, there is no record of that privilege being granted to a woman whose husband had deserted her.

Women were particularly vulnerable in early Nova Scotia. In the 45 recorded incidents of abuse or assault identified in the early court records, 20 of the victims and five of the assailants were females. It is interesting that in nine of these cases, the women were not assaulted by family members, employers or fellow servants, but by unrelated individuals in the community. In June 1778 Mary Dugan of Falmouth appeared before the Justice of the Peace, Robert Walker, to lay a complaint against Henry Lyons, also of Falmouth.[12] Mary Dugan testified that Lyons had come to her dwelling house with an axe and demanded that she leave the house. She refused to do so without an order from the court. "And on her refusal to quit the house ... he raised his hand with the axe over her head and threatened to cleave her down, if she did not hold her tongue, and using many other threatening expressions, put her in bodily fear of her life." She went on to tell the court that six days later he returned and tore the house down. Lyons was evidently within his rights by the standards of the time

---

10   Hants County Court of Quarter Sessions Records 1787-1812, 29 October 1793, PANS, RG 34-313, P, Vol. 1.

11   Kings County Court of General Sessions, PANS, RG 34-316, P, Vol. 5, 7 June 1781.

12   The relationship here is uncertain. Henry Lyons was probably Mary Dugan's landlord but there is no direct evidence.

because the bond of recognizance under which he was bound to appear before the court was discharged and no further penalty was incurred.[13]

Servants were held in even less regard than women by the Nova Scotia courts. An indentured servant was considered the property of his or her master until the term of the indenture had elapsed and the courts were very slow to break that legal agreement. "Thomas Little a servant boy of Between fourteen and fifteen years old belonging to Abel Mitchener of Falmouth, complains that on Saturday the 7th day of September instant, the said Abel Mitchener his master did with an Ox Goad, cruelly beat, wound, bruise, and abuse him, the said Thomas Little, near the barn of the said Abel Mitchener in Falmouth, and prays for Justice, etc." Abel Mitchener had been the captain of a slave ship engaged in the triangular trade out of Newport, Rhode Island, prior to coming to Nova Scotia as a Planter. His name comes up several times in Kings County assault charges. The two justices of the peace for Kings County, Lebbeus Harris and Nathan Dewolf, heard the complaint, investigated the circumstances and ruled that "Thomas Little hath just cause of complaint, and that the same is well grounded, we do therefore ... Discharge the said Thomas Little from his said apprenticeship ...." Mitchener appealed the ruling to the next Court of Quarter Sessions which overturned the magistrates' decision and reordered the apprentice to his service.[14]

There are two recorded cases in which slaves were the victims of violence. In one, in which the slave owner was acquitted of murder, the evidence or circumstances are not available.[15] In the other case, a hired servant, named George Burrows, was accused of seducing Dr. Samuel Willoughby's slave and later beating her "with an iron flesh fork." Both the doctor and his wife gave evidence concerning the man's behaviour while in their employ, including his theft of wine from their cellar, his abuse of the black woman, and his threats against themselves when apprehended. In return, Burrows charged that his employer had had "criminal connection with the black woman before he himself had." Having heard the evidence, the jury found Burrows not guilty.[16]

It is worth noting that two of the heaviest sentences for assault were imposed on two Kings County grantees who assaulted a Mi'kmaq named Bartholomew Noucot. The two charges were heard the same day in August 1763, but it is unclear exactly what the context of the assaults was. Jeheil Dewolf of Horton and John Arnold Hammond of Cornwallis were charged with grievously

---

13   Chipman Collection, Vol. 183, #172-73.

14   Chipman Collection, Vol. 182, #53.

15   Hants County Court of Quarter Sessions Records, PANS, RG 34-313, P, Vol. 1.

16   PANS, MG 100, Vol. 115, #13.

assaulting and beating Noucot. Dewolf pleaded guilty and was fined 40 shillings. Hammond admitted that he had hit Noucot with a stick, but claimed that he had not hurt the man. He believed that Noucot's injuries had been inflicted by some "horses [which] ran over him said Indian as he lay drunk in a foot path where the horses passed."[17] Arnold was found guilty and fined three pounds. Both fines were ordered to be paid directly to Bartholomew Noucot, "As recompense for his suffering," and it was noted that "the Indians were well satisfied and promised that they would do everything in their power to maintain a good understanding between them and us."[18]

A comparison of lists of the accused assailants and victims with the Poll Tax lists tells very little about the economic status of those involved in violence. They span the spectrum from dependents and labourers to merchants and prosperous farmers. One case involved two of the most prosperous men in Cornwallis Township, Samuel Starr and John Chipman. Samuel Starr was a merchant and tavern keeper in Cornwallis. John Chipman, son of Handley Chipman, was a merchant and one of the justices of the peace for Kings County. They both may be found in the highest tax bracket in the poll tax lists. One day in the summer of 1772 they met on the road. Starr testified that he was going home with a pail of water when he met Chipman who asked him to stop. He stopped and put down his pail. Chipman then said, "You have accused me with taking a false oath, and have kill'd my Turkeys." Starr said that he had not done either, on which John Chipman "struck Starr with his fist several times and knocked him down three times and hurt him very much ...." Chipman pleaded guilty and apologised. He was fined 40 shillings plus court costs.[19]

Some of the records of violent encounters between the Planters, such as the one just described, have an almost slapstick quality to them, particularly those in which the abuse consisted of name calling, using such epithets as "damned old foolish puppy,"[20] or "saucy old lying hag."[21] There are also very serious incidents of assault in which people's lives were threatened. Specific causes of domestic violence are difficult to assign given the evidence available. Isolation from family and established structures in New England, might have played a role in the early years, but there were few reported cases of assault during those years. Poverty and boredom were undoubtedly factors in some cases. Alcohol was named as a factor in the evidence or in the judge's decision in six cases.

17 Chipman Collection, Vol. 181, #68-71.

18 Kings County Court of General Sessions, PANS, RG 34-316, P, Vol. 1, 17 Aug. 1763.

19 Chipman Collection, Vol. 182, #21.

20 Chipman Collection, Vol. 183, #78.

21 Chipman Collection, Vol. 182, #62.

The one firm cause that can be identified is a misplaced excess of religious zeal. There are two well-documented cases which have an established religious root: the ritualistic rape of Sarah Hammond and Sarah Garrison by Archelaus Hammond and John Lunt in Gagetown in 1793, and Amos Babcock's murder of his sister in Shediac in 1805. These cases are fairly well known and are documented in D.G. Bell's *Newlight Baptist Journals of James Manning and James Innis.*[22] The New Light Movement, in its extreme form, was characterized by certain excesses. Theologically known as antinomianism—the belief that once a person's soul is saved they can do no wrong because, being led in all things by the Spirit, their thoughts and actions are dictated by that Spirit—these excesses usually took the form of rather lax sexual standards.

Late in 1792 a group of families separated from the Sheffield Newlight Church and formed themselves into a society, calling themselves "Hammondites" after one of their leaders, Archelaus Hammond. One of their members, John Lunt, later described by the local sheriff as "an abandonate profligate character, a sort of necromanser and fortune teller," convinced the others that he was a true prophet of God and under the direct guidance of the Holy Spirit. Prominent among his teachings was that "once converted, it was no sin for lambs of God to play all together." The records are sketchy, but it seems that this translated into some sort of ritual sexual activity in the context of church meetings. The Sheriff, Walter Bates, whose testimony may not be altogether reliable, wrote later that, "At one of his popular meetings held late of night, a young lady having more modesty, or not suffitiently converted as to comply with his spirit; one of his pure converts by the name of [Archelaus] Hammon attempted to assist him in his design." Eventually two young women, Hammond's daughter, Sarah Hammond who was 26 years of age, and Sarah Garrison who was 17, went to the authorities and charged Lunt with rape. Hammond was charged with assisting in the rape of his own daughter. The trials were held, many witnesses presented evidence, and the two men were acquitted, probably due to the uncertainty of whether consent had been given.[23]

The other incident of domestic violence which can be directly related to an excess of religious zeal was the murder of Mercy Hall in the Shediac area on 14 February 1805. A local revival was underway and two teenaged girls, Sarah Cornwall and Mary Babcock, began prophesying in an apocalyptic fashion. On the night in question there were 13 residents in the Babcock household: Amos Babcock, his wife and nine children, his brother Jonathan and their sister Mercy. Amos decided, late in the evening, that the end of the world was at hand, the

22   D.G. Bell, ed., *Newlight Baptist Journals of James Manning and James Innis* (Hantsport, N.S., 1984), 80-83, 183-186, 331-54.

23   H.T. Hazen Papers, New Brunswick Museum, Shelf 66, F3.

stars were falling, and that he was the Angel Gabriel. He did not want his sister, who was a sinner, to be in his household at the time of judgement so he ordered her to remove all her clothes and kneel on the floor. He then proceeded to disembowel her in front of his assembled family and buried her body in a snowbank. Brother Jonathan escaped at that point and alerted the neighbours. Amos Babcock was arrested and found guilty of murder. In June 1805 he was hanged at Dorchester.[24]

These two incidents are isolated and extreme; however, it would be reasonable to consider them to be representative of a whole body of unreported cases of physical "discipline" and emotional abuse which was perpetrated in the name of religion.

Based upon the limited amount of evidence that is available, we may conclude that the New England Planters accepted a certain amount of violence as a natural part of their relationships with each other in families and communities. It is, however, impossible to estimate how much domestic violence actually occurred in Planter society. Even if the reported cases are considered to be the proverbial "tip of the iceberg," it may be a fairly small iceberg. There was no given year for which there are records of more than six charges of assault being laid in all of the three categories — spousal, abuse of a servant, or assault of a neighbour or extended family member. Heads of households (at least male heads of households — none of the females accused of assault were heads) were considered to have a certain jurisdiction over persons residing within their households and, while charges could be, and were, laid, the penalties were not severe enough to serve as an effective deterrent.

24 New Brunswick Museum, F55

Capitalists, Merchants and Manufacturers in Early Nova Scotia, 1769-1791: The Tangled Affairs of John Avery, James Creighton, John Albro and Joseph Fairbanks

Julian Gwyn
Professor of History
University of Ottawa

If credit is the sinew of commerce and industry, debt is its necessary companion. In business in the eighteenth century, as today, failure was far more common than success. Yet economists ignore bankruptcy and insolvency, while bulky business management textbooks dismiss the subject in a couple of paragraphs. By contrast lawyers write thick books on the subject. Treatment by historians is, at best, uneven. They usually adopt a creditor-debtor adversarial model, and forget that creditors are always also debtors, while debtors frequently act as creditors.

To find evidence for this contention, we need look no further than the courts where civil actions took place. In early Nova Scotia, these include the two principal institutions, namely the Inferior Court of Common Pleas and the Supreme Court. They also included the Court of Chancery, whose jurisdiction covered the entire colony of Nova Scotia, and which acted as the only court where mortgages could be foreclosed, and where complainants turned for relief through injunctions either to stop procedures simultaneously being carried on in other courts or to suspend and reverse their judgments. Some three-quarters of the cases in Chancery were for foreclosure, while 90 percent of the cases before county courts dealt with debt. For historians interested in the social and economic position of women in early Nova Scotia, there is no better source than the thousands of civil actions in which women found themselves as litigants.[1]

The story to be told here is, perhaps regrettably, not about such women, but about four men, three from New England and one from Old England. Although none is a household name, each deserves our attention if we are to understand some of the essential elements of New England Planters' economic world in the era of the American Revolution. Together, the four will serve as quite sufficient props to illustrate the aggressive capitalist world which they inhabited, and the folly of so much economic activity.

The first of these characters is John Avery.[2] Born in Lebanon, Connecticut, he traded out of Windsor in the late 1760s, and then in the 1770s resided in

1 "Female Litigants in the Civil Courts of Nova Scotia, 1749-1783," paper presented to the 10th Atlantic Canada Studies Conference, Fredericton, N.B., May 1994.

2 Avery on 6 June 1757, sold, for NE£66, a lot amounting to 116 acres in Lebannon, Connecticut, to his brother, Robert. Connecticut State Library, 974.62

Halifax as a merchant. At first a partner of Isaac Deschamps, he was part of the Fundy-Minas Basin distribution network, selling a variety of goods, like tea, sugar, rum, molasses, salt, pork, flour, tobacco, candles, ironware, blankets and soap, all brought from Halifax. In return, he purchased sawn lumber and other wood products, as well as livestock and crop surpluses, to fill government or commercial contracts in Halifax.

Avery was a litigious fellow, who pursued his debtors with vigour; there are records of 36 suits brought by him and six against him between 1767 and 1779, an average of four a year. A man of strongly held opinions, he was given to direct action. In one case he was sued for £200 for defamation by the Windsor trader, Richard Heyzan, whom Avery had accused of keeping a half-bushel measure which was far too large, calling him, in the hearing of "diverse of his Majesty's subjects, a knave, rascal and liar."[3] In a second action for defamation, he was sued for £60 damages by the Windsor blacksmith, John Felmore, who claimed that Avery drove him out of his place of work by taking up "a bar of steel" and pursuing him down the street threatening that, "if he did not hold his impertenence he would knock him down."[4] In 1783 he was sued for £10,000 by the Solicitor General, Richard Gibbons, Jr., for defamation for having cried out at a meeting of freeholders in the court house gathered to elect an MLA for Halifax. His words, on that occasion, were reputed to have been: "Who will vote for him but Hell? ... He is a damned rascal, a damned scoundrel, a diabolical villain ... and shall never be in the House. He shall never be elected!"[5] Gibbons was defeated in his election bid and believed he had been slandered. The jury disagreed, and, on the balance of probabilities, always the measure in civil suits, acquitted Avery.

49da Main Vault. He was a lieutenant in the Company of Militia, Windsor Township, 21 May 1774. Public Archives of Nova Scotia [hereafter PANS], RG1, Vol. 168, 358. On 10 August 1776 Avery received a crown grant of land in the Parsboro-Partridge Island area, with Jacob Bacon and John Lockhart. Mount Allison University Archives, Webster MS Collection 7001/249. On 13 October 1777, Thomas Ratchford, of Parrsboro, contracted to supply Avery with 2,000 bushels of wheat. PANS, Chipman Papers MG 1/183, #73.

3   Heyzan withdrew the suit, when arbitrators were appointed to decide the matter. RG 39, Series C, Box 9, *Heyzen v. Avery*, Supreme Court, writ of summons, 2 August 1771.

4   Suit withdrawn by the plaintiff. RG 39, Series C, *Felmore v. Avery*, Supreme Court, writ of summons, 20 April 1778.

5   RG 39, Series C, Box 25, *Gibbons v. Avery*, Supreme Court, writ of summons 20 March 1783. For details on Gibbons, see Barry Cahill, "Richard Gibbons," 'Review' of the Administration of Law in Nova Scotia, 1774," *UNB Law Journal*, Vol. 37 (1988).

How had Avery, a New England Planter from Connecticut, and resident of Horton Township, graduated so rapidly from the attentions of the traders and craftsmen of Windsor to the heart of provincial authority in Halifax? In August 1780, while holding a small contract to supply fresh beef to the Royal Navy, then in the midst of the American War of Independence, Avery brought a case in the Court of Chancery against James Creighton, a Halifax merchant from Glastonbury in Somerset,[6] and the second of our characters. Avery brought the case out of some desperation. In May 1780 he had purchased six oxen, which were then delivered to the slaughter house of a Halifax butcher. At the same time, an ox owned by Creighton strayed from his farm at Birch Cove, overlooking Bedford Basin. A week later Creighton, accompanied by his wife, Elizabeth, David Doliff, a yeoman of Halifax (who owned one-half of the yoke of oxen, of which the missing ox was part), and two other witnesses went to the tanhouse of John Albro, another New England Planter. Creighton claimed that one of the oxhides in Albro's tan yard was that of the missing ox.[7]

After taking a week to consider his tactics, Creighton went to a printer, and published a handbill offering a reward of 20 guineas ($84) to be paid anyone who would supply information about the stray.[8] Suspecting Avery, Creighton and his friends began to put it about through the town that Avery had stolen the ox. To give concrete shape to his belief, Creighton brought an action in the Supreme Court against the naval contractor, claiming damages of H£60 ($240), including the ox, on which he placed the outrageous over-value of H£40 ($160).[9]

Before the judge and jury, Creighton and his witnesses insisted that the hide, seen in the tannery, came from the carcass of his ox. Other witnesses, brought by Avery, who protested his innocence, claimed it was off an ox which Avery had bought from Samuel Bent, a New England Planter from Granville Township. Despite the conflicting evidence, the jury found for Creighton, and Avery was promptly taken by the provost marshall and committed to jail. To regain his liberty, Avery paid over to the court officials H£33.16.10. ($135), which included H£22 ($88) for the ox, by the jury's evaluation.

---

6   James Creighton, Esq. died April 20, 1813 aged 80, *Acadian Recorder*, 24 April 1813. He married Elizabeth Woodin on 4 June 1758 and by her fathered many children: John (1759, predeceased his father in Philadelphia), Alexander (1760-1824), James (1762-1828), Elizabeth (1767), William (1769-1814), Mary (1770-1819), Anne (1772-1837), Lucy Charlotte (1780-1822). There were three other children, born in 1774, 1775 and 1777 but each died shortly after birth. An elder brother, John Creighton served as MHA for Lunenburg County from 1770 to 1775.

7   RG 36a, 3 June 1780, *Avery v. Creighton*, Court of Chancery.

8   13 June 1780.

9   RG 39, Series C, Box 21; *Creighton v. Avery*, Supreme Court; writ of summons 17 June 1780.

Shortly afterwards, the carcass of an ox was discovered "in the woods near" Creighton's farm. Here was proof of Avery's innocence, but the case was closed. To recover his funds and clear his name, Avery, through his attorney, turned to the Court of Chancery for relief. Here Chancery was being used as an unofficial court of appeal, there being no right of appeal from verdicts of the Supreme Court. It transpired in the testimony which was gathered in the new case — all such evidence had to be in writing in the Court of Chancery — that this ox, now becoming newsworthy, had not strayed at all. The evidence brought before Chancery showed conclusively that it had been stolen, slaughtered and partially devoured by eleven starving deserters from the Loyal Nova Scotia Volunteers, then garrisoning Fort Sackville. Three of the deserters provided the necessary testimony.

One might have expected Creighton to withdraw gracefully. Instead, he instructed his attorney to argue that, since the case had been decided in the Supreme Court, the masters of Chancery could not now hear it. As the contrary precedent had long before been set, the court quickly brushed this objection aside. This was the beginning of a series of delaying tactics by Creighton, knowing his case was meagre, with the probable intention of forcing his opponent to abandon the case, in the face of what he believed was Avery's own acute financial and commercial embarrassment. Perhaps it was simply a matter of inexperience of the courts, for Creighton had rarely before been involved with suits, as far as is known from the surviving records, although his brother, John, was a litigious merchant, who aggressively pursued his debtors.

Meanwhile, the case before the Court of Chancery drew in a new set of witnesses, through whose hands the ox had, or might have, passed. These included three Horton men, and two Annapolis men, as well as Samuel Bent of Granville.[10] At length, in May 1781, the interrogations took place first at the inn of Joseph Pierce and James Phillis at Horton, and a week later at the house of Mary Harris in Annapolis Royal. Later in July, Thomas Cochran, Esq. of Halifax also provided testimony about the remains of the carcass found near Fort Sackville.

Not very surprisingly, the court found for Avery, and ordered Creighton to pay his costs, which, by March 1782, amounted to H£133.10.1 ($536).[11] Creighton refused, and got his attorney on various specious grounds to ask the court to set aside the judgment. There followed a series of petitions and counter-petitions by Avery and Creighton, the one trying to bring the case to a final end, the other attempting to put off the day of reckoning as long as possible. At one point they agreed to select two Halifax merchants and formidable figures in public life — Hon. Richard Bulkeley and William Nesbitt,

10   RG 36a, Case 50, Doc. 21.

11   14 March 1782, RG 36a, Case 50, Doc. 56.

Esq. — one the provincial secretary and the other the attorney general, to arbitrate a settlement; and the court made their decision legally binding. Merchants in dispute frequently had recourse to this method of accommodation. When their finding favoured Avery, Creighton petitioned to have the arbitration overturned. The issue, to the enrichment of the Halifax bar, was no longer the long dead ox, but the procedures used in the arbitration. Again Creighton lost.

Finally on 31 January 1783, Governor John Parr, as Chancellor of Nova Scotia, gave the written judgment of the Court of Chancery, which, after reviewing and reciting all the evidence, confirmed the earlier arbitration. Undeterred, Creighton petitioned to appeal the verdict, which was his right; and the appeal was heard late in March following.[12] Predictably the appeal was promptly dismissed, and Creighton was ordered to pay Avery's costs, now amounting to H£240 ($960). Richard John Uniacke was appointed to receive the money from Creighton, who at first absolutely refused to pay. We can presume he finally capitulated, for there the paper trail vanishes.

How much was $960 worth in 1783? To answer this question, let us look at contemporary wages. Wartime conditions in Nova Scotia had almost doubled the wage rates which had obtained before the outbreak of war. When Creighton was told to pay Avery his costs in 1783, the common labourer received $1.20 a day, and a ship's carpenter, the best paid of the skilled workers, $1.80. At those inflated rates, it would have taken 800 days' work by a common labourer or 530 by a skilled worker to meet the cost!

The red and white ox in question had weighed, according to the estimates made by the witnesses, only between 400 and 430 pounds, at the age of six years.[13] This was not unusually small for the 1770s and 1780s. Mitchell, for instance, has calculated from records of steers supplied during the American war, then raging, that the live weight of a range steer was 550 lbs, with a carcass weight of some 55 to 60 percent of that or 300-330 lbs.[14] The average estimated weight of 22 steers for Horton, Liverpool and Shelburne between 1774 and 1788, was 443 lbs, a little heavier than Creighten's stolen beast.[15]

---

12 27 March 1783.

13 To calculate the weight of an ox, divide the sale price by the current price of beef, which will give the slaughtered weight. Assume that the liveweight is 40-45 percent greater. To be sure, the Halifax newspapers occasionally mentioned cattle of exceptional size which were paraded to the butchers through the streets of Halifax. I have found no such examples before the 1820s.

14 Robert Mitchell, "Agricultural Change and the American Revolution," *Agricultural History*, 47 (1973), 123-24.

15 Details of the sources, in various manuscript business papers in PANS and Dalhousie University archives, are available from the author upon request.

By 1780-82, wartime inflation had doubled the price of fresh beef to 6 pence (about $0.12) a pound, from its pre-war level. A 430-lb carcass might have produced 258 pounds of edible meat, bone and organs. Thus, by the time Creighton had paid his own and Avery's court costs, his unflagging pride might have cost him perhaps $1,920. This was meat and bone at $7.44 a pound, in the dollar value of 1783: a poor bargain even for a man who owned, until it was purchased by the crown, Citadel Hill and much more!

What sort of a man was Creighton that he would have persisted so long, and at such great cost, in a case which, for him, could have only one certain outcome? As neither personal papers nor contemporary comment which might otherwise shed some light to explain his motives has survived, the historian is poorly placed at a distance of more than two hundred years to hazard a guess. A key to unravel his motives may lie in the only surviving letter in Avery's hand. It was written in 1783 at the time of his trial over the alleged defamation of Richard Gibbons. In it he explained to his solicitor, Richard John Uniacke, his unusual relations with Gibbons. "He has spared no pains to persecute and distress me from the year 1779 to this day." It continued:

> That upon Mr. Creighton having lost his ox in the month of May 1780, and a suspicion that it had come into my possession, Mr. [John George] Pyke advised Mr. Creighton to have the matter determined by arbitration, but Mr. Gibbons opposed such an amicable accomodation [sic], and declared to Mr. Creighton that if he did not prosectute [sic] me that he would prosecute him.
>
> That a few days after the Election considering that my inadvertency in expressing myself unguardedly had done myself an injury, I wrote him a letter ... and personally called on him offering to make any reasonable concessions he would require. That Major Monk, his intimate friend, had at my request applied to him for an amicable accomodation [sic]. But he was deaf to every remonstrance, and was determined, if possible, by some quirk to extort from me a sum of money.[16]

Creighton's undoubted tenacity was a much desired character trait in any first generation Halifax settler. Yet at some undefined point the virtue of perseverance might evolve into the vice of perversity. Long before the final piece of paper relating to this most unfortunate case endured the pen, a dispassionate observer would surely have advised James Creighton to cut his accumulating losses. As it was, that damnable ox cost him and those closest to him the loss of

16 RG 39, Series C, Box 25, *Gibbons v. Avery* Supreme Court, writ of summons issued March 1782.

at least two years' peace of mind, and unjustly inflicted on Avery an equally un-settling experience. In terms of the law, it was certainly the highlight of Creighton's life as a litigant, a remarkable piece of folly. Despite this serious set-back, he died in his bed possessed of a substantial estate.[17]

The case of the missing ox lifted Avery from his relative obscurity to some public notoriety. Yet it only partially explains why Gibbons thought him a suitable target for a defamation suit. As a result of the maritime war then raging with the American rebels, Avery had lost several vessels to privateers. Unwisely, in September 1778 he had prepared two sets of papers, one true and one false, for one of his cargoes aboard the sloop *Experiment*, one-eighth owned with John Ritchie, a Scotsman who had arrived in Annapolis Royal from Boston in 1775.[18]

Avery's problems suddenly multiplied when Ritchie, Amos Sheffield and Jonathan Card swore incriminating statements against him in Halifax in February before William Nesbitt. Sheffield claimed that, while in Boston, in June 1778, as a prisoner, his ship having been taken by an American privateer, he heard that the sloop *Elizabeth*, James Littlefield, master and owned by John Avery, had been recovered to the great disappointment of the American captors. Littlefield, who then sailed to the West Indies for a cargo of molasses and returned to Cornwallis Township, claimed that he had no fear of capture as he carried two sets of papers and had cleared the examination of both the king's

17   His will left his 678-acre estate in Dartmouth to his son, James, who also received house and town lots on Duke and Hollis streets, Halifax. He left his son, Alexander, a £750 legacy and the Halifax house he occupied. To his son, William, he left £250 and a small house and lot on Cornwallis Street, Halifax. He left his daughter, Nancy, a £350 legacy and a Halifax house, called Grenadier Fort, which she shared with him. To his two daughters, Mary and Lucy Char-lotte, he left legacies each of £750, and an equal share in a field near the North Barracks on Cornwallis Street. Lucy Charlotte was also given Hill Farm in Dartmouth. She, with her two sisters, shared the silver, linen and furniture. He left each of the six surviving children of his deceased son, John, a legacy of £250. He also left legacies to Richard Woodin, the brother of his late wife and to Ann Proud, Richard's sister, and to Ann Mullins. There were assets enough in 1813, when he died, to distribute all the legacies he had assigned. See PANS, Reel 19400.

18   See Barry M. Moody, "John Ritchie, 1745-1790," *Dictionary of Canadian Biog-raphy*, IV (Toronto, 1979), 674-75. Ritchie had emigrated to Boston in 1770 to join his uncle, Andrew Ritchie, who had been established there as a merchant since 1753. His move to Annapolis Royal in 1775 appears to have been con-nected with commerce. Ritchie was probably incompetent or unlucky, perhaps both. In 1780 he conspired with one Christopher Prince to purchase for H£20 at public auction a 5,500-acre holding on the Annapolis Basin, formerly the property of Col. Jonathan Hoar, another insolvent intestate. See RG 36a, Case 63. Ritchie likewise died intestate and insolvent, leaving a defenceless widow and several small children.

ships and the privateer which stopped him.[19] Ritchie, for his part, claimed that in September 1778 he received a packet from Avery to be put into the hands of William Hanover, master of the sloop *Experiment*, then at Annapolis Royal. The packet contained papers which Avery claimed were invented solely to mislead should the vessel be taken by an American privateer. The papers included a letter from Avery to Edward Grey, a Boston merchant, which acknowledged an earlier transaction carried out on Avery's behalf by Captain Littlefield, as well as instructions to Hanover, if he was taken prisoner to Boston, to deliver the papers to Grey.[20] Labelling their statements "false and malicious," Avery said he wished only to mislead an enemy vessel which it might encounter. It is certainly true that this was a very common practice by merchants in wartime. According to Avery, Ritchie himself was fully aware of the scheme, supported it and handed the false manifest with instructions to the vessel's master at Annapolis for its voyage to Halifax.

For that alleged offence, Avery had been briefly imprisoned in March 1779. He was soon released, but only after posting bail bonds for H£2,000 ($8,000), a huge sum, with the promise of good behaviour. He also promised he would not engage in illicit trade, and would not leave the province without permission for a period of two years. There matters stood until the July following, when the Halifax Grand Jury found a bill of indictment, which accused Avery of trading with the rebels on four occasions, in May and December 1777 and in June and September 1778.[21]

Avery put down his predicament to the hostility of Richard Gibbons, the solicitor general, arising from "disputes and altercations"[22] between them. As Avery later explained to Uniacke:

> That upon the information given against me in the month of March 1779, Government were soon satisfied of their falsity, and the malevolence of my accusers ... until ... July 1779 when Mr. Gibbons, unknown to the King's Attorney [General] and contrary to his opinion, did prefer a bill before the Grand Jury with such aggravating circumstances, as caused them to find the Bill, which this defendant never could bring to trial to this day.[23]

---

19 RG 1/342, #52, #54. See also deposition by Jonathan Card. RG 1/342, #53.

20 RG 1/342, #55.

21 RG 1/342, #56.

22 RG 1/342, #51.

23 RG 39, Series C, Box 25, *Gibbons v. Avery*, Supreme Court.

As no trial occurred "to the great prejudice of his character," as "his innocence lays concealed," he petitioned Chief Justice Finucane in July 1781 to have the trial take place.[24] As this was fruitless, a year later he petitioned two of the justices, Isaac Deschamps, Esq., his former Windsor partner, and James Brenton, Esq., to ensure that at the next Supreme Court sitting he would be able to respond to the indictment and thereby "repair the injury done to his character." Finally in November 1783, in an act unprecedented in eighteenth-century Halifax, Avery paid for the publication of a letter in the *Nova Scotia Gazette,* which was printed prominently on the first page, together with a remarkable letter he had sent to Ritchie in 1781, in which he outlined his case and bitterly attacked his former commercial correspondent at Annapolis.[25]

For his part, Ritchie replied in a letter, which Avery characterized "as too futile, too full of duplicity, for me to be at the expence of publishing." By turning, in effect, king's evidence, Ritchie escaped any official censure. Rather, he was well rewarded, as he was first made a Justice of the Peace for Annapolis township in 1779, later became a justice of the county's Inferior Court of Common Pleas, and finally was elected to the Nova Scotia Assembly.

Avery's public protests and private petitioning either to dismiss the charge or to be tried on it were unavailing. The damage to his commercial interests, first from his brief imprisonment and then from having to conclude bail bonds, would have been tangible. Such a public act of criticism brought Avery no satisfaction, while it left Ritchie unharmed. No trial ever took place, as far as the surviving court records indicate; and the H£2,000 bond, as a consequence, was never returned to him. Thus the war, with its vastly extended opportunities and equally heightened risks, had proved no boon for Avery.

The peace, characterized by its large influx of Loyalist competitors, much reduced British government spending, and the collapse of commodity prices from their wartime levels brought no recovery to his affairs. Late in 1783, he absorbed a serious loss on an uninsured shipment of salt from Windsor and Cumberland, when a poorly maintained vessel he hired allowed seawater into the hold.[26] In 1785, he acted as a broker for those importing rum from Antigua. When he later refused to acknowledge their ownership of the rum, they gave evidence against him; and he was successfully prosecuted by the crown.[27] The

---

24 RG 1/342, #51.

25 Nova Scotia Gazette, 25 November 1783.

26 RG 39, Series C, Box 27, *Avery v. Andrew McKenzie,* Supreme Court, writ of summons issued 13 November 1783.

27 RG 39, Series C, Box 32, *Gracie v. Avery* and *Rex v. Avery,* Supreme Court writ of summons issued 2 July 1785. See also Box 35 for *Avery v. Gracie* Supreme Court, summons issued 26 July 1784, where the jury awarded Avery only £1.5s but without costs for a debt owed him for the rum transaction.

final blow came the following year, when he was sued by the Halifax merchant, Samuel Ferrand Waddington for a debt of H£274.[28] He was taken into custody by the sheriff, and obtained bail only by borrowing H£400 from Joseph Fairbanks, and as security gave him his personal bond for the penal sum of H£800. When he failed to repay the debt on demand, Fairbanks had him arrested and his household effects attached.[29] The inventory lists two desks, two dressing tables and dressing glasses, a square dining table, two smaller dining tables, a round tea table, a square birch table, six mahogany chairs, six birch chairs, six easy chairs, three feather beds, bedsteads, curtains and quilts, six pairs of sheets, six pairs of blankets, two carpets, a chamber table, a schooner *Mary* worth H£65, a black slave, named Cato, valued at H£30, one cow and two chaldron of coal, and all his china, glass and utensils. It was a sorry ending, which soon brought about his death, after the humiliating poverty of moving, when aged 40, to Chezettcook and trying to make his living as a fisherman.[30]

Not too many tears should be shed for John Avery. Livestock dealers are and were a shrewd lot, with deep pockets and ready cash to attract the hard-pressed, cash-poor grazier, and as full of guile as of rum, in roughly equal proportions. Someone must occasionally have had the better of Avery in such dealings, but perhaps not. If John Avery was wronged by James Creighton, there were probably husbandmen enough in the Annapolis Valley in wartime who felt Avery had got the better of them, and did not rejoice at Creighton's ultimate discomfiture, and perhaps took some satisfaction from Avery's collapse.

The third and fourth characters, in this tangled saga, are John Albro and Joseph Fairbanks. It is the same John Albro, at whose tanhouse Creighton believed he had identified the hide of his missing ox. It is also the same Joseph Fairbanks who reduced John Avery in 1785 to insolvency.

Albro, like Avery, was a New England Planter, but from Rhode Island, who settled in Newport Township, and made his livelihood there as a shoemaker and sometime tanner.[31] In March 1775 he opened a shop in Halifax "at Mr. Samuel

---

28 RG 39, Series C, Box 41, *Waddington v. Avery*, Supreme Court, writ of summons issued 6 January 1785. They had done £600 worth of business.

29 RG 39, Series C, Box 36, *Fairbanks v. Avery*, Supreme Court, writ of summons issued 7 May 1785.

30 See RG 39, Series C, Box 50, *William Taylor v. Avery & Fleming*, Supreme Court, writ of summons issued 19 September 1787. His last suit was brought in November 1789; and is presumed to have died shortly thereafter.

31 In a 1771 Halifax Supreme Court case brought by James Kelly against Samuel Albro and John Albro, Samuel was described as a husbandman of Newport and John as a shoemaker of Cornwallis. RG 39, Series C, Box 8. The case related to a promissory note given Kelly by John Albro in 1770 got £8 8s. to be paid in "merchantable leather or good shoes at the cash price."

Albro's house on the beach."[32] A year later he began to devote himself exclusively to the tanner's trade, at the suggestion and with the financial backing of Joseph Fairbanks, Esq., a well established Halifax capitalist, who, by the 1780s, was best known as a timber merchant, but who dealt also in lime and bricks and other building materials.[33] Fairbanks, born in Sherborn, Massachusetts, in 1718, had served as a lieutenant at the 1745 siege of Louisbourg. He had come to Nova Scotia in 1749, settled in the newly-founded town of Halifax and made his life there. Although Albro later claimed that he had asked Fairbanks for regular articles of partnership to be drawn up between them, they were never drafted. Still, they were accepted as co-partners by those with whom they did business.[34]

---

32 7 March 1775, *Nova Scotia Gazette.*

33 Joseph Fairbanks, 1718-1790 was born 17 September 1718, and died 10 July 1790. He was MHA 1758-59 and 1776-85. He held a number of positions in local government, Captain Lieutenant in the Company of Militia for Halifax County, 27 Sept 1762, RG 1, Vol. 164, #199; and later captain, RG 1, Vol. 164, #229 (section B); JP for Halifax County, 9 Oct 1762, *ibid.*, 203 and on 10 Feb 1772, RG 1, Vol. 168, #144; one of the overseers of the poor in Halifax town, 1762-63, RG 1, Vol. 165, #293; member of the Quorum, Halifax County, 18 March 1774, RG 1, Vol. 168, #353, 354; trustee in matters concerning the repair of the Halifax to Windsor road, RG 1, Vol. 169, #30. Twice married, in 1752 he obtained a divorce a *mensa et thoro*, subsequently married again, Lucy Blagden, and then sought a legislative confirmation. A private member's bill was passed by the Assembly, but rejected by the Council, *Journals of the House of Assembly*, 19 September 1760. A similar bill passed both houses in 1762, but Lieut Governor Belcher refused his consent. See Belcher to Board of Trade, 2 July 1762, CO 217/19. Fairbanks left a will, made on 5 July 1790, by which he left Miss Elizabeth Blagden a house on Windmill Hill, Dartmouth, with 9 acres "all improved land," as well as all his late wife's apparel and jewels, half of all the household furniture and plate and £25 per annum. He left Miss Lydia Prescott, the daughter of Jonathan Prescott, of Chester, a dwelling house and cooper's shop at the south end of Water Street, Halifax, and left Samuel Prescott, Lydia's brother, all his estates in Chester Township. He left Richard Fortnum, his old and faithful servant, £10 for life, and to an old servant, Robert Waite, the dwelling house he then occupied and half the garden for his life. He left additional legacies of £50 each to his nephews, Joseph Fairbanks, son of his brother, Ebenezer, and £50 to Joseph Fairbanks Blagden, but £100 to Rev. Eleazar Fairbanks of Boylston, Massachusetts, £50 to his sister in law, Miss Mary Blagden, £100 to Joseph Prescott, another brother to Lydia. The residue was to go to his nephew Rufus Fairbanks, one of his executors.

34 RG 36a, Case 93, *Fairbanks v. John Albro*, Bill filed 3 April 1789; decree 13 March 1789.

Over the next decade, according to Fairbanks, large sums were annually advanced by him to Albro. When serious difficulties emerged between the partners in 1785, Fairbanks instructed Brittain, his accountant, to prepare a statement to reflect his understanding of their mutual affairs. According to that statement, Fairbanks was owed H£4,108, as Table 1 indicates, of which less than £247 was secured. This sum grew to £4,511, as further interest accumulated, and as Fairbanks inflated his demands. When Fairbanks demanded that this huge sum be secured with his personal bond, Albro refused.

Table 1
Capital Advanced by Fairbanks to Albro, 1776-1786

1776	H£178.	15.	1.	
1777	741.	1.	6.	
1778	952.	4.	4.	
1779	682.	0.	5.	
1780	101.	5.	4.	
1781	92.	13.	11.	
1782	97.	10.	0.	
1783	191.	17.	4.	
1784-5	32.	0.	0.	
1786	81.	2.	0.	[land sold to Albro]
1786	200.	17.	6.	[bond: principal + interest]
1786	46.	0.	0.	[Albro's promissory notes]
Total Capital	3,397.	7.	7.	
Total Interest	783.	6.	2.	@6% 1 Jan 1777-23 May 1783
Grand Total	4,180.	13.	9.	

Immediately Fairbanks brought suit against Albro in the Supreme Court of the County of Halifax for the recovery of his claim. It should be noted that, by 1787, Fairbanks was no stranger to such proceedings, having been involved either as a plaintiff or defendant in 25 actions before the Inferior Court of Common Pleas and 17 actions in the Supreme Court. By contrast, Albro had brought but two small cases before the Supreme Court as plaintiff, while being defendant in four other actions since 1771.

In launching the suit, Fairbanks insisted that bail be set at not less than H£2,000.[35] When the sheriff presented Albro with the writ of summons, Albro refused him entrance, and barred all his windows and doors. Despite repeated shouted demands from the sheriff to open his premises for inventory, Albro

---

35 RG 39, Series C, Box 51, *Fairbanks v. John Albro*, Supreme Court, writ of summons issued 23 May 1788.

resisted. Nevertheless the sheriff put the value of £1,600 on Albro's property. To this appraisal, Fairbanks objected, as was his right, as being far too generous. So the sheriff appointed a new set of appraisers, who, "not being permitted to see ... nor to examine the state of the buildings inside," made their assessment from the outside of Albro's property on Water Street. Knowing the site contained 17 large and small tan pits with tubs, they assigned the much lower appraisal of £1,135.[36]

On 19 June 1788, Alexander Reid was deputed by the sheriff to serve a writ of attachment on Albro, and entered his house at about 6:00 a.m., the front door being left ajar by a maid servant, as he claimed. When he entered, the door was suddenly closed and bolted by two persons, who then, according to his sworn testimony, violently assaulted him. Albro suddenly appeared in the hallway, where the altercation occurred. Reid claimed that he was then doused with a burning liquid and was ejected bodily out of the window into the adjoining yard. He testified further that the substance, which he called *aqua fortis*, had caused him great pain by the liquid entering his mouth and eyes and occasioning "violent inflamations" by which he had been rendered incapable of "getting his livelihood."[37] He later sued Albro for £500 damages and summoned the surgeon, Donald McIntyre, who had attended him.[38] McIntyre had found his right eye totally closed, his mouth much blistered and inflamed and his face and neck almost wholly excoriated. This, he believed, had been caused by the burning liquid. Reid, in a precarious state for several days, took three weeks to begin to recover the use of his eye, and be freed of any danger to his life.

Sworn statements were also collected on 17 July from Elspat Fraser, Albro's illiterate domestic servant, and two of his apprentices in the tannery, Frederick Major[39] and Henry Hentz. Elspat, on the day in question, had entered the bedroom of John Albro and his wife, they still being in bed, in order to get the key to the back door. Mrs. Albro told her to be careful how she opened the door

---

36   29 May 1788. The appraisers were all socially prominent merchants.

37   RG 39, Series C, Box 51 and Box 53; sworn 19 June and 8 July 1788.

38   McIntyre had first come to Halifax as a surgeon with the 43rd Foot Regiment from Boston in 1776. See Allan Everett Marble, *Surgeons, Smallpox and the Poor. A History of Medicine and Social Conditions in Nova Scotia, 1749-1799* (Kingston & Montreal, 1993), 294 n255.

39   Perhaps the son of Venitia Major, who was buried in St. Paul's graveyard 15 October 1768. Marble, *Deaths, Burials, and Probate*, 17. An apprenticeship indenture had been signed on behalf of Major in December 1780, when he was 13, signed on the one hand by the Halifax overseers of the poor and on the others by Messrs Fairbanks and John Albro. Major was to be apprenticed until his 21st birthday (14 September 1788) in the tanner's trade, taught to read, write, cypher and to be instructed in the Protestant preinciples of the Christian religion,

for fear of Mr. Fairbanks' people attempting to rush in, and not to open the door until some of the men servants were present. When Hentz came down she unbolted the door, and looking through the key hole to see if someone was there, the latch was suddenly lifted and the door violently forced open by Reid, thrusting the latch into her breast and wounding her. Hentz ordered Reid to stand off at his peril, but Reid rushed forward and struck Hentz in the face, and forced himself into the house. Hearing a great noise from the kitchen, Major summoned Albro. Afraid to re-open the now bolted door they shoved him out of the kitchen window. They denied that Reid had said anything about a writ of attachment, and the matter of the burning fluid.

Albro's sworn statement, recounting the events of May and June, added a few details.[40] On 23 May he was coming out of his store adjoining his dwelling house when he saw sheriff Mathew Cahill, Esq., and Rufus Fairbanks, Joseph Fairbanks' nephew, in his yard. The sheriff explained that he had come to attach his property. Rufus gave the sheriff a tour. The value was set at £1,600. Albro would not permit his household goods to be attached, especially as he was convinced he would not lose his case with Fairbanks, who, Albro said, had tried to force him to "consent to the prostitution of his own wife," whom Fairbanks had tried to seduce. The sheriff advised him to find a bondsman for £400 to make up the difference. When this was about to be consummated Fairbanks raised his objection to the appraisal, and sent two men to watch Albro's place. They kept Albro's "family in a continual alarm beating and abusing the dogs which" Albro "kept to watch his tan yard." Reid was one such person in Fairbanks' employ who carried with him a stick with a bayonet fixed to it and once pointed it menacingly at Mrs. Albro. Albro also denied throwing any burning liquid at Reid.

When the jury gave their verdict in October 1788, again on the balance of probabilities, they stated that Fairbanks had failed to prove Albro was indebted to him in any form. Nor did they comment on Reid's obvious injury. To Fairbanks' intense dismay, Albro was awarded his legal costs.

Albro now brought a counter suit against Fairbanks, his nephew, the sheriff and the unfortunate Reid for £5,000 in damages, arising from their attachment of his property. The inventory, which earlier he had refused to supply the sheriff, provides rare details of a tanyard. It included 100 chords of bark, 10 barrels of train oil, 50 gallons of vitroil oil, 100 lbs. of lamp black copras and alum, a barrel of 224 lbs of sugar, a sleigh, harness and horse, 500 board feet of lumber, 300 dressed calf hides, 300 hides of tanned sole leather, 188 boot legs, 20 dozen

and to find and provide good and sufficient meat, drink, washing, lodging and apparel, and at the end of it to dismiss him with all his wearing apparel and one new suit of clothes. RG 36a, Cause 93.

40 17 July 1788.

calf skins and 50 ox hides in the lime pits, 10 hides of horse heather, 60 miscellaneous tanned small skins, all of which he valued at £2,000.[41]

Of more importance, Fairbanks, having been thwarted in the Supreme Court, resolved to bring his case before the Court of Chancery, as if it was a court of appeal. In this he acted as many had before him. If equity could not be found in the county courts at the hands of a jury of his peers, or of justices who were his social equals, then he felt it must reside in the professional bench at Chancery, which accepted only written testimony. In April 1789, Fairbanks submitted a lengthy stylized statement to the Chancery Court to recover this debt.

Albro's response, prepared for the court in July 1789, denied that he had agreed to Brittain preparing an account as stated by Fairbanks, and accused Fairbanks of listing in his accounts all sorts of items which had nothing to do with the partnership. Albro claimed to have pressed Fairbanks many times for an accounting, but that Fairbanks regularly, through one excuse or another, delayed. In 1785 Albro had instructed his usual suppliers among the butchers to send him no more hides. This so alarmed Fairbanks, according to Albro, that Fairbanks then went around to the same butchers to assure them that Fairbanks & Albro would continue to receive their hides for tanning. In 1786 Albro offered to dissolve the partnership, taking the "whole of the buildings, utensils and stock in trade of every kind to his own account at the first cost and charge thereof" at the rate of H£100 per annum, to which Fairbanks agreed and had documents drawn up. When Albro viewed them, he saw that they manifestly falsified the purport of their arrangements, and refused to sign them. Albro's goods were thereupon attached. Furthermore, Albro claimed that Fairbanks had sworn a false oath before a Halifax Justice of the Peace, claiming that Albro had decoyed him into one of the buildings, confined him, violently assaulted him and put a pistol to his breast unless he immediately executed a release and discharge of all of Albro's debts to him. This Albro utterly denied. A special jury was impanelled to hear the case and Albro was acquitted by the Supreme Court in Halifax. He was again acquitted, when immediately thereafter Fairbanks brought a bill of indictment against him in the Court of Sessions for the County of Halifax.

Brittain, when interrogated closely by Richard Bulkeley in August 1789, pointed out that in 1779 he was told by Fairbanks to open a separate set of books between himself and Albro, and that, until 1786, he was employed to maintain the books. Fairbanks, he added, kept an account open for Albro "in his own private books." Brittain considered that Fairbanks was the principal capitalist "who advanced the money for the stock and materials to prosecute the business and that Mr. Albro had nothing to contribute but the working part or superintendance." It had been Brittain's idea that one half the money advanced

---

41   RG 39, C, Box 51, *Albro v. Joseph Fairbanks, Rufus Fairbanks, Matthew Cahill, Alexander Reid*, Supreme Court, writ of summons 23 May 1788.

by Fairbanks to set the business going should be considered as so much lent to Albro. In order to wind up the partnership, he had been employed by them to draw up their separate accounts, Fairbanks from his own books of what Albro owed him and Albro likewise from his own books and the company books of what he was owed by Fairbanks. Mr. Sterns was employed to draw the necessary agreements. He believed that the partnership was dissolved long before the settlement.

At length, Albro made a fatal tactical error. After being pressed many times by Fairbanks, he agreed on 15 June 1790 to arbitration of any two of Benjamin Mulberry Holmes, Benjamin Salter and James Strachan. The accounts, prepared by the arbitrators and accepted by the court, afford us a rare insight into the details of a tanning business. Over a 10-year span, the business grossed almost H£1,000 annually, by processing, on average, 669 ox or cow hides, 421 calf hides and 132 sheep skins, purchased from dozens of suppliers. Surviving details are summarized in Tables 2 and 3. It was their finding that indeed Albro was indebted to Fairbanks, but for H£2,686, or less than 60 percent of the H£4,511 claimed by Fairbanks in 1787. The arbitrators allowed Albro to retain possession of all the partnership stock, debts and utensils which were on hand or due. They ruled that Fairbanks was not chargeable with any damages for the lengthy interruptions and stoppage to Albro's business, caused by his litigation.

Table 2

Albro's Tannery, Production and Revenue, 1777-1788

Year	Ox/Cow Hides		Calf		Sheep	Horse	Value		
	Sole	Neats	Skins	Hides	Skins	Hides	H£		
1777*	14	68	63	2	-	-	8	10	8
1778	83	68	156	62	-	-	192	8	6
1779	362	304	365	21	-	-	689	17	8
1780	373	500	653	176	-	-	934	5	9
1781	626	605	356	23	-	-	1,061	7	0
1782	669	679	387	33	-	-	1,301	1	0
1783	699	552	309	14	207	1	1,250	1	11
1784	417	414	196	7	-	-	704	11	4
1785	606	369	371	5	252	6	910	1	1
1786	899	500	541	6	28	-	1,225	17	1
1787	488	389	254	9	12	-	750	18	7
1788**	494	175	349	6	41	-	655	15	4
Totals	6,042	4,626	4,049	308	566	7	9,864	15	1
Average	604	463	405	31	57	-	986	9	0

* part year only; ** to 23 May only.

Table 3

Suppliers of Hides & Skins to Albro's Tannery, 1777-1788

Supplier	Hides			Skins		Value		
	Ox	Cow	Horse	Calf	Sheep	H£		
Samuel Albro	704	349	-	122	-	595	0	0
S. Albro & J. Avery	519	241	-	54		414	0	0
John Avery	84	7	-	1	-	53	6	0
Andrew Bauer	11	-	-	160	-	26	12	0
S.H. Binney	-	-	-	120	-	113	18	6
George Brehm	53	35	-	185	-	73	4	0
Philip Brehm	11	6	-	22	-	11	10	0
Richard Cleary	352	160	-	173	-	292	4	6
John Creighton	95	21	-	1	-	65	8	2
John Cunningham	505	263	-	-	-	498	12	0
John Dean	11	-	-	-	-	6	9	0
John Edwards	-	-	-	168	-	108	14	0
George Glashan	9	2	-	-	-	5	4	6
John Hutchinson	451	124	-	111	-	330	18	0
John Kennedy	9	4	-	-	-	6	19	6
John Kinselagh	34	11	-	-	-	23	0	0
William Martin	4	9	-	-	-	6	14	0
John Ort	-	-	-	32	-	3	10	0
Frederick Ott	13	12	-	286	-	45	10	0
F. Ott & S. Albro	120	67	-	-	-	129	10	0
Piers & Hill	-	-	-	17	12	9	1	3
Edmund Phelan	-	19	12	-	1	20	7	6
John Prince	-	1	-	-	-	8	0	
William Proud	375	184	-	220	-	373	15	0
Robert Robertson	23	-	-	-	-	13	16	0
James Ryley	90	28	-	570	47	150	18	6
John Sedgwick	152	69	-	62	-	155	1	0
William Thomson	64	33	-	5	-	52	3	0
Michael Tobin	103	54	-	297	-	135	19	6
M. Tobin & Brehm	10	9	-	7	-	12	14	0
John Tyson	155	17	-	-	-	99	0	0
Michael Wallace	4	-	-	-	-	2	8	1
Sundry persons	429	565	5	1,984	1,263	736	12	9
Totals	4,409	2,283	5	4,208	1,322	7,392	10	2
Average	441	228	-	421	132	739	5	0

To consummate the agreement, their attorneys were instructed to prepare the necessary releases to each other as quickly as possible.

This was prevented by Fairbanks' sudden death three days later on 10 July 1790,[42] Albro, nevertheless, was desperate. According to Elizabeth Richards, an illiterate black servant of James Forbes, the Halifax merchant, who lived opposite Albro's dwelling house, toward the beginning of August, for two or three nights, a number of people living in Albro's house had been "employed in removing articles ... supposed to be furniture from out of the house,"[43] This she told William Albert, servant to Rufus Fairbanks, Joseph Fairbanks' nephew, and one of his executors. Richards normally went over frequently "for water and upon other errands." Three or four days later she went again to Albro's house and passed through several rooms, and almost all the furniture, "particulary the window curtains, carpets, chairs and tables," had been removed. At the end of the month, on the advice of his solicitor he petitioned the Chancery for an injunction. Although the injunction was granted, the executors immediately applied to revive the suit in Chancery.[44] They also secured from the Supreme Court a writ of *capias ad respondum* against Albro, asking for and receiving bail set at H£2,000. Unable to carry on his business and unable to raise "so large an amount," Albro was given a month to appear to state why the suit in Chancery should not be revived by Fairbanks' executors.

Before he could submit his reply, he was arrested on a Supreme Court writ *ne exeat regno*, as Rufus Fairbanks suspected he was about to take ship to the United States. This dramatic event happened on Sunday, 10 October, when he stepped out of his house on his way, as he claimed, to divine services at St. Paul's. Albro was, in his own words, "forceably arrested and made prisoner in the public street at the time the bells were ringing for public worship by one William Barry and another person," identifying themselves as constables.[45] He was told to accompany them to the sheriff, James Clarke Esq., where he was informed that he was a prisoner by virtue of a writ issued out of the Supreme Court on the suit of Fairbanks' executors, and that he must remain in custody until he raised H£2,000 in bail. He offered the best bail he could procure, but this the sheriff refused. For four days he was kept a close prisoner in the sheriff's house, before removal to the Halifax common jail. Utterly denying that he intended to leave the province, he petitioned Chancery on 8 November 1790 to issue an injunction.

42 *The Royal Gazette and Nova Scotia Advertiser*, 13 July 1790.

43 On 14 September 1790, she swore this statement, RG 36a, Case 93.

44 13 September 1790.

45 When the sheriff was interrogated by the Court of Chancery, he said that Albro was going to show a kinsman, lately arrived from the States, a horse which he kept on his lot, and that he had mentioned nothing about divine service.

From his miserable confinement, Albro now responded to the arbitrators' award. He argued that it ignored the private debt between the parties, even though they were expressly told to take it into account. It ignored the severe damages done his business by the vexatious lawsuits brought against him by Fairbanks. Nor had they adjusted the accounts of the co-partners in the tanning business, as they had been instructed. On the whole, he claimed, they had greatly exceeded their powers, and had made a final award, when their instructions were special and conditional, all of which he argued would induce the court to set aside the award. Such objections, however substantial, were dismissed by the Court of Chancery, when on 13 March 1791 the Chancellor issued his final decree. It confirmed the award made by the arbitrators, together with the sum of H£123 in costs against Albro.

Albro was released from prison, and in the Supreme Court sued the sheriff for H£2,000 damages for imprisoning him for 454 days since October 1790 "without any reasonable cause."[46] When this failed, Albro left the province, with the help of his tenant on a 400-acre Cow Bay tract which he used to supply firewood for his tannery. John Morris, a poor fisherman, carried Albro away from his adopted land "in a boat."[47]

What conclusions can we make from these two inter-connected stories? Julian Hoppitt, in *Risk and Failure in British Business, 1700-1800*,[48] noted correctly that, in most economic activity, failure is much more common than success. Yet historians seldom accord it much space and attention. Commercial failure and personal insolvency are usually neglected by both social and economic historians. For Nova Scotia, only the legal historian, Philip Girard, has brought attention to the matter from the perspective of early nineteenth-century

---

46   RG 39, "Hfx," Box 62, *Albro v. James Clarke*, Supreme Court, writ of summons, 22 March 1791.

47   RG 36a, Cause 127. Bill filed by Frederick Major, 5 August 1798, described Albro "late of Halifax deceased." Major purchased for £71 at public auction the 400-acre tract from Alexander Brymer, Jr. and found John Morris on the tract, who recounted to him the story about Albro's lamentable departure from Nova Scotia. Albro and after his death, his heirs, retained the right of redemption to the land, if they could pay off Albro's debts which had occasioned his loss of ownership. Albro's heirs [his widow, John and Samuel Albro, and Ann (Albro) and John Bennet] convinced Morris himself to launch a suit of trespass against Major, when he cut an estimated 400 cords of firewood on the tract. Morris won damages of £50. Major then applied to Chancery for an injunction to have the award set aside, as he had not been allowed to justify his title. Chancery confirmed the award and was taxed £55 in costs.

48   (Cambridge, England, 1987).

law reform,[49] while Lewis Fischer, the shipping historian, mentions insolvency among pre-1776 Halifax merchants.[50]

Hoppitt raised, for England as a whole in the eighteenth century, a number of questions which can be applied to Nova Scotia with equal effect. He called business bankruptcy "an eighteenth-century growth industry."[51] Where business was brisk in rapidly developing economic activity, bankruptcies were common, and bankruptcy rates rose. In regional economic backwaters a tendency to declining rates of bankruptcy were observed. Finally, Hoppitt discovered that bankrupts in England before the nineteenth century tended to be younger, less experienced men. As the economy grew and expanded, business involved larger amounts of credit and decisions became more risky, not less. Such risks were compounded as the domestic economy became more integrated with the international economy with its regular trade or business cycles of boom and bust. In wartime the additional costs and risks made failure more probable, as business prospects expanded and became more enticing.

All of these elements were present in the stories which are told here. In the first instance — and this is perhaps the least important element — it was the younger men, Avery and Albro who failed, and the older men, with a dozen or more years more of experience, Creighton and Fairbanks, who survived and profited. Economic success and wealth accumulation are also associated with longevity. Both Avery and Albro died in their late 40s, while Fairbanks died in his 73rd year and Creighton in his 81st.

The second point to be noted is that to be imprisoned for debt, which both Avery and Albro experienced, was utterly ruinous. The debts here were huge sums, insisted upon by the plaintiffs by way of attachment for bail, in view of the excessive damages claimed. In Avery's case, the £2,000 insisted upon by the crown was as absurd as it was catastrophic. In Albro's case, the much reduced second appraisal of his property dashed his early hope of readily borrowing the difference, and left him a prisoner in his own house. His immediate arrest, when he finally ventured out, and the long imprisonment which followed, during which his brother, Samuel, probably supported his family, brought his domestic economy to such a low point that he could not, without borrowing anew, even

49 "Married Women's Property, Chancery Abolition, and Insolvency Law: Law Reform in Nova Scotia 1820-1867," in Philip Girard and Jim Phillips, eds. *Essays in the History of Canadian Law, Vol. III: Nova Scotia* (Toronto, 1990), 80-127; esp. 92-105.

50 Lewis R. Fischer, "Revolution without Independence: The Canadian Colonies, 1749-1775," in Ronald Hoffman, et al, eds. *The Economy of Early America. The Revolutionary Period 1763-1790* (Charlottesville, 1988), 88-125.

51 Hoppitt, 176.

set up as a tanner. Without house, implements or yard he was left almost destitute.

In the economically depressed world of the New England Planters of the late 1760s and early 1770s, John Avery, a capitalist on the make, clawed his way up over the whitening bones of his Horton neighbours, the yeomen, husbandmen, craftsmen and mariners of Cornwallis, Cumberland, Falmouth, Newport and Windsor. Stephen Bentley, Isaac Bigelow, Richard Boyd, Stephen Chase, Jonathan Crane, Robert Crowel, John Davison, Ephraim Deane, Moses Delesdernier, John Felmore, Armetstead Fielden, Josiah King, Caleb Lake, Nathan Longfellow, Andrew McKenzie, Able Michener, Alexander Morrison, James Mosher, Amos Sheffield, Samuel Starr, John Steele, Alexander Stewart, Amos Walley and Peter Wheeler all suffered at least a little, as defendants, at his hands. Prepared to use or evade the law, whenever it suited him, he was perhaps utterly typical of all avaricious men, with a litigious bent, who lived as his contemporaries. The grandson of a Connecticut clergyman, within a decade of coming to Nova Scotia he had reached, through his early modest commercial successes, the outer fringes of social success. He was married in 1772 at St. Paul's, Halifax, the foremost symbol of the Anglican establishment.[52] Within three years, he was an officer of the local Windsor militia. Described initially as a trader, by 1771 he had transformed himself into a merchant, a title he retained until his humiliating decline in the mid-1780s. Yet in so doing, he had made dangerous enemies, even among the socially and politically prominent. No gentleman himself, nevertheless, when snared in a trap of his own making, he complained publicly of Ritchie's ungentlemanly behaviour toward him. If a man as assertive as Avery could not be frightened, he could be broken and cast aside. This, in effect, is what, by exploiting his folly, Gibbons did to him; while Fairbanks merely gave him the *coup de grace*.

Albro, as a shoemaker and occasional tanner of his own leather, started at a much lower level of the social and economic scale, than had Avery, who had inherited land in Connecticut. He made the strategic move to migrate from Newport, with its limited economic horizons, at the very moment Halifax was about to surge, through war induced public spending. By doing this, he was following his brother, who had earlier established himself as a successful Halifax butcher. Plying his trade as a tanner, with Fairbanks' capital, he established a substantial and apparently successful undertaking. Why Fairbanks should have sued him is unclear. If they were partners, in the absence of articles of partnership it would be assumed that theirs were equal shares. Fairbanks' half would have been the capital he injected into the operation, while Albro's skill as

---

52 7 November 1772, Margaret Deily, a spinster.

a tanner and the overall day-to-day management of the tannery accounted for his share. Any profits then would have been split equally. Instead, Fairbanks claimed that the money he advanced was by way of loan to Albro, as if the tanner was the sole proprietor, and therefore the capitalist had a right to interest receivable on the capital advanced. Albro, for his part, stated that, if they were not partners, then he was prepared to refund Fairbanks £100 a year by way of rent for the buildings, "utensils and stock in trade" on the condition that he would retain whatever profits the business had produced. In 1786 this would have meant he owed £1,000, at the very moment when Fairbanks was pressing for the inflated sum of £4,511. When the Supreme Court verdict awarded Fairbanks nothing, and as Albro's offer seemed too paltry, Fairbanks understandably went to the Court of Chancery. Once arbitrators became involved, a world with which Fairbanks was utterly familiar, but about which Albro was wholly inexperienced, an altogether different verdict emerged. To have split the difference the arbitrators would have recommended £2,755 for Fairbanks, so when they hit upon £2,686, they were not far off this mark, although they offered no explanation for their figure. By then Fairbanks believed that Albro had tried to cheat him out of his just share of the financial arrangement they had carried on since 1776, while Albro believed that same of Fairbanks.

If nothing is known about Albro's reputation as an evenhanded man of business, Fairbanks, by contrast, had the reputation as a hard-nosed dealer. The following anecdote was written down in 1789 about him:

> There is a droll story told of F about a bag of nails. The people say he met once a negro man, who had found a bag, in digging under some foundation of an old building. The man, it seems, had not examined it. F, putting his hand upon the bag and finding it solid & weighty, says to Mungo, why this is only a bag of old nails! and paying him a trifle for it, carried the bag home, which, on examination a second time, perceived by his eye what before his fingers had directed him to judge of, but his heart would not consent to declare. For it proved to have been a deposit of Cash.[53]

True or not, the story made the rounds at the very moment when the battle with Albro was raging, while nothing like it every circulated about Albro. If Albro was partly the naive village shoemaker, Fairbanks, by contrast, shows unmistakably the hard face of the capitalist.

Albro's insolvency, perhaps, was thus unavoidable from the moment he first agreed to deal with Fairbanks. His failure, through inexperience, to establish

---

53 MS dated 22 August 1789, MG 1, Box 1911, File 16/17, Charles Bruce Fergus-
    son Fonds. Information kindly given me by Barry Cahill, PANS.

clearly Fairbanks' exact role, whether as his landlord, financial backer or partner, proved a fatal flaw in his arrangements, and shows both his credulity and relative poverty, which Fairbanks, a much richer, more experienced and shrewder man of business, was able to exploit. Albro's economic horizons had broadened by his move to Halifax and by the encouragement given him by Fairbanks. His wealth and standard of living probably rose significantly as a result of this large infusion of capital. Both collapsed in a business scheme, perhaps hatched by John Brittain, Fairbanks' astute book keeper, by which one half of the money advanced by Fairbanks was considered as a loan to Albro. It was the acceptance of this principle, wholly unsupported by any legal document or personal correspondence, first by the arbitrators, and secondly by the Court of Chancery's decree, that directly undid Albro. This allowed almost all his worldly goods to pass into the possession of Rufus Fairbanks, the inheritor of the Fairbanks' fortune, who had done nothing to create a farthing of its value. By contrast, despite Albro's skills and continuous application to his craft, there was an upward limit to his capital. The size of his debt to the Fairbanks' estate, which Chancery determined and which surprised and horrified the tanner, was far greater a sum than Albro could liquidate, and still retain his trade. Hence his plan to escape! His testimony that he was either on his way to divine services, as he said, or to inspect a horse, with a view to its purchase or sale, as reported to the sheriff, cannot be accepted. His credibility had been lost when he obviously lied in the matter of the vitroil thrown at Reid, Fairbank's henchman and the sheriff's agent. Once Chancery issued its verdict, Albro's escape to New England, perhaps to his Rhode Island home which he had left as an adolescent a generation earlier, seemed the only way to avoid insolvency. It was a path many before him had taken. In this way, ill-fated and unfortunate John Albro, now utterly undone, was snared, when Fairbanks was able to reach out, as it were, from the very grave, through the agency of his nephew, Rufus, his residual legatee. It was a strange and cruel world, which had swallowed Avery in 1785, and which then swamped and sank Albro by 1791, while allowing Creighton and Fairbanks both to die rich in their feather beds.

Isaac Backus and the Struggle for Disestablishment in New England[1]

Stanley J. Grenz
Carey Theological College
Vancouver

The demise of the French military presence and the deportation of the Acadians made Nova Scotia attractive to colonists from New England. Yet the potential settlers were largely Congregationalists — whether members of the Standing Order or those who, touched by the Great Awakening, had withdrawn from it. In either case they were reluctant to risk the uncertainties associated with life under an Anglican establishment. Only after the Proclamation of 1759 "guaranteed" liberty of conscience and exemption from religious taxation to dissenters did they come in great numbers.

In relocating to Nova Scotia, the New England Planters were the recipients — at least until the subsequent coming of the United Empire Loyalists — of a religious freedom that the Congregationalists of New England were unwilling to grant to dissenters from the religious establishment their forebears had constructed. Therefore, while the migration of Old Light Congregationalists may have been motivated largely by economic concerns, the New Lights, Separates and Baptists who swelled the ranks of the Planters could anticipate both greater economic opportunity and wider religious freedom in the northern land. The emigrants were leaving behind the ferment that was already threatening the social fabric of Massachusetts and Connecticut, and which would soon erupt into a political and religious revolution.

What was this revolution that was beginning its sweep through New England just as the Planters were relocating to their new homes? This study will focus on a pastor who became the most significant figure in the struggle for religious liberty — Isaac Backus.

The Context: Cracks in the New England Way

From its beginnings, New England was established upon religious concerns. The first English settlers, representatives of the exiled Separatist church of John Robinson, came to Plymouth in 1620 in search of religious freedom. More important for the subsequent shape of the colony was the arrival of non-separating Independents (or Congregationalists) who established Boston in 1630. The situation under the British monarch had led them to lose hope that reform would come to the English Church any time soon. In contrast to England, Massachusetts offered them both freedom from persecution and a land in which they

---

1   The essay is based on Stanley J. Grenz, *Isaac Backus — Puritan and Baptist*, NABPR Dissertation Series #4 (Macon, GA., 1983), 37-81.

could realize their dreams of a Christian society molded by pure, independent churches. They envisioned living in obedience to both magistrate and religious conviction, because the former would enforce only the God-ordained church order. The New World also afforded these Puritans an opportunity to undertake something which would benefit England, even the entire world. They would show that when Congregationalism — the one true religion revealed in the Bible — was patronized by the godly magistrate, it could remold society and bring about the goal of the reformers. In short, these Puritans were establishing a *new* England to serve as a model for the reformation of old England and all of Christendom. The New World, therefore, provided the context for them to establish "a city upon a hill" as a source of light to the hopeful, watching eyes of the world.

The Bay colonists codified their understanding of Congregationalism in the Cambridge Platform (1648). This document asserted that the true church is not national or provincial but congregational; the local assembly of the covenanted people of God is the church. Each local church, however, was to be a silent democracy under the direction of a "speaking aristocracy." Although the people elected elders for the church, once elected, the latter were empowered to govern as they saw fit.

This Congregationalism shaped the Massachusetts approach to church and state. As Puritans, the colonists believed that the magistrate should support true religion. But because independency meant that no church existed except for the local, particular churches, no state church in the strict sense could be established, only independent churches protected by the state. And the colonists set forth rigid boundaries between church and state. A church could excommunicate a religious offender but not inflict corporal punishment, whereas the state was empowered with the latter but not the former. In practice, however, a partnership arose between the two spheres. The colonists limited voting privileges to church members, which served to enhance the civil influence of the clergy.

Despite their best efforts, the colonists found it impossible to maintain their carefully-designed blueprint for the new Christian society. To insure that the church remained pure, the Cambridge Platform stipulated that all candidates for church membership bear witness to a religious experience through which God himself had given them assurance of elect status. This experiential membership requirement, however, lay beyond human power to fulfil. The first generation Puritans assumed not only that God would continually bring the elect into the church, but that his promise to Abraham indicated that most, if not all, children born to the elect would later experience a confirmation of their own elect status. But the expectations of the early Puritans did not materialize. New waves of immigrants could not meet the strict membership requirements, and God did not visit the children of the saints with the religious fervour of their parents.

To resolve this problem, the Puritans compromised the pure church ideal. Following the lead of the ministerial council of Massachusetts and Connecticut which, in 1657, had approved "certain 'half-way' measures," a synod summoned in 1662 by the Massachusetts General Court adopted what came to be known as the "halfway covenant." Those who had been baptized as infants and acknowledged church doctrine but could not give convincing evidence to election were granted a "half-way" membership status, allowing them to bring their children for baptism but not to receive communion or vote in congregational meetings. This solution received widespread, but not universal acceptance in New England. During the next hundred years it remained a source of contention. To enhance the influence of the church over the increasingly unchurched population of the colony, Massachusetts passed a series of laws requiring all residents to attend preaching services, assigning to ministers responsibilities for the entire community, and strengthening the ministerial societies.

In addition to compromising the pure church ideal, the Puritans modified congregational polity. The worsening financial situation of the churches caused by the decline in membership and the poverty of the population as a whole led Massachusetts in 1638 and Connecticut in 1644 to abandon the principle of voluntarism and pass laws taxing all residents for the support of the clergy, lest they be forced to leave their parish duties to support themselves. In 1652, these laws were expanded to include taxation for funding the construction of meeting houses. Then, the Reforming Synod of 1680 made certain alterations in the Cambridge Platform, including the elimination of "plebeian ordination" (i.e., performed by the laity in the absence of church officers) and the softening of the stringent church membership requirements by allowing private pastoral examinations of candidates to replace oral public testimonies.[2]

In 1691, the British king drew up a new charter for Massachusetts which dealt a heavy blow to the Puritan establishment. It extended the franchise, which formerly included only church members, to all property owners, and it granted "liberty of conscience ... in the worship of God to all Christians (except Papists)."[3]

During the next fifty years the struggle to retain the old establishment in the face of the new situation produced a radically altered Congregationalism. To ensure that all residents would receive the benefits of the Puritan clergy, the Massachusetts legislature enacted the Act for the Settlement and Support of Ministers and Schoolmasters (November 1692), which demanded that the voters of each town select and settle a town minister. But because the franchise now included all property owners, this act robbed the local churches of the right to elect their own ministers. To offset this handicap, the act was revised in

2   Mary Louise Greene, *The Development of Religious Liberty in Connecticut* (Boston, 1905), 126-27.

3   The Charter of 1691, as quoted in Susan Martha Reed, *Church and State in Massachusetts 1691-1740* (Urbana, IL., 1914), 17.

February 1693, giving those citizens who regularly attended worship services veto power over the choice made at the town meeting and exempting Boston from the entire act. Noncompliance by various towns called forth two further laws, which constructed a council from the neighbouring churches to handle refusals to settle a town pastor (1695) and stipulated that the minister procured by the general assembly for a noncomplying town must be acceptable to the settled ministers in the area (1715). In this manner the attempt to ensure church domination of society transformed Massachusetts Congregationalism into a territorial parish system with a Presbyterian polity.

The Massachusetts establishment was also increasingly plagued by dissenting religious groups who chafed in the face of the discrepancy between the liberty of conscience clause in the colonial charter and a religious taxation system which required all citizens to support the Congregational Church in spite of personal religious preference. Finally, in June 1728, Massachusetts passed an act which exempted those persons who, because of conscience, could not pay tax, if they usually attended Sunday service in a Baptist or Quaker meetinghouse within five miles of their home, provided their church submitted a membership list to the local government. In 1731 and 1734 laws were passed, first for the Quakers and then the Baptists, omitting the five mile limitation and replacing the membership lists with a certificate system. Each church should issue certificates to its members stating that they were indeed bonafide dissidents; these were then turned in by the members themselves. But to prevent the Baptists from gaining a majority in any new settlement, the law added that the exemption would not be granted until the town had settled an "orthodox" minister and built a meetinghouse.[4]

By 1740, the situation in Massachusetts was outwardly peaceful. Although the pure church ideal had been abandoned, few within the establishment raised much objection. The church-state alliance had retreated to accommodate minority sects. In Connecticut, however, the situation was quite different.

Unlike Massachusetts, Connecticut was relatively free from dissent until 1710. And when widespread dissention did come, it was not spearheaded by sectarians but by disgruntled members of the Standing Churches. Further, the source of dissent lay not in the intolerance of the church-state alliance, but rather in lay mistrust of what they perceived as a dominating and unorthodox clergy. The problem was ignited by the Saybrook Platform (1708) which altered certain provisions of the older Cambridge codification of "the New England Way."

In attempting to counteract certain abuses of the Cambridge Congregationalism,[5] the Saybrook Platform of 1708 organized the churches by

4   William G. McLoughlin, *New England Dissent 1630-1833: The Baptists and the Separation of Church and State* (Cambridge, Mass., 1971), 237.

5   Richard L. Bushman, *From Puritan to Yankee: Character and the Social Order in Connecticut, 1690-1765* (Cambridge, Mass., 1967), 150.

counties and established for each county a "consociation" composed of the ministers of, and lay delegates from the churches within, the county. The Platform also stipulated that the decisions of the consociation required a majority vote of its clergy membership. In essence, the Saybrook architects transferred ecclesiastical power from the local church to the consociation and from the laity to the clergy. Even if an entire church differed with its pastor, his decision would be binding so long as it was in harmony with the consensus of his clerical peers.

The adoption of this platform was met with a wave of protest.[6] Whole congregations rejected it entirely. It introduced conflict within other locales, and it set loose an undercurrent of mistrust of the clergy. In 1724 Solomon Stoddard added fuel to the fire in a sermon in which he questioned the piety of his colleagues and blamed them for the spiritual decadence of the churches. Stoddard's claim that many clergymen lacked a personal experience of saving grace which prohibited them from preaching to the emotions of the people revealed a growing theological split within the clergy. Evangelicals, such as Stoddard, saw the will and the emotions as the control-centre of a person. The rationalists, in contrast, distrusted the emotions and appealed instead to the rational faculty, an outlook which won for them the scandalous label of "Arminians" from their opponents.[7]

On two occasions in the 1730s the distrust led to schism within a Standing Church. The first occurred in Guilford, where a minority established a separate assembly for public worship when it became clear that their objections to the settling of an "Arminian" minister would be ignored. Because Connecticut law forced the General Court to release a schismatic congregation from paying religious taxes to the established church, new legislation was quickly enacted which declared that no one thereafter could qualify as a dissenter who held to the "congregational or presbyterian persuasion."[8] This act was passed early enough to require the schismatic group in Milford, who likewise left the established church because of the settling of an "Arminian" minister, to pay taxes to the older church even as late as 1750.

Thus, in contrast to Massachusetts, the Great Awakening arrived in Connecticut at the time when the Standing Churches were themselves torn by dissent and already polarized into two factions, the one favouring a return to the polity and piety of the early Puritans and the other advocating Presbyterian polity and rationalistic theology. It is not surprising, therefore, that the post-Awakening Separate movement began in Connecticut and then spread to Massachusetts.

---

6   Ibid., 154.

7   *Ibid.*, 178-80.

8   *Ibid.*, 176.

The Lifespan of Isaac Backus

Isaac Backus's life covered a crucial period in the history of New England. Being only sixteen years old at the outbreak of the Great Awakening, he was both deeply affected by its theology and in a position to play a key role in the outworking of that theology in the subsequent years. Likewise, his lifespan covered the traumatic era, during which the American conflict with England reached its climax and the new nation was born. He lived in an age in which "liberty" and "freedom" were popular slogans, but in which full religious freedom remained the dream of only a few. In the aftermath of the Great Awakening the struggle against the New England Standing Order was rekindled, a struggle which was waged first by the schismatic Separates and then by a rejuvenated Baptist denomination. Backus played an important leadership role in both of these religious groups.

The Norwich church was among those in Connecticut which did not readily accept the new Saybrook Platform. When the pastor of the church finally approved the innovations, one of the town's leading citizens, Joseph Backus, withdrew from the congregation in 1714, an act which resulted in his expulsion from the Connecticut legislature.[9] So great was his dislike for the Platform that Backus travelled to Massachusetts to seek the support of the leading Puritan pastors for the Norwich schismatics. The mission was unsuccessful. Nevertheless, the rebellious group stood firm, returning to the fold only after the minister resigned and his replacement agreed to follow the old Cambridge Platform.

Joseph Backus's son, Samuel, and his wife, Elizabeth, joined the Norwich church under the provisions of the halfway covenant in 1718, six years before their son, Isaac, was born. Isaac's first sixteen years were typical of any New England farmboy until the sudden death of his father in November 1740, two months after George Whitefield's first tour through New England touched off the Awakening in the area. The loss of her husband drove Isaac's mother into a grave state of depression in which she continually asked why God had allowed such a calamity to occur. Her depression lasted until the next summer, when James Davenport, a Whitefield protégé, brought the revival to Norwich at the request of its pastor, Benjamin Lord. During Davenport's stay, Elizabeth Backus's faith was renewed,[10] her depression left, and she became a fervent revival enthusiast, opening her home for prayer and exhortation meetings.

Young Isaac was deeply impressed with what he saw happening in Norwich, and he desired the conversion which so many others had come to enjoy. Not knowing how one received such an experience, he went to his minister. Because

9   Thomas Bufford Maston, *Isaac Backus: Pioneer of Religious Liberty* (Rochester, N.Y., 1962), 12.

10   Isaac Backus, *Gospel Comfort under Heavy Tidings* (Providence, R.I., 1769), appendix, i.

of his acceptance of the outlook of New England rationalist theology (if a sinner leads an upright life, God will in due time grant salvation), pastor Lord suggested to his inquirer, "Be not discouraged, but see if God does not appear for your help."[11] Backus found this advice totally unacceptable. He continued his search for salvation until finally concluding that personal striving was totally useless. It was only then that Backus's quest was rewarded:

> As I was mowing alone in the field, August 24th, 1741, all my past life was opened plainly before me, and I saw clearly that it had been filled up with sin. I went and sat down in the shade of a tree, where my prayers and tears, my hearing of the Word of God and striving for a better heart, with all my other doings, were set before me in such a light that I perceived I could never make myself better, should I live ever so long. Divine justice appeared clear in my condemnation, and I saw that God had a right to do with me as he would. My soul yielded all into his hands, fell at his feet, and was silent and calm before Him. And while I sat there, I was enabled by divine light to see the perfect righteousness of Christ and the freeness and riches of His grace, with such clearness, that my soul was drawn forth to trust him for salvation. And I wondered that others did not also come to Him who had enough for all. The Word of God and the promise of His grace appeared firmer than a rock, and I was astonished at my previous unbelief. My heavy burden was done, tormenting fears were fled, and my joy was unspeakable.[12]

Soon after his experience of "divine light," Backus received the "inner witness" which assured him that he was indeed a true saint predestined for salvation.

The experiences of Elizabeth and Isaac Backus were repeated in great numbers during the years 1740-1742, not only in New England, but along the entire Atlantic seaboard. In fact, so widespread and far-reaching was the revival, that it has been termed America's national conversion. The Awakening drew the colonies together, uniting them by means of a common experience and giving them a consciousness that they were part of a single whole.

The catalysts for the Awakening throughout the colonies were the evangelists. These itinerant preachers conducted tours throughout the land, always emphasizing the need for a conversion experience. Although Jonathan Edwards ought not to be classified with the itinerants, by his Calvinistic preaching in the

---

11   Isaac Backus, "Isaac Backus's Life: An Account of the Life of Isaac Backus" (unpublished manuscript), 11. Also found in "Isaac Backus, his writing containing Some Particular account of my Conversion" (unpublished manuscript), 5.

12   Backus, "Account of Life," 16-18. Also in Backus, "Account of Conversion," 5-6.

Connecticut Valley in the late 1730s, he had set the stage for George Whitefield, the most famous of the travelling preachers.

The success of the Awakening was due to many factors. Being completely free from denominational ties and ecclesiastical concerns, the itinerants took religion to the people. In contrast to the complex soteriological systems of the churches, this religion emphasized a simple, dramatic and highly emotional conversion experience, based on the simplified, three-stage process enunciated by Jonathan Edwards. The message of the need for, and the method of salvation was repeated in each location by masters of rhetoric who were able to use voice variation and well-chosen anecdotes to appeal to the emotions and thereby move the wills of their audiences.

In addition to the revivalistic technique, the Awakening was successful because of its democratic presuppositions. In an era when aristocratic establishments were already under heavy attack, the itinerants stated that all persons, regardless of class, status and education, were in the same desperate situation, needed the same conversion experience and, when converted, received the same Holy Spirit who gave spiritual gifts to every believer.

But the same factors which led to the spread of the Awakening produced difficulties as well. The democratic spirit often became antinomian and anticlerical. Many unlearned and ungifted converts joined the ranks of the evangelists, invading parishes uninvited and denouncing the local clergy. Similarly, the emphasis on a traumatic experience often gave birth to a haughty, judgmental attitude toward those whose experience did not conform to the new norm. And the emotionalism often led to an overemphasis on mere outward signs.

These extravagances led the more conservative elements in New England to dismiss the revival. When this occurred in Connecticut, the division already present in the Standing Church became a quickly-growing schism. Even if extravagances had not occurred, it is still possible that widespread schism would have taken place. An increasing number of nominal church people, dramatically converted through the Awakening, began to call into question the ecclesiastical structure of New England. These new converts wondered why conversion and revival had not come sooner. The answer to their question led right to that system which, by abandoning the original membership requirements and by instituting the new parish system, not only allowed the unconverted into the church, but also gave the unconverted the power to place unconverted clergy over the church. And even if the converted gained a majority in a town, the county consociation prevented them from ridding their church of corruption.

In essence, then, the Awakening sparked a revival of the old Puritan piety, which ignited a new interest in the original Congregationalist ideals. Yet the Awakening was not merely a "re-vival," a return to a previous ideal. Added to this backward longing for the original polity was something new. The revival brought a new democratic tendency. This was noticeable, for example, even in

George Whitefield. The fiery Englishman preached not only the universal need of all for conversion, but also the existence of fundamental divine laws, obedience to which empowered the individual Christian with the right to question and even to break any human law that ran contrary to God's law.[13] The addition of this democratic element to the revival of the older Puritan piety led the new enthusiasts eventually to call into question the whole New England concept of a rigidly institutionalized religion. Eventually this brought down the curtain on the Standing Order.

The evils the Awakening set loose upon the land brought a swift and forceful response from the Connecticut clergy, who appealed to the state to come to their aid. Assistance arrived in 1743 in the form of laws against the uninvited entrance of itinerants into a parish, laws usurping the right of counties to license dissenting churches, and laws which deprived persons sympathetic to the Awakening of seats in the legislature.

These actions, however, were not the direct cause of the first separations, which occurred in two towns near Norwich where relatives of Backus happened to be living. Rather, the Canterbury and Plainfield schisms were the result of controversies over the settling of a new minister, as had been the case in the two separations of the previous decade.

The Canterbury schism occurred in 1743. New Lights comprised the majority of the church membership, but they constituted only a minority of the larger parish population. The Windham County Consociation declared that the Old Lights constituted the church and then ordained their ministerial choice, who of course had been ratified by the parish.

In Plainfield the situation was exactly opposite. In 1744, the Consociation made an opposite ruling, ordaining the candidate favoured by the Old Light majority in the church against the will of the New Light majority in the parish. In each case, the New Light faction withdrew and formed a separate church. For this they suffered persecution.

The schism in Norwich was more typical of the manner in which Separate churches were formed. Similar to many of his colleagues, Benjamin Lord at first welcomed the revival but then turned against it after seeing the extravagances it brought. For their part, Backus and the Norwich New Lights, like many others who had been touched by the Awakening, joined the Standing Church only after much personal debate and then with the hope of reforming it from within.[14] But

---

13 Alice M. Baldwin, *The New England Clergy and the American Revolution* (Durham, N.C., 1928), 57-58.

14 In his diary he reports, "And now I had thoughts of joining to the church but then I saw so many corruptions among them; that these together with some other things, kept me off for near a year but then on July 11, 1742, I joined with the church in Norwich town and so I lived several years." Isaac Backus, "Diary," (unpublished manuscript), I, 2.

Lord, armed with the 1743 laws, clamped down on the presence of lay exhorters who had been holding meetings in several homes in his parish and forbade even the more moderate itinerants from returning to Norwich. The New Lights, however, remaining intent on reformation, proposed that the church adopt a new membership requirement stipulating that no one be admitted without first giving oral evidence of a conversion experience (February 1745). The proposal was defeated. The New Lights began holding separate worship services, citing in their defense four conditions in the established church which they held to be intolerable:

1. Neglect of church discipline, and coldness and want of application in preaching.
2. Lack of adherence to the gospel qualifications of church membership.
3. Laity prohibited from exhortation and prayer.
4. Acceptance of Saybrook Platform and new anti-Awakening laws.

The schismatics were charged with covenant breaking and censured, but never excommunicated.[15] Nevertheless, a Separate or Strict Congregational church was organized in Norwich on 16 July 1746, following the original method of the New England Puritans: oral testimonies of conversion were heard, a covenant was signed, and a minister, who was later ordained, was chosen.

Within a decade, Separate churches had sprung up throughout Connecticut and Massachusetts. Two months after the formation of the Norwich Separate Church, while he was again alone in the woods, Backus received an "internal call" to preach the gospel, an experience that the New Lights valued more than the earned degrees which were the prerequisites for ministerial positions in the Standing Churches. The next Sunday he "tested his gift" and his call by preaching in the Separate church of which he and his mother Elizabeth were now members. Upon hearing the sermon, the congregation confirmed that God had indeed called and gifted Backus to preach. The young minister spent the next year in the itinerant circuit. His travels took him to Hartford in June 1747, where

---

15 William G. McLoughlin, *Isaac Backus and the American Pietistic Tradition*, in the *Library of American Biography*, ed. Oscar Hardlin (Boston, 1967), 30. However, C.C. Goen claims that the Norwich church excommunicated the schismatic party on 17 October, 1745 (C.C. Goen, *Revivalism and Separatism in New England,1740-1800: Strict Congregationalists and Separate Baptists in the Great Awakening* [New Haven, CT., 1962], 216). Backus never mentions that he had been excommunicated, although he does use the term "censure" in his diary entry, 22 April, 1788, in which he reports having preached in the Norwich church: "Thus the leaders of the church who censured me above forty years ago, can hear me preach in their place of worship, without any retraction on either side, so full is the world of inconsistencies." "Diary," Vol. 11, 57.

he visited and was inspired by John Paine, a Separate who had been jailed for similar unsolicited exhorting.

That December an elder from Backus's church took him to Massachusetts to preach in a strife-torn parish, which straddled the townships of Bridgewater and Middleboro. Since its formation in 1743, Titicut parish had been without a minister. After they heard him preach, it seemed that Backus would be accepted by all factions, that is, until a question over his ability to be installed within the framework of Massachusetts law caused the conservative elements in the parish to oppose his coming.[16] The New Lights, however, having already decided on Backus, asked him to form them into a church. On 16 February 1748, he drew up a church covenant and articles of faith, which included regenerate membership, strict congregational and democratic polity, voluntarism and openness to "further light." On the following 13 April, Backus was ordained the minister of a Separate church.

The presence of a schismatic congregation in Titicut was not welcomed by the parish as a whole, for it would now be difficult for them to obtain an orthodox (i.e., college-educated) minister. Nevertheless, the process was begun on 31 March with the levying of a 500 pound tax on all residents for the completion of the meeting house. The Separates, of course, saw no reason for paying a tax to build a meeting house which they would not be using. Their refusal brought in the civil government. Many Separates were imprisoned, a fate which Backus only narrowly escaped — someone paid the tax for him.

On 21 November, the Separates wrote a letter of protest to the parish in which they suggested that their fellow parishioners either "return" and unite with the Separate church or, out of obedience to the golden rule, condone the presence of the New Light congregation in their midst. To this the parish committee sent a lengthy reply. They rejected flatly the first suggestion, because the strict Separate admission standards made experiential conversion the norm for admittance and because, in their view, it was the Separates who had departed and thus needed to do the "returning." Next, the committee voiced their disapproval of Backus. Finally, they declared that they could not exclude the

---

16 McLaughlin, *Backus*, 35-46. Goen suggests that the problems in Titicut were the result of the unwillingness of the two neighbouring churches to release their members to form a church in the newly created parish (Goen, *Revivalism*, 217-18). Goen's assertion does reflect the situation as described by Backus ("Isaac Backus, his Book containing some particular Account of my first Setling (sic) in the Ministry in the joining border of Bridgewater and Middleborough" (unpublished manuscript, 6-7). Nevertheless, the full accounts of the entire process indicate that whereas the neighbouring parishes had previously been reluctant to release members, the arrival of Backus caused a split between the radical New Lights, who were ready to form a church without following the legal process, and the moderates, who valued fidelity to the legal process above the immediate formation of a church.

Separates from the tax because duty required the schismatics to pay it. They argued that it is neither persecution nor contrary to the golden rule and liberty of conscience to compel the Separates to comply with "their duty as it is pointed out by the laws of God or the good and wholesome laws of the land" and to seek to bring them back from their departure into error.

The refusal of Titicut parish to exempt the Separate church from the religious tax catapulted Backus into a struggle over the relationship between church and state which was to occupy the central place in his entire life. His lifelong involvement began merely as an effort by a group of Congregationalist schismatics to gain for themselves the same exemption status enjoyed by the Baptists, Quakers and Anglicans.

On 18 April 1749, Backus wrote to three neighbouring churches proposing a special conference on 24 May for the purpose of drafting a petition to the legislature requesting exemption status on the basis of the Charter of 1691. After the conference, he travelled to the Cape Cod area, gathering signatures from other Separates, bringing the total to 183 signers. The petition declared that God had given each person the inalienable right to worship according to the dictates of conscience, a right which God himself had always defended, but especially in the case of the Puritan founders of the colony. The legislature was not moved by the argument. But Backus was not in a position to launch a new attempt to achieve exemption. Another issue was arising within the Separate ranks which was soon to split the schismatics.

Because they rejected the idea of baptismal regeneration, the New England Puritans had continually struggled to find an adequate theological justification for the baptism of infants (pedobaptism). The first settlers had legitimized the rite by resorting to an analogy from the Abrahamic covenant. They declared that because God's covenant with them extended to their "seed," in due time God would grant that their children would also experience confirmation of their elect status. When these hopes did not materialize, the ideal of the national Christian commonwealth took precedence over that of the pure church. With the halfway covenant, the Puritans altered the meaning of baptism. The Great Awakening, however, rekindled interest in the pure church. By calling into question the previous compromise, the revival raised anew the issue of the meaning of baptism. It is therefore not surprising that the radical New Lights, imbued with the pure church ideal, struggled with this explosive issue.

The issue arrived in Titicut on 7 August 1749, in the form of the advocacy of antipedobaptism by two members of Backus's church. Although he set out to refute the two, Backus found himself agreeing with their arguments. After preaching a hastily composed sermon in defense of the Baptist position, he recanted, returning to an uneasy acceptance of his former view. These events began a two-year personal struggle over this complex but weighty issue. Backus realized what was at stake, namely, the entire Puritan covenant theology. To abandon pedobaptism was to secede from the Separate movement just when success appeared on the horizon. On the other hand, Backus was beginning to see that not only was the New England form of covenant theology not taught by the Bible, it was being used to justify the ecclesiastical evils of the day — the pollution of the church through the halfway covenant, the parish system, religious taxes, and the aristocratic structure of the established churches.[17] Finally on 25 July 1751, Backus came irrevocably to the antipedobaptist position. He was then baptized by immersion on 22 August.

Decisions such as Backus's were triggering a crisis throughout the Separate movement. Backus himself tried desperately to maintain an open-communion church and keep peace between the two factions. But the task was difficult. The next two and a half years were marred by internal chaos. The disorders at Titicut and elsewhere precipitated a series of synods, called with the hope of finding a solution to the controversy. Finally on 29 May 1754, by a vote of 37 to 35 with 6 abstentions, a Separate synod withdrew fellowship from the antipedobaptists, claiming that the two positions were irreconcilable: either the baptism of infants was a sin or the withholding of that rite was.

In spite of this vote and his ouster from the denomination, Backus sought to maintain an open-communion congregation. In the end, however, he too concluded that the attempt was fruitless. 16 January 1756 marked the end of a five year effort. On that day he helped form a close-communion, immersionist church in Middleboro (a church in which membership, and even the distribution of communion, was restricted to those who had been baptized by immersion as believers). This congregation, in turn, ordained him as pastor on 23 June.

When Backus established the church in Middleboro, the Baptists of New England were hopelessly divided. On the one hand, the old Baptists were split into several groups which differed with each other over the great theological issues of the day — reflecting the same spectrum present in the Standing Churches — and over minor practical issues. They were joined by the independent congregations recently expelled from the Separate denomination. These included the antipedobaptist churches (like Backus's newly formed Middleboro congregation) and those churches which gallantly remained open-communion. All of these former Separate churches, of course, had hopes of being granted dissenting status.

The altered theological and ecclesiological situation of the new close-communion churches generated a new problem for the establishment. Although they were now clearly Baptist in polity, these churches had previously belonged to the old order. Consequently, their members remained obligated to support financially the Standing Churches.

---

17 McLoughlin, *Backus*, 62.

A squabble over this issue occurred as early as 1750 in Sturbridge, Massachusetts. To forestall any future problems and to prevent any loop-hole by which these Separate-Baptists might claim dissenting status, in 1753 the Massachusetts legislature added a new requirement to the Exemption Act for the Baptists. It stipulated that the exemption certificates issued by individual churches must be validated by three other "Anabaptist" churches in the region.

The law failed miserably. It alarmed the old Baptists, who held a series of meetings in order to organize themselves against it. They drafted a remonstrance to the Massachusetts general court and raised funds to send a representative to England with their grievances.[18] Further, in that the act failed to define "Anabaptist," it created an even bigger loophole, for the Separate-Baptist churches merely validated certificates for each other. Finally, the law accelerated the movement of open-communion churches to close-communion status and heightened the awareness among the close-communion churches of their fundamental ties first to each other and then with the old Baptists, whom they themselves had previously ostracized. In short, the Massachusetts law initiated the rejuvenation of the New England Baptists.

The process of unifying and enlivening the Baptists in the New England colonies received impetus from two other sources. The first was Issac Backus, who saw almost immediately the importance of close ties among all churches holding Baptist beliefs. Between 1756 and 1767, he travelled nearly 15,000 miles within the region,[19] visiting old Baptist churches, open-communion congregations, and new groups which sought his help in the task of organizing as churches.

The Philadelphia Baptist Association was the second impetus. Key leaders, such as James Manning, Hezekiah Smith, Samuel Stillman and John Davis, travelled north to encourage and assist their New England co-religionists. In so doing they also brought to the region a sense that these churches belonged to a national denomination, one which encompassed all the colonies. The leadership of the Philadelphia Association resulted in the establishment of Rhode Island College (now Brown University) in the 1760s and the founding of the Warren Baptist Association in 1767. It also contributed to the short-lived victory of moderate Calvinism, which Backus shared, as the reigning theology in the entire denomination.

The Warren Association had originally been established for the purpose of aiding local churches. Yet, it soon took on a more political role, becoming the arm of the New England Baptists in a renewed struggle against the Standing

---

18   Jacob C. Meyer, *Church and State in Massachusetts from 1740 to 1833: A Chapter in the History of the Development of Individual Freedom* (New York, 1968 [original edition 1930]), 49.

19   Robert George Torbet, *A History of the Baptists* (Philadelphia, 1950), 253.

Order. This struggle did not begin because the Baptists had reached a new theological position on the church/state question, but because some of their churches faced difficulties with the Standing Order. Specifically, the situation in Ashfield, Massachusetts, set the Association machinery in action.

The original exemption laws had stipulated that Baptists living in new areas would be required to pay the religious tax until the town was incorporated. But incorporation in 1765 did not bring the sizeable Baptist population relief from the taxation. After some initial disputes, the legislature passed the "Ashfield Act" in June 1768, which legally required the Baptists to continue paying the tax. Word of this development reached the Warren Association, which had also received complaints from other areas about injustices in the administration of the exemption laws.

In 1769 the Association appointed a grievance committee to collect the complaints of the churches, to write a suitable petition, and to present it to the legislature.[20] Backus was largely responsible for the content of the petition. In keeping with public sentiment of the day, it condemned the certificate system as "taxation without representation" and spoke of liberty of conscience as a natural right. But the Standing Order discarded the Baptist plea, replying that natural rights were in this case superseded by the civil obligation to contribute to the moral good of the community through the financial support of the parish minister.[21]

After this initial defeat, the committee placed an advertisement in the Boston *Evening Post* of 30 August 1770, asking the harassed churches to bring their grievances to the Association meeting in Bellingham, which would launch an appeal to the king if necessary. The legislature then passed a new, milder certificate law, but did not repeal the Ashfield Act. Meanwhile, through the funding of the Philadelphia Association, Hezekiah Smith was dispatched to England in November 1770, and the king annulled the offending law. Nevertheless, the certificate system remained in place, and injustices in its administration continued. This led to a turning point in Backus's own thinking, as he became convinced that only through the disestablishment of the Standing Order could the Baptists obtain their natural, legal and Christian rights.

At this time (1772-1773) Backus developed his theory of the two governments. God had appointed two kinds of governments, he said, the civil and the ecclesiastical, which ought never to be "confounded" together. Backus concluded that the union of the two governments in the New England colonies must be broken if America were to become a truly Christian land.[22] In September

20 Bynum Shaw, *Divided We Stand: the Baptists in American Life* (Durham, N.C., 1974), 63.

21 See McLoughlin, *Dissent*, 539.

22 See McLoughlin, *Backus*, 123-27.

1772, the grievance committee was reactivated, this time under the leadership of Backus himself. Using his theory as well as its corollary, the right of the Christian to disobey when the governments had indeed been "confounded," the committee suggested to the Association meeting of September 1773, a new program — the mass refusal by the Baptists to turn in exemption certificates. The Association voted to leave this decision with each individual church but to aid financially those who suffered because of their non-compliance with the certificate law.

During this time the struggle between the colonies and England was also intensifying. The first Continental Congress was scheduled to meet in Philadelphia on 5 September 1774. Seeing this as their opportunity to appeal to a body higher than the Massachusetts legislature without appearing to be disloyal, the New England Baptists sent Backus and Manning to join forces with the Baptists and Quakers of Philadelphia. At the suggestion of the Quakers, a meeting was sought with the Massachusetts congressional delegation together with several sympathetic delegates from other colonies. Manning opened the meeting, held on 14 October, by reading a memorial written by himself, Backus and Robert Stettle Jones. The piece included Backus's two-government theory and the Baptist arguments on behalf of their concept of liberty of worship.[23] The Massachusetts delegates, however, contended that the complaints listed were not at all matters of conscience. To this Backus replied that he could not turn in the certificates without acknowledging "that power in man which ... belongs only to God."[24] Again John and Sam Adams defended the Massachusetts system, stating that although an establishment existed it was "a very slender one."

In the end the meeting proved to be a mistake. Not only did the Baptists fail to accomplish their goal of focusing national attention on their plight, their association with Tory Quakers and neutral, if not Tory, Philadelphia Baptists added to the suspicion in New England that they too were unpatriotic. Having failed in Philadelphia, the Baptists were forced again to appeal to the Massachusetts assembly, doing so in July 1775. Soon after, the revolutionary war began.

Unlike many of their colleagues in the middle colonies, Backus and the New England Baptists closed ranks with the Congregationalists behind the war effort. They had come to believe that religious liberty was more threatened by the English Anglican establishment than the New England Puritans. Therefore, they viewed the revolutionary struggle as one phase of their own. The war was a providential act that would set the stage for the final overthrow of the New England establishment. With this in mind, the Baptists seized the opportunity

---

23   *Ibid.*, 131.

24   Quoted in Torbet, *History*, 237.

given them to have one of their own, Samuel Stillman, deliver the election sermon of 1779. Having received help from Backus, Stillman sounded again the theme that religious taxation was taxation without representation. He then repeated the Separate argument that because humanly instituted ecclesiastical laws constituted a usurpation of Christ's power and because his kingdom was not of this world, Christ's Christian subjects were under obligation to no religious laws, except those given by their Lord.

Later that year, the opportunity to institute real change came. A September convention was called for the purpose of writing a new state constitution. Backus lobbied intensively and even drew up a proposed bill of rights. Nevertheless, the new proposed constitution which was finished on 2 March 1780, did not totally separate church and state nor fulfil Backus's desire that it leave the "rational soul" free to find "true religion" as expressed in the Bible. The cause of disappointment was Article III. This section altered the Massachusetts system drastically by guaranteeing public financial support to all Protestant ministers, not just Congregationalists. Yet, it retained the principle of compulsory religious taxation, which violated the Baptist conscience, and it suspended all exemptions from that taxation.

The proposed constitution was to be debated until a statewide vote scheduled for 9 June 1780. During this time Backus and the Baptists argued untiringly against Article III. They did not object to the idea of the Christian commonwealth and its goal of the diffusion of public worship throughout the state. Rather, they pointed out that this goal was best served by voluntarism, because any state coercion inevitably leads to infringement on conscience, the thwarting of faith, and public support for error.[25] Hence, Backus did not disagree with his opponents concerning the value of Christianity for the welfare of society. Instead, he took issue with their assumption that this somehow gave the legislature the power to establish and demand support for public worship.

The dissenters' cause was further enhanced by a series of articles in the Boston newspapers, published by a New Light Congregationalist under the name Philanthropos. In these essays the author denied that the support of religion was a civil duty and that Christianity was essential to preservation of the state. Philanthropos then redefined piety as "heart religion," and concluded that the state has the right to support only ethics education, for only morality or "natural religion" and not piety is essential to good government.[26]

The debate over Article III was actually an internal Puritan discussion. At issue was the best method for attaining the Puritan goal of a Christian land. This

---

25 McLoughlin, *Backus*, 149.

26 McLoughlin, *Dissent*, 618; John M. Mecklin, *The Story of American Dissent* (Port Washington, N.Y., 1968 [original edition, 1934]), 305-06.

question, however, led to a deeper issue which had been simmering for some time, namely, the definition of piety. True to the rationalist tradition, the defenders of the establishment saw piety as something which, being reasonable and somewhat social, could be taught. Hence, they continued to uphold the Christian society built upon the alliance between church and state. The post-Awakening groups, on the other hand, viewed piety as a matter which also included the emotions and was radically individual. Consequently, they envisioned a society which was Christianized by the leavening influence of its Christian citizens and in which the government merely created a climate conducive for the spread of the faith.

Although it is doubtful that Article III obtained the two-thirds majority needed for passage, the legislature declared it law on 25 October 1780, a decision which the Baptists protested in vain. During the wave of renewed persecution against the Baptists who refused once again to pay the religious tax, the legislature ignored completely any petitions and protests. Now the struggle shifted to the courts.

The Baptists won a great victory in the Balkcom Case of 1782. But the decision was reversed two years later in *Cutter v. Frost*, which made the situation worse by stating that only legally incorporated religious societies were entitled to legal recognition. For the Baptists this meant that, whereas local churches had previously been able to receive a proportionate share of all taxes collected, they would now receive nothing unless they sought legal incorporation. Against the advice of Backus, many churches began complying with the law, seeking incorporation, paying the tax, and then suing to have their taxes go to their own minister.

The Baptist efforts to eliminate religious taxation had not been successful. Nevertheless, by 1785 a climate of broad acceptance and toleration of the denomination had been attained. In this new situation the group turned its attention away from the political struggle to the task of evangelism.

Backus also found himself devoting much of his effort to other needs. He sought to counter the inroads of new sects and non-Calvinist theologies. Through sermons and tracts he attacked what he saw as heresy and gave literary definition to the outlook which he had experientially found to be true. Middleboro honoured its Baptist minister by electing him as a delegate to the Massachusetts convention which debated the newly-proposed United States Constitution. After giving much attention to this trust, he finally voted against the consensus of his constituents and in favour of ratification.

The new evangelism impetus of the denomination drew Backus's attention as well. At the Warren Association meeting on 6 September 1788, Backus called for a renewal of the struggle against the establishment. The Association appointed a committee to write a petition and present it to the legislature at its own discretion. Then it presented Backus with a new challenge — a southern journey to aid in a revival currently taking place there. This he did, returning enthusiastic in 1790, but unable to produce a similar renewal in his home state.

Backus continued his ministry in Middleboro, where he had served since organizing the Titicut church. But after his health began to fail in 1798 and his wife's death in 1800, his congregation began to see the need of obtaining an assistant for their aging pastor. In 1804 they called to this post Ezra Kendal, who, as a member of the new generation of Baptist pastors, held certain Arminian views. The year 1806 was Backus's last: he suffered a stroke in March, preached his last sermon on 3 April, suffered a second stroke on 23 April, but lingered until 24 November, on which day the eighty-two year old Baptist statesman died.

The final victory of the cause for which Backus struggled was not achieved within his lifetime. Yet it did come, partly through the efforts of his denominational heirs.

The incorporation issue against which Backus could not mobilize the Baptists was settled in 1811 by the Religious Liberty Act. This legislation reversed the Cutter Case by interpreting Article III as applying to all churches regardless of their incorporation status. The struggle then returned to Connecticut, which had produced the first Separate churches but had receded to the background behind the shadow of its larger neighbour. On 3 May 1818, the Baptists, now led by John Leland, submitted a petition to the legislature calling for religious freedom not only for all Protestants, but, returning to the position of Roger Williams, for "infidels" as well. That same year religious taxation was abolished in the state.

Fifteen years later, on 11 November 1833, Massachusetts finally disestablished the Congregational church as well. It was the last of the original thirteen states to take this radical step.

The revivalists among the Planters who left New England in the midst of the struggle spearheaded by Isaac Backus offered fertile soil for ideas about conversion, baptism and church order similar to those espoused by the Middleboro minister. It is not surprising, therefore, that many of them were receptive to the Baptist message as it was carried northward by Ebenezer Moulton and subsequent evangelists.

"The Rage For Dipping": Joseph Crandall, Elijah Estabrooks and Believer's Baptism 1795-1800

George Rawlyk
Professor of History
Queen's University

The Planters who came to the old colony of Nova Scotia in the 1760s held a variety of Protestant religious beliefs, but the majority were either Old or New Light Congregationalists. At the end of the eighteenth century, many Planters became enthusiastic converts to Baptist beliefs and practices, the most characteristic of which was a demand that believers undergo a ritual baptism by immersion. The "rage for dipping"[1] or what has recently been called the "Baptist reformation"[2] was not simply a carefully orchestrated policy implemented by recently minted Baptist ministers determined to impose their unique kind of hegemonic order over a deeply divided popular and radical Evangelical movement. Most of the so-called Maritime Baptist Patriarchs in the 1790s — men like Harris Harding, James and Edward Manning, Thomas Handly Chipman, Theodore Seth Harding and Joseph Dimock — were, in fact, extremely reluctant Baptists. Their fear of the excesses unleashed by Antinomianism (which stressed that the truly converted Christian was not subject to moral law) as well as their growing preoccupation with respectability, prestige and order, without question, moved some of the Patriarchs from a radical New Light position to a more-or-less Massachusetts Calvinist Evangelical Baptist one. But these men, it should be kept in mind, could have instead followed their former friend and close associate, John Payzant, into New Light Congregationalism in order to avoid Antinomian anarchy. However, if they had done so, they must have suspected that few of the growing number of Radical Evangelicals would have followed them. The Patriarchs may also have briefly considered Methodism, but here, too, they confronted the very real possibility that few of their followers would have even considered coming along. Rather, the Baptist Patriarchs became ardent Baptists largely because they were compelled to do so, in order to survive as ministers. Their role as spiritual leaders was profoundly challenged by a powerful popular movement which swept through the Yankee heartland of Nova Scotia and the Chignecto-Shepody region of New Brunswick and the St. John River Valley in the late eighteenth and early nineteenth centuries. At the centre of this movement was an intense and widespread demand for "believer's" baptism.

---

1 Quoted in E.M. Saunders, *History of the Baptists of the Maritime Provinces* (Halifax, 1902), 115.

2 D. Bell, ed., *Newlight Baptist Journals of James Manning and James Innis* (Hantsport, 1984), 23.

How does one account for what Bishop Charles Inglis spitefully referred to in 1800 as an almost irrational obsession with "total immersion" in Yankee regions of Nova Scotia.[3] According to Professor David Bell, it was yet another manifestation of the Radical Evangelical concern with religious and spiritual innovation. "Baptism by immersion," according to Bell, "was just the latest phase of a whole generation of religious novelties that had begun with Alline himself."[4] Yet this explanation begs a further question — why this particular novelty? Why not "speaking in tongues," or "divine healing," or "intense Sanctification?" There were some outbreaks of "glossolalia" in 1793 in New Brunswick and then in Nova Scotia both a little earlier and a little later. Surely speaking in tongues was as innovative a practice, if not more radically innovative, than believer's baptism by immersion in the context of the 1790s. Both believer's baptism and glossolalia were, of course, marvellous examples of Christian primitivism — an emphasis on the return to the pristine purity of Apostolic Christianity. And Christian primitivism was, furthermore, a powerful force at work in late eighteenth-century Maritime Canada as well as in Central Canada. "Believer's baptism," however, unlike other Primitivist practices endorsed by the New Testament, was a ritual permeated not only by religious meaning but also by folk belief and by a sense of almost medieval magic. It was a ritual which, like the camp meeting, was energized from the bottom up and could be so effectively controlled from the top down.

One must never underestimate what Mary Douglas has perceptively referred to as a universal belief in "the revivifying role of water in religious symbolism."[5] And according to Marcel Eliade:

> In water everything is "dissolved," every "form" is broken up, everything that has happened ceases to exist; nothing that was before remains after immersion in water, not an outline, not a "sign," not an event. Immersion is the equivalent, at the human level, of death at the cosmic level, of the cataclysm (the Flood) which periodically dissolves the world into the primeval ocean. Breaking up all the forms, doing away with the past, water possesses this power of purifying, of regenerating, of giving new birth .... Water purifies and regenerates because it nullifies the past, and restores — even only for a moment — the integrity of the dawn of things.[6]

---

3 Quoted in Saunders, *History of the Baptists*, 115.

4 Bell, *Newlight Baptist Journals*, 21.

5 Mary Douglas, *Purity and Danger: An Analysis of the Concepts of Pollution and Taboo* (London, 1979), 161.

6 M. Eliade, *Patterns in Comparative Religion* (London, 1958), 194.

"Believer's baptism" by immersion was, among other things, a purity ritual which helped both to create and to consolidate "a sense of community shaped by an intense public experience."[7] In theory, this new community was, because of the purifying power of "believer's baptism," "a new society which would be free, unbounded and without coercion or contradiction."[8] Maritime Baptists were inspired by Paul's letter to the Galatians (Galatians 3:28), "In being baptized into Christ, you have put on Christ: there can be neither Jew, nor Greek, neither bond nor free, neither male nor female, for you are all one in Christ Jesus." "Believer's baptism" was, moreover, the means whereby thousands of Maritime Evangelicals reversed the widespread Protestant "tendency to suppose that any ritual is empty form," and that "any external religion betrays true interior religion."[9] In "believer's baptism," Maritime Baptists appropriated for themselves their own unique, New Testament and Christ-inspired ritual. It permitted them to gain control over their total universe, where the cosmic overlapped with the mundane world, and it also provided them with a divinely sanctioned framing function which enabled them, in a profound psychological sense, to "shut in desired themes or shut out intruding ones."[10] We are always trying to create boundaries for ourselves to help to define who we are and who we are not. "Believer's baptism," in a sense, sanctified the rejection of the world and the acceptance of Christ's salvation triggered by conversion. It was the outward and visible sign of the acceptance of "Christ as Saviour and Lord."

As the eighteenth century blurred into the nineteenth, an increasing number of Maritime Radical Evangelicals, particularly those who would become Baptists, began to regard the moment of baptism as being as important or even more important than the actual instant of conversion. There is some fragmentary evidence suggesting that for some early Baptists there was such a thing as baptismal regeneration. "Believer's baptism" for some new Baptist Christians thus helped to "frame" the precise moment when they "became new creatures in Christ."[11] The ritual encapsulated the entire conversion and sanctification process. While intensely individual and personal, adult baptism was also a reaffirmation of community. It was a public, not a private ritual and it was one which only an ordained Baptist minister could administer. A lay baptism was worse than worthless; it was perceived to be both evil and anti-Christian.

In the pre-1812 period, there is, in the available hundreds of pages of records, not one instance of a Maritime layperson baptizing another layperson.

---

7   Douglas, *Purity and Danger*, 2.

8   *Ibid.*, 158.

9   *Ibid.*, 61.

10   *Ibid.*, 63.

11   See *ibid.*, 64.

Only an ordained Baptist minister, it should be stressed, could immerse a new convert. Some isolated converts would wait for months, and even for years, to be baptized by a Baptist itinerant preacher; others, including women in their eighties, would be baptized by immersion in large holes cut out of the St. John River ice in the midst of winter because a Baptist minister was at last available. Why would men and women risk pneumonia or worse in order to be baptized by a visiting ordained Baptist minister, often a stranger, at such an inconvenient time and in such horrendous circumstances? What factor or factors actualized into Maritime reality, at a specific time, a growing popular preoccupation with the Baptist ritual of purification and cleansing?

There was, it seems, at the popular grassroots level, whether in the Yankee heartland of Nova Scotia or the St. John River Valley of Loyalist New Brunswick, a powerful primitive belief in the regenerative efficacy of "believer's baptism" by immersion. The Baptist minister who alone could administer the ritual to a believer, to someone who had first publicly declared her or his conversion, was believed to possess special spiritual powers. In baptizing a believer in the name of the "Father, Son and Holy Spirit," the minister was not only obeying the command of Christ to "make disciples of all the nations baptizing them in the name of the Father and of the Son and of the Holy Spirit," but he was actually transforming the temporal into the cosmic by spiritually purifying the individual for eternity. In late eighteenth-century New Brunswick and Nova Scotia, there was a growing popular belief (some would call it a primitive prejudice) that without conversion *and* "believer's baptism" one could not "enter the Kingdom of Heaven." In Christ's words as captured by John 3:5: "Except a person be born of water and the spirit, the person cannot enter into the Kingdom of God." It is noteworthy that in this key verse, upon which the "doctrine of Baptismal Regeneration is usually rested,"[12] being immersed in "water" is explicitly referred to before being born of "the Spirit." But the question of why this popular belief swept certain regions of New Brunswick and Nova Scotia in the late eighteenth century is not necessarily answered, in a satisfactory way, by merely stressing either the extraordinary convergence, in many minds, of the New Light conversion experience and baptism by immersion or the primacy given to baptism by "water" over "the Spirit."

What seemed to exacerbate significantly the "rage for dipping" was a growing and widespread belief that the end of the world was imminent and that Jesus Christ would soon return to earth and gather into his presence only those who were indeed "born of water and the Spirit." Many seemed to devote inordinate time and attention, at the turn of the century, to "listening intently for

---

12. *Christian Messenger*, 12 February 1841.

the 'Midnight Cry.'"[13] One of these men was Elijah Estabrooks, a New Brunswick New Light who, in 1800, was baptized by immersion. Estabrooks, we know, soon after his baptism in the St. John River:

> asked the patience of the people, till he communicated his thoughts of the near approach of the millennium day, when Christ will reign a thousand years. Mr. Estabrooks had spoken but a few minutes before his mind seemed to awake in possession of the glorious day. A divine spark catched in the hearts of Mr. [Theodore] Harding, Mr. [Joseph] Crandall, and some others, and increased to a mighty flame. One sang glory, glory, glory to God in the highest, and others hallelujah, hallelujah, amen, so let it be; indeed, sir, the people were overshadowed with power divine.[14]

Other New Lights in the Cornwallis region, a few years earlier, and in the eastern extremity of New Brunswick, a few years later, also emphasized the imminent return of Christ especially as they looked forward to the coming of the new century and viewed the myriad and complex repercussions of both the French and American revolutions.[15] There was a powerful compulsion to return to the practices of the New Testament church in order to usher in the "End Times."

There is yet another way to try to come to grips with something of the appeal and something of the socio-psychological substance of the "rage for dipping" by looking at the purification ritual as a crucially important element in evolving Maritime popular and radical Evangelicalism at the turn of the eighteenth century. The approach is a largely biographical one, an attempt to see and to understand "believer's baptism" from the immediate vantage-point of a Baptist minister Joseph Crandall (1771-1858) and a person he actually baptized —Elijah Estabrooks (1756-1825). A rather general and largely theoretical approach is only one way to provide answers to the problem of the remarkable growth of the "rage for dipping." The biographical approach obviously is much more specific and explicit both in terms of time and space. But the two approaches, when sensitively combined, may provide some convincing clues to the actual origins of the so-called "Maritime Baptist Reformation."

According to Crandall's most recent biographer, the New Brunswick Baptist Patriarch was, without question, "the most influential and venerated Baptist

---

13   Bell, *Newlight Baptist Journals*, 184.

14   Z. Estey to James Manning, 10 March 1802, Acadia University Archives (AUA), Fredericton Baptist Churchbook, 271,

15   See Bell, *Newlight Baptist Journals*, 184-85, 257-58.

leader" in the colony "during the first years of the nineteenth century."[16] It would be a serious mistake, however, to argue, as I.E. Bill did in 1880, that "probably to him more than to any other single individual, this Province [New Brunswick] stands indebted for the diffusion of correct sentiments regarding the matter of civil and religious liberty."[17] As a politician in the New Brunswick Assembly from 1818 to 1824, Crandall accomplished virtually nothing and was certainly neither "a radical" at odds with the political and religious establishment nor "a regional power broker."18 His contemporaries knew him for what he was, a very successful Baptist evangelist, nothing more and nothing less.

Joseph Crandall was born in 1771 in Tiverton, Rhode Island.[19] While still a child, he accompanied his emigrating parents to Nova Scotia "the year before the American Revolution, and settled in Chester."[20] In his highly stylized autobiography, penned near the end of his life, Crandall described his being "called to the death bed of my mother." Crandall was, apparently,

> much alarmed to see my beloved mother so pale and deathlike. She said to me "that she had sent for me to hear her last farewell." She said "she was going to leave us all and go to her Saviour where she would be happy." After some time she looked earnestly at me and said "Joseph the Lord has a great work for you to do when I am dead and gone."[21]

Well after the event, Crandall was absolutely certain that his mother was indeed "under the influence of the Holy Spirit," and it is clear that her words would haunt him for the rest of his life. Nor would Crandall ever forget what his father told him soon after the latter had heard Henry Alline preach for the first time: "that this preacher Henry Alline was a 'New Light' and that the 'New Light'

---

16   J.M. Bumsted, "Joseph Crandall," *Dictionary of Canadian Biography*, VIII (Toronto, 1985), 179. There are some major typographical errors in this biography, for example the date of birth of Crandall is given as 1761 instead of 1771 and the age at death 97 instead of the correct 87.

17   I.E. Bill, *Fifty Years With the Baptist Ministers and Churches of the Maritime Provinces of Canada* (Saint John, 1880), 213.

18   D. Britton, "Joseph Crandall: Preacher and Politician," in R.S. Wilson, ed., *An Abiding Conviction: Maritime Baptists and their World* (Hantsport, 1988), 110.

19   See *ibid*, 111.

20   Bill, *Fifty Years*, 204.

21   J.M. Bumsted, ed., "The Autobiography of Joseph Crandall," *Acadiensis*, III, 1 (Autumn, 1973), 81. Hereafter referred to as *Crandall Autobiography*.

were the people of God for they were Christians and that none could go to Heaven unless they were converted."[22]

Despite the New Light commitment of his parents, and despite hearing New Light evangelistic sermons preached in Chester in the mid 1780s by Thomas Handly Chipman and Harris Harding, Crandall found that his "heart was hard and unmoved and I thought at the time that the Lord had left me to perish in my sins and justly too for I was one of the greatest sinners on earth."[23] Disoriented because of the death of his parents, Crandall, though still only in his teens, was keen to make a new start in life, and he made his way to Liverpool where he "was employed ... in Cod fishing."[24] Finding himself "more hardened in sin and ... often in despair," he soon returned to "Chester, from there I went to Falmouth and then to Newport — was engaged for a time in freighting lumber from Shubenacadie to Windsor."[25] In July 1795, the now 24-year-old Crandall attended a New Light "Sabbath morning" service in a private home in Onslow, where Harris Harding preached a memorable sermon. The disciple of Henry Alline had been "high" in Crandall's "esteem since the time of the reformation at Chester."[26] The service was also attended by Joseph Dimock who was at the time pastor of the Chester New Light Congregational Church. Crandall described what J.M. Bumsted has recently referred to as his almost stereotypical New Light "adult conversion experience"[27] in the following evocative Allinite manner:

> When I entered the house the glorious majesty of the Divine Being appeared to open before the eyes of my understanding (I beheld no object with my bodily eyes) and I saw myself justly condemned to endless misery. I saw no way of escape until suddenly a glorious light shone from the excellent Majesty and I saw the way of Salvation was Gods work and not mine. I felt as I had never felt before although among strangers. I could not hold my peace. My hard heart was at last broken and I had such a view of a perishing world lying in ruin as I never could express.[28]

---

22 *Ibid.*, 81.

23 *Ibid.*, 82.

24 *Ibid.*

25 *Ibid.*

26 *Ibid.*

27 Bumsted, "Joseph Crandall," 179.

28 *Crandall Autobiography*, 82-83.

Then to the "great surprise of all present," an excited and agitated and seemingly inspired Crandall "began to speak and try to tell what I felt and saw."[29] He was absolutely convinced, years after the unforgettable event, that:

> My mind was completely absorbed in the solemn and marvellous scene. It appeared to me that the whole human race lay in open ruin and were altogether at the disposal of that Holy Being whose bright glory had so overwhelmed my soul. I saw mercy so connected with the justice of God that they were both one that what God had done in the person of Christ was alone sufficient to save all that came to God for mercy through Jesus Christ. I felt that the whole world ought to know what I felt and saw for indeed it appeared of more importance to me than the whole world.[30]

Words of testimony and exhortation, shaped by his parents' New Light faith and his own former "despair," poured out of the new convert's mouth "for more than an hour" since he "could not hold my peace."[31] Crandall's salvation, which involved, for him, the infusion of the Holy Spirit, "was a stream of living water flowing into my soul and then bursting forth like a stream from an overflowing fountain."[32] Crandall, while exhorting, experienced the Almighty's powerful and unmistakable "call" to preach the gospel; it was a distinct "call" within a context of a "vision" or "scene," in which, "The work of sinners lay before me like a broad field to which I could see no end."[33]

Crandall's totally unexpected hour-length exhortation amazed Dimock and Harding and moved them to uncontrollable "weeping" and many others in the crowded room found themselves "weeping with them."[34] Crandall remained in the Newport-Onslow region in the summer and "the *World* had no charms for me now."[35] Instead, he discovered, much to his delight, that he "had no comfort unless I was praying or exhorting which I did whenever opportunity offered."[36] And there were many opportunities for Crandall in the Onslow region and then in his home town of Chester where he returned in the autumn. But by the late

---

29 *Ibid.*, 83.

30 *Ibid.*, 83.

31 *Ibid.*

32 *Ibid.*

33 *Ibid.*

34 *Ibid.*

35 *Ibid.*

36 *Ibid.*

autumn, Crandall was no longer satisfied with merely "praying and exhorting" after Dimock had preached his sermon; the new convert wanted to preach and not play ministerial second-fiddle to any other man, even his much beloved pastor. Opposition to Crandall's becoming a minister — actually being ordained — was, as he put it, "like thorns to my soul."[37] Then towards the end of 1795, Crandall had a dream, a dream very much in the Allinite tradition and one which also seemed to have been influenced by the "world of wonders" inhabited by Harris Harding. It was, according to Crandall, a "strange dream," a dream which he experienced late on a Saturday night or early on a Sunday morning. The former fisherman dreamed that:

> I was standing by a broad stream of smooth water thousands of men and women were floating down the stream in a standing position with their heads and shoulders above the water, they seemed quite unconscious of their danger. I watched them until they reached the cataract below when they suddenly disappeared. All below the rocky cataract was dense darkness. I also saw in the dream a man with a long pole and a bow on the end of it: He came to me and told me to wade in and save all the people I could. I thought in the dream that I did so and all that I could throw the bow over I led to a delightful bank covered with green grass and beautiful flowers and there they united in singing the praises of God in a delightful manner.[38]

While Crandall was "musing on this strange dream," early on the Sunday morning, "the 28th chapter of Matthew came to my mind and when I came to the two last verses I was struck with a great surprise."[39] The two verses contained the last words of the resurrected Christ to his disciples:

> 19. "Go therefore and make disciples of all the nations, baptizing them in the name of the Father and of the Son and the Holy Spirit;"

> 20. "Teaching them to observe all things that I have commanded you; and lo, I am with you always, even to the end of the age."

The "strange dream" (only "part of which" Crandall was willing to "relate" in his "Autobiography"), when taken in its entirety compelled the New Light convert to view "believer's baptism" by immersion not as Alline and his followers still viewed it as "a nonessential," but as a divinely ordained absolute essential.

---

37 *Ibid.*

38 *Ibid.*, 83-84.

39 *Ibid.*, 84.

"Had I been present when John baptised the Saviour and stood on the bank of the Jordan and witnessed the whole scene," Crandall declared, "I could not have been more convinced."[40] The Sunday morning "divine illumination" had, in a remarkable and unanticipated manner, driven away all the existing doubts that Crandall still had "about my conversion" and "calling."[41] In addition, it had suddenly transformed him into an ardent advocate of "believer's baptism." On "That same sabbath day," probably in late October or early November, Crandall, after pressuring his pastor, "was buried with my Lord in a watery grave by Elder Joseph Dimock."[42] This public baptism by immersion in the frigid waters of Chester Basin became the defining experiential religious moment for Crandall who, from that precise moment, "never since had one doubt about my conversion nor mode of baptism."[43]

From Crandall's own account, at least, there were three major reasons why he became a Baptist. First, his memorable "dream," something he considered to be an amalgam of "divine impression" and "command," persuaded him that to "save all the people I could," he would have "to wade in" the "water," in a deep ritualistic sense. Second, the dream compelled him to see the urgency of Christ's command to go "and make disciples of all nations, baptizing them ...." It was obviously not enough to help convert people to Evangelical, even New Light, Christianity; conversion had to be followed by baptism by immersion because this was what Christ commanded. Third, Crandall powerfully connected the "believer's baptism" imperative of the last two verses of Matthew and Christ's own baptism in the Jordan River by John the Baptist. If baptism by immersion in the Jordan River by John the Baptist was good enough for the Saviour, it was good enough for Joseph Crandall. The "dream" had enabled Crandall to see the Scriptures in a radically different manner and through a newly-ground lens provided by the Holy Spirit. By November 1795, Crandall had his message and his empowering ritual, a ritual which had touched, it seemed, almost in every conceivable way, the innermost recesses of his being.

In late November 1795, Crandall accompanied his spiritual mentor, Harris Harding, to Liverpool where the two men helped to preach a religious revival into existence. Crandall then spent most of the next four years itinerating throughout Yankee Nova Scotia and the eastern corner of New Brunswick. Despite his 1795 obsession with the efficacy of "believer's baptism," there is absolutely no mention of any of his converts being baptized by immersion in 1796, 1797, 1798, or in 1799, the year when, on 8 October in Sackville, New

40 *Ibid.*

41 *Ibid.*

42 *Ibid.*

43 *Ibid.*

Brunswick, he was finally ordained as a minister of the gospel. The timing of Crandall's ordination on 8 October 1799[44] is of critical importance in explaining why his preaching did not produce baptisms. Of course, he could not baptize any of his converts until he was properly ordained; Crandall knew this and so did the hundreds of Nova Scotians and New Brunswickers who had flocked to hear his New Light evangelistic message. Moreover, his mentor in the faith, Harris Harding, was not baptized by immersion until 1799, four years after Crandall had been. And even after his baptism Harding still regarded the question of baptism in strictly Allinite light — as a matter of little real consequence. What remained absolutely central for Harding, throughout the latter part of the eighteenth century and early years of the nineteenth was the New Light conversion experience. Furthermore, despite his own baptism by immersion as early as 1787, Joseph Dimock, Crandall's pastor, never considered the ritual to be of special significance, until at least 1811. Even after that date, Dimock, who ministered in Chester, continued to place more stress on the centrality of the New Light New Birth than he did on "believer's baptism."[45]

Without ministerial support from his closest colleagues and friends for the gospel of "Conversion-baptism" the 27-year-old Crandall found himself, by late 1798, increasingly dysfunctional. A mood of intense and disconcerting spiritual immobilization had been intensified by his recent marriage and his move to the Salisbury area of eastern New Brunswick, where he now farmed "quite in the wilderness."[46] His "troubles of mind became almost overwhelming" and he was afraid, as early as 1796, that "there was a possibility that I had deceived myself, and if myself, then others."[47] Under these depressing "fears," he resolved "to preach no more."[48] By early October 1799, however, it is clear that Crandall's "depressing fears" had disappeared and his ordination, even as minster of "a mixed church" — where the immersed and the merely converted were members — was the means whereby he could both spread his gospel of "believer's baptism" and also implement it.

Less than two months before Crandall's ordination Harris Harding was finally baptized by immersion by James Manning in Yarmouth. Manning described his baptism in the following manner:

> At the time, the ordinance of baptism was administered the people looked as solemn as the grave. Mr. Harding's coming to the water

---

44   Bumsted, "Joseph Crandall," 179.

45   See G.E. Levy, ed., *The Diary of Joseph Dimock* (Hantsport, 1979), passim.

46   *Crandall Autobiography*, 86.

47   *Ibid.*

48   *Ibid.*

seemed like Christ coming to Jordan. After he came from the water he prayed with the people in the street. It seemed as though he had a double portion of the Spirit. Some of the dear christians broke forth in praises to God and the Lamb.[49]

The Harding baptism poured fuel on the revival fires which had begun to blaze down the Annapolis Valley in 1798. By 1800 this religious and social movement had become what David Bell has accurately described as "the first distinctly" Baptist "reformation in Maritime history,"[50] and had spread to the Yarmouth region and to neighbouring New Brunswick. In the Spring of 1798 the "mass immersions began under Thomas Chipman,"[51] in the Annapolis-Granville region. Within 13 months, Chipman had "dipped 173 persons"[52] and scores of others were baptized by immersion in Kings and Yarmouth counties.

By 1800, the "Baptist reformation" had begun to concern Bishop Charles Inglis. According to Inglis, the new Baptists "Formerly ... were Pedobaptists, but by a recent illumination, they have adopted the Anabaptist scheme, by which their number has been much increased and their zeal inflamed."[53] Inglis stressed the popular, almost populist, impulse within the new Baptist movement. And he knew, from his local Anglican sources in "Annapolis-Granville, Wilmot and Aylesford,"[54] that this was indeed the case. The New Light ministers were themselves being swallowed up by what Inglis spitefully referred to as the "rage for dipping."[55] This "rage for dipping," Inglis reported to his superiors at the Society for the Propagation of the Gospel,

> or total immersion prevails all over the western counties of the Province, and is frequently performed in a very indelicate manner before vast collections of people. Several hundreds have already been baptized, and this plunging they deem to be absolutely necessary to the conversion of their souls.[56]

---

49 J.M. Cramp, "History of the Maritime Baptists," AUA.

50 Bell, *Newlight Baptist Journals*, 23.

51 *Ibid.*, 21.

52 *Ibid.*

53 Quoted in Saunders, *History of the Baptists*, 1145.

54 *Ibid.*, 115.

55 *Ibid.*

56 *Ibid.*

Inglis explicitly connected, as has already been pointed out, the popular Baptist movement to what he explicitly called a "democratic ... general plan of total revolution in religion and civil government."[57] "All order and decorum are despised by them," he railed. "Fierce dissentions prevail among the most intimate; family government is dissolved; children are neglected and become disobedient."[58]

Despite his somewhat exaggerated claims, there were flashes of shrewd insight to be found in the Inglis report. There was indeed a "rage for dipping" in the Yankee heartland of Nova Scotia in 1798 and 1799, a rage not created by the "Baptist Patriarchs" from above but forced on most of them from below. The "Baptist reformation" had, of course, more than just religious implications. There was to be found, as Inglis perceptively realized, in the ritual of cleansing, a powerful democratic and egalitarian impulse. The disconcerting question which hovered over the "Baptist reformation," for some Anglicans at least, was whether the "rage for dipping" would be channelled or deflected from the largely religious realm to that of the secular sphere. Most of the Baptists involved in the movement, however, considered the question to be an irrelevant one, since, for them, the religious realm was everything.

As he itinerated throughout New Brunswick, Crandall would carry with him, after October 1799, his own version of "total immersion," this version which owed virtually nothing to the "Baptist reformation" in southwestern Yankee Nova Scotia. In early January 1800, Crandall felt a call to preach the "true gospel" along "the River Saint John."[59] At this time, there was only one tiny Baptist Church, Crandall's own, in the entire colony of New Brunswick and only a handful of people who had been immersed. Thus, out of a total New Brunswick population of approximately 20,000 inhabitants in 1800, fewer than 50 were Baptists.[60] Seventy-one years later, out of a total population of some 285,594, 70,595 or 25 percent was Baptist, almost one half of the Protestant population.[61] During the first six decades of the nineteenth century the religious life of New Brunswick had obviously been significantly affected by the "Baptist reformation," a development which might also be referred to, with good reason, as the "Baptist revolution."

Assisting in the transformation of Yankee New Lights into Nova Scotia Baptists was one thing; being part of the same complex transformation process

---

57   *Ibid.*

58   *Ibid.*

59   *Crandall Autobiography*, 87.

60   Bell, *Newlight Baptist Journals*, 249-50.

61   See my *Ravished by the Spirit: Religious Revivals, Baptists and Henry Alline* (Montreal, 1984), 171.

in Loyalist New Brunswick, where demographic heterogeneity and not homogeneity was the norm, was a radically different thing — or so it would seem.[62] The 1798-1800 "Baptist reformation" in Yankee Nova Scotia brought like-minded Yankees together by enabling them to continue "to regard themselves as a people with a unique history, a distinct identity, and a special destiny."[63] In New Brunswick, unlike Nova Scotia, the "Yankee" element was of little numerical consequence and most of the population was of Loyalist background, a rough cross-section of American colonial society before the revolution. These Loyalists shared little in common except a sense of defeat and despair. But as far as David Bell is concerned, this apparent obstacle had, in fact, become a Baptist advantage at the turn of the century. "Economically and demographically the colony was stagnant," he has argued. "Politically," he goes on,

> [New Brunswick] was bitterly factionalized. Far from becoming the boasted "envy of the American states" New Brunswick was reduced to the status of a remote backwater in the empire's struggle against the revolutionary French. One symptom of this loss of hierarchical consensus is the fact that some Loyalists felt free to demonstrate that they had no more regard for the elite's Church of England than the Church had shown for them.[64]

Consequently, according to Bell's very persuasive analysis:

> The Loyalist frontier needed the social organization religion could provide, and Baptist preachers arrived at a time when many no longer feared taking a stand with religious dissent.[65]

Bell could have also mentioned that the first Baptist itinerant to arrive in New Brunswick in the first decade of the nineteenth century was greeted by large numbers, Loyalists and Yankees alike, who needed little, if any, convincing to be immersed. They too were caught up in the "rage for dipping," part of a complex tendency natural among neighbouring societies to borrow, despite the absence of explicit and direct contact, "cultural elements from one another freely."[66]

---

62 See E.C. Wright, *The Loyalists of New Brunswick* (Fredericton, 1955), passim.

63 See my *Nova Scotia's Massachusetts* (Montreal, 1973), xvi.

64 Bell, *Newlight Baptist Journals*, 85.

65 *Ibid.*

66 G.P. Murdoch, "Ethnographic Atlas: A Summary," *Ethnology*, I (April 1967), 112.

Joseph Crandall, in January 1800, was the human agent largely responsible for actualizing what may be regarded as the pro-Baptist process of cultural osmosis then affecting certain regions of New Brunswick. In January 1800, Crandall was 28, and according to Jarvis Ring who met him at this time, "a seallator [slender] Lacky [lanky] man not clothed much like a minister."[67] His "voice" it was said, was especially "commanding, and his intonations at times peculiarly touching."[68] He was always an eager itinerant and saw in his first expedition an opportunity to spread his New Light-Baptist message up and down the St. John River Valley. But he still wondered "where my path of duty lay."[69] In his autobiography, Crandall stressed that, "It was now midwinter and how to get there I could not tell but it seemed by going there was the only door of hope open to my troubled mind."[70]

What did Crandall really mean when he wrote that, "it seemed by going there was the only door of hope open to my troubled mind?" Why was itinerating in the midst of winter in the St. John River Valley Crandall's "only door of hope?" Here was Joseph the Baptist going to convert and to baptize New Brunswickers, people with whom he had so little in common, at the time of the year when all the available rivers and lakes were covered with thick ice. And why was Crandall again suffering from a "troubled mind," only months after his ordination? Was it because he felt himself to be hypocritical in that he was minister of a church, as he put it, that "was organized on gospel grounds with the exception that unimmersed Christians might commune?"71 He was obviously caught on the horns of a real dilemma. In order to be baptized by immersion, he needed to be an ordained minister; and in order to be ordained by Edward Manning, Joseph Dimock and T.S. Harding, the three ministers who actually ordained him in October 1799, Crandall had to accept "mixed communion," a practice buttressed by the Allinite conviction that the form of baptism was not an "essential." How could Crandall resolve his dilemma without splitting his church and without being immobilized himself? In good New Light and Allinite fashion, Crandall could leave his problems behind, however temporarily, by itinerating far from home. And this is precisely what he decided to do, at a most inappropriate time it seemed, especially for a Baptist itinerant, in early 1800.

67   Jarvis Ring Papers, AUA.

68   Bill, *Fifty Years*, 214.

69   *Crandall Autobiography*, 87.

70   *Ibid.*

71   *Ibid.*, 86.

Crandall finally arrived at Waterborough, on the St. John River, apparently his intended destination, "uninvited and unknown towards the middle of March."[72] On his journey to Waterborough by snowshoe and later by "a sleigh on the ice," during which time he preached frequently, Crandall maintained that he only met one person — a "Mrs. Case ... who had been immersed."[73] At Waterborough where there was a small Allinite congregation led by "A very Godly man ... Elijah Easterbrooks,"[74] Crandall spent time with the members but not with Esterbrooks who "was absent during my visit."[75] Crandall felt that his preaching had helped the "spirit of the Lord" affect "the minds of the people" but only "One or two ... found mercy."[76] Somewhat disappointed, Crandall decided to strike out towards the west towards Kingsclear, a few miles beyond the provincial capital of Fredericton, an area where "Edward Manning had had his most spectacular success in 1793."[77] At Kingsclear Crandall seemed to discover a totally unanticipated pro-Baptist sentiment. According to Crandall:

> The Lord wrought wonders in ... Kingsclear. On the Lord's day a pious woman asked me how she could proceed in order to be immersed. I pointed out the way, and announced that sister Cole would be immersed at ten o'clock the next day at a certain place. Long before the hour arrived people came in from all directions for many miles around.[78]

It is noteworthy that the initiative for a winter baptism by immersion definitely came from "sister Cole"; once she asked Crandall, he merely "pointed out the way."[79] The "pious woman" had obviously already experienced the New Birth, most likely under the Allinite preaching of Edward Manning in 1793. She now demanded "immersion;" immersion was, it is clear, not forced upon her by a manipulative Crandall. Moreover, the news about her imminent baptism spread quickly throughout the region, triggering an amazingly positive popular response. The novelty of the ritual of "believer's baptism," a ritual which both fascinated and attracted them, without question, drew many people.

---

72 Bell, *Newlight Baptist Journals*, 85.

73 *Crandall Autobiography*, 87.

74 *Ibid.*, 88.

75 *Ibid.*

76 *Ibid.*

77 Bell, *Newlight Baptist Journals*, 85.

78 *Crandall Autobiography*, 88.

79 *Ibid.*

"Four or five hundred people surrounded the watery grave," at ten in the morning, and what they saw would leave an indelible impression on their collective memory:

> The ice being open the candidate related a clear experience and was immersed. When we came up out of the water, two men came forward and related what the Lord had done for their souls. We could not leave the water until fourteen happy converts were immersed in the same manner as our Saviour. Truly this was the Lord's work .... it was wonderful to see the young converts going around among the people they came out of the cold water praising the Lord and exhorting others to come and embrace the Saviour. Surely this was the beginning of good days, the work of the Lord spread in every direction. As they returned from the meeting they said the bible was altogether a new book to them.[80]

Crandall had, in his preaching and his dipping, provided the Kingsclear area residents, with a new pro-Baptist grid to apply to their reading of the New Testament. This grid transformed the Bible into an "altogether ... new book." Thus, the divinely inspired "Word of God," read by an increasingly literate population, through divinely inspired Baptist eyes, enabled Pedobaptists, whether Anglicans or Congregationalists or Presbyterians, to become Baptists in a complex process which sanctified their primitive urge to be purified, thus blotting out a bleak and disconcerting past and also restoring a faith, however fragile, in the future both in a local and cosmic sense.

The Kingsclear baptisms are noteworthy because they were administered in frigid waters; Crandall, in immersing 14 men and women, would have had to have spent, at the least, 20 minutes, up to his waist, in the frigid St. John River. Each candidate would have walked, over some slippery ice, to "the watery grave" and then gradually each made her and his way into the water to stand near the minister. Neither person, of course, had special waterproof boots and clothes for the occasion. Once they were in place and their feet firmly on the flat bottom of the river, Crandall would use his left hand to grasp the two hands clasped in prayer of the candidate and his right would cup the candidate's neck. Just before the immersion, Crandall would shout out to those hundreds crowded along the shore, "I baptize you" and then he would include the name of the individual, "in the name of the Father, the Son, and the Holy Ghost." The candidate then would fall slowly into the water, Crandall would be careful to ensure that the person was completely immersed and that she or he would be quickly lifted back into an upright position. There were a number of instances of

---

80 *Ibid.*

people not being totally immersed who demanded to be rebaptized properly. Both minister and candidate would probably leave the water, Crandall to get warm and dry, if for only a moment, and the candidate to put on dry clothes.

The Kingsclear winter baptism must have been both an exhilarating and physically debilitating experience for both baptizer and baptized. Moreover, the extraordinary conditions in which these ceremonies were performed must have also added an almost ethereal quality to the occasion, a quality readily exaggerated, in a myriad of ways, as those who were actually there told others about the amazing event, soon afterwards and then over and over again as the years passed.

Revitalized by the baptisms, Crandall moved up to present day Woodstock "preaching and immersing believers."[81] Then in late May he returned to Waterborough. Because of heavy flooding in the region, Crandall "could not see how the Lord's work could be carried forward just then as the people could not attend the meetings."[82] Crandall had, however, underestimated the power of the St. John River Valley system of oral communication. Just when he "began to think it was about time for me to return home," Crandall saw, arriving from east and west, "boats ... loaded with anxious inquirers asking about the reformation up the river for they had heard about such numbers being immersed."[83] This unexpected intelligence had compelled "many ... to read their bibles and were prepared to yield obedience to the Lords commands." An astonished Crandall was quickly surrounded by scores of men and women and soon "the Lords Work commenced and a number rejoiced in the Lord."[84] "It was wonderful" for the visiting preacher "to see the aged, the middle aged, and the youths relating in the language of the Holy Scripture what the Lord had done for their souls."[85] The revival fires were fanned by the enthusiasm and support of "Brother Elijah Easterbrooks."[86] Not only did Estabrooks support the revival preaching of Crandall, but the old Allinite also unequivocally accepted the Baptist immersionist argument. Within a few days, "There were about thirty immersed," including Estabrooks and Zebulon Estey, hitherto a vociferous opponent of "believer's baptism." Estey, according to Crandall, was "an old New England Congregationalist rooted and grounded in the old puritan practice of Infant sprinkling."[87]

---

81 *Ibid.*

82 *Ibid.*

83 *Ibid.*

84 *Ibid.*

85 *Ibid.*

86 *Ibid.*

87 *Ibid.*

On first meeting Crandall, Estey declared, "I see you are going to break up our church." Crandall replied, "Sir, if your church is built on Christ the gates of hell cannot prevail against it." "Do you not call us a church of Christ," Estey shot back, only to be told by the New Light Baptist itinerant, "I consider you are a company of pious christians but not walking in the order of the gospel as commanded by Christ." A furious Estey turned his back on Crandall and spat back at him, "my parents had given me up to the Lord in infancy and from that I would not depart." Before Estey could leave, Crandall confidently declared, "Squire, I have one word to say to you. The Scribes and Pharisees rejected the council of the Lord against themselves not being immersed."[88]

The confrontation with Estey had taken place on Saturday during a ten-hour long "Conference meeting" where it was announced that the special Baptismal service would take place on the following morning "being Lord's day ... at the water side at 9 o'clock."[89] "There was a great host of people assembled to see the effects of the new religion" and to Crandall's "great surprise" Estey, an "old gentleman who was determined 'never to depart from his infant sprinkling,' was the first to yield obedience to the commands of Christ."[90] He was followed into a somewhat warmer St. John River "watery grave" by his close friend Elijah Estabrooks and eight others. Crandall maintained that "such a day of the Lord's power was I believe rarely witnessed on earth." He went on:

> This meeting did not break up until after the sun had gone down. And it was truly solemn and delightful as well to hear the praises of the Lord sung by great numbers of happy converts returning home in their Boats from the solemn scene. The work of that day I can never forget. The clear setting sun, the broad expanse of smooth water spreading over a large extent of land, the serenity of the atmosphere, the delightful notes of the feathered songsters and the solemn tone of the hymns from the many happy voices presented to me an emblem of the very presence of God. It seemed as though the very Heavens had come down to earth and I was on the brink of the external world.[91]

On the following Monday, Crandall "passed over the river and at 8 o'clock in the morning immersed a number," 21 in fact, "that came into liberty the day before."[92] He then, early in June, began his return to his Salisbury home and his

---

88   *Ibid.*, 88-89.

89   *Ibid.*, 89.

90   *Ibid.*

91   *Ibid.*

92   *Ibid.*

Baptist church. On the way he "preached several times and immersed quite a number," always, he was certain, under "the watchful eye of God over me and mine."[93]

Crandall would often return to the St. John River Valley; he was a very effective Baptist itinerant during his long ministerial career which only ended with his death in February 1858. But Crandall, as one of his biographers, I.E. Bill, observed in 1881, was not a particularly successful pastor. "The fact is," Bill observed, "that steady pastoral guidance, in connection with an individual Church, was not his *forte*."[94] "Notwithstanding" that he "was in his eighty-seventh year, he nevertheless died with his armour on." According to Bill, who knew Crandall well,

> Only six weeks before he died, he preached the Gospel to the people, supported by two of his deacons, and took his leave of his affectionate and weeping Church; and during his last illness, though his sufferings were at times severe, yet he staggered not at the promise through unbelief, but was strong in faith, giving glory to God. Sensible to the very last, he met the King of terrors with perfect composure, and feeling that death was doing its work, he closed his eyes and died without a struggle.[95]

Elijah Estabrooks, at the time of his 1800 baptism by Joseph Crandall, was 44 years old. Estabrooks was born in Haverill, Massachusetts, in May 1756; his parents "belonged to the Church of England, and educated him conformably to the sentiment of that denomination."[96] In 1763 the Estabrooks family joined thousands of New Englanders as they moved north-eastwards to settle in Nova Scotia. After three years in the Horton region, the Estabrooks moved, in "about 1768, to St. John (N.B.)" and then nine years later, in 1777, "they settled in Waterbury, on the River St. John."[97]

At the age of 22, Estabrooks, in the early summer 1778, experienced a New Light conversion brought about by a powerful evangelistic sermon preached by a Yankee itinerant, Elisha Freeman.[98] Throughout his life, Estabrooks

---

93 *Ibid.*, 90.

94 Bill, *Fifty Years With the Baptists*, 214.

95 *Ibid.*, 215.

96 "Memoir of the Rev. Elijah Estabrooks," *The Baptist Missionary Magazine of Nova Scotia and New Brunswick*, 1, 1 (April 1829), 289. Hereafter referred to as "Estabrooks Memoir."

97 *Ibid.*

98 Bell, *Newlight Baptist Journals*, 35.

remembered Freeman's text from John VIII: 36 *"If the Son therefore shall make you free., ye shall be free indeed."* A "deep and permanent impression" was made "on his mind" but it was not until August that he actually experienced "regeneration," what he referred to as obtaining "a hope in Christ, — *a good hope through grace."*[99] A year later, Estabrooks first heard Henry Alline preach and soon afterwards became a member of the local New Light Congregational Church. According to a contemporary, at this time,

> He was much esteemed for his exemplary piety, and it soon became manifest, that he possessed gifts for public usefulness. After a few years he commenced preaching and laboured to general acceptance.[100]

It is known that "about the year 1790," Estabrooks was very active in Allinite New Light services being held in the Waterborough area. At these house services, there would be prayer, some exhorting or witnessing and "Alline's hymns were commonly sung."[101] It is also known that in the summer of 1791, the Black Loyalist Baptist, David George, became the first "Baptist to preach and immerse on the River St. John."[102] George may or may not have made contact with Estabrooks; it is certain, however, that his Black disciple Sampson Colbert did later in the year. These Baptists failed to persuade the Allinites to accept their New Light Black Baptist gospel. Instead, Estabrooks and some of his friends seemed to become enamoured with Radical Evangelical Methodism. At some of these New Light-Methodist meetings in Waterborough in 1792, a British Calvinist Methodist missionary, John James, observed "about 25 or thirty have been bawling as loud as they could at the same instant of Time consisting of Male and Female, old and young, and many of them Persons of infamous Character."[103] These men and women were transformed into "preachers by the mere impulse of a heated imagination."[104] And according to the Scots traveller Patrick Campbell who, by a "remarkable coincidence,"[105] was visiting Water-

---

99 "Estabrooks Memoir," 289-90.

100 *Ibid.*, 290.

101 Bell, *Newlight Baptist Journals, 72.*

102 *Ibid.*

103 John James to unidentified, 18 October 1792, transcript in the possession of G.A. Rawlyk. The original letter is in the archives of Westminster College, Cambridge, U.K.

104 *Ibid.*

105 Bell, *Newlight Baptist Journals,* 77.

borough at the same time as Jones, the Jones description was indeed an accurate one:

> As we were conversing along, I heard a great noise in a house at some distance, on which I stopped to listen, and told the gentleman that there were some people fighting in that house; at which he smiled and answered, "That he knew the place well; that it was a house of worship, where a number of religious fanatics assembled at all hours of the night and day, there no body preached, every one prayed for himself, and the louder they roared, the more sincere and devout they were supposed to be; so that the one vied with the other who should bawl out loudest." When we had come nearer, I was struck with amazement at the hideous noise they made ... I asked him if he supposed they would permit me to go in to see them; he said I might, provided I behaved properly, and did not laugh, or offer to ridicule them in any shape; that they would not prevent me, or give me the least trouble; thus encouraged, I went in, and found they consisted of about three score persons, of both sexes, all on their knees, and in tears, every one praying for himself ... and bawling out, O Lord! O Lord! which were the only expressions I understood of what they said. After standing a few minutes in the house, my hair almost standing on end at the horror of the scene these miserable people exhibited, I returned, and just as I was passing the window of their apartment, someone called out, that the devil was among them; upon which they all gave a yell, louder and more horrible than any Indian war hoop I had ever heard; and if the devil himself was to show his physiognomy in all the frightful grimaces ascribed to him in the middle of them, every door bolted, so that none possibly could escape his clutches, their screaming could not have been louder or more horrible.[106]

Though the Scot traveller Patrick Campbell had little sympathy for what he called New Brunswick New Light "fanaticism,"[107] he certainly did notice in the worship service, the importance of lay preachers and exhorters, gender equality, and enthusiasm. In all likelihood, Estabrooks, now 36 years old, was one of the men on his knees, praying and yelling, and almost delirious in his Allinite ecstasy. Being ecstatic was one thing for Estabrooks, but he drew the line at actually having sexual relations with women during worship services, as some reportedly did. These Antinomian excesses, called by some "liturgical sex," split

---

106 P. Campbell, *Travels in the Interior Inhabited Parts of North America: in the Years 1791 and 1792*, edited by H.H. Langton and W.F. Ganong (1793, Toronto, 1937), 255-56.

107 *Ibid.*, 256.

these Waterborough Allinites late in 1792 and 1793 into two major camps. The Antinomian one was led by John Lunt, described by a contemporary as "an abandoned profligate character, a sort of necromancer and fortune teller"[108] and the other — spitefully referred to by the Luntites as the "pharisaical" — was apparently led by Estabrooks and Estey.[109]

A rape charge against Lunt, heard in the Queen's County circuit court on 29 June 1793,[110] seemed to strengthen Estabrook's resolve to create theological distance and space between his position and that of his former close friends. In 1794 or 1795, it is known that Estabrooks was seriously considering being ordained a Methodist minister; but during his "public examination" Estabrooks stubbornly refused to accept certain key features of Wesleyan Arminianism because of his deep commitment to the Allinite emphasis on the "perseverance of the Saints."[111]

After his flirtation with the Methodists, Estabrooks returned to his struggling New Light congregation which, according to David Bell, had "become consciously more formalistic."[112] For the latter half of the last decade of the eighteenth century, Estabrooks, though still active as a New Light preacher, though not ordained, began to raise serious and disconcerting questions about "the correctness of some of his sentiments."[113] While "endeavouring to maintain the views which he then entertained," Estabrooks found that "his mind was seriously exercised with doubts."[114] According to a friend, who knew him very well at the time, Estabrooks had slowly come to the realization, late in the 1790s, that many of his Allinite views "had been adopted without a due examination of the Scriptures."[115]

> [He] proceeded, therefore, to a prayerful and attentive investigation. This terminated in a full conviction, that salvation is wholly of grace, proceeding from the *eternal purpose* of JEHOVAH. On pursuing a similar inquiry relative to the ordinances of the Gospel, he came to the

---

108 Quoted in Bell, *Newlight Baptist Journals*, 80.

109 Quoted in *ibid.*, 80.

110 This trial is superbly dealt with in *ibid.*, 81-83.

111 Jarvis Ring Papers, AUA.

112 Bell, *Newlight Baptist Journals*, 84.

113 "Eastabrooks Memoir," 290.

114 *Ibid.*

115 *Ibid.*

conclusion, that the immersion of a professed believer in Christ is the only scriptural baptism.[116]

Estabrook's religious and spiritual trajectory from Allinism to Baptist Calvinism may not have been seen as straightforward as his biographer seemed to suggest in 1829.[117] What is certain, however, is that by "About the commencement of the year 1800," Estabrooks had definitely replaced Allinite "impressionism" with "a due examination of the Scriptures" and New Light anarchy with an almost exaggerated emphasis on decorum and order.118 Moreover, like hundreds of New Brunswickers inhabiting the St. John River Valley and thousands of Yankees in Nova Scotia, Estabrooks had seen in "believer's baptism" not only a possible answer to the various complex problems unleashed by manifestations of New Dispensationalism, but also a powerful ritual actually endorsed and experienced by his Saviour. Perhaps his double espousal of Calvinism and "believer's baptism" was more common than many have assumed. But the available contemporary evidence suggests that it was not, especially at the popular level. Calvinism was, it seems clear, espoused first by some members of the Baptist ministerial elite, influenced by events and personalities in Massachusetts and by their almost palpable desire to become respectable and not, as one of their members put it, to be "looked upon as nobody."[119] Estabrooks, early in 1800, had abandoned the Allinite indifference to the mode of baptism and now considered "believer's baptism" to be an "essential" of the Evangelical Christian faith. His espousal of Calvinism and closed communion would come later despite what some of his Baptist contemporaries might have thought in the 1820s. These men were eager to rewrite the Baptist past and in many respects, until quite recently, they were amazingly successful in their mission.

By late May, 1800, Estabrooks, "Having embraced" his pro-immersion "sentiments ... did not hesitate to make a public avowal of them."[120] On that early Sunday morning, he saw his close friend Zebulon Estey baptized by Joseph Crandall. After Estey's baptism, Estabrooks entered the "watery grave." He walked out on the firm sandy bottom to where Crandall was standing up to his hips in the St. John River water. Estabrooks was dressed, in all likelihood, simply in homespun trousers and a light shirt; he was also barefooted. When he

---

116 *Ibid.*

117 For a further discussion of this problem with respect to some of the other "Baptist Patriarchs," see my *Ravished by the Spirit*, 73-105.

118 See *Ravished By the Spirit*, 88-93

119 Quoted in Cramp, "History of the Maritime Baptists," AUA.

120 "Estabrooks Memoir," 290.

reached Crandall, Estabrooks looked back and saw scores of his friends crowded along the flat river bank; there were many others to be seen further up the bank, men, women and children who did not consider themselves to be believers. There was symbolic space therefore between those who believed and those who did not, something which both groups almost instinctively created for themselves. Those crowded along the river felt that they, like the Hay Bay Camp Meeting Methodists, were on sacred ground. And they regarded the water contiguous to them as sacred space as well, their New Brunswick Jordan. In this sacred space, the events of the New Testament could indeed be replicated. As had been the case when John the Baptist had baptized Jesus or when the apostle Philip had baptized the "Ethiopian eunuch," the Holy Spirit was expected to be present in its full transforming power. Estabrooks proudly faced the shore; and then, while Crandall gently grabbed Estabrook's hands clutched together in prayer with his left hand and placed his right behind the former's neck, the Baptist minister shouted for all to hear "I baptize you" Elijah Estabrooks in the name of the Father, the Son and the Holy Spirit." Then Estabrooks bent his knees slightly and Crandall both pushed and guided him under the water. Estabrooks closed his eyes and his mouth and held his breath. He felt himself transported through centuries of time to the Jordan and, in Crandall's touch, he felt the touch of his Saviour. Immersed in the St. John River, Estabrooks experienced again his New Light regeneration of 1778 and the boundless grace of Christ's ultimate sacrifice. For a brief and glorious moment he felt almost one with the divine. Then suddenly, he found himself being helped to his feet by Crandall. And as Estabrooks wiped his face and straightened his trousers, and regained his balance, he may have seen Crandall look at the people on the shore and then slowly bend over and lift in the palm of his right hand some water. After doing this, while he let the water dribble back to the St. John, Crandall might have shouted out the question, quoting from Acts 8, "See here is water what hinders *you* from being baptized?" It is noteworthy that for Estabrooks, as had been the case for Crandall, the public baptism by immersion became the defining moment of his religious life. In addition, the actual mode of and style of immersion would become the New Brunswick nineteenth-century Baptist norm. There would be some additions such as antiphonal singing and testimonies and even some sermonizing from "the watery grave." Yet, at the core of the ritual of "believer's baptism," there was to be found the "revivifying role of water in religious symbolism" and the almost magical powers of purification and regeneration dispensed by the ordained minister, but always within a narrowly-conceived New Testament framework.

Estabrook's baptism led to his ordination on 15 September 1800 as a Baptist minister.[121] It was hoped that he would be the human means in spreading the "Baptist reformation" up and down the St. John River Valley. And he was,

---

121 *Ibid.*

despite some setbacks along the way. When New Brunswick's Baptist "Elijah"[122] was on the verge of death in September 1825, it seemed that "the spirituality and comfort which he had enjoyed while labouring successfully in the cause of his dear Redeemer, appeared to continue unabated, and even to increase, as he approached the close of his mortal existence."[123]

The Crandall-Estabrook story provides something of the particular "New Brunswick Character" necessary to evaluate the essential nature of the more generalized "Baptist Circumstance." Social anthropological theory, the description of virulent critics and that of unreconstructed supporters, when applied to the actual accounts of two of the principal actors involved in the "Baptist Reformation," adds both depth and substance to a descriptive analysis of a crucially important social and religious movement — the "rage for dipping." This Baptist ritual significantly influenced Maritime Evangelical culture at the turn of the eighteenth century and beyond. The widely perceived transforming power of this ritual, moreover, was so obvious to contemporaries that it seldom drew much serious attention either from them or from some twentieth-century scholars who remain critically suspicious of the obvious — especially in the realm of religion.[124]

122 *Ibid.*, 294.

123 *Ibid.*

124 This is a revised version of a chapter to be found in my *The Canada Fire: Radical Evangelicalism in British North America, 1775-1812* (Montreal, 1994), 162-84.

The Reverend Jonathan Scott
Planter, Preacher, and Patriarch

Gwen Guiou Trask CG(C) and F. Stuart Trask
Yarmouth, Nova Scotia

Almost everything we know about Jonathan Scott comes from Jonathan Scott's own writings. He kept a journal of which only the first volume, ending in November 1777, has surfaced.[1] Further volumes may have been lost in the fire at Minot, Maine, in February 1807 that destroyed his home and in which his youngest child died, although from 1897 to 1910 people, in their correspondence, quoted passages from Scott diaries which they said they had seen.[2]

Jonathan Scott lived in the Planter community of Jebogue/Chebogue in western Nova Scotia. He wrote *The Records of the Church of Jebogue in Yarmouth* for the period 1766 to 1795 (Figure 1). These became his account of his execution of the duties and responsibilities as pastor of a Congregational church and society.[3]

In 1793 and again in 1794, Jonathan Scott went to preach in Bakerstown, Maine, and was called to be the first pastor of the Congregational Church in Minot, moving there with his family in the spring of 1795. He recorded the events in that church and Planter community with the same attention to detail as he had done in Jebogue, until his death in 1819.[4]

In addition, Jonathan Scott wrote *A Brief View, ...*, a book that analyzed the writing and preaching of Henry Alline and his followers. This book was devoted mostly to Congregational doctrine and order but, in his examples, Scott provided some description of Planter family life. By the way, the title filled the first page and the book was over 330 pages long, anything but brief![5]

---

1   Henry E. Scott Jr. ed., *The Journal of Jonathan Scott* (Boston, 1980). Hereafter, *Journal*.

2   For example, in her letter to Chaplain Seymour Tribou under cancellation date 3 May 1895, the Scott scholar Lizzie Washburn wrote, "I have seen nine diaries." New England Historic Genealogical Society (Boston), SG TIN 30. Hereafter, NEHGS.

3   Gwen G. Trask et al, eds. *The Records of the Church of Jebogue, 1766-1851* (Yarmouth, N.S., 1992). Hereafter *Jebogue Church Records*. Handwritten originals at The Public Archives of Nova Scotia [PANS].

4   A photocopy of these records is stored in the Library of the Androscoggin Historical Society, West Auburn ME. Hereafter Androscoggin Records.

5   Jonathan Scott, *A Brief View of the Religious Tenets and Sentiments Lately Published and Spread in the Province of Nova Scotia ...* (Halifax, 1784).

Jonathan Scott kept a separate record of the marriages he performed.[6] As well, we have the assignment of his properties as a grantee, and all the exchanges of property covered in Yarmouth Township deeds.[7] Most of the entries in the Scott family bible were made by him.[8] We can only hope that further Jonathan Scott writings, particularly the missing small diaries, or even the original handwritten first volume of his journal, will surface and be available to further reveal the mind of this remarkable man.

Jonathan Scott — Planter

The Planters of Yarmouth Township, in Scott's time part of Queens County in Nova Scotia, had been arriving from New England in varying size groups

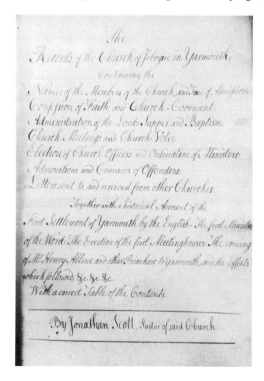

1. Title Page, Jebogue Church Records handwritten by the Reverend Jonathan Scott, PANS Collection. Photo: Stuart Trask

6   *The Mayflower Descendant*, Vols. IX (1907), 40-198, X (1908), 3-5.

7   Yarmouth Township Deeds, Courthouse, Yarmouth, N.S..

8   *Mayflower Descendant*, Vol. VIII (1906), 80-84.

since the three original families came to stay in June 1761.[9] Long before the first grant was finalized and mapped in 1787, these settlers had partitioned Yarmouth Township, creating three areas, First Division, Second Division and Third Division. A committee of the township did its best — these Yankees were old hands at this sort of paperwork — to settle property boundaries which were determined in at least the First Division by their appointed surveyor, Paul Gowen. An effort was made to make the claims official of those already situated on the land of their choice while awaiting confirmation of the grant. To make up the number of acres due each Planter, allotments were also drawn in the Second and Third Divisions by each First Division proprietor.

Jonathan Scott was 20 years old when he first appeared in Yarmouth Township in 1764. He had completed his apprenticeship as a shoemaker (cordwainer) in Roxbury, Massachusetts and, "... having a mind to look a Settlement for myself in life ...," he joined his brother Moses, who had been his guardian since their father's death in 1756. Moses had settled on the Jebogue River in Yarmouth Township in 1763, but was very ill during the summer of 1764 and needed Jonathan's help with his business. Jonathan made the trip from Boston on the vessel of Captain George Ring, worked for Moses for six months, and then returned to Roxbury, having had a dreary, and expensive, time of it in Nova Scotia. Roxbury did not pan out either as he did not get on with William Goddard, his master in the shoemaking trade, with whom he had been apprenticed at age 14. Unable to make a living on his own, he decided early in 1765 to go back to Nova Scotia and his brother. While still in Boston he undertook to fish for the summer with Captain Seth Barnes of Jebogue, and returned with him to Nova Scotia.[10]

He was not cut out for life at sea but he did earn enough that summer to pay for his passage and to finance the building of a log house on the east side of the Jebogue/Chebogue river, "... having pitched on a lot of land to settle on ...." He had it ready enough to take up solitary housekeeping by late 1765. He described his new home: "I built me a log House, on my lot 14 feet long, and 12 feet wide, and covered the roof with Boards, and built a stone Chimney therein, all with my own hand, in about four weeks time ...."[11] He took up farming and, to provide for himself further, he fished for the summers of 1766 and 1767 with Captain George Ring. These endeavours met with some success.

He rated ½ share in the First Division of land, 99 acres and 72 perches, and was settled officially on lot #37. He shared 625 acres, lot #83 in the Second Division and 167 acres and 10 perches in the Third Division, so designated on

---

9   *Jebogue Church Records*, 1.

10   *Journal*, 10.

11   *Journal*, 10.

the Grantees' Map. From then until his departure in 1795 he was involved in many real estate transactions up and down the Jebogue River.[12]

Meanwhile, the 14-year-old daughter of Captain Ring, Mistress Lucy Ring, caught his eye. With her parents' consent, they "kept company." Jonathan was much influenced by Mr. and Mrs. Ring with whom he "... conversed freely on the Things of Religion and the state of my Soul ...," resulting in, among other things, his conversion. An account of his personal covenant with God was included in his journal.[13]

In true Planter fashion Jonathan Scott determined to improve the housing situation for his future wife despite "...having little Ability, and not seeing how I could accomplish it ...." January and February could not have been a good time to start building by that tidal river, but start he did. As soon as Lucy was 16 they were married with the Rings' "... free and hearty consent ...," on 14 March 1768, by the Reverend Ebenezer Moulton, a Baptist minister then in Yarmouth Township. Moulton's sermons had been an early influence in the life of Jonathan, although, by 1770, Moulton was the centre of some contention in the society and congregation at Jebogue.

By pre-arrangement Lucy lived on at the Ring home following their marriage and that summer, after he had "... proceeded with the cellar, raised the roof of the house and boarded ye roof ...," he again went fishing with his father-in-law. In the fall of the year the house was habitable, but Lucy remained at home to give birth to their son John on 21 November 1768. The end of November and early December can be very bleak along the Jebogue River, but on 7 December 1768, with her brother Samuel along to give Jonathan a hand with the rowing, Lucy and 16-day-old John, along with "Household Stuff," arrived by boat at their new home.[14]

Jonathan Scott — Preacher

In 1766 there was a religious revival in Yarmouth Township. Ebenezer Moulton preached there and Jonathan Scott expressed delight in what he heard. He recorded that he learned more of the way of Salvation by hearing Moulton a few times than all he had learned previously, "... for he insisted chiefly on the doctrines of Grace, which I had never heard much before."

That fall, Jonathan Scott and others gathered in private meetings for prayer and religious conference, and at these meetings Jonathan was put forward to pray and read, to lead in singing, and to speak. John Frost of Argyle Township came to Yarmouth to lead in these meetings four or five times. In October 1768

---

12   Yarmouth Township Deeds, Courthouse, Yarmouth, N.S..

13   *Journal*, 17.

14   *Journal*, 17.

Jonathan Scott began to lead in public worship, but in May 1769 John Frost was brought to Yarmouth Township to live and preach to the people in Jebogue, and was ordained to the pastoral office. Whenever Jonathan Scott was home from the sea on a Sunday, John Frost asked him to preach one part of the day. Scott also preached at John Frost's ordination, 21 September 1769, the first protestant ordination in Canada.[15]

Many years later, in the record of the church at Minot, Jonathan Scott wrote in his same fine handwriting the following account of his time in Yarmouth. (Note the use of the third person throughout.)

> At the Age of twenty-four Years, in the Month of October, 1768, at the Desire of the Church in that Town, he first began to preach the Word of God to the Church and Congregation in that Place, and continued to preach (though not every Sabbath) until the Year 1772, when he, unanimously, was invited by the Church and Congregation to settle in the Gospel Ministry among them. By the Desire of the People, and his own Consent, Mr. Scott was sent, and a Committee of three Persons with him, to Plymouth County, in Massachusetts State, for Examination and Ordination. He left Home in Nova-Scotia on the twentieth Day of March, 1772, and in the beginning of April, following about the seventh Day, he arrived at the House of Rev. Sylvanus Conant of Middleborough, where he tarried three Weeks, under the Tuition of Rev. Mr. Conant, to whom he had been recommended, and at whose House an Ecclesiastical Council was conven'd for the Purpose of Ordination: And on the twenty-eighth Day of April, A.D. 1772, Mr. Scott was ordained to the pastoral Charge of the Church and Congregation in Yarmouth in Nova-Scotia. The Ordination was performed in the Meetinghouse of Rev. Sylvanus Conant, Pastor of the first Church in Middleborough ....[16]

> ... Mr. Scott having received Ordination, set out for Nova Scotia the next Day, and took Passage at Plymouth and went to Boston, and thence, together with the Committees, to Yarmouth in Nova Scotia. The Proceedings of the Ecclesiastical Council were acceptable to the People, and Mr. Scott was received in quiet, for ought that appear'd.

> Mr. Scott, at the Time of his Ordination, had a Wife and three small Children, and but little Support from the People, which laid him under

---

15 *Journal*, 19; Maurice W. Armstrong, "The First Protestant Ordination in Canada," *The Dalhousie Review* (1947), 52.

16 Here Jonathan Scott copied Sylvanus Conant's account to the church in Yarmouth of the Ordination. A full description of the event and a duplicate of this account was entered by Scott in the Records of the Church of Jebogue.

Necessity to labour hard and constantly with his Hands for the support of himself and Family. His Situation was two Miles from the Meetinghouse, and across a River in a Boat, or on the Ice in Winter; and by Water, separated from near two Thirds of the People to whom he was related as a Pastor, and under the Necessity rowing in Boats, to attend Worship, visit the People, or do Business from.

The Situation of the Church and People was about one hundred Miles from any Church or gospel Minister; (except the French Roman Catholics, who were on both Sides of the Town) and there was no Roads convenient to ride on Horseback to any other Town, for the Space of more than 25 Years from the Time the Town was first settled. In the Period of twenty Years while Mr. Scott was Pastor in Yarmouth, he never had Opportunity to exchange one Day with a regular Ordained Pastor of his own Denomination; though there were two or three Candidates for the Ministry, who came to the Town at different Times in the Course of twenty Years, who preach for Mr. Scott divers Times.

These Circumstances rendered Mr. Scott's public Employment very trying, wore down his Strength, and broke his animal constitution. But the Providence of God which occasioned his Dismission from the People in Yarmouth, was their being divided and broken by wild, erroneous, disorderly, ignorant, separate Preachers. The first of this Sort, who broke in upon both Church and Society, was Mr. Henry Alline, and soon after him a Number more, much of the same Description, rushed in, until Order, Union and Peace were destroyed. Mr. Scott continued seven or eight Years in this trying State of the People, often requesting a Dismission, and the People refusing to grant it.

At last, Mr. Scott made a particular and full Statement of his Circumstances and obtained a Dismission from the Church and Society in Yarmouth, Nova Scotia.[17]

At his ordination in April 1772 Scott was admitted to membership in the Association formed by the ministers of the Congregational churches of Middleborough, Bridgewater, Plymtown, Plymouth, Halifax and Rainham, in Massachusetts. Back in Yarmouth Township he assumed his pastoral responsibilities, which he took very seriously. In March 1773 he returned to New England to consult with other ministers and with the Association about doctrine and parish matters. In Boston he talked with three ministers, then spent several days in Middleborough where the Reverend Sylvanus Conant advised him on church discipline. Scott wrote out some questions for Conant to lay before the Association to have its judgment about them.

---

17 Androscoggin Records.

Jonathan Scott's brother David Scott returned with him to Nova Scotia, arriving 13 April 1773. Even with the advice he received, he had some difficulties in coping with discipline cases. He felt that too often he came off second-best. Then, on 20 December 1777, Lucy died, leaving Jonathan with six children under ten years of age.

By this time the animosity between England and its colonies in New England had caused the removal of more than 20 families from the Society of Jebogue. Some families had gone to Halifax, some to New England, some to the River St. John and other places. In the summer of 1778 Jonathan Scott described his situation to the church and society of Jebogue: a single parent with six children, the oldest not ten and the youngest under 2, financial support averaging £32 a year, living two miles and on the other side of the river from the meetinghouse, unable to develop his farm, no time to train his children or give them any schooling, and now "above thirty-five Dollars" in debt. These conditions rendered him unable to do the work of a gospel minister among the society and unless they could be corrected, he expected the society would be willing to dismiss him from the work of the ministry among them. At this point he felt he was a failure as a Planter, as a Parent, and as a Pastor.[18]

He distributed his children among the people of Jebogue, leased his farm for a year and, with the permission of the society, and in answer to a request from the Cornwallis church, he went to Cornwallis Township for the winter of 1778-1779. When he returned in April, the society had made arrangements to provide land around the meetinghouse and nearly £50 toward building a house, and subscribed £50 for the year 1779. The title, however, was clouded. As well, some members wanted the land for the society, and it was rumoured he was after more money or that he had a call to Cornwallis, so he gave up any plan to move and continued as pastor in Jebogue as before.

The preaching and proceedings of Henry Alline had divided the church in Cornwallis, and subsequently had attracted followers in Horton, Annapolis, Granville and Wilmot townships. In 1779, after his ordination by lay persons as an itinerant preacher, Alline visited the River St. John and attracted many followers, which split the Maugerville church. The people of Jebogue knew little of Henry Alline, but Jonathan Scott had learned a lot about him while in Cornwallis the previous winter, when he experienced what he described as opposition and trial from Alline and his followers. The book by Henry Alline entitled *Two Mites &c.* was printed in Halifax in 1781. In this book his religious opinions were presented with his reasons and justification for holding them. Jonathan Scott laid these opinions before a number of the people of his charge. He described their reaction. "They looked upon them very erroneous and horrible and expressed a very low esteem of the author of them."

18 *Jebogue Church Records*, 79-86.

When Alline came to Yarmouth Township, in October 1781, Jonathan Scott provided lodging one night, invited Alline to pray in the evening with his family and next day to return thanks at the table. But he refused to give Alline any countenance or assistance as a minister, and presented the arguments that later were developed fully and published in the book titled *A Brief View, &c.*

Alline preached twice in private homes in Jebogue before going on to Argyle, Barrington and Liverpool townships. Alline's theology has since been described as "... a strange mixture of Calvinism, Antinomianism, and Enthusiasm ...." The religious influence that accompanied his preaching in different places was reaching the level of a reformation.[19]

Jonathan Scott's explanation for this phenomenon was the lack of ministers to teach and instruct people in gospel order and ordinances, and the fact that many Planter communities had not had schools for the instruction of youth for more than 20 years. Bishop Charles Inglis, in 1801, was direct in describing *itinerant* preachers, "... without any liberal education, or even tincture of learning — scarcely able to read a Chapter in the English Bible ...."[20] E.J. Monaghan reports that the research suggests nearly all of the Planters coming to Nova Scotia were functionally literate, but there is a general impression (as yet unsupported by research) that literacy skills degenerated over the next generation. Initial settlements had no schools and the new settlers had to devote all their time and energy to such essentials as food and shelter.[21]

A member of the Jebogue church, Cornelius Rogers, joined with another Alline supporter, Major Jeremiah Allen, and, with the help of Henry Alline and another itinerant preacher, Handley Chipman, set up separate worship. Rogers encouraged others to join him. Scott reported on this activity:

> As Mr. Alline had employed his Art in exciting high and boisterous Affections and Passions in his Hearers, and mightily succeeded therein: Mr. Rogers took the Advantage of these Affections, and advised and persuaded Persons thus affected, not to go to the Meetinghouse where Mr. Scott preached, lest they should loose[sic] their Convictions, and so never obtain Mercy.

19 M.W. Armstrong, "Neutrality and Religion in Revolutionary Nova Scotia," *The New England Quarterly* (March 1946), 58.

20 D.G. Bell, ed., *Newlight Baptist Journals of James Manning and James Innis* (Hantsport 1984), 316.

21 E. Jennifer Monaghan, "Literacy in Eighteenth Century New England", *Making Adjustments: Change and Continuity in Planter Nova Scotia 1759-1800,* Margaret Conrad, ed. (Fredericton, 1991), 43-44.

Some members blamed this separation on Scott's failure to receive and countenance Alline when he first arrived in Yarmouth, others on his failure "... to reprove, convince or reclaim Mr. Rogers ...." Some members claimed the right to go to hear any minister that came to the township. Church member John Crawley said that Scott, "... neglected to visit the people and seek to remove their Difficulties and Suspicions ...."[22]

Convinced that his position as Pastor required him to act and speak and write exactly as he had done, Jonathan Scott found himself treated as the chief offender in these difficulties, and powerless to remove the disagreements or to promote unity. Having been elected by the church and society to be Pastor, he felt he had been abandoned by his chief church members, men and women who had signed the Jebogue Church covenant promising to "... watch over one another, ... give daily frequent Exhortations to Duty, ... Admonitions in case of Sin and Failing ...." He again considered himself to be a failure as a Pastor. He wanted his dismission.

The church brethren were also troubled and looked for unity. On 22 October 1782 at a conference at Scott's house, with most of the church members present, Deacon Daniel Crocker declared with an audible voice and fervour of speech, "I am ready to do all that is in my power to maintain the worship, ordinances, order and ministry, according as I have covenanted; and look upon myself bound so to do."

Esquire John Crawley answered, "So am I."

Mr. Amos Hilton said, "So am I."

Since these were three leading voices in the support of Henry Alline and in the opposition to Jonathan Scott, they were giving Scott the opportunity to restore order, recover his flock, and start the unifying process. Within a month, however, his zeal for perfection resulted in attempts to discipline Cornelius Rogers. This emphasis on past covenant violations instead of on teaching and instructing in gospel order and ordinances led to more disruption, and Jonathan Scott believed that he was now generating opposition within the church. Letters arrived from Liverpool and Maugerville requesting that Scott come to those places to administer sacraments, preach and to advise their broken churches. By this time the Jebogue church difficulties were such that consent for him to go could not be obtained from the Jebogue brethren.[23]

In the spring and summer of 1783, he wrote his book, *A Brief View, &c.* Scott set out with the manuscript on 15 September 1783 by land, by way of Annapolis, to Halifax. In Halifax he was successful in arranging for the book to be printed the following spring, and he returned to Annapolis in November expecting a prearranged passage to Yarmouth. Scott recorded that this

22 *Jebogue Church Records*, 138-47.

23 *Jebogue Church Records*, 182.

arrangement fell through and, with winter setting in, he was not able to return by land. He was compelled to remain in Annapolis where, on 8 December 1783, he married Elizabeth Bass, fourth of nine children of Joseph Bass and Lydia Searle.[24] Scott employed his time during this winter, "... in preaching and assisting the broken and scattered Churches and Congregations of Annapolis, Granville, and Cornwallis; all which were now destitute of Pastors .... And these broken Flocks manifested much Gratitude and Thankfulness for the Pastor's Labour among them ...."[25] Scott returned to Yarmouth Township in May 1784.

In July 1785 Jonathan Scott stated to the brethren of the Jebogue church that, since he was regarded as an offender, he was unfit and unlikely to bring about a reconciliation. He asked them to call a Council to settle the difficulties or to give him a dismission from his pastoral relation.

Again on 16 March 1786 he asked for a dismission. The church appointed a committee to seek reconciliation and, one after another, members declared they could not give their consent to a dismission. In July 1791 a majority of the church and society voted their consent for Scott to put his request for dismission before other churches, to have their counsel and advice. Then at the 2 November 1791 meeting, Scott read aloud what he had prepared to lay before a Council. The representations occupied more than five pages and included a summary of the proceedings following upon his first request for a dismission in 1786. In essence, his case was that, though the church and society had called him to the pastoral office over them, they had, since the coming of Henry Alline, limited his ability to conduct baptisms, administer sacraments, maintain the discipline of the church, and lead in the healing and removing of offenses. When the society heard this representation they voted to give Scott his dismission. The church did not, at this meeting, but did so at a meeting 2 April 1792.

He was immediately called to be the pastor of the church in Cape Forchu, also in Yarmouth Township, but he declined. Then both Cape Forchu and Jebogue churches requested him to preach, and this he agreed to, devoting half time to each. Freed from pastoral responsibility he seemed satisfied with this arrangement.

Was there to be life after Jebogue for Jonathan Scott? Yes indeed. In October 1793 he received an invitation to Bakerstown, Maine. He preached there from November 1793 until June 1794 when he returned to his family. He went again in August and this time received a call to the church in Bakerstown, which he accepted. He returned to Yarmouth Township in November to collect his family and moved to Bakerstown in April 1795.

---

24 *Journal*, 183. The Bass family moved to Annapolis Township from Dorchester, Massachusetts, in 1760.

25 *Jebogue Church Records*, 183.

Bakerstown became four towns over the next 30 years (Mechanic Falls, Poland, Minot and West Auburn). Jonathan Scott's church was at Minot. Once again, as Pastor, he became involved in discipline problems, but in Minot Deacon Chandler Freeman was an important mentor who counselled Scott to be conciliatory. Scott felt bound to act on advice he had solicited and the result was more satisfactory than had sometimes been the case at Jebogue. He did request his dismission from the church which was fast expanding into three meeting houses. Separate churches were formed and, immediately after he was dismissed on 22 August 1805, he was called to the first church in Minot and remained as Pastor there until his death in 1819. In Maine he was instrumental in forming a consociation of churches; he also participated in missionary activities and was a founder of the Maine Missionary Society. All his parishioners, in Yarmouth and in Minot, liked to boast about the ability of Jonathan Scott to quote scripture to suit any occasion, complete with chapter and verse. At least three Yarmouth Township families moved and settled in Minot following Scott's relocation there.[26]

Jonathan Scott — Patriarch

Historians, scholars and theologians have chronicled the Reverend Jonathan Scott's influence on the religious and social structure of western Nova Scotia, but it falls to genealogists and family historians to pursue his well-documented and detailed background in early New England. His brothers' descendants as well as his own are broadly represented in succeeding generations in Nova Scotia and in the United States and, what is more, his 13 children, six by his first wife Lucy Ring and seven by his second wife Elizabeth Bass, all qualify as Mayflower descendants through their mothers. Not all of these children had offspring.

Lucy's line goes back to Stephen Hopkins, William Brewster and John Howland, and Elizabeth's to John Alden. Both wives are of Planter stock, each coming when young from New England as part of a family unit, Lucy to Jebogue and Elizabeth to Annapolis.

Jonathan Scott's father John Scott came before 1729 from Ireland to Massachusetts and first lived at Cambridge where he met Lydia Thwing. They were married in nearby Boston in 1729. Lydia was fourth generation, her great grandfather Christopher Lawson having first come to Kennebec from England.[27] His marriage to Elizabeth James is listed in Torrey's *New England Marriages Prior to 1700*. Their daughter, Elizabeth Lawson, was born 1645 and her marriage to Edward Thwing is also listed by Torrey, as is the marriage of

---

26 Maine Vital Records.

27 *Journal*, 120.

Edward's parents, Benjamin and Deborah Thwing.[28] Edward and Elizabeth's son, Edward, married Lydia Smith, and they were the parents of Lydia who married John Scott.[29]

John and Lydia Scott settled at Lunenburg in the province of Massachusetts Bay where they had six sons and two daughters. Jonathan, born 12 October 1744, was the youngest son. His father, John, was killed 5 November 1756 and Moses, Jonathan's oldest brother, became his guardian.

This is the Moses Scott who, by 1763, was a Planter on the Jebogue River in Nova Scotia. For some reason, when Moses was an infant, he was "put to nurse" at the house of one Samuel Spear who brought him up as Moses Spear, and for "a considerable time" his parents were kept in ignorance of his name and his whereabouts. Four years before the death of his father, in January 1752, Moses, then over age 21, successfully petitioned the General Court of Massachusetts Bay to acknowledge his parents John and Lydia, living at Braintree, and to be called Moses Scott. His father would have preferred he be called John, the name he was given at birth.[30] Moses and his wife Sarah Gridley had seven children born in Yarmouth: Sarah, Abigail, Hannah, James, Rebekkah, Elizabeth and John Flavil.[31]

The other brother who shows up in Yarmouth records is David, born 1 April 1742 and died at Yarmouth in 1839. He was one of the Yarmouth militia scooped up by privateers from New England and held hostage on board two schooners in the harbour at Cape Forchu for three weeks in December 1775.[32] His obituary spells out details of this interesting man.

> DIED On Saturday the 19th inst., at the advanced age of 98, Mr. David Scott, the oldest inhabitant of this Township. He was one of the last, (perhaps the VERY last) survivor of those who, more than 80 years ago, served in the British Army, under Amherst and Wolfe, at the capture of Louisburg.[33]

---

28 Clarence A. Torrey, *New England Marriages Prior to 1700* (Baltimore, 1985), 456, 741.

29 See H.E. Scott's genealogical charts, NEHGS, Boston.

30 Massachusetts Archives, Boston Mass. Petitions, Vol. 105, 408.

31 Gwen G. Trask, ed., *Early Vital Records of the Township of Yarmouth, NS* (Yarmouth, 1982), Bk 1, 38. Hereafter *Yarmouth Vital Records.*

32 *Journal*, 71.

33 *Yarmouth Herald and Western Advertiser*, 28 January 1839.

The *Yarmouth Vital Records* also state that David and Mary Scott had two sons, John Welwood and Benjamin. Thus Jonathan was surrounded by close relatives on the Scott side, not to mention the connections through his in-laws, the Rings.

Thanks to Jonathan Scott's diligence in setting down important matters such as the dates, and time of day, of the births of his children, in his journal as well as in *The Records of the Church of Jebogue,* we are blessed with primary sources. His six children by Lucy Ring, who died at age 26 in 1777, are also recorded in *Yarmouth Vital Records.* The August 1906 publication of *The Mayflower Descendant* included details of the Scott Family Bible, providing not only birth, but death, records of the first and of the second family, the children of his second wife, Elizabeth Bass.

Jonathan fathered 13 children, so he obviously did something beside rowing and writing. Several did not make it to maturity. Elizabeth's daughter Lucy, born at Jebogue, died there at age 6 and is buried beside Jonathan's first wife Lucy. Joseph died at 14 after the move to Minot, and Sylvanus, the only child born in Maine, died at age 11 in the tragic fire in Minot in February 1807.

Jonathan and Elizabeth's removal to Minot by 1795 allows us to differentiate two lines of descent geographically, because some of the offspring remained in Chebogue, having established families there, and some went with Jonathan and Elizabeth to Maine. The Yarmouth Township Nova Scotia line began with his oldest son John, born 1768. He married Ruth Hilton (Amos Hilton's daughter) in 1791, and established a strong Scott line by producing 11 children, six girls and five boys, who, in turn, married into easily-recognized Planter families — Allen, Clements, Trefry, Flavel, Haley, Cook, for example, and had enormous families.

Jonathan and Lucy's fourth child, Jonathan Edwards Scott, named for the New England New Light theologian, graduated from Harvard University in 1802 and died at Wiscasset, Maine, in 1822.[34] He is the ancestor of Henry Edwards Scott Sr., the historian of the family who succeeded in getting his hands on the original journal of Jonathan Scott, 1764-1777, and whose son Henry Edwards Scott Jr. handed us a prepublication manuscript of his edited work, *The Journal of the Reverend Jonathan Scott with Genealogical Notes,* later published by The New England Historic Genealogical Society. Even he, however, could not come up with succeeding volumes.

Lucretia married in Poland, Maine, in 1796, Timothy Redding; Olive married John Tedford and died at Topsham, Maine. Their older sister Lydia married at Jebogue, Nova Scotia, in 1788, Ebenezer Ellis, son of the Ebenezer Ellis who was one of the first Planters to come in 1761. They had five children born at Jebogue,[35] but after Ebenezer was lost at sea in 1799 she disposed of her holdings in Nova Scotia and in March 1800 took her children over to Maine to

---

34 Sibley, *Harvard Graduates.*

35 *Yarmouth Vital Records,* Bk 1, 38.

the home of her father and stepmother and their six surviving children. The trip from Jebogue to Minot at that time of year with small children must have been dreadful. Her story has a happy ending, as in 1804 she married Davis Verril of a prominent Minot family and had three more babies. This explains the connection of many Ellises in Maine.[36]

Of Jonathan and Elizabeth's brood, only Benjamin and Mary married. Their other daughter, Elizabeth, born 1786, lived to be 82 and died in 1869, unmarried. Joseph died in 1800, at 14, and was the first of the family buried in Minot on his father's property in what is now known as the Scott Burying Ground (Figure 2). George was lost at sea at age 34 and young Sylvanus, only 11, died in the burning of their house. Lucy had died at Jebogue when only 6 years old.

Descending from the two branches of the Scott family, nine generations of Planter stock worldwide can readily trace their ancestral roots either in western Nova Scotia or in Maine straight to the progenitor, the Reverend Jonathan Scott.

Conclusion

Jonathan Scott considered himself, for the most part, to be a failure, or so it would seem from his lamentations so profuse in his writings. Because what we know of him nearly all comes from his own pen, we might be led to the same conclusion. Such was not the truth — he was highly regarded by his peers in the ministry and by his congregation at Jebogue which, from 1785 to 1790, resisted his repeated requests for dismission until they finally acceded in 1792,

> ... At the same time expressing our most sincere Sorrow and Grief at the Necessity of such a Measure. And looking forward with the deepest Concern to the gloomy Prospect before us, we feel the most painful sensations at parting with our Rev. Pastor, who by his life and conversation has adorned the Christian Name and Profession ....[37]

Earl B. Eddy claims that the title of Bishop best describes the role of Jonathan Scott.

> He was the first young man in Nova Scotia to be chosen by a church and society to be set apart for the Christian ministry; he served his home church for nearly a quarter of a century as its minister; he stood for Congregationalism at its best, the *gathered* Church with its flanking Society, the Covenant, the Confession of Faith, strict discipline, and the use of Church Councils for wisdom and fellowship. Jonathan Scott was the only minister of a Congregational Church in rural Nova Scotia to

---

36 Minot, Maine Vital Records, Maine State Archives, Augusta.

37 *Jebogue Church Records*, 206

2. Scott Family Burying Ground on Jonathan Scott's property at Minot, Maine. His headstone is second from the left. Photo: Stuart Trask

3. Gravestone of the Reverend Jonathan Scott, Burying Ground, Minot Maine. Photo: Deborah Trask

withstand the Newlight division; his call to help three other congregations in their troubles showed true episcopal responsibility.[38]

Jonathan Scott was also highly regarded by his congregation at Minot, which placed a splendid tombstone (Figure 3) upon his grave, inscribed as follows:

In memory of
REV^d JONATHAN SCOTT
Pastor of the 1st church in Minot
26 years in the christian
Ministry at Yarmouth, Nova Scotia,
and 25 in this place,
who died Oct. 15, 1819
Aged 75 years

"My flesh shall slumber in the ground,
Till the last trumpet's joyful sound;
Then burst the chains with sweet surprise,
And in my Saviour's image rise."

In testimony of their esteem the Church of
Christ of which the deceased was the
worthy Pastor has erected
this monument

---

38 Earl B. Eddy, "The Uncrowned Bishop of Congregationalism in Nova Scotia," *United Church Bulletin*, No. 9 (1956), 34.

The Moultons and Their Contribution to Religion and Education in Canada

Beatrice Corbett
M.A., Department of English
Queen's University, Kingston, Ontario

The name of Ebenezer Moulton, 1709-1783, is reasonably well-known to Planter scholars, and there is a plaque to his memory in Wolfville United Baptist Church. But there was another Moulton of the same New England family, who came to Canada: Susan Moulton, 1819-1916. These two had a common background, some common characteristics, and each was steadfast in the Baptist faith. One, a Planter, was the first to preach the Gospel in parts of Nova Scotia. The other was closely associated with the founding of two Canadian educational institutions.

Their circumstances could not have been more different. In 1761 Ebenezer Moulton, a Baptist preacher, fled from Massachusetts to Nova Scotia, with his creditors snapping at his heels. He returned to Massachusetts in 1771. In 1871 Susan Moulton Fraser, an affluent widow, married Senator William McMaster, one of Canada's most successful entrepreneurs, and came to live in Toronto in the four-year-old Dominion of Canada.

Robert, the first Moulton in Massachusetts, came in 1629, and was a member of the first House of Representatives until he was disarmed for holding views dangerous to the state.[1] This independence of thought leading to civil disobedience and sometimes arrest, has continued — to the present time — but the Moultons came by it honestly, for the strands that make up the family line include Mayflower Pilgrims, Puritans from the Massachusetts Bay Company and French Huguenots. George Levy's point is well taken when he writes of Ebenezer Moulton: "Dissent was in his veins."[2]

Ebenezer, seventh in his family, was born at Windham, Connecticut, in 1709, into a family of Congregationalists, or members of the Church of the Standing Order. It was a time of religious turmoil, with New England on the brink of the Great Awakening, the religious revival led by George Whitefield and Jonathan Edwards, whose followers were known as New Lights. In 1736 we find Ebenezer at Wales, Massachusetts, and he has become a Baptist and a New

---

1   J. Gordon Jones, *Greatness Passing by: Biographical Sketches of some Canadian Baptists, Emphasizing Their Contribution to Our National Life from 1867 to 1967* (Toronto, 1967), 7.

2   George Edward Levy, *The Baptists of the Maritime Provinces, 1753-1956* (Saint John, 1946).

Light, at a time when Baptists were regarded as religious radicals of the most dangerous sort.[3]

In 1741 he was ordained elder, but his tenure at Wales Baptist Church was marked by controversy. When, in 1749, he baptized 13 Congregationalists at Sturbridge, he so enraged the authorities that he was dragged out of town and thrust into jail as a vagabond and a stroller. No doubt community outrage was fuelled by financial considerations. Baptists were exempt from paying taxes for the support of the Church of the Standing Order and his action had removed 13 taxpayers from the list. On his release from prison, unrepentant, he continued to preach throughout Massachusetts, and many were converted, or influenced, including Isaac Backus.[4] To support his family, Moulton had become a merchant as well as a preacher, but during the Seven Years' War he got heavily into debt, and in 1761 fled to Yarmouth, Nova Scotia, where his family followed him, and where, as a Justice of the Peace, he was active in establishing the town during its first difficult years.

But Elder Moulton's sense of mission was still strong, and at Cape Forchu he found a group of dissidents and preached to them. His rallying cry was, "I have a message from God and I am in haste to deliver it."[5] Then he set his feet upon the road of itinerant preaching: to Barrington by sea, overland to Cornwallis and Horton. At Horton he found a congenial settlement, and a group of New Lights who were searching for a preacher. He ministered to both Baptists and Congregationalists, and a meetinghouse was built. Then difficulties arose, the Congregationalists won out, and Elder Moulton left Horton. Mrs. Israel Harding expressed the feelings of many; "The Lord sent Mr. Moulton to Horton, but the devil sent him away."[6] He apparently preached with such conviction and power that many were deeply moved.

What happened to Moulton's little church of 30 souls at Horton? Some scholars say it died out,[7] but in an article, *Origins of the Maritime Baptists: A New Document*, J.M. Bumsted discusses a letter written four years after Moulton's departure by three members of the church, referring to it as extant:

3   Maurice W. Armstrong, "'Elder Moulton' and the Nova Scotia Baptists," *Dalhousie Review*, 24 (October 1944), 320.

4   Jones, *Greatness Passing By*, 8.

5   Jones, *Greatness Passing By*, 9.

6   Ronald Stewart Longley, *The Wolfville United Baptist Church*, (Kentville, 1954), 5.

7   E.R. Fitch, *The Baptists of Canada: Their Progress and Achievements* (Toronto, 1911), 19.

During the stay of the said Moulton with us we thought it our duty to join ourselves in solemn covenant. Hence call ourselves the Baptist Church of Christ in Horton in King's County .... we have continued assembling ourselves together and endeavour through divine assistance to keep the Worship of God according to the Best Gifts bestow'd on us.[8]

If this letter is accepted, it may be argued that Moulton's church did survive and that it formed the basis of Horton Baptist Church, founded in 1778.

When Elder Moulton arrived back in Yarmouth in 1767, he found a Congregationalist meetinghouse had been built there. He also found within that congregation a group of dissidents to whom he could preach as a Baptist, and he thus effected a separation within this church in 1769. A separation is said to occur when some members of an existing congregation break away and form their own church. Ebenezer Moulton's last stand in Yarmouth Township took place in 1770 when he was introduced to speak in the meetinghouse unbeknownst to Jonathan Scott, the right and proper minister. There was a second separation within the church (known as Jebogue Church), and henceforth Elder Moulton preached in private houses. His attempts to set up a Baptist church failed and in 1771 he returned to Massachusetts. It is encouraging to know, for those who consider Moulton's efforts to have been worthwhile, that, as Armstrong tells us, "in 1779 his heart was gladdened by a religious revival of great intensity which more than doubled the membership of his old church," at Wales, Massachusetts.[9]

What influence did Ebenezer Moulton have in Nova Scotia? At one end of the spectrum Edward Manning Saunders traces an unbroken line from Moulton through the Horton Baptist Church to Horton Academy and Acadia College.[10] At the other extreme, Gordon Stewart, in his entry on Moulton in the *Dictionary of Canadian Biography* writes: "After a decade of religious service in the Yarmouth area, he was left without a following and without a role."[11]

Maurice Armstrong offers a fair assessment of Moulton:

The significance of Elder Moulton lies not so much in the Baptist seeds he scattered here and there among the settlements, but rather in the fact

---

8   J.M. Bumsted, "Origins of the Maritime Baptists: A New Document," *Dalhousie Review,* Vol. XLIX (Spring 1969), 91.

9   Armstrong, "Elder Moulton," 323.

10   Edward Manning Saunders: *History of the Baptists of the Maritime Provinces* (Halifax, 1902), dedication page.

11   Gordon Stewart, "Ebenezer Moulton," *Dictionary of Canadian Biography,* Volume IV (Toronto, 1980), 564-65.

that in him the attitudes and travails of the Preloyalists are most clearly distinguishable. He is representative of several thousand pioneers who have left no such definite memory of themselves.[12]

Thirty-six years after Ebenezer Moulton's death, Susan Moulton was born, in 1819, in Glenville, Connecticut. There is strong evidence that she was the greatgreat niece of Ebenezer. Her memoirs, now at McMaster University Library, tell of a happy New England girlhood. These Moultons were Congregationalists, but Susan's mother was a Quaker. Susan was educated at Ipswich Seminary, where she was greatly influenced by her teacher, Mary Lyon, who pioneered higher education for women in the United States and later founded Mount Holyoke College. Susan's first marriage, to James Fraser, a Scot who had prospered in the lumber business, took her to Michigan and a life of adventure and excitement on the frontier. She writes: "A New England girl found plenty for her ambitious longings in going to a new, partially undeveloped country."[13] Her life in Toronto as the wife of her second husband, Senator McMaster, was filled with Baptist activity and grand occasions. Susan Moulton Fraser McMaster was highly adaptable.

Susan's strong religious faith had its roots in her childhood. When she was eight years old she had a stirring religious experience. When she was 16 she was converted to the Baptist faith at Norwalk, Connecticut, and she broke the ice to plunge into a running stream. In Michigan she worked hard for the Baptist cause. By the time she went to Newburgh, as a widow, she was a prominent member of the Northern Baptist Convention. The Baptists had come a long way since Ebenezer's time.

When William McMaster met Susan Moulton Fraser at the home of Baptist friends at Newburgh, he could not have been unaware of her suitability as a second wife for him. She was a committed Baptist, an affluent widow; she could take her place in the social circles he enjoyed, and she could help him in his ambition to make the Baptist Church in Canada respectable. In his interesting and otherwise excellent work on McMaster University, Charles Johnston writes simply of Susan: "She was a native of Newburgh, New York."[14] (She lived there for five years). If her New England background and her life experience are ignored, it is not possible to understand who she was and what she accomplished.

---

12 Armstrong, 323.

13 Autobiography of Susan Moulton McMaster, 1906, Mills Research Collections, McMaster University (Hamilton), np.

14 Charles M. Johnston, *McMaster University, Vol. 1, The Toronto Years* (Toronto 1976), 22.

In Toronto, William McMaster had gathered round him a circle that included former Prime Minister Alexander MacKenzie, and George Brown of *The Globe*. In *Canadian Baptists and Higher Education,* George Rawlyk articulates perceptively and clearly the outlook and attitudes of McMaster and his circle in the late nineteenth century. These people managed to reconcile their evangelical fervour with their financial success, and led the way in developing attitudes that reflected a strong appreciation of the material side of life.[15] This is borne out in the Toronto section of Susan's memoirs with its proud descriptions of Rathnelly, the McMaster home, and the entertaining that was done there.[16]

By the 1870s William McMaster had come to realize that there were two things the Canadian Baptist Church needed: a cathedral and a university. The principal Baptist church in Toronto was Bond Street Baptist Church, a rather modest edifice. To this came as pastor, in 1873, the Reverend John Harvard Castle. What induced this distinguished American clergyman to forsake the gardens of Philadelphia for the untilled fields of Ontario? Undoubtedly a factor was that Dr. Castle had been her pastor at Newburgh, when Susan had lived there.

The cathedral which William McMaster craved came into being in 1876 as Jarvis Street Baptist Church, a handsome church built with a handsome contribution from the senator. Dr. Castle was the first pastor. The strong American influence of Mrs. McMaster and Dr. Castle was fiercely resented by many Canadian Baptists, both in the smaller centres and in Toronto. Some seeds of later Baptist dissension may have been sown during the McMaster reign.

The university which Senator McMaster envisioned was incorporated in 1887 as McMaster University in Toronto.[17] A large donation of McMaster money went into this project. Six months later, William McMaster died. Susan Moulton McMaster's part in the founding of this university has been cloudy, but it has been well known that she had a significant influence on her husband. In Johnston we read that several times after the turn of the century Mrs. McMaster had mentioned that she would state the facts of the case in this matter, but her recollections were never put down on paper.[18] Well, actually they were, and I quote from her memoirs (Emaline is her daughter, "he" is the senator):

> Six weeks after reaching Rathnelly, Emaline and her governess came on, and I commenced to feel that this beautiful home should be dedicated to

15 G.A. Rawlyk, *Canadian Baptists and Higher Education* (Kingston and Montreal, 1988), 38-40.

16 Autobiography of Susan Moulton McMaster, np.

17 Rawlyk, 38-40.

18 Johnston, 48.

the Lord. So one afternoon when we were sitting under the pines in some garden seats, I asked him if he knew what I would like him to do with Rathnelly. He said he was sure he did not. So I told him I wanted him to build a theological seminary there and have the house for the professors to live in and thus dedicate the whole thing to the Lord. "Oh," he said, "that's impracticable." However I was not discouraged. I went over the same ground next evening and the next, and kept at it until my sister told me I would surely bore him to death. I told her I felt the need of such a thing so much and was determined that it be done. On one occasion he replied, "We'll see." I felt encouraged in my belief that it would be done. And soon Dr. Castle came on from Philadelphia, who was our pastor for many years, and he helped the project very much. The result is McMaster University — McMaster Theological Seminary. Mr. McMaster gave $1,100,000 for the founding and endowment. He had previously had his mind on building a hospital as a monument. I am thankful that his mind was led in a different direction.[19]

In 1888, after her husband's death, Susan McMaster surrendered her interest in the McMaster house on Bloor Street in Toronto and entered into an agreement with the university that it would be used for a girls' school, to be named Moulton Ladies' College. This school, strongly denominational, thrived (under difficulties) from 1888 to 1954 when it was closed by McMaster University, on very short notice, on account of funding problems. Susan Moulton McMaster had an extremely strong influence on the school she founded, and, as late as 1942, she was still referred to as "Our Founder-Mother."[20] She visited the school frequently and always held discussions with small groups of girls, discussions which centred on the Christian life, for she had set up Christian womanhood as the ideal to be attained.[21]

In his essay on Moulton College, Paul Bennett remarks that when the college closed, its time had passed.[22] Perhaps this was true of the form and facilities of the school, but not of its members. Some 1500 girls went through Moulton, and they have been represented in many professions and occupations. Their contributions, past and present, are notable. An active Moulton Alumnae Association provides nondenominational scholarships at the university level. At

---

19 Autobiography of Susan Moulton McMaster, np.

20 Carrie J. Holman, "Susan Moulton Mc.Master: Our Founder-Mother," *Moulton College Alumnae News* (Toronto), November 1942.

21 Autobiography of Susan Moulton McMaster, np

22 Paul W. Bennett, "Fitting Young Girls for 'Christian Womanhood': the Moulton Ladies' College Experience," course 1462F essay, *Ontario Institute for Studies in Education.* 1987, 30.

McMaster, Moulton Hall is now a women's residence. In all these, a guiding force and mentor has been Alfreda Hall, a former Moulton teacher.

Both Ebenezer and Susan Moulton brought to their lifework the energy and vitality, the courage of conviction and the belief in Christian principles, which marked the Moultons. With Ebenezer, this meant the courage to dissent and, in the face of failure upon failure, to persist in the faith. With Susan, it meant that, with her position and influence, she was able to put her ideas into reality. In the best sense of the term both these Moultons served their time well.

John Duncanson, Planter Scholar

by James Snowdon
Acadia University

Over the past decade the term "Planter" has become an accepted part of the Canadian historical vocabulary. The fact that this, our third such Planter Conference, has been so successfully attended and that scholars from various disciplines have willingly shared with us their interests and research on a wide variety of topics relating to the family and community in Planter Nova Scotia bear vibrant testimony to the maturation of Planter studies.

It is not any exaggeration to suggest that John Victor Duncanson is in large measure responsible. No, he did not organize the banquet or beg for funding. He is not a member of the organizing committee, nor did he present a 'knock-em-down' paper. Rather, John Duncanson set a standard for meticulous research and community studies long before many of us understood the significance of the Planter era in old Nova Scotia. His *Falmouth, A New England Township in Nova Scotia, 1760-1965* was published in 1965 and introduced the concept of linking family history, migration and community organization. For his pioneering efforts, John was awarded the Canadian Historical Association Local History Award. His next two volumes were *Newport, Nova Scotia: A Rhode Island Township* (1985) and *Rawdon and Douglas: Two Loyalist Townships in Nova Scotia* (1989). In addition, he worked on the Bishop Family history project and is presently delving into the history of shipbuilding and shipping in the Minas region.

John Duncanson is not a professional historian — his career was in the field of labour relations. But community and family history was his real interest, a love nurtured by the fertile lands of Falmouth — by the lore of those who had farmed the dykelands and fought to retain them during the preceding generations. From the time he was a wide-eyed teenager (more than a few years ago, I might add) the stories of the Acadians, of the Deportation and of the Planters were told and re-told — sowing the seeds of inquiry and starting John on a lifetime of research and writing.

Today, John willingly shares his expertise with others. His knowledge of the pre-deportation Acadian community is astounding, and I am told that if you really wish to get a feeling for that era, and have the stamina — go on a field trip around Falmouth with John Duncanson. The *Duncanson Papers* form an integral part of the genealogical and community studies holdings of the Public Archives of Nova Scotia — a legacy to future generations of scholars.

In recognition of this lifetime of accomplishment and unselfish contribution to the historical community, the Committee for Planter Studies at Acadia University proudly awards John Victor Duncanson the title "Planter Scholar."

INDEX for
Intimate Relations: Family and Community in Planter Nova Scotia

MARGARET CONRAD, ed., *Intimate Relations: Family and Community in Planter Nova Scotia 1759-1800*, 1995, 310 pp.

A fascinating new look at 18th century family and community life, *Intimate Relations* is the latest in a series of publications on the pre-Loyalist New England immigrants to the Maritime Provinces. Individual chapters examine childhood, widowhood and family relationships, inheritance patterns and economic life, clothing, furniture, religious belief and cultural values.

ISBN 0-919107-42-7
Paper only: $21.95

MARGARET CONRAD, ed., *Making Adjustments: Change and Continuity in Planter Nova Scotia, 1739-1800*, 1991, 280 pp.

The second in a series of publications on the New England Planters in Maritime Canada produced by the Planter Studies Centre at Acadia University. Topics range across a broad spectrum of the Planter experience, including economics, politics, religion, literature, music, material culture, relations with the Micmac and Black populations, and the larger geopolitical forces transforming the North Atlantic world in the late 18th century.

ISBN 0-919107-33-8
Paper only: $21.95

MARGARET CONRAD, ed., *They Planted Well: New England Planters in Maritime Canada*, 1988, 321 pp.

The first major collection of studies of the 18th century pre-Loyalist migrations from New England. Among the 25 contributors are Jack Greene, George Rawlyk, Murray Young, Graeme Wynn, Thomas Vincent and Esther Clark Wright. They explore a variety of traditional and innovative approaches and discuss future directions in the field.

ISBN 0-919107-20-6
Paper only $19.95

The above titles are available from Acadiensis Press. Shipping: $2 for one title, $1 for each additional title plus 7% GST for Canadian orders. Send order to:

Acadiensis Press
Campus House, University of New Brunswick, Fredericton, N.B.
Canada E3B 5A3